The Portable Lawyer
for Mental Health Professionals

Other Books by the Authors

The Portable Ethicist for Mental Health Professionals: An A-Z Guide to Responsible Practice (2000) John Wiley & Sons, Inc.

The Pocket Manual for Mental Health Professionals: A Compendium of Answers to Questions Most Frequently Asked by Professional Counselors, Social Workers, Psychologists, Marriage and Family Counselors, Family Therapists, Pastoral Counselors, Addictions Counselors, and Others (2000), by Thomas L. Hartsell, Jr. and Barton E. Bernstein. A collection of published and unpublished articles, statutes, board rules, and other information helpful to mental health professionals of all disciplines (available by contacting Thomas L. Hartsell, 6440 North Central Expressway, Suite 402, University Tower, Dallas, TX 75206, Tel: 214-363-0555, Fax: 214-369-3590, tlhartsell2@aol.com).

The Portable Lawyer
for Mental Health Professionals

An A–Z Guide
to
Protecting Your Clients,
Your Practice, and Yourself

Second Edition

Barton E. Bernstein, JD, LMSW
and
Thomas L. Hartsell, Jr., JD

WILEY

JOHN WILEY & SONS, INC.

This book is printed on acid-free paper. ∞

Copyright © 1998, 2004 by John Wiley & Sons, Inc. All rights reserved.

Published by John Wiley & Sons, Inc., Hoboken, New Jersey
Published simultaneously in Canada.

Library of Congress Cataloging-in-Publication Data:
Bernstein, Barton E.
    The portable lawyer for mental health professionals: an A–Z guide to protecting your clients, your practice, and yourself / Barton E. Bernstein and Thomas L. Hartsell, Jr.—2nd ed.
        p.   cm.
    Includes bibliographical references and index.
    ISBN 0-471-46551-8 (pbk. : alk. paper)
    1. Mental health laws—United States. 2. Mental health personnel—Legal status, laws, etc.—United States. I. Hartsell, Thomas L. (Thomas Lee), 1955– II. Title.
    KF3828.Z9B47   2004
    344.7304′4—dc22
                                                                                    2003068779

Printed in the United States of America.

10 9 8 7 6 5 4 3 2 1

To Donna, my fiancée, for her constant inspiration, with deepest love, affection, and appreciation.

To my children, Alon, the merchant, Talya, the lawyer, and son-in-law, Misha, the musician.

To my late aunt, Anita Springer Bloch, who took me in when I was discharged from the Navy and who patiently nurtured me and my career during my entire life.

To my cousin, Mallyn Rose Bloch.

To my sisters, Rona Mae Solberg and Dr. Berna Gae Haberman, and brother-in-law, Wolf (Bill) Haberman.

And in loving memory of my father, Samuel Bernstein, and my mother, Suetelle Springer Bernstein Antine.

In memory of Dr. Myron "Mike" Solberg, Professor Emeritus, Rutgers University.

Tom Hartsell, who always reminds me by both words and example that law is a noble, distinguished, and learned profession; a friend and solid support.

B. B.

To my wife, Barbara, who continues to endure with patience and love the long hours I spend working on book manuscripts, running a law practice, teaching, and lecturing. I love you so much.

To my earliest mentors, my parents, Tom and Julie Hartsell, who, by admonishment and example, taught me the value of education and knowledge and instilled in me the independence and discipline to seek them both. Mom and Pop, I owe you everything.

To my professional mentor, Bart Bernstein, who helped teach me the practice of law, the joy of being an educator, and so much more that I can never hope to repay him. Along the way, he inspired me and challenged me to become a better lawyer and educator and, in the process, became a true and dear friend. Bart, you are truly an inspiration.

To my boss and friend, Dr. Tony Picchioni, the program director for the Alternative Dispute Resolution Program at Southern Methodist University, who never ceases to amaze me with his extraordinary vision and the talent and wisdom to make dreams reality. You too are an inspiration. I appreciate greatly the opportunities you made possible for me. Lead on.

To my sons, Ryan and Jason, who still haven't read our first book but who are rounding into fine young men anyway and who make me very proud. I love you guys.

To my new best pal, Dexter, my Jack Russell Terrier, who has become my therapy dog, warming my heart and soul with his antics and never-ending love and affection.

T. L. H.

Preface

Lawyers don't know what therapists really do, so how can they know when (if) they do it wrong.
      —Anonymous; first heard by the authors about 30 years ago.

Years ago, few licenses were granted to or required of a mental health professional. You earned a degree from an accredited institution, hung a diploma, and began to practice. Now, most states require a graduate degree plus a license to practice independently. But the license is not permanent; it is "loaned" to the licensee, who may act only within the authority granted by the license. If a license violation occurs because of an ethical infraction, as defined by the licensing law; or continuing education credits are not sought and maintained; or a renewal is late; or a check for renewal does not clear the bank, the license can be revoked or suspended, thus ending or interrupting a professional career. The power of the licensing board is awesome and seriously applied. Also, malpractice suits have both intended and unintended consequences.

The need for continuing education has increased. Mental health professionals face harsh consequences if they act negligently or unethically with clients, the institutions with which they are associated, or both. They may not be allowed to renew their malpractice insurance policies; or they may fail to qualify as managed care providers because of a blemish on their record. In short, accountability requires in-depth knowledge of the law as well as published ethical standards that are promulgated by all licensing boards and most national organizations.

The Portable Lawyer is primarily directed to mental health professionals of all disciplines who can benefit from a quick and up-to-date reference to legal and ethical issues. The book covers over 35 general topics. When practitioners/ providers of mental health services have a question or situation that has possible legal or ethical overtones, they can consult the contents and index and be guided to rules and principles that apply to the specific problem, without extensive research. Armed with fundamental knowledge and examples of relevant documents, together with the answers suggested in this text, practitioners can make informed decisions, including consulting with a lawyer for further clarification and advice.

The Portable Lawyer is also directed to consumers of mental health services who feel something has gone wrong with the services available or already being provided. Because of the mystique surrounding mental health (from the consumer's point of view), the recipients of mental health treatment often do not know where to go to discover whether the actions of a therapist or provider are appropriate. This book discusses what can go wrong so that the consumer can decide whether the treatment received was appropriate or actionable. We hope that the therapy will be competent, caring, appropriate, and helpful.

Following the publication of the first *Portable Lawyer* in 1998, the authors continued to conduct workshops and seminars, and to teach graduate classes on mental health and law. Although students and workshop participants appreciated the general outline of do's and don'ts comprising the interrelationships of law, ethics, and mental health that the *Portable Lawyer* and seminars provided, the authors observed that many providers and students (especially those in practicum) had specific, case-oriented questions that came up again and again for which they wanted unambiguous and practical answers.

General principals are important to understand but mental health professionals are also looking for guidance in specific situations. For example, when could a seemingly innocent remark or bit of private advice become *involuntary therapy* and create liability? Or what would you do if two clients met at a singles church group and suddenly each, not knowing you knew the other, asked your advice about dealing with the other person?

In this second edition, we build on the general principles described in the original book by providing answers to frequently asked questions and adding additional information and knowledge. We use the questions as a technique for teaching the law that applies to mental health professionals. We encourage readers to seek the advice of an attorney in their jurisdiction for clarification of explanations and principles included in this book.

In addition to the questions, we have modernized and supplemented the forms from the previous edition to reflect the literature and current case law. For example, professionals now seek more protection under their client contracts, and ethical statements and licensing laws require that clients have additional information in their quest for "informed consent."

Finally, the *Portable Lawyer*, Second Edition, includes critical information on the Health Insurance Portability and Accountability Act of 1996 (HIPAA) and it's implications for the delivery of mental health services. The privacy rules promulgated by the Department of Health and Human Services pursuant to HIPAA that became effective April 14, 2003. One goal of this federal law is to create a national floor for the protection of the privacy of health information. It will not supercede state law that is more protective of health care information and will require mental health professionals to review each form used in their practice.

When these rules were first announced, many mental health professionals assumed that if they did not "electronically" send or receive health care information they would not have to be compliant with HIPAA.

That is not correct. Many state laws provide that health care providers must comply with the HIPAA provisions relating to notice of privacy practices and the access, amendment and uses and disclosures of protected health information even if they do not engage in electronic transactions.

In this second edition, we have included the new rules and regulations that apply to practitioners and developed new forms that are compliant with HIPAA's requirements. As a result, readers have a firm foundation on which to build and adjust their individual practices and procedures in order to be compliant.

BARTON E. BERNSTEIN
Dallas, Texas   THOMAS L. HARTSELL, JR.

Acknowledgments

In the process of writing this book, the authors had many friends, acquaintances, and colleagues who provided inspiration, nurturing, and mentoring—all necessary for any work worthy of publication.

We want to thank our editor at John Wiley & Sons, Inc. for creating the idea, and Tracey Belmont, senior editor, and Isabel Pratt, assistant editor, who helped to reorganize the chapters, and who were able to digest legal concepts and help us translate legalese into English as well as inspire a second edition. Thanks to Linda Indig, senior production editor at Wiley, Brenda Hunter and the staff at Publications Development Company of Texas who reviewed, organized, edited, and helped to make this book more useful.

Encouragement came from many special friends, some of whom we want to mention by name. James W. Callicutt, PhD, Graduate School of Social Work, University of Texas, Arlington, was Bart's mentor, initial source of inspiration, and first contact in the interactive field of law and mental health. He helped organize the first course in law and social work and has facilitated the interaction ever since. Myron (Mike) F. Weiner, MD, Department of Psychiatry, Southwestern Medical School, and a friend for over thirty years, bridged the gap between psychiatry and law, encouraging participation in the residents' program at the Medical School and service on the adjunct faculty. David Shriro, a close friend and confidant for almost 40 years, for constantly encouraging (some might call it nagging) an addiction to writing; and to Anthony Paul Picchioni, PhD, for emphasizing the need for continuing education in the area of ethics and malpractice. Also to Dr. Martin J. Davidson, Professor Emeritus, University of North Texas, for constantly lighting the lamp of inspiration, and encouraging further academic achievement.

Sample Forms

CLIENT FORMS

HIPAA FORMS

CONSENT FORMS

WAIVER FORMS

MISCELLANEOUS FORMS

Contents

SECTION FOUR

FEES

SECTION FIVE

FORENSIC ISSUES

SECTION SIX

PRACTICE MODELS

SECTION SEVEN

HOW TO AVOID MALPRACTICE CHARGES

SECTION EIGHT
MANAGED CARE

SECTION NINE
TEAMWORK

SECTION TEN
UNUSUAL PRACTICES

SECTION ELEVEN
THE HEALTH INSURANCE PORTABILITY AND ACCOUNTABILITY ACT (HIPPA)

SECTION ONE

CLINICAL RECORDS
Protected or Not

1

Clinical Notes

Melody had been a client of Ms. Ford, MSSW and a licensed clinical social worker, on and off for about five years. Melody called Ms. Ford during times of crisis but ignored her in between. There had been a 16-month lull since Melody's last visit, and Ms. Ford assumed Melody was doing all right. Melody had called once, indicating she was in love and had found the ideal man. Ms. Ford dutifully recorded the call in Melody's file. Within a few years, Melody married and had a child. Then her marriage began falling apart. A contested divorce followed, in which custody or conservatorship was the issue. Both Melody and her husband petitioned the court to be designated as the primary parent of the child—the parent with whom the child would live and who would receive child support. The other spouse would be allowed visitation only at specified times. As part of the custody battle, a process server showed up at Ms. Ford's door with a subpoena, seeking all the clinical records Ms. Ford has maintained in Melody's file.

Does Ms. Ford have to turn over the original records to the process server? If there is a deposition, does Ms. Ford have to appear and bring all of Melody's clinical records to the deposition? If there is a court hearing and Ms. Ford receives a *subpoena duces tecum* (she is to come in person and bring all Melody's records), does she have to comply and testify, revealing every aspect of the records and during cross examination comment on each response given?

The ultimate question is: Are the records of a mental health professional protected from the curious or interloping eyes of the information-seeking public *or* an investigative reporter *or* the attorney for the opposition in a contested suit? Does whatever the therapist writes down for purposes of therapy become part of the public domain? Have we discovered a true intellectual conflict when clinical notes created to assist in the therapeutic process become involved in the legal process in a manner that was never intended? Does every therapist need to keep notes with the "withering cross-fire of cross-examination" in mind?

Are the records of a mental health professional protected?

Clinical Records/Clinical Notes Must Be Maintained

Gone are the days when therapists could keep clinical records in their heads. When a threat of malpractice arises or when a complaint is filed with the licensing board, the clinical notes are often the first line of defense. The board or the attorney for the plaintiff requests all clinical notes as the initial procedure in the investigation.

Whether we like it or not, clinical notes—including computer files—cannot be fully protected from the intrusive eyes of the legal system.

Every therapist must keep and maintain clinical notes.

Every therapist must keep and maintain clinical notes, in some cases preserving them for five to seven years for adults or five to seven years past majority for clients who are minors. The Health Insurance Portability and Accountability Act (HIPAA) Privacy and Security Rules mandate a minimum six-year retention requirement for some records regardless of state law.

A change of therapists is another reason for keeping complete, current clinical notes. Vacation, disability, retirement, job change, death, or other circumstances may require having a new therapist take over a client. The clinical file is the only up-to-date professional record of assessment, diagnosis, prognosis, and treatment.

Customs of the profession indicate what records must be maintained. What notes should a reasonable and prudent therapist keep? In addition, the ethical canons of many jurisdictions, usually stated in guidelines published by the various licensing boards, require that certain records be maintained for each client.

For example, in various states, the code of ethics and professional standards of practice might include these themes:

- **Therapist shall base all services on an assessment, evaluation, or diagnosis of the client.** This standard suggests that therapists must maintain notes that contain clinical information and the rationale for the assessment, evaluation, and diagnosis of the client. It also implies that the treatment plan should be supported by the same factors.
- **Therapist shall evaluate a client's progress on a continuing basis.** The notes on each client must be maintained and updated throughout the treatment process. All changes in the assessment, evaluation, prognosis, and diagnosis, as well as the treatment plan, are updated continuously, as long as the client is in treatment. When terminated, the record should record the reason for termination.
- **For each client, the therapist *shall* keep records of the dates of services, types of services, and billing information.** Routine, accurate billing records, and third-party payment forms provide the means of fulfilling this requirement.
- **Therapist shall not disclose any confidential information [but will take] reasonable action to inform medical or law enforcement personnel if the professional determines that there is a probability of imminent physical**

injury by the client to the client or others, or there is a probability of immediate mental or emotional injury to the client. Although the confidentiality requirements vary greatly from jurisdiction to jurisdiction, confidentiality canons should always raise a red flag. In general, confidentiality is to be protected. But when the specter of homicide or suicide appears, the state statute must be consulted. In some jurisdictions, there is a duty to warn the identifiable, apparent intended victim; in others, the therapist *must*, or sometimes, *may*, alert the police or a medical facility. In some instances, the therapist is required to call a client's family to prevent a possible suicide; in other states, such a call might be a breach of confidentiality and could have secondary consequences including personal liability. Research the requirements of your state carefully when confidentiality is at issue. The federal HIPAA statute, discussed more thoroughly in Section Eleven, attempts to create a minimum floor for the protection of confidential health care information. Careful review reveals, however, that most preexisting state law exceptions to confidentiality survive HIPAA's bold intentions.

Research the requirements of your state carefully when confidentiality is at issue.

Can Clinical Records and Notes Be Protected?

Statutes granting the therapist-client privilege vary, so make sure to consult the statutes in your state and federal HIPAA law. In general, the confidentiality of mental health information is guaranteed. But, in some cases, a different maxim is operative: "What the big print giveth, the small print taketh away." That is, the guarantee of privilege is made hollow by exceptions to the statute. For example, generally there is *no mental health privilege* when a parent-child relationship is involved and custody is an issue, when a crime has been committed, when the mental health of a party is an issue in litigation, when there is child or elder abuse, or when a suit is filed against a therapist.

There is no mental health privilege in parent-child custody situations.

When professionals discuss the confidentiality of mental health records, they have to inform clients of the limits of confidentiality, as mandated by the state and federal law. For the therapist's protection, the limits on confidentiality should be clearly spelled out in the original intake and consent form signed by the client before therapy begins, as well as in the Notice of Privacy mandated by HIPAA's Privacy Rule. (See Chapter 2 and Appendix F for sample forms.)

Practitioners must also keep in mind that the privilege (i.e., the desire to protect the record) belongs to the client. If the client tells the therapist to make the record public, the therapist must do so. (The client's request should be written, signed, and dated. In some states, it may have to be notarized. HIPAA's Privacy Rule also requires specific language to be included in a client's authorization.) If a therapist feels, as a matter of professional judgment, that the file should not be made public, he or she may file a motion with the appropriate court to restrict publication of the file. This motion will lead to a hearing and a judicial determination. The therapist does not possess the right

Privilege belongs to the client.

to refuse to disclose the file if the client and court determine it should be made public. The burden of proof is on the therapist. The court must be shown that revealing the file to the client would be harmful to the client and that the best interest of the client would be served by keeping the file confidential, even from the client. In several relatively new cases, therapists were able to protect and preserve the confidentiality of a child's file from parents by showing the court that revealing the file to parents or the court would damage the child and would not be in the best interest of the child.

Two remedies are available when the therapist seeks to preserve the confidentiality of a file when a subpoena is served: (1) a motion to quash and (2) a motion for a protective order. Generally, a motion to quash points out a technical problem that renders a subpoena invalid. A motion for a protective order acknowledges the validity of the subpoena but argues against the scope of the subpoena. A therapist who wishes to introduce either of these legal remedies would be well advised to seek representation and engage an attorney. When the court rules on the motions, the therapist must abide by the ruling.

Answers to Frequently Asked Questions about:

Subpoenas

Subpoenas duces tecum

Fees for evaluation

Fees for court appearances

Problems when clients change attorneys

? *Question: Honoring Subpoenas*

I am in the final stages of conducting a custody evaluation. I have a signed agreement from both parents and both parents' attorneys agreeing to a fee structure, security deposit, and an understanding that both evaluation and any court testimony would be provided at a predetermined fee; that is, I would be compensated at my customary rate. During the latter part of the evaluation, one of the parents changed attorneys; then the new attorney subpoenaed me to court after his new client had fallen far behind in payments to me for the evaluation and had already lost the security deposit due to nonpayment. Should I honor the subpoena (not a bench subpoena from the judge but from the new attorney's office)? Are there other ramifications of this situation?

! *Answer*

In some states, attorneys have the legal authority to issue subpoenas to which you must comply. This includes a subpoena duces tecum, whereby you have to bring the client's records with you. (Take a copy as well as the original so the copy may be introduced into evidence if required, and you keep and preserve your original clinical notes.) Assuming this is true in your jurisdiction, you must appear in court at the time and date specified in the subpoena, even though one or more of the parties have breached their contractual obligation to pay your fees.

Further assuming you have consent from the parties who hired you to disclose their confidential or privileged information, you must give testimony and produce subpoenaed records. If you are uncomfortable or unwilling to do so, you should retain an attorney to file a motion to quash the subpoena or a motion for a protective order. In our opinion, it is unlikely the court will quash the subpoena, since custody is an issue in the case and you may have relevant information on that issue. Since the parties and prior counsel agreed that you would be paid a predetermined fee for courtroom testimony, announce to each side what that fee is. Mail or fax a letter to both parties and their current counsel telling them what your fee is and that you expect payment *prior to* your appearance in court. Let the defaulting party and his or her attorney know the total charges due to you from that party. Send copies of each letter to the court. It is important to let the judge know what the agreement of the parties was concerning your services and what fees are due to you. The judge may be able to make a ruling on how, when, and by whom you get paid.

It is possible you will have to testify without getting paid what is owed you. An option is to file suit for your fees against the breaching party after the case is concluded. It usually (i.e., almost always) is unwise, however, to sue a client for a fee, although fee collection cases give rise to an exception to confidentiality. Suits over fees often result in malpractice and ethical complaint counterclaims, especially if the party sued is unhappy with the court's ruling on the case in which the therapist gave testimony. It is better to chalk it up to a bitter learning experience, and consider it a reminder to charge future clients sufficient retainer fees upfront, that is, in advance, to cover your evaluation time and courtroom testimony.

💡 Additional Thoughts

- Honoring a subpoena is important. If a subpoena is issued and it can be avoided at this time, it is still better to make arrangements to appear in court with the records, if required. Defects in a subpoena can easily be cured, and, usually, all dilatory actions do is delay the inevitable.
- Suing a client for a fee, though legal and justified, is never a good idea.
- We, as lawyers, have defended many a therapist before licensing boards when unhappy clients filed seemingly frivolous complaints inspired by collection efforts.
- Create a trust fund account. Whenever there is an evaluation or the possibility of a courtroom appearance, have the client make a deposit "in trust."

If the fund is used for professional services, the therapist keeps the trust money. If unused, it is cheerfully refunded to the client.

- Such trust funds are mandated for lawyers who often are in possession of sums of money belonging to clients. Your lawyer can help you set up the fund, as can your banker and accountant.
- If this client is angry with you to begin with, and further, if the client loses the case, the client will try to blame someone other then himself or herself. Who is the obvious person to blame? You. And a complaint or malpractice suit is likely to follow, costing you time, money, and emotion.
- You are entitled to be paid for court appearances, making copies of clinical files, and professional evaluations. Put it in a contract, get the money in advance, insist on trial preparation, but, if you don't get paid, forget it. Unpaid bills are a business risk.

The Bottom Line

- Clinical records must be maintained on every client.
- Clients have to be informed about what is confidential and privileged and what is not confidential and privileged. Ms. Ford has an ethical and legal obligation to inform her clients what is and is not confidential and privileged.
- Subpoenas cannot be ignored. The therapist has to take affirmative action to protect a file.
- Computer records are subject to subpoena.
- If a discipline issues a state license, the licensing board usually publishes guidelines that set out the minimum standards necessary for clinical records and notes.
- A therapist can maintain only one set of records. Private records, or personal notations (sometimes called the "sticky paper note files"), are usually subject to subpoena. Court testimony indicating that the therapist had two sets of records, one for the client and the other for the therapist, can be embarrassing. HIPAA's Privacy Rule provides (with the usual exceptions) that psychotherapy notes (i.e., a therapist's notes on what was said by the client and therapist during a session) can be disclosed only with client authorization.
- Questions about homicide, suicide, and other "duty to warn" situations are in a constant state of legislative and judicial flux. When a problem arises, call your lawyer and your malpractice insurance carrier. A court decision or a new statute can change the rules between the time of publication and the time of the incident.
- If a record, in the interest of the therapist and the client, is to be protected, both, as a team, should consult a lawyer, who can then take the necessary legal steps to protect the file, the therapist, and the client.

Because the therapist records, protects, and maintains the file, keep in mind that every note contained in the file should be written with the possibility of disclosure in court, under oath, with a judge, lawyers, parties, possibly members of the public, and a court reporter present.

Clinical notes can never be fully protected, even when they may contain information detrimental to the client. Efforts can be made to protect confidentiality. The privilege that safeguards records must be exercised when necessary. Both clients and therapists must know the limits to confidentiality imposed under the law.

Clinical notes can never be fully protected, even when they may contain information detrimental to the client. Efforts can be made to protect confidentiality. The privilege that safeguards records must be exercised when necessary. Both clients and therapists must know the limits imposed by law.

Legal Lightbulb

- A privilege must be granted by statute or there is no privilege.

- Don't promise clients that everything they tell you will be kept confidential. In the intake and consent form along with the HIPAA Privacy Rule Privacy Notice, set out *in writing* all the *exceptions to confidentiality.* Don't worry if the form is lengthy. Remember, the purpose of the consent form, carefully drafted by *your* lawyer, is to protect you.

- It takes a lawyer to protect a file.

- It takes only an evening to:

  ⇒ Read the state statutes concerning privilege and confidentiality and the federal Privacy Rule.

  ⇒ Read the state board requirements regarding clinical records and the duty to warn when a client is a danger to self and/or others.

  ⇒ Read the state and national standards for record keeping, if published.

- If a therapist attends a lecture, reads a book, or takes a class concerning therapy and law, the words of the lecturer are educational and *not* the practice of law. That is, a student or seminar participant can't sue the professor if the participant follows the professor's advice given in a lecture and the advice turns out to be incorrect. Hiring a lawyer is a different matter. If a lawyer is engaged, the lawyer is professionally responsible for the advice given. There is a difference, for professional liability purposes, between the practice of law and the educational experience.

2

Consent Forms

A client's lawyer calls and says he wants a copy of all your records regarding the client—now—including all your personal notes. He says it is okay to send them directly to him; after all, he is the client's lawyer.

~

An investigator from the district attorney's office briskly walks into your office and insists on seeing you immediately. Your startled receptionist interrupts you in a therapy session, and you come out to see what the fuss is all about. The investigator gives you his card and demands the opportunity to review the original files of one of your clients, who has been criminally charged with sexual assault of a child.

~

A husband and wife come to you for couples therapy as well as individual counseling sessions. Eventually, the wife discontinues therapy and files for divorce. The husband asks you for a copy of both his and his wife's records.

~

What do you do?

Disclosure to Third Parties and Clients

Under what circumstance should a therapist produce records upon receipt of a request for information or records pertaining to a client?

Have you maintained separate records for each client, or are the records commingled? Can they be easily separated?

The general rule is: *Never* release records or information about a client without the informed, and usually written, consent of the client. There are circumstances when a therapist has a duty to warn or make a report, and serious consequences will be imposed on a therapist who fails to do so. Securing a client's consent to the release of documents or information under duty to warn or duty to notify such as in child abuse cases is not required. There also may be occasions when a therapist will have to provide records or information about a client in response to a subpoena or a court order. Even under these circumstances, it is best to attempt to secure the client's consent via a consent form.

When should you use a consent form? Every time a request for information or records is received from a person or entity other than the client. A therapist's arsenal of protective weapons should include ready-to-use, HIPAA-compliant (lawyer-drafted) client consent forms. The consent form should include:

Never release records or information about a client without the informed, and usually written, consent of the client.

- Client's name.
- Address, telephone number(s), and social security number of client.
- A direction to the therapist to produce clinical or billing records, or a copy thereof, to a specifically identified person or entity, and, if possible, the time period during which the consent is in effect.
- A description of the records to be produced or a reference to "any and all records."
- Any restrictions on the time period during which the authorization will be in effect.
- All language required by HIPAA's Privacy Rule. (See discussion in Chapter 41.)
- An itemization of any records that *should not* be produced.

Always give the client a copy of any form he or she signs. Once you secure the client's signature on a written consent form, the specified records or information can be disclosed with impunity as long as the disclosure is consistent with the scope of the written consent. You may use the sample form, Authorization for Use and Disclosure of Protected Health Information, Appendix G as a model when preparing a consent form.

Always give the client a copy of any form he or she signs.

The HIPAA Privacy Rule provides that a client has the right to revoke an authorization to disclose his or her confidential information and that a client must be advised by the treating mental health professional on how to accomplish the revocation. As with consent or authorization, an attempt should always be made to secure written revocation from a client. See Chapter 41 for further discussion on the Privacy Rule's authorization and revocation requirements and Appendix L for an example of an Authorization Revocation Form.

The sample consent form would offer protection in the scenarios outlined at the start of the chapter. For example, if a lawyer telephones and says, "Send me my client's records," you should politely respond, "My policy is that if and when I receive a consent for release of records from any client, I will comply with the request." Until that time, it is inappropriate to admit or acknowledge that a particular individual *is* a client.

If an investigator from the district attorney's office starts to throw some weight around, you might state, "In connection with criminal investigations, it is my policy that, upon receipt of a court order or a signed consent for release of records from a client, I will comply with the request."

If one spouse in marital therapy requests both partners' records, you may say something like, "I will be happy to supply you with copies of *your* records, but, until such time as I get a signed consent from your spouse to release your spouse's records to you or anyone else, I cannot comply with your request."

Do not blindly trust any person concerning disclosure of records—not even lawyers or law enforcement personnel. Be wary and be vigilant in protecting your client's right to confidentiality. Beware of a pushy attorney, an aggressive investigator, or an ingratiating caller who seeks information. Such contacts often come from the individuals who are least entitled to the information. If someone enters your office seeking client records, ask for and photocopy the person's driver's license, business card, and photo ID (if there is one). Most government personnel have permanent identification cards. Even with official identification, make sure the proper consent has been obtained.

Make sure that everyone on your staff is well aware of confidentiality policies and professional guidelines concerning confidentiality. HIPAA compliance requires formal, documented training of all personnel. (See Appendix G, Authorization for the Use and Disclosure of Protected Health Information.)

Be wary and be vigilant in protecting your client's right to confidentiality.

Disclosure among Therapists

In many instances, consent forms not only offer a valuable means of protection against disclosure to third parties, but also, when a change of therapist occurs, provide the new therapist with a way to review the prior therapeutic history and an indication of the progress or success of earlier methods of treatment. In a therapist-to-therapist disclosure, the client should complete a consent form that will allow the release of records or information to the new therapist. To make sure there is proper identification of the client and the relevant records, this form should include the address and social security number of the client. The form should also specify the precise information that the client is agreeing to have disclosed. If, in addition to record transmittal, there will be an oral follow-up conversation from therapist to therapist, seek and obtain permission in writing for this consultation to take place (see sample Consent to Therapist-to-Therapist Disclosure form).

Sample Form

CONSENT TO THERAPIST-TO-THERAPIST DISCLOSURE
OF CLIENT RECORDS/INFORMATION

TO: James Longley, LPC

     2407 Forest Lane, Suite 624
     Dallas, Texas 75208

CLIENT: Henry Joseph Harrison
            Birthdate: 6/14/52
            Social Security #453-67-8932, Phone # 972-991-2345

I, the undersigned, hereby consent to, direct, and authorize James Longley, LPC, to release or disclose to Dr. Anthony Kindheart, 6880 N. Central Exp., Suite 402, Dallas, Texas 75206; (214) 452-7698, confidential records or information pertaining to my treatment with James Longley, LPC, for the period of time from January 1, 1996, through the date this consent is signed by me. The information or records to be released or disclosed should include:

_____ Initial evaluation/history

_____ Psychiatric/psychological reports

_____ Medical information

_____ Psychotherapy notes

_____ Billing records

_____ Transfer/termination summary

_____ Tests taken and testing scores

_____ Other _____

_____ Any and all records/information

(continued)

Sample Form
(continued)

I also authorize the above named therapists to consult with each other concerning my therapy.

I acknowledge that I have the right to revoke this authorization in writing at any time to the extent James Longley, LPC, has not taken action in reliance on this authorization. I further acknowledge that even if I revoke this authorization, the use and disclosure of my protected health information could possibly still be compelled pursuant to law as indicated in the copy of the Notice of Privacy Practices of James Longley, LPC, that I have received and reviewed.

I acknowledge that I have been advised by James Longley, LPC, of the potential of the redisclosure of my protected health information by the authorized recipients and that it will no longer be protected by the federal Privacy Rule.

I acknowledge and understand that I am waiving my right to confidentiality with respect to the records and information released pursuant to this consent and hereby release James Longley and his staff from any and all liability arising from release and disclosure of the information and records to Dr. Kindheart.

I further acknowledge that the treatment provided to me by James Longley, LPC, was not conditioned on my signing this authorization.

SIGNED this _____ day of _____ , 20___ .

_____   WITNESSED BY:

Client

_____

Address

_____   _____

City and State   Anthony Kindheart, LPC

_____   _____

Telephone Number   James Longley, LPC

I acknowledge that I received a copy of this signed authorization from James Longley, LPC, on this _____ day of _____ , 20_____

                                 _____

                                 Client

Answers to Frequently Asked Questions about:

Consent for release of information

Revocation

❓ Question

What are the laws with respect to the release of confidential information? Can a consent for release of mental health information be revoked? What do we do if we have already released information pursuant to a signed release and the client subsequently revokes the release?

❗ Answer

A client can revoke consent to a release of information. The revocation is not effective with respect to all action previously taken by the therapist in reliance on the release. It is preferable that the revocation be in writing, dated, and signed. The HIPAA Privacy Rule requires that authorizations for release of protected health information contain a statement that the client may revoke the authorization in writing. Some may infer from this requirement that only a written revocation is effective, but until there is more definitive law to refer to, oral revocations will pose a problem. If a client verbally revokes a written consent, you should at least confirm the client's verbal revocation in writing with the client and then make a clear and unmistakable notation in the file. Documentation of the revocation is key. When confronted with an oral revocation, you may wish to consult with an attorney practicing in your area or contact your licensing board for any information they might have.

💡 Additional Thoughts

- If a clinician receives a request for a client's records from a third party along with the client's signed release but learns that the release has been revoked, the clinician should seek and obtain a *current* release of information form, signed by the client. The clinician should call the client to make sure the client and the clinician have the *same understanding concerning whether the clinician may or may not share the clinical file with anyone.*
- If information is released *after* the consent to release information was revoked, the release might be a breach of confidentiality. Consult the professional liability insurance carrier at once.
- Even if the practitioner knows the law concerning "revocation of consent," the mental health professional should not indulge in offering advice on the subject to the client. It might constitute practicing law without a license. *It is*

Legal Lightbulb

- Information contained in a client's records should not be shared without written consent signed by the client. Written consent is advisable before admitting, acknowledging, or implying that a person *is* a client. Front office personnel should be trained to repeat the phrase: "Without written consent, we cannot either admit or deny that any individual is or has ever been a client. Thank you very much. Goodbye."

- HIPAA's Privacy Rule specifically states that a therapist's psychotherapy notes may not be disclosed without the written authorization of the client. This gives a therapist additional legal authority to refuse to provide information about a client without written authorization.

- The more aggressive the person asking for information, the more reluctant the therapist should be to divulge information.

- In certain situations (e.g., child abuse, elder abuse, sexual exploitation of a client by a former therapist), information may be required by statute to be reported. State statutes set the limits of disclosure and the guidelines. Ethical canons require that these exceptions to confidentiality be disclosed to clients *before* therapy begins.

- Photocopy the driver's license, business card, and photo ID of any person seeking information about your client. *Show a copy of the file* and don't leave anyone alone with the original file. If the original file must be produced, remain present while it is being reviewed.

- A supply of limited and general consent forms should be a part of the therapist's office inventory and available to be signed by clients whenever appropriate. *Always keep and maintain a copy in the client file and give a copy to the client.*

- Spouses and lawyers do not, by virtue of their marital or legal relationship, have a right to review their spouses' and clients' files.

- Certain blank test forms cannot be released because of a contractual and proprietary relationship between the therapist and the owners or creators of those tests.

- All forms should be periodically reviewed and updated to ensure that they are current and conform to the most recent legal and state licensing board requirements.

- If the sample forms in this book are to be used as models, they should be reviewed by a local attorney to see whether they conform to state and federal requirements.

bad form, at best, to offer advice that might interfere with the professional relationship between a client and a former clinician. Don't put yourself in a position where you are suggesting answers to legal questions propounded by a new client. Send that person to a lawyer.

- This is the time for the clinician and lawyer to associate as an interdisciplinary team, serving the best long-range benefit of the client.
- Be careful in situations where the consent to release was in writing and the revocation was oral. Questions always arise in cases like this concerning whether the revocation was clear, unmistakable, unambiguous, and in a context where the revocation was definite. Sometimes a passing remark means one thing to one person, the speaker, and has another meaning to the listener.
- In the future, instruct clients who have signed consent to release information forms that the best practice is to revoke in writing and obtain a signature that the revocation was received. HIPAA requires the release itself to advise clients that the release may be revoked in writing.
- Remember the maxim: "An oral revocation is not worth the paper it is written on."

See Appendix L for an Authorization Revocation form.

3

Correcting Errors

A client, Bob, presented himself for marital counseling concerning difficulties with communication. Bob had had five sessions with the therapist when he called to tell her that his wife had filed for divorce and had accused him—in a written pleading filed with the court—of being physically abusive. His wife was seeking custody of the couple's children and permission to move to another state. Bob also informed the therapist that, according to his attorney, his wife and her lawyer might subpoena his therapy records. Bob wanted to sign a consent for release of a copy of his file to his attorney. The therapist complied with Bob's request and released his record to his attorney.

On review of the file, the attorney for the husband was startled to find the following note in Bob's records: ". . . discussed his physical abuse of Karen." (Karen was Bob's wife.) The attorney immediately called Bob, who advised him that what he and the therapist had actually discussed was Karen's recent behavior. She had spit on him and hit him on the back with a stick. Bob and his attorney called the therapist and demanded an explanation and the removal of that specific word or line from the notes. The therapist recalled the conversation and realized she had meant to write down "his physical abuse by Karen." This error in the clinical record could be devastating to Bob if quoted verbatim as part of the trial testimony.

In this situation what should the therapist do, and what is she permitted to do? Would the situation change if the wife's attorney had been able to secure a copy of the therapist's notes first without review?

Therapists are human, and mistakes are inevitably made with respect to mental health records. But a careful approach to transcribing records and reviewing them soon after they are transcribed can help prevent mistakes from surfacing months or even years in the future. Therapists should get into the habit of reviewing notes and records soon after they are written, when recollections are fresh and strong. But even the best procedures and the most diligent concern for the accuracy of records will not prevent occasional errors.

Most states do not have statutes or regulations concerning corrections to health care records, but several do. The rules prescribed by these states establish

A careful approach to transcribing records and reviewing them soon after they are transcribed can help prevent mistakes from surfacing months or even years in the future.

sound safeguards and guidelines to be followed by a mental health practitioner who wishes to correct a client's record. In Arkansas, pursuant to "Rules & Regulations for Hospitals & Related Institutions in Arkansas," Section 601 G (1988), errors in medical records must be corrected by drawing a single line through the incorrect entry, dating it, initialing it, and labeling it as an error. Pursuant to Massachusetts Regulations Code, Title 105, Section 150.013 (B) (1990), Massachusetts health care facilities are prohibited from erasing mistakes, using ink eradicators, or removing pages from the record.

How to Make Corrections

Common sense would dictate that only the person who originally made the error should correct it. When an error is made, the credibility of the record and of the person who made the entry is at stake. In litigation, attorneys must establish the credibility, or lack thereof, of witnesses and admissible evidence introduced at trial. When examining a therapist about a client's file in a deposition or at trial, a prudent attorney will ask whether any corrections, alterations, additions, or deletions were made to the records after they were originally transcribed. A therapist who has made an undisclosed change to a record is under oath and is faced with two choices: commit perjury or admit to changing the record. A therapist who has "whited out" or erased information and then written over it will have a more difficult time explaining his or her actions than a therapist who has drawn a single line through the error, initialed it, dated it, and marked it "Error." Much more suspicion will be raised in the minds of a judge, jury, and opposing counsel when an entry is completely removed and no one but the therapist knows what was originally recorded. Indecipherable notations are always suspect. (In the Nixon tapes, far more attention has been paid to the 18 missing minutes than to the hours of accurate audiotape.)

Only the person who originally made the error should correct it.

If you need more space than the record allows to correct an entry, attach an addendum on a separate sheet of paper and reference the addendum at the point in the record where the mistake occurred.

Bob's therapist should correct her record by striking through the word "of," marking it "Error," inserting the word "by," and then dating and initialing the correction. The same procedure should be followed regardless of when the error is discovered—even if the records have already been produced in a lawsuit, with copies delivered to all concerned. In such a case, make the correction, date and initial it, then send the correction to all parties.

Correct an error by drawing a single line through it, labeling it "Error," inserting the correction above it, and dating and initialing the correction.

In case you are tempted to make undisclosed changes to a mental health record, remember that such conduct could lead to revocation of a professional license for unethical conduct and criminal prosecution for perjury or evidence tampering.

Computer records present a unique problem because a hard drive or disk can be easily deleted and corrected. Be very careful when correcting computer copies, especially if hard copies have been printed. If a therapist testifies that a recent printout is correct and then a different, older hard copy is located, the consequences are dire—charges of perjury, loss of credibility, and ethics concerns.

When correcting a computer record, do not delete but insert, in parentheses, the date of correction and the initials of the person modifying the record. The computer record should then contain both the original and corrected versions.

The Bottom Line

- Never surreptitiously change a client's record.
- If an error is made, correct it by drawing a single line through it, labeling it "Error," inserting the correction above it, and dating and initialing the correction.
- License revocation and criminal prosecution await those who make undisclosed changes to mental health records.
- Jurors and judges are as willing to forgive an admitted error as they are a repentant sinner, but they have little sympathy for a therapist who erases or "whites out" to hide an unpleasant fact.
- If there is a state regulation concerning the procedure to correct an error, the therapist must become familiar with that procedure.
- When an error is discovered, review the error, the reason for the error, and the reason for correcting the error. Be prepared, should the case come to trial and testimony be required, to explain the error.
- Consult state statutes when correcting computer records.
- *If any changes are to be made in the file*, remember, it is better to *correct a file now* than wait until the letter request is received. At that time any changes you make might be viewed as self-serving and suspicious.
- If there is any technical jargon in the file, make sure you understand its meaning and can explain it in lay terms if called on.

Answers to Frequently Asked Questions about:

Client's right to review session notes

Response to request to view file

Review and correcting file

What it said before, what it says now

Case records

❓ Question

I am a social worker in private practice. What are the legal and ethical issues concerning a client's request to read session notes? I have seen this client for three years and some of the notes could be troubling. In fact, when I reviewed the progress notes, I discovered an error of only a few words, which would substantially change the focus of the therapy. The actual therapy was correct, but I made an error in noting a particular statement. She has not yet asked for the records, but I suspect she may do so and I want to be prepared.

❗ Answer

As you know, the client has a right to access his or her own mental health records. Ask for a request in writing. However, many states, including Texas, have statutes that allow a therapist to withhold requested records from a client if the therapist believes disclosure of information in the records would be *harmful to the client.* HIPAA's Privacy Rule has similar provisions. The client will then have the right to seek a court order compelling production of the records, and *the therapist will have the burden of proving the potential harm to the court.*

You should check with an attorney in your state or your state licensing board regarding the law where you practice. In some states, the clinician can refuse to produce "harmful" notes, and the client must file a motion for production; in other states, the clinician who wants to protect a client record must file to affirmatively protect the record and prove to the court that it is in the best interest of the client to keep the record confidential, even from the client.

The HIPAA Privacy Rule states that a client of a covered entity has the right to have a covered entity amend protected health information for as long as it is maintained by the treatment provider (45 CFR 164.526). A therapist does have the right to deny the request if the information was not created by the therapist (unless the creator is not available to act on the requested amendment) or if the information is accurate and complete. (See Appendix H for an example of a Client Information Amendment form.)

Consider this scenario: After careful evaluation of a client, a mental health professional gives a client the diagnosis of borderline personality disorder. The client, on review of the file, learns of this diagnosis and becomes upset and demands that the therapist change it. What is the procedure set out in the Privacy Rule?

1. The client has the right to request the diagnosis be amended. The client may be asked to do so in writing, stating specific reasons for the request.
2. If the therapist approves the amendment, the client should be so advised and the information amended. Any person or entity that received the incorrect or inaccurate information should be notified of the amendment.

3. If the therapist believes the original information is accurate, he or she can then deny the request and should do so in writing, setting forth the reasoning.

4. The client then has the right to submit a statement of disagreement in writing, which must be maintained in the client's file and must be sent to any person or entity that the client's protected health information is disclosed to in the future.

5. The therapist is required to act on the client's request for amendment within 60 days of receipt of the request, but may extend the response time for an additional 30 days if necessary as long as the client is informed in writing of the reason for the delay and given a date when the therapist will complete action on the request.

🔆 Additional Thoughts

- Be careful what you write down; it may come back to haunt you, especially if it contains words indicating bias, prejudice, or unsubstantiated conclusions, which cannot be professionally drawn from a careful perusal of the clinical file.
- Some clinicians prefer to give the client a free oral report or a written case summary in lieu of the complete file.
- *If any changes are to be made in the file,* it is better to *correct a file now* than wait until the letter request is received. At that time, any changes you make might be viewed as self-serving and with suspicion. Correct an erroneous entry upon discovering the error, line it out, date, and initial so that any person viewing the file can easily discern what it contained in the past and what it contains now.
- Motions to protect the *confidentiality of the file from the client* require that you show the court that information in the file will harm the client. The burden is on you.
- Be careful and prompt in responding to a client's request for amendments.

Answers to Frequently Asked Questions about:

Changing progress notes

Correcting notes when inappropriate

Practicing without a license

Clinical supervision by a nonclinician

❓ Question

I work full time in a community mental health center. Most of the time a licensed clinician (LCSW) directs the weekly staffing meeting. On more than one occasion, however, a nonlicensed person who has an advanced degree in a nonmental health field directs the staffing meeting. I have objected to this directly to him and to others and have, on occasion, refused to do what he has asked, for example, change a diagnosis or add something to a progress note. He is my administrative supervisor and just this week cited me in a formal review for being noncooperative with him. When I asked him for examples, he mentioned the incident about not changing a clinical progress note. How should I handle this situation?

! Answer

The fact that an unlicensed, advanced (MA, PhD) degree holder conducts staffing in and of itself does not present a problem to us. We assume this person is not supervising you with respect to practice hours necessary for licensure, nor supervising your cases as a clinical supervisor. You should always use your own independent clinical judgment, though, regarding a change in your client notes. *You are responsible for accurate record keeping,* and you should not make corrections or changes that you do not believe are correct and accurate. If you decide, in the exercise of your clinical judgment, the change sought by your supervisor should not be made, you should not do it. This stance could cost you your job, but it might save your license. If this person insists on changes, let *that person* make, date, and initial the change, indicating that the administrative supervisor made the change, not you. Show a copy of your licensing law and code of ethics to this person, and inform the administrative supervisor about your responsibility for accurate progress notes as you understand the code. As a last, but not lovable action, ask the supervisor to put the request for changes in writing. Usually such a request ends the discussion.

♥ Additional Thoughts

- If you are responsible for a file, suggestions made by nonlicensed personnel should always be considered *suggestions* and not *orders*.
- Your responsibility for and to the client is clearly set out in the national codes as well as state ethical standards. No change can be made that is not appropriate and in accordance with your perception of the diagnosis, treatment plan, and prognosis.
- If the supervisor wants some insertion, have that person prepare an independent, signed memo and indicate you will insert the memo in the file.
- Make sure any differences are professional and not personal. Sometimes nonclinicians and nonlicensed individuals have good ideas, and those ideas should not be rejected out of hand. If the request is reasonable and appropriate, insert it. Don't reject it just because it was made by an unlicensed person.
- Ultimately, the responsibility for the clinical file or progress notes rests with the treating clinician. The buck stops there.

Legal Lightbulb

- Clinical records must be maintained for *every* client, with no exceptions.

- Most states have requirements or minimum standards for the type of records to be maintained.

- Errors will occur. When they are discovered, they should be acknowledged and corrected, dated, and initialed.

- There are few consequences when an error is corrected openly and honestly.

- There are many consequences for hiding, concealing, or lying about making an error.

- Clinical records may be carefully examined by clients, attorneys, juries, and judges. They must be corrected appropriately so that any appearance of impropriety is avoided.

- Hiding a mistake is more difficult to explain than correcting one.

- Clients have the right to request amendments to their health care information pursuant to the HIPAA Privacy Rule. Familiarize yourself with the procedure mandated by the Privacy Rule and document requests and denials accordingly.

- Even lawyers and authors make errors and are forgiven.

4

Discharge or Termination

A depressed client, Joshua, failed to appear for a scheduled appointment with a therapist and did not call to reschedule. Joshua had been in counseling approximately six months and told family members he was functioning well and didn't need to continue therapy.

In reality, Joshua was seriously depressed, and the therapist had concerns about his stability and well-being. When Joshua failed to appear, the therapist tried to reach him by phone and e-mail but was unsuccessful. Afterward, the therapist, who had a busy practice, put Joshua out of her mind.

One month later, the therapist received a call from Joshua's sister, who notified the therapist that her brother had committed suicide. When the sister began to ask probing questions, the therapist refused to discuss the matter with her, citing confidentiality concerns. The sister was ultimately appointed executor of her brother's estate by the probate court and used this legal authority to secure copies of the therapist's records. On review of the records, the sister accused the therapist of malpractice for failing to advise her brother of the therapist's concerns and of the brother's need for continuing mental health services when he stopped coming to therapy.

~

Amy was terminating therapy. Both the therapist and Amy were pleased with the results. They both realized the goals of therapy had been achieved. Amy was very satisfied and had become capable of coping with the problems of life. The time had come for Amy and her therapist to shake hands and go their separate ways.

What should the therapist do?

What is the appropriate method to terminate when the client has essentially voluntarily terminated the therapy, but the therapist feels that therapy should have continued? A continued "no show" sends a message. The therapist should be especially concerned when clients who are obligated (perhaps by court order) to make an appointment fail to call to set up a date and time or consistently fail to appear.

What methods are used to appropriately terminate a therapeutic relationship?

What methods are used to appropriately terminate a therapeutic relationship, when either the client or the therapist does not feel continued therapy would be helpful, or when the goals of therapy have been accomplished?

There will come a point in every therapeutic relationship when termination should occur. Termination can result from the client's achieving all therapeutic goals, or it can occur when the client stops making progress and a referral to another provider is indicated. At that time, it is important to document the termination and the reason for it, in appropriate detail. At any point before termination, a client's file should reflect the need for continued therapy. As soon as the need ceases to exist, termination of the therapeutic relationship with that client should take place. The file should also reflect that a client is benefiting from the mental health services provided. If, after an appropriate length of time, it becomes apparent that the client is not benefiting from therapy, termination and referral should occur.

How Should Termination Occur?

A termination letter should be prepared, reviewed with the client, and signed by the client.

It is best to schedule an exit session or termination interview with the client so the therapist can be sure that the client fully understands what is taking place, the reasons behind it, and any future recommendations the therapist has for the client. A termination letter should be prepared, reviewed with the client, and signed by the client. The client should be given a copy of the signed termination letter when the session ends. The termination letter should indicate that the therapist will:

- Be happy to consult with any subsequent therapist with client's request and written consent.
- Make the file available to other professional individuals in response to a written request from the client and the signing of a consent form.

Obtain a phone number and alternate mailing or e-mail address where the client can be contacted, and obtain authorization to contact the client at that particular phone number, regular mailing address, or e-mail.

- Be available personally, if possible, should the client feel, in the future, that further therapy is needed.
- Provide a tickler follow-up file if desired by the client. The therapist would then check, at specified times, how the client is doing. The client would furnish an acceptable phone number(s) or address(es) for future contact and give written permission to the therapist to contact the client at the number or location furnished to the therapist. *Note:* Many professionals use the tickler file to facilitate a steady flow of business.

It is advisable for therapists to note the client's e-mail address in the file. Both termination letters and tickler files can easily be communicated with a convenient e-mail address. The confidentiality of the e-mail must be secured and HIPAA regulations followed.

If an exit or termination interview session is not possible, a phone conference should be attempted, and a copy of the termination letter should be sent
to the client at the mailing address authorized by the client or by e-mail. If neither an office visit nor a phone conference is possible, two copies of the termination letter should be sent to the client: one by certified mail, with return
receipt requested, and another by first-class mail. This procedure should be followed when a client skips an appointment and then stops all contact with the
therapist, especially if the therapist believes the client is in need of additional
mental health care. Don't dismiss a client who drops out of sight and refuses to
return phone calls. Write and/or e-mail the client, explain the need for continuing mental health services, and recommend at least three competent referral
sources. If using e-mail, keep a hard copy.

*Don't dismiss a
client who drops
out of sight and
refuses to return
phone calls. Be
assertive in
locating the client
and document in
the file.*

Termination Letter Checklist

The termination letter should include the following:

- Client's name, address, social security number, and phone number.
- Date therapy began.
- Termination date.
- Primary (and any secondary) diagnosis.
- Reason for termination.
- Summary of treatment, including need for additional services.
- Referral sources, including addresses and phone numbers (try to list at least
  three).
- A statement that the client understands what termination of treatment
  means and accepts the responsibility to seek further treatment if needed or
  appropriate.
- Signature lines for both the therapist and the client and a date line for each
  signature.
- Enclose a self-addressed, stamped envelope, and indicate "Enclosure" at the
  bottom of the termination letter.
- If sent by e-mail, keep a hard copy of the e-mail including any evidence that
  the e-mail was received. If a client, in a conversation, says: "I received your
  termination e-mail," make a note in the file.

Closing a File

It is imperative for the therapist to document the completion of a client's file
with a termination letter or form or e-mail hard copy similar to the one suggested here. A therapist has an ethical obligation to terminate a client who is

Make notations in the client file of all attempts to contact the client.

not benefiting from the relationship and to make an appropriate referral when the client can be better served by another provider. The surest way to prove compliance with these ethical obligations is to maintain a written record in the client's file. Don't put yourself in the same situation as the therapist described at the beginning of the chapter. Make some proactive efforts when a client "no show" becomes a voluntary termination. *Be proactive;* document your file.

A similar letter is necessary for voluntary termination, when both the therapist and the client agree that the therapy has accomplished its goals. Most important would be these provisions:

A client's record is not complete until it has a written record of termination.

- The therapist is available for future sessions if the client desires.
- The therapist will make the client's file available to any future therapist, if the client consents, in writing, to its release. In addition, the therapist will consult, if requested, with subsequent therapists.
- If the client leaves the area, referrals can be made to a therapist in the new location.

Be proactive; document your file.

Answers to Frequently Asked Questions about:

Abandonment

Termination

The hostile/angry client

Avoiding abandonment

? Question

I've been seeing a patient in psychotherapy who has never been consistent in her attendance, despite my accommodations to her schedule and despite discussions of how difficult it is to make progress absent regular attendance. She has now asked to be seen once every three to four weeks, and I suspect that it will even be less frequent than that because of her numerous cancellations. I'm unwilling to do this, in part because it is not nearly commensurate with the severity of her problems and would, therefore, constitute inadequate treatment, and in part because my practice is organized around a model of at least weekly sessions for active cases. I told the patient that I could not agree to an ongoing arrangement that would render her treatment ineffective/inadequate. I said that I would meet infrequently on a temporary basis, so that she could take steps to improve her financial position (she works only part time but could increase her hours and thus her income), but with the understanding that we could increase back to at least once weekly within a specified period of time.

Sample Form

CLIENT TERMINATION LETTER

ANTHONY KINDHEART, LPC
6894 Forest Park Drive
Suite 268
Dallas, Texas 75206
July 17, 20_____

Mr. Kevin Jones
1425 Centenary
Dallas, Texas 75210

Re: Termination of Treatment

Dear Mr. Kevin Jones:

It has become necessary, for the reasons stated below, to terminate our professional and therapeutic relationship. I will maintain your records for the period required by law and will make copies of your records available to you or a subsequent therapist upon written request. You may be charged a reasonable fee for the cost of duplicating the records.

Our work together began on July 1, _____, and ended on this date. During this time, we worked on improving your occupational and social functioning and alleviating your depression by addressing factors that may have caused, contributed to, or aggravated your depression.

In the exercise of my professional judgment, I have concluded that you have not made satisfactory progress in improving your social and occupational functioning and with your depression. I believe you are in need of additional mental health services for treatment of your depression and possible chemical dependency. These services can be best provided to you by one of the following:

Richard Lewins, MD (214) 489-3624, 1900 Main Street, Suite 120, Dallas, TX 75201

Sylvia Jones, LCDC (972) 270-9142, 689 LBJ Freeway, Suite 410, Dallas, TX 75214

Harold Jones, PhD (214) 814-3621, 48764 Mockingbird, Suite 206, Dallas, TX 75206

(continued)

Sample Form
(continued)

I recommend you contact one of these providers or another provider of your choosing as quickly as possible to schedule an appointment. With your written consent, I will consult with any professional you may select and will forward the file or a summary of your treatment to my successor.

Your primary discharge diagnosis is: 296.32 Major Depression, recurrent.

This termination is not due to any personal reasons but solely due to my desire for you to achieve the highest possible level of mental health wellness and social and occupational functioning. I believe referring you to one of the providers listed above presents the best possibility for this to occur. I wish you success and want you to know that I will make myself available for consultation with anyone you choose to work with, in order to make this transition as easy as possible.

Sincerely,

_____

Anthony Kindheart, LPC

I acknowledge receipt and review and accept and understand the terms of this termination letter, dated the 17th day of July, 20____.

_____   _____

Kevin Jones   Date

_____

Social Security Number

I also offered her a referral to a low-fee clinic as a way of acknowledging her percep-
tion of financial incapacity (and avoiding abandonment).

The patient responded with some anger, saying I wasn't "understanding" her
situation, and she has broken off all contact with me. It appears she has elected to
terminate her treatment; however, I don't want this to appear at some later time
as abandonment. Am I correct in thinking I have no obligation to see her in a
manner I believe to be inadequate relative to her diagnosis . . . or must I see her
on whatever basis she requests? Should I send her a letter, and if so, what should
the letter say?

❗ *Answer*

We believe you acted appropriately with this client. Now that the *client has*
broken off contact, we think you should send the client a termination letter or
e-mail. This letter should set forth your opinion as to the client's mental
health treatment needs and the names, addresses, and phone numbers of at
least three appropriate referral sources whom the client may call if further assistance is needed.

If a client is uncooperative and refuses to follow through with your treatment recommendations, we feel termination and referral to another therapist,
who may be better able to get through to the client, is usually sound clinical
practice. We don't see how you could be an effective therapist if you were to let
clients control your practice and treatment methods.

However, be careful and tactful. This is exactly the type of hostile and
angry, perhaps controlling client, who will vent their anger, hostility, and control with a licensing board and/or consult with an attorney. You will be on
solid ground with careful documentation of every step you take and a carefully
prepared intake and consent form. The intake and informed consent form
should authorize termination of professional services when, in the opinion of
the professional, the client is not progressing in therapy for any reason. Reasons for termination might include failure to follow agreed-on therapy plan,
delinquent payment schedules, failure to keep appointments or to cancel as
per agreements, and so on.

💡 *Additional Thoughts*

- A practitioner need not be intimidated by clients, but should be aware of
  angry clients and how that anger may be brought to the surface.
- When a client self-terminates by either not making another appointment or
  by breaking off all contact, send a termination notice or letter, both certified
  and regular mail, or by e-mail to the authorized address. Keep a hard copy of
  any e-mails. Include your recommendations for further treatment and your

referrals. Indicate, in the letter, that it is her responsibility to follow up on her need for continuing treatment. Keep the certified receipt and the letter sent by regular mail if it is returned to you or a copy of the document indicating the e-mail was received. If not returned, make a note in the file.

- See if your national organization or licensing board rules cover situations such as this. If they contain a procedure in cases of this type, follow the stated procedures carefully.

Legal Lightbulb

- The therapeutic relationship with a client should continue only so long as it is benefiting the client.

- A client's file should always reflect the need for additional mental health services. When that need ceases, it is time to terminate.

- Try to schedule a face-to-face termination session and have the client sign the form or letter in your presence. If an exit interview isn't possible, try to make phone contact with the client. Either way, mail the form or letter to the client's authorized mailing address. It's a good idea to make two copies of the letter. Send one by certified mail, with return receipt requested, and the other by regular mail. Regular mail is delivered; certified mail can be refused. E-mail is acceptable if you have the correct e-mail address and you are authorized by the client to use it.

- If termination is necessary and the client needs additional mental health care, provide the client with at least three competent referral sources. (Remember, a tort action can be brought against you for "negligent referral.") Any person, agency, or organization on your referral list must be capable of treating the client, on terms the client can accept financially and clinically. (See Chapters 27 and 28 for more specifics.)

- Documentation is critical. It is your best defense.

- Proper closure is important to the client, the file, and the provider.

5

Electronic Records

A worried therapist called his lawyers. He had taken his personal office computer to a major repair facility and returned two weeks later to pick up the instrument. However, it could not be found! After a long and diligent search of the repair service, the shop offered to replace it with an upgraded computer—a new state-of-the-art product with double the market value of the lost PC. The only problem was that the original computer's hard drive had not been erased (nor a complete backup file created), and some person now had possession of numerous client files, all of which were privileged, confidential, and private. Fortunately, there had been no repercussions. Whoever had the computer was probably interested only in the hardware and was ignorant of the significance of the stored, intimately personal data. The therapist responsible for the security of the file had been lucky—there had been no reported breaches of confidentiality. Prayer had worked so far. On the other hand, the therapist lost all the data and notes that had been saved on the hard drive. This is a potentially explosive situation.

In the current electronic age, therapists are using desktop computers to create, store, and design client files, and are transmitting documents via fax and e-mail. In addition, new client records are constantly being created, generated, and maintained on computers, and the need for hard copies stored in voluminous, space-eating files is diminishing.

Because maintaining floor space for files costs money, many mental health professionals prefer the convenience of a disk to the bulk of a thick paper file. When a client file is needed, the press of a few buttons retrieves the file onto the screen or printer in a matter of seconds. The main concern when a therapist chooses to convert to computerized record keeping and storage of client files is whether the computer system will preserve both the confidentiality and the integrity of client health care information and whether this system will be in operation and available in 20 years (for minors) should the file be needed at that time.

HIPAA imposes stringent rules on all health care providers with respect to electronic health care information. The specifics of the HIPAA Privacy and Security Rules are discussed in Chapters 38 and 46.

A computer system should preserve the confidentiality of the client's information.

HIPAA imposes stringent rules on all health care providers with respect to electronic health care information.

Maintaining Correct Files and Confidentiality

A mental health professional's obligation to maintain the confidentiality of a client's file is not altered by a change in the method by which the record is created or stored.

Access to computer files can be safeguarded with codes, but absolute security cannot be guaranteed. Always do the best you can and, preferably, have a competent technician design a system for you.

With a printed paper file, it is easy to secure client information. The office and the file cabinets can be locked, and only designated persons can have access to the file on a "need to know" basis. Paper files can also be counted on to survive the time period for which the therapist is required, by law and good practice, to maintain and preserve case records. However, with computers, the rules and procedures of storage have changed. Indeed, there is little similarity between a computer disk and a printed, paper-intensive file secured in a cardboard file folder.

Gone are the days when a hard copy of each client file was maintained in a neat manila folder, which could be pulled out when needed. Now, in addition to hard copies, there are floppy disks, hard drives, and, possibly, central storage systems. Maintaining security, confidentiality, privacy, and privilege has become a clinician's nightmare and a hacker's delight.

A mental health professional's obligation to maintain the confidentiality of a client's file is not altered by a change in the method by which the record is created or stored. It does not matter whether the file is created by hand, computer, audiotape, or videotape. Computerization of client information, however, does increase the risk of unauthorized disclosure to hackers—individuals who, for the sheer pleasure of displaying their technical expertise, randomly invade, disclose, or rearrange files. Access to computer files can be safeguarded with codes, but absolute security can usually not be guaranteed.

System security measures, such as user passwords or computer locks, should be considered. To satisfactorily comply with a therapist's legal and ethical obligation to preserve the confidentiality of a client's record, including duties mandated by the HIPAA Security Rule, reasonable efforts must be made and reasonable safeguards must be implemented.

Call for Backup

Back up all files regularly.

Every mental health provider, regardless of discipline, should back up each file regularly, perhaps daily, to a CD-ROM, floppy disk, tape, or some other backup system. Clients have a right to copies of their files, and they will take a dim view of a therapist or provider who has, by negligence or inadvertence, allowed a file to be lost, destroyed, or negligently placed into the public domain. In addition, HIPAA provides for administrative fines and penalties for such violations.

As a precaution, when a computer needs repair, copy information to the backup system, and erase the files from the hard drive. If the computer is lost or stolen, only the computer is lost, not client information, substance, or material. Remember, the client has not given informed consent for a computer repairer to review his or her file. If a computer is to be repaired, it is better to have the technician come to the office and repair the equipment under the therapist's watchful eye. Under these circumstances, it is also a good idea to have the technician making the repair enter into a Business Associate Contract to ensure confidentiality and compliance with HIPAA in case some confidential information comes to the technician's attention. (See Chapter 38.)

Computer files can easily be deleted, lost, erased, corrupted, or overwritten. The typical system—whether as a result of inadvertent or accidental operator error, or unforeseen events such as electrical storms, major power surges, or power shortages—can lose data very quickly. Frequent backup is a necessity.

The therapist should give thought to the durability of a computerized record—the medium on which the information is stored. A disk or tape will have to survive for at least the minimum time period the therapist is required to maintain records. (See Chapter 7.) In addition, technology is rapidly advancing and changing. If a therapist upgrades his or her computer system, it is important for the new and the old systems to be compatible. If they are not, old equipment may have to be preserved and maintained so the therapist can comply with retrieval requirements for the minimum record-keeping period.

How should the therapist keep computerized records?

When a computer needs repair, copy information to the backup system, and erase the files from the hard drive.

Hints for Keeping Computerized Records

- Make sure the hard drive and any backup disks are locked and secure at all times. They should be protected against fire, flood, curious cleaning people, and inquisitive clients who have the habit of draping themselves over the therapist's or receptionist's desk and peering at the computer screen.
- A password protects access to the computer system; secure passwords from detection.
- If a celebrity is in treatment at any time, devise a fictitious name and keep all records under the assumed name. Have the "key" to the name in a protected place. (Investigative reporters and private detectives have been known to gain entry surreptitiously and copy files. A diligent hacker can access most instruments.)
- Back up the computer to a disk, tape, or other backup system regularly, and give the backup system the same respect as the hard drive.
- Copy the records to a disk, tape, or other backup system, and then delete the hard drive whenever the computer is taken in for repair or whenever a repairer must examine it. Understand how to protect stored information and the durability of the different mediums (i.e., disk or tape) used to back up and store information.

Regular or temporary support staff who have access to computer files should sign a confidentiality form and be fully trained on the entity's Privacy and Security Rule safeguards.

- Have *every person* who will have access to files *read and initial* a published protocol that indicates the importance and relevance of safeguarding mental health files. This is especially important for temporary and other support staff who may not be aware of or trained in important principles concerning the sanctity, privacy, or absolute confidentiality of clients' records or names.
- Adequately train yourself and the support staff about the computer system employed. Know how to use it properly.
- Consider the files of all clients to be valuable property that, if lost or stolen, produces dramatic obvious, foreseen, and unforeseen consequences.
- Position computer monitors so that only the operator can see the screen.
- Use virus protection software.
- Take the potential problem of computer theft or crash seriously enough to establish reasonable safeguards.

The New Communications Media

Advances in technology help communication; however, use caution when dealing with faxes, pagers, voice mail, and e-mail.

Technology has created new methods of communication and has the capacity to put into the public domain information that is thought to be private and personal. Many of the current communication methods were not available even a few years ago. These methods make communication and publication easier, but confidentiality and privacy are more difficult to maintain.

New transmission media include the Internet, fax machines, cordless telephones, cellular telephone communications networks, computer communications, private network communications, semipublic network (password-protected or encrypted) communications, unencrypted Internet e-mail, and other creative methods of communication.

All are in use, and many are presumed by clients to be private and confidential—and perhaps privileged as well. But all these methods are relatively new in the global, long-term view of legal history and case precedents, and legal determinations have not yet been solidified into dependable rules of law. HIPAA is a comprehensive attempt to connect the world of technology to the privacy of health care information. To some extent, the rules of computer technology and the responsibility of therapists to create, maintain, and guard records are in the process of evolution. To date, there are few case precedents, and most lawyers give advice with a caveat: "This is my best guess regarding the legal consequences as of this day. Tomorrow it may change." HIPAA's Privacy and Security Rules are new and will be subject to judicial review and interpretation.

Modern communication methods permeate all phases of mental health practice, from the keeping and maintaining of clinical records to the written and oral transmission of information over the wires and air waves of mass communication. Speed and accuracy are mandated, but so, too, is confidentiality and, where appropriate, privilege. Each method of communication has its own developing body of law. Remember, not all forms of communication will bring a therapist within the purview of HIPAA. Using a telephone or phone-to-phone fax transmission currently falls outside the scope of the HIPAA. The mental health professional who has "gone modern" should stay abreast of the developing law in his or her jurisdiction and federal law before going public with information that might place a client, and later the provider, in jeopardy.

Alongside the benefits of technology, there are some disadvantages to consider. Copy machines offer an opportunity for roving eyes to glance at documents that were intended to be private. Fax transmissions can go to the wrong place because of the simple error of pressing the wrong digit. Telephone answering machines can generate messages to unidentified listeners, or information may be offered before the absolute identity of the original caller is determined. Cellular phones carry conversations over the air waves, and anyone with the proper equipment can listen in while a call is being made. Voice pagers can blurt out information in closed sessions. The caller assumes confidentiality and will have no idea that the voice message has entered the public domain. Voice mail messages are often unprotected if the access code is in writing and placed near the machine. Computer terminals are often in plain view, so a person can peer around the counter or workstation and see the mental health history of a client on the screen.

In these circumstances, common sense must prevail. No rules are always fail-safe in all situations. However, certain standard methods of protection can be practiced in most office settings, and individual therapists will create others to satisfy their own needs and purposes.

Not all forms of communication will bring a therapist within the purview of HIPAA.

Stay abreast of the developing law.

Suggested Safeguards

- Prevent the copy and fax machine from becoming a social gathering place. Make sure that discarded copies are shredded and not left to be viewed by anyone who might glance at or go through the trash.
- Turn down the volume on your telephone answering machine, or turn it off, when third parties are in the room.
- When answering a message left on your answering machine, verify the identity of the person who made the call, and make sure you are alone in the room.
- On a cellular phone, assume "Big Brother" is listening in on your call. You can't be too careful. Careers have been ruined by talking too freely to a wrong, and unseen, person. "Big Brother" can be a gossipy neighbor, an investigative reporter, a government agency, or a political rival.
- Don't use a loud voice pager in public. Turn the volume down or off.

As always, the therapist is responsible for maintaining the confidentiality of a client's file, regardless of the method by which the record is created or stored.

- Ensure the integrity of your voice mail code. Only the mental health professional and others who have a real "need to know" should have it available.
- Ask for the client's written consent before sending any fax or e-mail transmissions. Advise the client of the potential risk of disclosure. In some cases, ask the recipient to wait by the fax machine while the fax is being sent. Ask for confirmation of receipt.
- Consider encryption technology for e-mail transmissions.
- Contact the intended recipient before transmission to advise that a transmission is imminent.
- Double-check all fax transmissions, and keep the printout (staple it to the transmission) so there is always evidence of the recipient's number.
- When using the fax, have a fail-safe system to see that all numbers are accurately pressed. Include a confidentiality page in each transmission.

Advancing technology will continue to create new difficulties and areas of exposure—in terms of liability and professional ethics—for the mental health practitioner. The client assumes everything shared with the professional is confidential and will be kept confidential. The best way for the therapist to maintain that level of confidentiality is to continue to be cautious.

When in doubt, call your lawyer, the malpractice hot line, your professional organization, or the licensing board. New laws will be published on a regular basis. Read the latest bulletins on law and therapy and on the need for confidentiality preservation and maintenance of electronic and computer files. Knowing the content of the most current bulletin will help you in the future and may even save your license and your practice.

Answers to Frequently Asked Questions about:

>   Admissibility as evidence
>   Electronic charting
>   Computer repairs
>   Retention and preservation

❓ Question

How does electronic charting, record keeping, or maintenance of progress notes (instead of the handwritten in black ink style) hold up legally? I would like to change over to electronic charting for all my clients because computer records are easier to write, maintain, correct, preserve, and forward to another facility, an insurance company, or the client. But, if it is going to be challenged legally later on, I won't switch.

❗ *Answer*

Generally speaking, there is *no legal difference* between electronic record keeping and traditional handwritten files. The same rules apply with respect to content, preservation, and confidentiality. (See Chapter 46.) There are some additional considerations such as whether the electronic records are to be kept on a computer hard drive or on a 3½-inch floppy disk, a CD-ROM, tape, or zip disk. Each medium must be *secured from prying eyes* and *preserved* for the time period required in your state and by your discipline. Computers should be *password protected*. Files maintained on hard drives should be backed up in case of failures. These are minimum safeguards required by HIPAA's Security Rule. (See Chapter 46.) Repairs to the computer present their own unique problems, as illustrated.

A client requesting a copy of the file is entitled to a hard copy. The information stored electronically will have to be printed if, as, and when requested. We are not aware of any rules or laws that make electronic records illegal. Rather, health care delivery is moving toward an all electronic system. Check with your state licensing board or a knowledgeable attorney in your area if you have any doubt.

💡 *Additional Thoughts*

- Electronic records can be introduced into evidence in a trial. They are as admissible as other business records and printed documents and are subject to the same rules of evidence.
- If electronic records are changed, corrected, or altered, remember, they cannot be lined out and initialed. Changes must be made indicating the original entry, what was changed, who changed it, the date, and the correcting entry. The same information required by a handwritten entry must be entered on a computer entry.
- Floppy disks, CD-ROMS, tapes, and zip disks all have life spans beyond which the integrity of the data cannot be guaranteed. We have tried, with conspicuous lack of success, to obtain a guarantee of use preservation in terms of years. All we obtain is a blank stare.
- Computer repairs must be made under the therapist's watchful eyes. When a computer crashes, after the initial hand wringing, remember: There are confidential files on it, and this confidentiality must be maintained and secured from repair people or any subsequent person who has access to the computer.
- Every ethics code requires an in-house procedure for the security, retention, and destruction of files. This includes electronic records.

Legal Lightbulb

- A computer file is the same as a hard file, when confidentiality, privacy, privilege, maintenance, and security are to be considered.

- Legally, files are files, regardless of the method of creation and preservation.

- Computers must be secure from roving eyes.

- Presumably, a client who has a right to view his or her file would have a right to a copy of that portion of the disk on which his or her files are stored.

- A lawyer who states "This is the law concerning computer files" is overstating the current status of the law and/or the facts. The law, including HIPAA, is in a developing stage and will be as long as computers are being constantly created, updated, and upgraded within a few years after their creation. Imminent obsolescence seems to keep the law and the anxiety level of lawyers on a constant fluctuating high plane. If a lawyer renders an opinion, ask him or her to reduce it to writing.

- The transmission of sensitive information using modern technology creates a legal nightmare. There is no fail-safe advice. Just be careful and HIPAA compliant.

- Most unintentional breaches of confidentiality are covered by professional liability malpractice policies. A therapist who is worried should increase his or her coverage.

- Be careful what you discard as trash. In this sense, old and obsolete computers, printers, disks, tapes, and paper files are not "trash." They are to be treated as confidential and potentially explosive historic documents or items—destroyed, not discarded.

- Create a therapist-employee (regular or temporary) contract. Employees have no reason to copy files onto a personal disk, and no client files, disks, or records should ever be removed from the office unless it is part of a supervised back-up system.

6

Intake and Consent Forms

Dr. Shapiro was notified by her licensing board that a complaint had been filed against her by a client whom she had reported to the state authorities for suspected child abuse—pursuant to Dr. Shapiro's legal duty to make this report. In the complaint to the licensing board, the client stated that he had sought mental health treatment from the therapist for problems when dealing with his children, and the therapist had never advised him that suspected child abuse was an exception to his right to confidentiality.

∼

Dr. Chen was practicing under supervision, with the approval of his licensing board. He received notice of a complaint filed against him with his licensing board for allegedly failing to advise a client that he was practicing under supervision. The client stated that the supervision was never disclosed to her, and she never would have consented to treatment with the therapist had she known about the supervision. She wanted the therapist to refund the $1,800 she had paid from her own pocket for counseling and therapy over a 15-month period. She was complaining only about the failure of the therapist to disclose to her that he was under supervision, not about the quality or professionalism of the therapy.

How does a therapist defend against these and other allegations from unhappy clients?

Many state licensing statutes require a mental health professional to discuss several important matters with a client before, or at the onset of, the very first counseling session with the client, that is, before therapy begins. To proceed with treatment, the therapist must have the *informed consent* of the client. *Uninformed consent is no consent at all.* Remember that licensing statutes have evolved primarily out of a concern for and in an effort to protect the consumer. Public policy demands a protected and well-educated consumer. Fortunately or unfortunately, the therapist has the task of educating the consumer/client.

To help accomplish that end, a mental health practitioner is required to discuss, at the outset:

Uninformed consent is no consent at all.

- The licensing of the therapist and restrictions on the license, if any.
- Supervision and restrictions.
- Information about the services to be provided.
- Purposes, goals, and techniques of treatment.
- Confidentiality and its exceptions. Note that federal law (see Chapter 44) requires specific "privacy information" be furnished to clients in a "Notice of Privacy Practices."
- Fees and payment.
- Consent for treatment.

The best evidence to present to the licensing board when a complaint is filed is an intake and consent form signed by the client.

Without a written record that these matters were discussed with the client, the therapist's word must stand against that of a client who complains to a licensing board. The best and easiest evidence to present to the licensing board when a complaint is filed is an intake and consent form signed by the client on the date of the very first therapist-client session.

There is no basis for argument when a written record indicates coverage of all the matters that need to be addressed. Prepare a consent form to use in conjunction with a HIPAA "Notice of Privacy Practices," go over it with the client, have the client sign it in your presence, and send the client home with a signed copy of the consent. If the client returns for a second session, he or she will find it even more difficult to support a complaint or to allege failure to cover the requisite matters.

Every intake and consent form should be carefully crafted for each therapist's individual practice and clientele.

This chapter gives you a checklist of issues to be addressed in an intake and consent form. The list should not be considered exhaustive. Mental health providers who are "covered providers" under the HIPAA Privacy Rule will have to prepare and implement a document that informs the client of the provider's privacy practices. Every intake and consent form should be carefully crafted for each therapist's individual practice and clientele.

Throughout this book, model forms are presented to cover specific problems. When constructing your own forms from the models, include all possible circumstances and eliminate areas that are so remote or statistically improbable for your practice that they do not need inclusion. For example, don't include clauses concerning children if your practice is limited to geriatric clients.

Anyone entering a hospital within the past few years signs an admission form consisting of pages and pages of small print. Anyone watching the procedure observes that arriving patients will sign almost anything placed in front of them when they need the service. Few question the admission form, which has been carefully crafted by the hospital lawyer *to protect the hospital, the attending physician, and the staff.* Mental health professionals might not need such detailed protection, but in our litigious society, the printed and signed form *is* important.

What to Include in Your Intake and Consent Form

1. A description of yourself and your credentials: Include information about your education, licensing status, restrictions, if any, and, if you are practicing under supervision, the name and address of your supervisor. State your relationship to any referring entity, such as: "Independent Contractor/ Provider for ABC Managed Care." Mention your employer if you work for a group or agency. If you are in private practice, advise the client of your independent status.

2. A description of the services you provide: Tell the client what you do during a typical session and what types of services you provide (e.g., "psychological services including but not limited to play therapy and psychological testing"). The idea is to make sure the client is an educated consumer. The client should acknowledge, in writing, what the therapist does and does not provide, the competence of the therapist in specified fields, and the limits of that competence.

Make sure the client is an educated consumer.

3. Procedures for appointments: Tell the new client how far ahead you schedule appointments and how much notice you expect for a cancellation. Provide the client with specific information on scheduling and canceling appointments, including the times and the numbers to call. *State whether there is a charge for canceled or missed appointments* and the charge for missing scheduled appointments.

Provide the client with specific information on scheduling and canceling appointments.

4. Length and number of sessions: Advise the client when a finite number of sessions is approved initially by an insurance carrier or managed care company. Start planning—and encourage the client to do so as well—the steps that will be needed if additional sessions are required. If there are no session limitations, advise the client that you cannot predict how many sessions may be required to appropriately address his or her problems or concerns. At least discuss managed care or insurance limitations and what the plan might be if third-party payments are not available.

5. Relationship between the therapist and client: Dual relationship and boundary problems can be effectively avoided if the therapist has a frank discussion with the client concerning the nature of the therapeutic relationship between therapists and clients. Explain to the client what a therapeutic relationship means and the limitations concerning nontherapeutic personal contact. Advise the client that, for your work to have the best chance of success for him or her, the therapeutic relationship is the only relationship the two of you can have. Advise the client that it is inappropriate for you to exchange or bestow gifts, spend time with each other socially, or attend family functions, graduations, marriages, or religious ceremonies.

Explain to the client what a therapeutic relationship means.

It is not appropriate for a client to try to engage you in conversation, in person or by phone, at your home or anywhere outside your office. Urge the client not to call you outside the office unless it is to discuss a future appointment or a genuine emergency.

A client can cross the line into a dual relationship with impunity, but the therapist can't. Many therapists have been unwittingly drawn across the line by a manipulative or zealous client. Deal with the issue when establishing the initial relationship, and advise the client that, if the line is crossed, you will have to terminate the therapeutic relationship and refer the client to another therapist. A periodic, gentle reminder might be appropriate. Blurred relationships or fuzzy contacts are to be avoided. When a therapeutic relationship begins to blur, handle the problem at once. Don't wait until the therapeutic contact becomes a crisis.

6. Goals, purposes, and techniques of therapy: Most licensing acts require a client to be informed of what the mental health professional will be doing with and to the client. This is an essential element of informed consent. You often see this described in licensing acts as informing the client of the "goals, purposes, and techniques of therapy." The client should be provided with this information and given the opportunity to ask questions and have input on the goals and treatment to be provided by the therapist.

Including space in an intake and consent form to record the initial goals, purposes, and techniques of therapy can help document informed consent.

In malpractice suits brought against mental health professionals, a common theme is the lack of informed consent due to the failure of the treatment provider to advise the client of alternative treatments or therapies available to the client. If the client is given only one option by the therapist, it can be argued that the client was not an informed consumer who made an informed choice to hire the therapist to treat the client's problem.

7. Fees/payment: Give the client accurate information about all special charges and about your fees for services you provide to clients. State when payment is due. For a managed care referral, calculate and communicate the amount of copays for which the client is responsible.

A matter not often addressed by mental health professionals is the time and expense that may be incurred in response to a subpoena to produce records or give testimony. Most often, a therapist will not be a *litigation expert witness*—someone who meets the client for the first time after a lawsuit has been filed and is retained to give testimony on behalf of the client. Usually, the therapist has provided mental health services to a client before any lawsuit is filed or even contemplated. For example, one therapist began treating a woman for depression and, six months later, was subpoenaed by the client's husband, who was filing for divorce and seeking custody of the couple's children.

Unfortunately, there is usually no court protection for therapists who may wish to petition for reimbursement for time and expenses incurred in responding to a subpoena. A therapist, like an eyewitness to an accident, can be subpoenaed to testify in court about what he or she has heard or observed. To give yourself an option to present an invoice for your time and trouble, include in the intake and consent form clauses that make the client responsible to pay a fee for your preparation, time, and expense spent in responding to a subpoena, regardless of who issued the subpoena.

Is it fair for the client to have to pay for the therapist's time if her husband and his attorney issued the subpoena? Perhaps not, but is it fair for the therapist to incur financial loss—in the form of canceled appointments and missed opportunities—and inconvenience because the client and her husband are seeking a divorce? It is fairer to place this unexpected loss on the client/litigant, who has more control over and more involvement in the events that gave rise to the litigation? As Abraham Lincoln would have said, had he been a therapist: "A therapist's time and advice are his stock in trade." If utilized, the clinician should be compensated. (See Chapter 1 for further discussion.)

8. Confidentiality and the duty to warn: Clients come into your office with the expectation that everything told to you will be kept strictly confidential and will not be disclosed to any third parties. They may believe that you will take their secrets to the grave and will never give them up or testify about them, no matter what the price. In reality, however, *absolute therapeutic confidentiality is a myth.* There are so many exceptions to confidentiality that, on consideration of all of them, a person might reasonably conclude that true or absolute confidentiality no longer exists.

A mental health professional has the duty to explain confidentiality to a prospective client and to reveal substantially all the exceptions. HIPAA's Privacy Rule does not impose a new duty in this regard for mental health professionals. Cover this matter thoroughly, whether you are "ensnared" by HIPAA or not. List as many exceptions as you can think of; use the clause "including but not limited to." Create and incorporate a HIPAA-compliant "Notice of Privacy Practices" by reference or directly into your consent form. (See Appendix I.) If you open a practice in a jurisdiction where it is unclear whether you have the right or duty to warn or contact an identifiable intended victim, have all your new clients authorize your right to contact any person in a position to prevent harm to the client or a third party. Consent is the number one exception to confidentiality. Ask the client to provide you with mail and e-mail addresses and phone numbers of specific persons you can contact if you reasonably suspect the client or a third party is in danger.

9. Addresses/phone numbers for communication with client: Be sure to have the client provide you with an address where mail and e-mail can and may be sent and one or more phone numbers (work/daytime, evening, weekend) where you can contact the client if necessary. Remember, disclosing client identity can constitute a breach of confidentiality, and area codes, phone numbers, and addresses change over time. Check the validity of your client information file at regular intervals.

10. Risks of therapy/counseling: Tell your new clients that therapy involves risks. Therapy sessions can be very painful at times. Clients may learn things about themselves that they don't like. Pain often precedes growth, and

Tell your new clients that therapy involves risks.

clients should be made aware that they may experience pain, sorrow, depression, and anxiety along the way. For example, marital therapy, which, in the mind of the client is to improve a marriage relationship, may lead to divorce. It's a risk.

11. After-hours emergencies: Clients should be given a phone number to call in the event of an emergency. If your practice provides 24-hour access to a therapist, provide clients with the phone numbers to call during and after normal office hours. If 24-hour service is not available, list on your intake form the phone numbers for hotlines or prevention organizations that should be contacted in the event of an emergency and for local hospital emergency rooms. Specify on your answering machine message the times you are not available.

12. Therapist's death/incapacity: Confidentiality survives death—the therapist's as well as the client's. Very few mental health practitioners consider what to do about client records or how clients should be contacted if the therapist should die or become incapacitated. Some states impose a duty on therapists *to plan for these contingencies,* but not all have specific statutory provisions or ethical canons that set out procedures to follow in the event of the death or incapacity of the therapist or the death of a client. One approach is for therapists to state in their wills that all of their records and files are to go to the appropriate licensing board in the event of the therapist's death. The therapist's concern is breach of confidentiality. It is not appropriate for a therapist's spouse, or any third party not consented to by the clients, to review files or appointment calendars when the therapist dies or becomes incapacitated.

Therapists can consider appointing the licensing board as the custodian for all their files and records.

There is an exception for court-appointed executors, administrators, guardians, or receivers, but it takes time to secure a court appointment. In the meantime, how should current and/or needy or desperate clients be protected? In your intake and consent form, provide for the client to consent to having another mental health professional of your choosing take possession of the client's file and contact the client in the event you become incapacitated or die. If the client wishes, he or she may designate the successor therapist as the recipient of the file on the death or disability of the treating professional.

Make sure you have a signed intake and consent form from a person with the legal authority to consent for a child.

13. Consent to treat: A client must consent to having you provide mental health services. When the client is a child, make sure you have a signed intake and consent form from a person who has the legal authority to consent for that child. Have the child sign the consent also if appropriate. (See Chapter 18.) The consent authorizes you to provide services, and it states the client's or a third-party payer's obligation to pay. It establishes a contract between you and the client, and it gives you all the rights and duties to provide professional mental health services for compensation.

A client must consent to having you provide mental health services.

One problem can plague the therapist. What happens when the appropriate call is made; authorization is given; therapy is offered, accepted, and concluded; then, after internal review, the insurance carrier or managed care company declines the claim as being unauthorized or inappropriate because of some technicality? In one case, the parties were divorced and the carrier was not notified. The divorce had terminated the client's coverage. Everyone acted in good faith and yet the claim was denied.

Provide specifically in the consent form that ultimate responsibility for the bill is with the client/patient and whoever signed the form in the case of minors. If the claim is later denied for any reason, the client/patient is fully responsible for paying the bill within a reasonable time period—for example, 30 days after the date the claim is denied. (In one case, the claim was denied after payment had been made, and the insurance company demanded reimbursement from the therapist a year later.)

The responsibility for payment is ultimately with the client; with children, it is with the individual who signs the consent to treatment form.

HIPAA does not address client consent but specifically leaves the issue of consent to state law. Mental health professionals should, therefore, obtain and document client consent consistent with their state law.

HIPAA leaves the issue of consent to state law.

14. Waiver of right to child's records/information: If you deal with children, especially adolescents, it may be advisable to secure a waiver of a parent's right to review information about a child, in the event that you determine it is in the best interest of the child to withhold information from the parent. Generally, parents have the right to access the mental health records and files of their children. But a teenager may be reluctant to be candid with a therapist if a parent will have access to the information shared in a counseling session. The waiver may prove helpful later on in dealing with difficult parent-child issues raised by the child. For the child to achieve success in therapy, trust and a right to ensured privacy are critical. The prying eyes of involved and intrusive parents are not always helpful to effective therapy. Your contract should provide that you control the file and who examines it.

It is advisable to secure a waiver of a parent's right to information about a child—if it is in the best interest of the child and is permitted by the HIPAA Privacy Rule.

HIPAA's Privacy Rule specifically provides for these types of waivers so if state law is silent on this issue or is not as protective of the child's privacy rights as HIPAA, the Privacy Rule should prevail. It clearly provides strong legal authority for therapists to enter into these kinds of waivers or agreements with parents.

15. Signature lines: After you have developed your intake and consent form with your lawyer and reviewed it with your client, don't forget to have the client sign it. You should also sign it and make a copy of the signed form for the client to take home. At that point, you should have a client who is a well-educated consumer and adequate proof of having satisfied your professional responsibilities in educating, informing, and advising the client.

Consider forms carefully, and engage the help of lawyers or other professionals who are familiar with the mental health statutes of your state.

It may be necessary to develop more than one information and consent form to satisfy different areas of your practice. A therapist who solicits forensic work may wish to tailor a form for criminal, custody, and other specific types of cases. Clients in these cases must understand that the therapist may come to a conclusion or be forced to give an opinion that is adverse to the client or the

*It may be
necessary to
develop more than
one information
and consent form
to satisfy different
areas of your
practice.*

client's position in a lawsuit. Do not use forms blindly; consider them carefully, and engage the help of lawyers and other professionals to make sure they suit your practice and give you maximum protection.

16. HIPAA: The HIPAA law can affect the intake and consent form. A review of Section Eleven will alert you to the requirements of this act. When revising your forms, make sure all HIPAA requirements are taken into consideration. Printed materials, workshops, and seminars are being prepared and presented all over the nation to alert mental health professionals concerning the new governmental requirements.

Answers to Frequently Asked Questions about:

No-show charges

Late cancellation charges

❓ Question

What is the legal status of no-show or late-cancellation charges? I advise potential patients of these charges in advance and in writing. In my own mind, I liken them to an airline charging for a nonrefundable ticket—you pay whether you use the seat or not—or to a rented apartment in which rent is owed whether you occupy the space or not. A clinician cannot bill an insurance company or third-party payer for a no-show because it is not actually a service rendered.

However, recently, I charged a patient for a no-show and he refused to pay, stating that such charges are illegal. He also quit treatment. I won't press the issue with this particular individual; however, I am eager to know whether these kinds of charges are in fact legitimate and "pursuable" in the eyes of the law.

❗ Answer

A therapist should clearly provide a potential client with the *therapist's fee policy in writing* before any services are provided. This would include the cancellation policy and the requirement that fees for sessions are to be paid if an appointment is not cancelled a specified numbers of days or hours in advance. Generally speaking, if the client is advised upfront that the failure to cancel an appointment in the manner prescribed by the therapist will result in the client's being charged the normal session rate for the skipped appointment, the therapist is free to bill the client the no-show charge. The fee charged must be reasonable, that is, not more than the normal session rate.

Be careful, however, to review any provider contract that you may have signed with a managed care or insurance entity that referred the client to you.

We have seen provider contracts that preclude the therapist from charging the client any fee except a copay. This kind of language in a provider agreement could prohibit you from charging for a skipped appointment.

Although we are not aware of any law that makes it illegal for a therapist to charge for a skipped appointment, we are not familiar with the laws in each state. You should consult with your state licensing board or a knowledgeable attorney in your area.

💡 *Additional Thoughts*

- No-show or cancellation policies *must* be in writing in order to avoid legitimate misunderstandings.
- Such charges, if they are in writing and signed by you and the client before therapy commences, are legal unless there is some prohibition in either an insurance policy or in some agreement that the provider (you) has with managed care.
- You may make these charges, but you are wise not to pursue them with enthusiasm. When a client refuses to pay for any reason, it is better to "eat" the loss rather than sue, turn the claim over to a collection agency or lawyer, or write unpleasant letters. Go on to the next client. Write it off.
- Not all legitimate debts are worth pursuing. Pursuing a client for any manner of unpaid bill usually brings about an automatic complaint to the licensing board and sometimes a legal counterclaim. It is just not worth pursuing. It is a business loss. The advice to therapists: Limit your accounts receivable and have the intake and consent form provide that the provider-client contract can be terminated if bills for services remain unpaid after a specified time period or after a specified accumulated amount remains unpaid.
- A good thought is to publish and post the therapist's no-show policy in a pamphlet and distribute the pamphlet to clients. Restate the no-show policy in the intake form and have the client acknowledge receipt of the pamphlet.

The Bottom Line

- Documentation is a therapist's best defense against a complaint lodged by a client.
- The most important document in a client's file is a detailed information and consent form that has been carefully drafted and reviewed by a lawyer familiar with mental health law and includes the Notice of Privacy Practices required by the HIPAA Privacy Rule.
- Without a signed, comprehensive information and consent form, it is the therapist's word against the client's in the event a fact dispute occurs, a complaint is filed against the therapist, or any other dispute arises.

Sample Form

CLIENT INFORMATION AND CONSENT

Therapist

The undersigned therapist is a licensed professional and chemical dependency counselor and a licensed marriage and family therapist engaged in private practice providing mental health care services to clients directly and as an independent contractor/provider for various managed care entities. In addition, as shareholder and employee, the undersigned therapist provides all mental health services through Life Experiences, Inc. d/b/a New Life Counseling Center.

Mental Health Services

While it may not be easy to seek help from a mental health professional, it is hoped that you will be better able to understand your situation and feelings and move toward resolving your difficulties. The therapist, using his [or her] knowledge of human development and behavior, will make observations about situations as well as suggestions for new ways to approach them. It will be important for you to explore your own feelings and thoughts and to try new approaches in order for change to occur. You may bring other family members to a therapy session if you feel it would be helpful or if this is recommended by your therapist.

Appointments

Appointments are made by calling _____ Monday through Friday between the hours of 9:00 A.M. and 5:00 P.M. Please call to cancel or reschedule at least 24 hours in advance, or **you will be charged for the missed appointment.** Third-party payments will not usually cover or reimburse for missed appointments.

Number of Visits

The number of sessions needed depends on many factors and will be discussed by the therapist.

Length of Visits

Therapy sessions are 45 minutes in length but may take longer for psychological testing.

Relationship

Your relationship with the therapist is a professional and therapeutic relationship. In order to preserve this relationship, it is imperative that the therapist not have any other type of

Sample Form
(continued)

relationship with you. Personal and/or business relationships undermine the effectiveness of the therapeutic relationship. The therapist cares about helping you but is not in a position to be your friend or to have a social or personal relationship with you.

Gifts, bartering, and trading services are not appropriate and should not be shared between you and the therapist.

Goals, Purposes, and Techniques of Therapy

There may be alternative ways to effectively treat the problems you are experiencing. It is important for you to discuss any questions you may have regarding the treatment recommended by the therapist and to have input into setting the goals of your therapy. As therapy progresses, these may change. The initial goals, purposes, and techniques of therapy agreed upon by you and the therapist are as follows:

_____

_____

_____

Cancellations

Cancellations must be received at least 24 hours before your scheduled appointment; otherwise *you* will be charged the customary fee for that missed appointment. You are responsible for calling to cancel or reschedule your appointment.

Payment for Services

The charge for your initial session is _____ and the charge for any subsequent sessions is _____. The undersigned therapist does not normally accept assignment of insurance benefits but may be required to do so in connection with certain managed care contracts. **The undersigned therapist will look to you for full payment of your account, and you will be responsible for payment of all charges.** Different copayments are required by various group coverage plans. Your copayment is based on the Mental Health Policy selected by your employer or purchased by you. In addition, the copay may be different for the first visit than for subsequent visits. You are responsible for and shall pay your copay portion of the undersigned therapist's charges for services *at the time the services are provided.* It is recommended that you determine your copayment before your first visit by calling your benefits office or insurance company.

Although it is the goal of the undersigned therapist to protect the confidentiality of your records, there may be times when disclosure of your records or testimony will be compelled

(continued)

Sample Form
(continued)

by law. Confidentiality and exceptions to confidentiality are discussed below. In the event disclosure of your records or the therapist's testimony are requested by you or required by law, you will be responsible for and shall pay the costs involved in producing the records and the therapist's normal hourly rate for the time involved in preparing for and giving testimony. Such payments are to be made at the time or prior to the time the services are rendered by the therapist. The therapist may require a deposit for anticipated court appearances and preparation.

Confidentiality

Discussions between a therapist and a client are confidential. No information will be released without the client's written consent unless mandated by law. Possible exceptions to confidentiality include but are not limited to the following situations: child abuse; abuse of the elderly or disabled; abuse of patients in mental health facilities; sexual exploitation; IDS/HIV infection and possible transmission; criminal prosecutions; child custody cases; suits in which the mental health of a party is in issue; situations where the therapist has a duty to disclose, or where, in the therapist's judgment, it is necessary to warn, notify, or disclose; fee disputes between the therapist and the client; a negligence suit brought by the client against the therapist; or the filing of a complaint with a licensing board or other state or federal regulatory authority. **FOR FURTHER INFORMATION, REVIEW THE NOTICE OF PRIVACY PRACTICES FURNISHED TO YOU BY YOUR THERAPIST IN CONJUNCTION WITH THIS CLIENT INFORMATION AND CONSENT DOCUMENT.** If you have any questions regarding confidentiality, you should bring them to the attention of the therapist when you and the therapist discuss this matter further. By signing this information and consent form, you are giving your consent to the undersigned therapist to share confidential information with all persons mandated by law and with the agency that referred you and the managed care company and/or insurance carrier responsible for providing your mental health care services and payment for those services, and you are also releasing and holding harmless the undersigned therapist from any departure from your right of confidentiality that may result.

Duty to Warn

In the event that the undersigned therapist reasonably believes that I am a danger, physically or emotionally, to myself or another person, I specifically consent for the therapist to warn the person in danger and to contact any person in a position to prevent harm to myself or another person, in addition to medical and law enforcement personnel, and the following persons:

Sample Form
(continued)

NAME   **TELEPHONE NUMBER**

_____

_____

_____

This information is to be provided at my request for use by said persons only to prevent harm to myself or another person. This authorization shall expire upon the termination of my therapy with the undersigned therapist.

I acknowledge that I have the right to revoke this authorization in writing at any time to the extent the undersigned therapist has not taken action in reliance on this authorization. I further acknowledge that even if I revoke this authorization, the use and disclosure of my protected health information could possibly still be permitted by law as indicated in the copy of the Notice of Privacy Practices of the undersigned therapist that I have received and reviewed.

I acknowledge that I have been advised by the undersigned therapist of the potential of the redisclosure of my protected health information by the authorized recipients and that it will no longer be protected by the federal Privacy Rule.

I further acknowledge that the treatment provided to me by the undersigned therapist was conditioned on my providing this authorization.

Contact Information

I consent for the undersigned therapist to communicate with me by mail, email, and phone at the following addresses and phone numbers, and I will IMMEDIATELY advise the therapist in the event of any change:

NAME   **TELEPHONE NUMBER**

_____

_____

_____

Risks of Therapy

Therapy is the Greek word for change. You may learn things about yourself that you don't like. Often growth cannot occur until you experience and confront issues that induce you

(continued)

Sample Form
(continued)

to feel sadness, sorrow, anxiety, or pain. The success of our work together depends on the quality of the efforts on both our parts and the realization that you are responsible for lifestyle choices/changes that may result from therapy. Specifically, one risk of marital therapy is the possibility of exercising the divorce option.

After-Hours Emergencies

A mental health professional or your therapist is on call when your therapist's office is closed and can be reached for emergencies on a 24-hour, seven-days-per-week basis, by calling _____. Emergencies are urgent issues requiring immediate action.

Therapist's Incapacity or Death

I acknowledge that, in the event the undersigned therapist becomes incapacitated or dies, it will become necessary for another therapist to take possession of my file and records. By signing this information and consent form, I give my consent to allowing another licensed mental health professional selected by the undersigned therapist to take possession of my file and records and provide me with copies upon request, or to deliver them to a therapist of my choice. I will select a successor therapist within a reasonable time and will notify the appointed licensed mental health professional.

Consent to Treatment

I, voluntarily, agree to receive Mental Health assessment, care, treatment, or services and authorize the undersigned therapist to provide such care, treatment, or services as are considered necessary and advisable.

I understand and agree that I will participate in the planning of my care, treatment, or services and that I may stop such care, treatment, or services that I receive through the undersigned therapist at any time.

By signing this Client Information and Consent form, I, the undersigned client, acknowledge that I have both read and understood all the terms and information contained herein. Ample opportunity has been offered to me to ask questions and seek clarification of anything unclear to me.

_____   _____

Client/Parent   Date

_____

Social Security Number and Address

Sample Form
(continued)

I may be contacted at the following:

Address: _____

Telephone number(s): _____

E-mail address: _____

as witnessed by:

_____   _____
Anthony Kindheart, MA, LPC,   Date
LCDC & LMFT, Therapist

I acknowledge that I received a copy of this signed intake and consent form from my therapist on this _____ day of _____, 20___

_____
                                                        Client

Sample Form

PARENTAL WAIVER OF RIGHT TO CHILD'S RECORDS

   I hereby waive my right as parent/guardian to obtain information from and copies of any records from Anthony Kindheart and New Life Counseling Center pertaining to the assessment, evaluation, and treatment of the following child: _____, age _____ .
I understand that Anthony Kindheart and New Life Counseling Center may refuse to provide me, or any third party acting upon my request or authorization, with information and records pertaining to this child's mental health evaluation and treatment, if disclosure *in the opinion of the child's therapist* would negatively impact the child or the child's evaluation and treatment. I hereby release Anthony Kindheart and New Life Counseling Center from any and all liability for good-faith refusal to disclose the child's information or records.

_____   _____
Parent/Guardian   Date

_____   _____
Parent/Guardian   Date

as witnessed by:

_____   _____
Anthony Kindheart, MA, LPC,   Date
LCDC & LMFT, Therapist

Legal Lightbulb

- A written contract is an enforceable legal agreement.

- Because we live in a consumer-oriented society, the intake form will be construed against the professional if there is a dispute. Therefore, it must be carefully drafted by a lawyer with protection of the clinician in mind and explained in detail. A copy or duplicate original should *always* be delivered to the client at the time of signing.

- There is nothing wrong with practicing defensive mental health therapy.

- Clients will generally sign any forms presented to them during an intake session.

- Before creating the information and consent form, contemplate areas of vulnerability and, if possible, contractually guard against them.

- A clinician cannot contract away liability for his or her own negligence.

- Sex, boundary violations, dual relationships, and conscious breaches of confidentiality are the subjects of numerous claims. Therapists must protect against them—in writing (and in personal conduct). Beware the aggressive client or the client who is overzealous or overexuberant, especially the client who enthuses: "You are the only therapist who can help me. I have complete faith in you and you only."

- In the event a client or therapist dies, postdeath provisions should be included in the contract. Every therapist should have a disability and a postdeath plan.

- Obligations to the client and the client's file survive the death of both the client and the therapist.

- Children's rights should be protected in the information and consent form. Some states have different rules if the child is 16 or 17 years of age, is married, is living apart from his or her parents, or is emancipated (the "disabilities" of minority have been removed).

- Generally, in disputes before a licensing board or in malpractice litigation, differences in testimony are resolved against the professional. Therefore, written instruments give the professional valuable support. If carefully drafted by the mental health professional's lawyer, the contract is the first line of defense.

- The lawyer you select to review your consent form should be familiar with state statutes concerning mental health, state licensing laws, and the cases that interpret them. Mental health law may not be a recognized specialty, but familiarity with local and national professional information is necessary to draft a coordinated contract that protects the professional.
- A contract is usually construed against the entity that has drafted it and presented it to the other party for signature. In our consumer-oriented society, a precise document is critical. This document should be drafted by the professional's lawyer with protection of the mental health professional in mind.
- The checklist is not complete. Each therapist must complete it with specifics that apply to his or her individual practice.

7

Maintaining Records

After practicing privately for 15 years in the same office, Richard, a therapist, was forced to relocate to a new office when the building owner decided to sell the land and building to a developer. Richard began searching for new office space and, because of financial restrictions, was forced to rent a smaller office. As moving day approached and the packing began, Richard decided to discard the retained client records maintained and preserved during the first eight years he was in practice. He had limited space in his new office and wanted to discard old files. State law required therapists to maintain client records for seven years. So Richard discarded files that were older than seven years and files for which the last contact had occurred at least eight years before.

Two months after he was happily situated in his new office space, he was visited by an investigator from the district attorney's office. Apparently a former client had mentioned to her current counselor that she once had a sexual relationship with Richard while in therapy. The current counselor was legally bound to report the alleged sexual exploitation to the district attorney and to Richard's licensing board.

Richard was charged with a criminal offense (sex with a client is a criminal offense in a number of states) and faced a licensing board hearing for revocation of his license. The accuser (alleged victim) did not realize that a sexual relationship was inappropriate until a few months before, when she was so advised by her present counselor. The statute of limitations for prosecuting sexual offenses in Richard's state is 10 years. Richard could not even recall whether his accuser had entered his office. There was no written documentation of any therapy and no recollection of this woman, at all. The alleged victim claimed she had paid in cash because she was married at the time and did not want her husband to know she was seeing a therapist.

Without a file, a recollection of the person, or any inkling of the incident, Richard's defense became even more difficult.

How Long Should Client Records Be Maintained?

The legal requirements set out by statutes, regulations, and licensing boards vary from state to state and within each mental health discipline and licensing body. These legal requirements are published and available to every practitioner. The average maintenance period appears to be seven years; the shortest term is five years, and the longest is 10 years. In light of Richard's problem, common sense would dictate a minimum maintenance period of 10 years after the last client contact, or 10 years after majority if the client is a minor. HIPAA's Privacy and Security Rules impose a six-year retention period not only for certain client records but also for the entity's privacy and security procedure information.

The most conservative and safest advice for mental health professionals is: Never destroy client records; maintain them even after death, at least until the deceased therapist's estate is fully probated. You can never know when a claim based on charges of professional negligence or misconduct will rear its ugly head. If the means are available to maintain and store client files permanently, keep them; if not, be sure to maintain them for at least 10 years.

In all jurisdictions, statutes of limitations define the time allowed for a client to bring a complaint to a licensing board or initiate a malpractice lawsuit for alleged negligent acts of omission or commission by a therapist. The limitation periods vary from state to state, board to board, and discipline to discipline. Limitation periods may be longer than the minimum record-keeping period, as seen in Richard's situation. Often, a *discovery rule* comes into play and further confounds the problem with respect to record keeping. The discovery rule provides that the statute of limitations does not begin to run until a reasonable person knows or should have known that he or she had a claim for professional negligence or misconduct against a therapist. If a client represses a memory and does not recover the memory until 10 years later, an argument based on a discovery rule could be raised to defeat a statute of limitations defense. The suit might be allowed based on 10 years after the client realized the action was wrongful or actionable, even though it was not brought within the 10-year limitation period.

As a result of these overlapping statutes and principles of law, it is abundantly clear that the only truly safe position a therapist can take is to preserve records for as long a period as possible. *A therapist's first, and often best, line of defense against allegations of misconduct is a well-documented client file.* Without documentation, even the most resourceful attorney will have a difficult time mounting a spirited, effective, and competent defense. In our consumer-oriented society, when conflicting evidence is admitted in court or before a licensing board, the word of the consumer is often given greater weight than that of the professional.

If the client is a minor at the time the mental health service is provided, all states require records to be maintained for a time period after the minor reaches the age of majority. (In some states, majority is achieved by marrying or having the disabilities of minority removed before the normal age of majority is reached—a procedure sometimes called "emancipation.") The general

Never destroy client records.

Limitation periods vary from state to state, board to board, and discipline to discipline.

The discovery rule provides that the statute of limitations does not begin until the person knows or should have known there were grounds for a claim of negligence or misconduct.

A therapist's first, and often best, line of defense against allegations of misconduct is a well-documented client file.

rule is that after a child reaches the age of majority, his or her records must be preserved for the same number of years a therapist is required to maintain adult records. For example, if the state requirement is seven years, a child's records must be maintained until the child reaches 25 years of age (18 + 7).

A therapist should know what his or her jurisdiction requires. Whatever the minimum legal requirement, it is suggested that records be kept for as long as possible and certainly well beyond the minimum required time period. If space constraints become a factor, save at least basic information: intake forms, dates of treatment, diagnoses, termination forms, and, perhaps, case summaries.

How Should Client Records Be Discarded?

When the decision is made to eliminate files in whole or in part, destruction of records must be accomplished in a manner that protects confidentiality. Have the records shredded or burned or, for preservation of the environment, opt for shredding and recycling. Be sure there is no possibility for any third party to determine client information from the discarded and destroyed files.

In one situation, a semiretired therapist, practicing part time in a small community, emptied old files "as is" into an outdoor dumpster. Later, local children playing in the dumpster found some very interesting reading material about people they knew, and soon the information was spread all over town. Former clients who had consulted with the therapist some 20 years earlier were very unhappy, and that was only the beginning of the story.

Take the time and expense to shred or burn all files selected for destruction. Oversee the process yourself to guarantee that the job is completely private and that prying eyes are not reviewing the contents before the files are consigned to oblivion.

There are commercial establishments in the business of confidentially destroying files. Hire one of these firms, secure a confidentiality agreement from them, and deliver the files with the assurance that they will be thoroughly ruined, undecipherable, deidentified, and totally beyond recognition.

Be sure there is no possibility for any third party to determine client information from the discarded and destroyed files.

Securing Files against Third Parties

Files should be secured at all times to prevent access or review by third parties. Only the therapist and office personnel who have a legitimate need to access information should be allowed contact with a client's file. Any access by office personnel should be limited to only the information needed. A staff person performing a billing function would not normally need to review the therapist's session notes to properly and accurately bill for services provided. Access should be permitted only under the supervision of the therapist. It is the

The therapist will be held accountable for breaches by office personnel or third parties.

therapist's legal and ethical duty and responsibility to safeguard the confidentiality of clients' records, and the therapist will be held accountable for breaches by office personnel or third parties.

Regardless of the recording medium used—paper, computer disks or tapes, microfilm, videotapes, or audiotapes—records should be kept under lock and key, with coded access. Individual cabinets and the rooms in which they are stored should be secured. A therapist will not be held liable if a burglar breaks into a locked room and pries open a locked cabinet to gain access to clients' files. But a therapist will be held liable if the files are not secured and, for example, a husband waiting for his wife to emerge from her therapy session slides down the hall, opens an unsecured door and a file cabinet drawer, and reads progress notes in his wife's clinical file about an undisclosed affair. The same liability would apply if the husband is a computer hacker and easily cracks the therapist's too simple security code.

A therapist will be held liable if the files are not secured.

It is important for every therapist to establish office procedures and policies concerning maintenance and security of and access to client files. (See Chapter 46, HIPAA Security Rule.) These procedures and policies should be clearly presented in an office manual and signed by each person working in the office or practice, including persons who might be engaged on a temporary basis to answer the phone and who would have no understanding of client confidentiality or the importance of protecting client files. Mental health records are different from all other records. Even a therapist practicing alone, without any support staff, should ponder these matters from time to time to ensure that every possible means of protecting and securing clients' records has been employed.

If there is ever a question about a particular person's access to a client's file, the therapist should seek written consent from the client.

Every mental health professional must have a death or disability plan in place, which provides for the ultimate protection and safeguard of the client's file in the event of the death or disability of either the client or the therapist.

Death or Disability Plan in Place

Every mental health professional must have a death or disability plan in place, made available to the office staff and the colleague who will take over the individual files with the preauthorized consent of the client, which provides for the ultimate protection and safeguard of the files in the event of the death or disability of either the client or the therapist. After the files have been preserved for the requisite number of years, the plan must provide for the confidential and total destruction of the files.

Answers to Frequently Asked Questions about:

Records: Husband and wife are clients
Family therapy: Separate versus joint records

Access to records

Subpoenas

❓ Question

I am seeing a couple wherein I suspect a divorce will occur. I have seen the couple twice, each individually, once, and will see the couple one more time. My concern: Who, if anyone, will have access to the records should a suit for divorce be filed? The case was opened in the wife's name. What do I do if I get a subpoena?

❗ Answer

Generally, a child custody case will give rise to an exception to confidentiality and allow either parent to gain access to the other's mental health records by subpoena. Absent a lawsuit, each parent could access only his or her own records. Because of the difficulty in segregating information during marital conjoint therapy (although we advise separate files), we suggest that for joint sessions you have the parties consent in writing for you to keep one file. As part of the agreement, either party can access and obtain copies. You would keep separate files for each client for individual sessions or therapy.

Although it is cumbersome and difficult to flip from page to page, better practice is to have separate files for each person in therapy: dad, mom, and children. This may appear to be an inconvenience, but if there is litigation, such files can be more easily accessed or protected. Remember, either parent can view his or her own file and that of the child or children, but spouses have no right to see and examine their spouse's file. Marriage does not grant that right.

💡 Additional Thoughts

If a subpoena is filed, a motion to quash or a motion for a protective order can be filed by either party. The judge will rule concerning the admissibility of the therapeutic file. The judge can also rule that *portions* of the file are admissible and proper for discovery and other portions are inadmissible and not subject to either discovery or examination.

- Whenever possible, it is beneficial to keep separate records for each individual client, including children. Merged or joint records are difficult to protect, legally, because they become part of the same record.
- Individual clients have access to their own records (absent an issue of harm) and usually that of their children. Access to a child's file can be waived *in writing by a carefully drafted waiver of access* form inserted in the file.
- Spouses do not have the *right* to access each other's file in the absence of a court order.

- In some states, a therapist has the right to seek confidentiality and privilege for the record of a child made while the child was in therapy if the therapist can prove it is *in the best interest of the child*. Such protection of the child's file and, consequently, the child, is difficult, if not impossible, if the file is merged with that of the parent or the parents. A judge usually has to make a protective ruling.
- It does not matter in whose name the file was opened. If the names of other parties are contained in the file and if they participated in the therapy, the file is part of *their* record.

Answers to Frequently Asked Questions about:

Records: Dad, child, and, possibly, mom in therapy

Response to subpoenas

Benefit of separate clinical files

Question

A 15-year-old female patient was referred to me by her father for depression related to her parents' breakup. Both the child and her dad signed the appropriate consent to treat form, but the dad is not a client. The father filed for divorce from the mother this year. They are not yet divorced and still reside together, although the father tends to spend the nights at his dad's home.

I've seen the patient four times—she is always accompanied by her dad. Mom is not a part of this therapeutic process so far. I have not yet asked her mom to come in, although I expect she will not, because I think she feels her husband and daughter are ganging up on her.

Let's say I do see the mom, also. Then one parent's attorney subpoenas me to testify in a child custody dispute. How can I protect the confidentiality of the other parent, and how can I continue to treat this family?

Answer

Although you are asking, "How can I continue to treat this family," you are not really treating the *family*. You are treating the child. Refer the mom and/or dad to another therapist for resolution of *their* problems. If you have conversations with either parent incidental to your treatment of the child and that information becomes part of the child's record, either parent can access it with or without a subpoena. Keep any and all records of conversations with the parents in two "mom" and "dad" separate files. Don't mix or blend, even slightly.

If you decide to provide therapy to either parent, the parent's records could be reached by subpoena by the other parent in a custody suit. Be sure to disclose this exception to confidentiality and document you have done so *before* you provide therapy to either one of the parents. Good judgment would indicate that every client be informed of *all* the exceptions to confidentiality. Indeed, this is a requirement of some state licensing canons. Such information should be contained in the intake form and signed by every adult and mature child.

If you do provide therapy to both parents in other cases and a divorce suit is subsequently filed, it would be wise to terminate with both parents at that point and refer each of them to different mental health professionals. Avoid the *appearance* of taking sides or being either parent's advocate. The child is the client and any relationship that is not in the best interest of the child should be avoided.

Remember, however, that whenever a divorce is imminent in any family situation, we suggest you confine your services to the child and refer both parents elsewhere.

💡 Additional Thoughts

- Either or both parents usually have a right to view the child's clinical file.
- If you continue to treat the child, your client, the record can be subpoenaed. You would have to file a motion to quash or a motion for a protective order to protect the child's file. Filing these motions, although the court might authorize a fee, would probably be at your own expense.
- Some courts will protect the child's file if it is demonstrably in the best interest of the child to keep the file confidential.
- Always have a list of other competent professionals to offer to clients/ patients and third parties at times like this.
- Perhaps have the mom or dad see another therapist and obtain written permission to consult with the other therapist.
- Review your informed consent form with a lawyer to make sure it contains all the necessary language as set forth in the state licensing law. (See Chapter 6 for a beginning form.)
- A powerful caveat: If a case such as this ever goes to trial, the losing parent—that is, the parent who does not receive custody or conservatorship of the child—is going to be angry. This parent often takes out his or her anger on the therapist who testified, assuming that, but for the unfavorable testimony of the therapist, he or she would have received the result he or she deserved. Think through the dilemma thoroughly. Consider the parents' feelings as well as the legalities. Be honest, objective, and professional, but avoid antagonizing the parties.

Legal Lightbulb

- Maintain files for *at least* the minimum time period required in your jurisdiction. (States do not coordinate with one another, nor do various national and state professional organizations.) Remember also HIPAA's six-year retention rules.

- Best practice is to *never discard* client files because it is impossible to know when a claim or complaint will be made by a former client.

- Remember that claims can be brought after a therapist is no longer required to maintain records or after a therapist retires, leaves the jurisdiction, changes agencies, or loses control of a file.

- The *discovery rule* provides that the statute of limitations does not begin to run until the person knows or should have known there were grounds for a claim of negligence or misconduct.

- If you must eliminate old client files, consider maintaining a partial file with basic information such as intake forms, dates of treatment, diagnosis, and termination forms. At least have some documentation of who your clients were and why they were there.

- If files are to be discarded, completely destroy them by shredding or burning them. Be present until the destruction is complete. Use a professional company whose profession it is to destroy confidential files.

- It is difficult to defend against a complaint or malpractice suit in the absence of a well-documented and complete client file.

- Secure all file cabinets, as well as the room in which they are stored. Where computer records are maintained for clients, create, establish, and provide for the computer equivalent of a lock and key; that is, have hacker-proof codes for each client and, where clients are well known, open files under assumed or fictitious names (as long as you can find them).

- Establish written policies and procedures for the maintenance and security of client files and the limitations on access to them. Review the policies with each permanent and temporary staff person. Have each employee, regular or temporary, initial the protocol cover sheet, and keep a file of signatories.

- Limit the number of people who have access to your office, files, and computers. Limit access to the information needed; do not open an entire file unless absolutely necessary.

- If in doubt about a person's right to access information, obtain written consent from the client.

- If a client or parent wants access to a file and you wish to prohibit access but the law does not allow you to withhold the record, seek a protective order from an appropriate court.

- Remember, the therapist has the ultimate responsibility for his or her client files and should not rely on others (i.e., support staff) to maintain and protect records.

Clients' Right to Access Files

Do clients have the absolute right to access their own records? Generally, the answer is "Yes," but the HIPAA Privacy Rule and many state statutes allow a mental health professional to withhold records or information from a client if the therapist, in the exercise of professional judgment, reasonably believes the disclosure would be harmful to the client. If a therapist is not a covered entity for HIPAA purposes and practices in a jurisdiction where there is no statutory authority to withhold information or records from a client, and the therapist believes the records should be withheld, he or she should petition an appropriate court for a protective order to keep the records from the client. The petition will be reviewed, a hearing will be set, and a ruling will be made by the court.

Ask the parent to waive his or her right to access the records before beginning therapy with the child.

Parents of a child generally have the right to access their child's mental health records, but a few jurisdictions allow the therapist, pursuant to statute, to withhold records from a parent. In the absence of statutory authority, a therapist who is concerned about a parent's access to a child's records should seek a protective order from a court of competent jurisdiction to keep records from the parent. As discussed earlier, it is good practice for the therapist to ask the parent to waive his or her right to access the records before beginning therapy with the child.

In a perfect world, only the client and therapist would ever have access to a client's records. But the world is far from perfect, and many eyes are legally entitled to gain access to a client's mental health information. It's the therapist's duty to limit, as much as possible, the number of contacts third parties have with a client's file. Although the confidentiality of mental health information is set down as a rule of law in many jurisdictions, the exceptions to the rule emasculate the perceived right to privacy. In most cases, the therapist has scant legal grounds for keeping a file absolutely private from everyone.

It's the therapist's duty to limit, as much as possible, the number of contacts third parties have with a client's file.

8

Treatment Plans

Jane attended regular therapy sessions with Dr. Gold for four years. Her problem was depression. She was in an unhappy marriage and was unsure of her legal, therapeutic, and ethical options. Finally, Jane, with the input of Dr. Gold and her attorney, decided to divorce her husband and seek custody of her two minor children. At the trial, Dr. Gold testified as an expert for Jane, but the court ruled in favor of her husband. Despite the expert testimony and evidence in her favor, Jane was given only standard rights of visitation and had to pay child support. She was angry, devastated, and humiliated. Jane felt that if Dr. Gold's testimony had been more enthusiastic and spirited, she would have won the custody battle. As time passed, and as she talked to her friends, she became gradually more furious. What did Dr. Gold write in the clinical file that offered such (in her opinion) lukewarm testimony? Jane called Dr. Gold and asked for a complete copy of her clinical records.

In years past, the client file belonged to the therapist. Clients had a right to review a summary of the therapy but did not have a right to peruse the file itself. This protection has changed with the times.

The client has the right to receive a copy of his or her file upon reasonable notice.

The client file now belongs to the client. Copying expense is billable, but the client has the right to receive a *copy* of his or her file upon reasonable notice. The file includes the treatment plan, assessment, diagnosis, prognosis, and any notes entered in the file.

Clients' Rights Concerning the Treatment Plan

Clients *cannot* enter the therapist's office unannounced and expect to have their file copied immediately while they sit tapping their fingers in the waiting room, nor can they suggest that the therapist should hand over the original file for review.

The client *can* call or write to request to see the file or to receive a copy of the file. The therapist must then make a copy (a reasonable fee can be charged for copying services) and allow the client to pick up the copy when ready. Or, the copy can be mailed or faxed according to the client's written instructions and authorization. The information in the client file, in theory, belongs to the client, and the client has a right to a copy.

On occasion, a file may contain information that the therapist, on reflection, feels would be detrimental to the client—material that, if known to the client, might be injurious psychologically. For example, during therapy, a client constantly talked negatively about her mother. However, after therapy concluded, the client was reconciled with her mother and then forgot the offensive and insulting phrases that were dutifully recorded in her file. If the client's file were to be disclosed, old wounds would resurface and create new hostility. In another case, a therapist was granted permission to investigate her client's background by meeting with a school counselor, a former teacher, a relative, and a good friend. This information, although hearsay in legal terms, remained in the client file. If revealed, the investigative inquiries would be disturbing to the client.

The intake and consent form should state that if the file is requested, the therapist may, if clinically necessary in the therapist's opinion, withhold information in the file that is or might be, in the therapist's opinion, injurious to the client. Clients can also waive, in advance, the right to full disclosure of tests, notes, or an investigative summary. The waiver must be in writing.

In another scenario, a client had taken a psychological test. The test results might be available, but the test itself was not, for contractual reasons. Again, the importance of an intake form must be stressed. The intake form should contain a paragraph stating that, in the course of therapy, certain tests might be administered. These tests and their contents cannot be revealed to the client, and the client must agree in advance that no request for them will be made. Many are proprietary; they belong to the creator of the test, not the therapist. Raw test results may not be disclosed unless interpreted by a competent professional because they might be misleading and misunderstood by a layperson.

Some therapists' ethical canons provide for maintaining test security. These canons state that therapists must make reasonable efforts to maintain the integrity and security of tests and other assessment techniques in a manner that is consistent with legal and contractual obligations and permits compliance with the requirements of ethics codes. A therapist who uses proprietary tests or copyrighted material has an obligation to protect the disclosure of the material. If the client insists on disclosure, the therapist must seek legal protection. This is a double bind—there is an obligation to release client information to the client and an obligation to protect a psychological test from disclosure, in accordance with the contractual relationship between the test owner and the therapist. Where appropriate, seek and obtain a court protective order.

A reasonable fee can be charged for copying services.

The intake and consent form should state that if the file is requested, the therapist may withhold information in the file.

The therapist has an obligation to protect proprietary tests or copyrighted material.

Treatment Plan: Basic Minimum Requirements

- Assessment.
- Diagnosis.
- Treatment plan: As a result of your diagnosis, what are you going to do to ameliorate the condition? State the techniques of treatment.
- Prognosis: As a result of what you are going to do, what is supposed to happen and when should it happen? What should be the end result of the treatment?
- Significant therapeutic or behavioral changes that will take place and client's response and adjustments.
- Itemization of consultations and referrals.
- If appropriate, termination and reason for termination.

A significant portion of a clinician's education is the appropriate documentation of a file. The file should substantiate all the conclusions reached by the provider and the client while they are in the therapeutic relationship, from initial intake to ultimate termination.

Therapist's Response to Demand to See Files

- Discuss the matter with the client. Ask whether the client will accept an oral summary of the file in a modified therapy session.
- If an oral summary is not acceptable, suggest that you furnish a written summary, rather than a complete file.
- Be sure to respond to the client's request in a timely manner. State law often imposes specific time periods for responding to requests for health care records.
- If the complete file is still demanded and the file is thorough, appropriate, and ready for disclosure, make a complete copy and deliver it to the client in the manner requested by the client. Insert *caveats* where needed; that is, clarify why raw test scores require professional interpretation or why certain material in the file was received from third parties, but the therapist cannot vouch for their truthfulness.
- Be sure to carefully review the file and appropriately correct any errors or omissions.
- Indicate to the client that certain tests, and perhaps other materials, are copyrighted, trademarked, or proprietary and cannot be disclosed. Most clients will accept this as a correct statement. Alternatively, the therapist can expect an angry letter from the client or the client's lawyer (with a release-of-information form attached), demanding the complete file. The therapist would then be wise to seek a court order to protect the file. A judge,

presented with the obligation to maintain test security, will usually issue a protective order guarding the right of the client to see the file while, at the same time, safeguarding the interests of the therapist. The judge will determine which part of the file is to be delivered to the client and which part is to remain in the therapist's sole control.

Answers to Frequently Asked Questions about:

Child, treatment of

Legal custody

Court orders

Recalcitrant parents or custodians

Treatment plans

❓ Question

I am treating a minor child who was brought to treatment by her mother. The child is fairly high functioning and has only some adjustment issues relative to her family situation. The parents are divorced. The mother has sole physical custody. However, there is joint legal custody with the father. (At least that is how I read the divorce decree. In this state, this arrangement is called joint managing conservatorship.)

For reasons he will not discuss, the father is adamantly opposed to the child's receiving any sort of mental health treatment. This does not seem to be specific to my treatment of the child. He has never met me, although I did invite him to be in touch with me if he had any questions or concerns, using a standard letter I send to noninvolved parents.

Do I have a legal or ethical obligation to discontinue this child's treatment, given this joint legal custodian's (the dad's) objection to continuing therapy? What should I document in the file to protect myself? How can I establish a treatment plan when the father is so resistant to any sort of therapy? How much grief can a belligerent father cause me? I do have the mother's written permission to be in touch with the family court counselor who oversees the case. Should I ask the family court counselor or the mother to raise the issue in court, in the hope of securing a court order signed by the judge permitting, authorizing, or allowing treatment, thus giving me some measure of protection . . . ?

❗ Answer

You must be absolutely clear that the mother has the legal right to consent to the child's mental health treatment. Start by reading the *most recent* court order concerning the custody of this child and, if you are not certain from reviewing the decree, consult with an attorney. Make sure the attorney interprets the court order as you do. If the mother doesn't have that legal right, do not provide services without a court order or the consent of the person who does have that right. Most decrees are clear concerning exactly who has the legal right to consent to medical, surgical, and psychological (mental health) treatment. For a foreign decree, secure a certified translation and obtain expert legal advice concerning the usage of language in the foreign country. Different states have different vocabularies for custodial and noncustodial parents. Whether in your state, another state, or a foreign country, make sure you are correct in your and the mother's interpretation of the court order.

Assuming the mother does have the legal right to consent, you have to then determine if the dad is opposed to you or if he, the recalcitrant parent, is opposed to mental health treatment regardless of the provider. If *you* are the objection, certainly stand aside and make a referral to several other competent therapists. Let the court, the attorneys by agreement, or the family court counselor make the decision. As a general principle, battling an angry parent is not cost effective.

If the dad is opposed to *any* form *or* provider of mental health treatment, you should still weigh carefully whether you want to get involved. Your facts indicated that the child is not experiencing any serious problems. You should try to determine if the dad would act out so badly when he doesn't get his way that stress and harm to the child are likely. If so, you may decide it would be better for the child that you not continue providing services.

Parents not on board with the therapy program can be a basis for ethically refusing to provide treatment. The friction, stress, or outright unhelpful conduct could subvert the therapy and the therapeutic progress. Don't be afraid to say, "No, thanks."

💡 Additional Thoughts

- Consent to treat a minor child must be signed by the parent or guardian authorized to give legal informed consent.
- When any parent adamantly opposes treatment and that parent is dissatisfied with the outcome of litigation, there is a good chance he or she will file a complaint with the licensing board or a national organization. Make sure your documentation contains all the substantiating data required of a treatment plan.
- Make sure you demand, obtain, and read the *latest court order*. Remember, where children are involved, most courts have continuing jurisdiction until the child reaches majority. Orders can be changed, often by agreement or by motion filed by either party and heard by the court.
- The role of the resistant parent can easily be used to render even effective treatment useless.

Sample Form

CLIENT WAIVER OF FULL DISCLOSURE CLAUSE

"... I have been advised I have a right to copies of my entire file but acknowledge some information may not be in my best interest to review. In the event my therapist, in the exercise of his/her professional judgment, determines that information in my file may be injurious to me, I waive my right to obtain such potentially injurious information and release my therapist from any and all claims, damages, and causes of action that I suffer or could assert for his/her refusal to provide me with the information requested. ... The therapist's discretion shall control."

Legal Lightbulb

- In general, the client is entitled to a copy of his or her file upon payment of a reasonable copying cost ($0.25 to $1.00 per page). Read and review the file *before* delivering a copy to a client. If there are any errors, clarifications, or changes, the time to make these changes is before hard copies are made and distributed. Check numbers and pronouns carefully. Make sure they refer to the proper person. There is a big difference whether "he" or "she" did it.

- Certain test materials must be protected, and the client has no right to them.

- The intake and consent form should contain a paragraph that protects proprietary or contractually protected rights and information.

- Some clients demand their files on impulse. A free session might dissuade such a client from proceeding further.

- It is better to review the file with the client than just hand it over.

- Clients who are angry because they have lost contested litigation, at great expense to themselves, often seek some third party to blame, and an obvious and vulnerable person is the therapist. *Handle every demand for records as a potential lawsuit or complaint to the board. Proceed gingerly.*

- Do not withhold a file because of nonpayment of your bill.

- Remember that information in client files belongs to the client. The therapist is only the custodian of the original record.

- The mother's attorney, in a case such as this, can file the necessary pleadings to support court-ordered counseling and provide for adequate compensation. Such an appointment would probably insulate you against any attack, although you would have to be careful to document carefully and provide excellent treatment.

- A careful assessment, diagnosis, treatment plan, and prognosis, updated regularly, would be the minimum requirements of progress notes. Entries in the clinical record should support the treatment plan, or the plan should be modified to indicate current information.

- Treat resistant parents with kid gloves. These are the individuals who are looking for "satisfaction," and, if the therapist is vulnerable, they will be vicious in their approach.
- To practice in peace, don't look for trouble. Find someone else to help the child, especially someone appointed by the court.

Therapists should be aware of the "nuisance factor" cases. In one situation, a mother engaged the therapist to evaluate her child. The father was silent and the mother was authorized to engage a therapist. When the case came to trial, the therapist testified in what she thought was an objective and professional manner. The court ruled in favor of the mother. The father was furious and filed a complaint with the licensing board against the therapist. The case was dismissed because it was clear to the board that this was a "sour grapes" case. The father did not want to accept responsibility for losing and, in acting out his anger, aimed at the therapist. However, the therapist had to answer the complaint in writing, agonize over the verbiage in the letter, review it with a lawyer, appear at the hearing, and then have the complaint, though dismissed, in her permanent file. In a way, this is a business or professional risk, but perhaps it can be avoided if carefully orchestrated. Remember, when it comes to complaints to the licensing board, all the complaining consumer has to do is fill out the proscribed form, sign and date it, and send it to the board. The board does all the work.

SECTION TWO

CONFIDENTIALITY

9

Couples, Family, and Group Therapy

Dr. Lowenstein, a licensed psychologist, conducted group sessions that included couples, single individuals, and teenagers. Before accepting each person into the group, he stressed the importance of confidentiality. What was said in the group session was not to leave the room. Each person had to affirm in writing that he or she understood the principle of confidentiality. For added emphasis, Dr. Lowenstein insisted that each person sign a "guarantee of silence" form—an agreement that he or she would not, under any circumstances, share with any person outside the group, what was revealed in the group. In addition, at the beginning and end of each session, Dr. Lowenstein stressed confidentiality and trust. Participants, he explained, would be removed from the program if there was any possibility that the information was repeated.

Four weeks into a 16-week workshop series, a group member, Jill, discovered that another member, Maria, was a personal friend of Jill's employer. Jill had talked freely for three weeks about her employer (her perception of the cause of all her stress) and felt that if her boss found out what she had been saying, she would be in trouble or be fired. She became very intimidated and hesitant about sharing stress-causing incidents.

Can Jill be guaranteed absolute confidentiality? Or, if she became involved in a major discrimination suit or personal litigation, could all the group participants be subpoenaed? Could Dr. Lowenstein be compelled to reveal the names of the group members? If he maintained session notes, could he be forced to bring these notes to court for examination?

How can a mental health professional who conducts group sessions protect the members of the group from a harmful breach of confidentiality? Are there differences when the group is small (a couple), slightly larger (a family in family systems therapy), or very large (an assembly of strangers who gather because they have a common problem)?

Managed care has created pressure to cut costs while increasing services, and this phenomenon has led to handling an increased patient load via group sessions and group therapy. Is there anything the therapist can do to *guarantee* absolute privacy?

Probably not, because, unlike the mental health professional, the group members are laypersons, and they are not obligated by professional ethics or codes of conduct to refrain from gossip. However, if they sign a form in which they acknowledge the principle of confidentiality and agree to abide by it, they are then contractually responsible. To date, there is no litigation in which group members have been sued and substantial recoveries awarded because information received in the group was repeated to outsiders. The principal reason to create contractual responsibility is to create a deterrent, not establish punishment. Group members will undoubtedly limit what they repeat if they realize they are responsible and liable financially, as well as morally and ethically, for what they say.

Group members are not obligated to refrain from gossip.

The best the therapist can do is make sure each prospective client in a group setting is aware of the confidentiality issue, as well as the limitations. The client must understand the risks involved in sharing facts and intimacies with strangers who might repeat what is heard, either inadvertently or as juicy gossip.

Make sure each client in a group is aware of the confidentiality issue.

These limitations should be spelled out in the intake and consent form that is signed before the initial group session and then signed by each individual who later enters the group. The original should be maintained by the therapist, and copies should be given to the clients. In this context, group and family members are all "clients."

When a client's signed statement acknowledging the limitations of or exceptions to confidentiality is in the therapist's file, the client, at a later date, would be hard pressed to claim ignorance concerning the need for confidentiality. Some states, in their ethical canons, require that clients be informed concerning the limits of confidentiality. It is always best to have this receipt of information in writing (i.e., that clients have been fully informed, in writing, that there are limits and exceptions to confidentiality; that they have been told what those limits are; and that they accept the risk of those clear and specified limits).

The confidentiality form signed by all members of the group should be lawyer crafted and legally enforceable. Confidentiality should be emphasized periodically to all group members and stressed to new members entering the group.

Protective Measures for Confidentiality

Although confidentiality cannot be guaranteed, there are some methods to protect the therapist in the event a group member does not take the confidentiality concept seriously enough, including:

- In group sessions, have each individual sign a confidentiality statement. In couples or family systems therapy, the same principal should apply. Each person should sign a confidentiality statement. However, should litigation commence between the parties, confidentiality will be more difficult to protect because of the nature of the relationship between the individuals and the matter litigated.

- Insert a *hold harmless* clause indicating that, should a participant breach confidentiality and should the facilitator be held responsible or sued, the participant will pay all damages incurred. This will serve as a deterrent to participants who feel that, as nonprofessionals, they are not liable for their own gossip. A legally drafted contract creates legally enforceable liability. Every adult knows this, or should know it. (It might also deter an investigative reporter who joins in a group for information rather than therapy.)
- The sign-in sheet must contain, in bold print, a confidentiality reminder.
- The policy of group therapy, enforced without exception, is that anyone who violates confidentiality will be dismissed from the group, forfeiting all payments made (and be liable for any damages he or she caused).
- Anyone in the group who hears of group gossip is obligated to report the infraction to the group leader, whether a therapist, a layperson, or a facilitator.
- Although there may be some "public policy" opinions against such language, the intake form should contain a clause that exonerates the therapist in the event a group member gossips inappropriately. Each person must sign an intake form before entering the group.
- Obvious exceptions to confidentiality include child abuse, elder abuse, abuse of the disabled, a subpoena to testify under penalty of contempt of court, a parent-child relationship problem before the court, litigation in which the mental health of the patient client is an issue, and some criminal prosecutions. The statutory exceptions to confidentiality vary from state to state and are situational. Professional legal advice should be sought before assuming that any of these circumstances justifies making therapeutic information public. And then, it is better to testify only when required by the court.
- Many therapists have brochures that contain abbreviated vitae as well as descriptions of the treatment offered. If the brochure has a statement that describes the limits of confidentiality in group sessions, participants can sign on the intake form that a copy of the brochure was received, read, and understood, and promise that they will not repeat anywhere what they heard in group sessions.

The sign-in sheet must contain, in bold print, a confidentiality reminder.

As group therapy, couples therapy, and family systems therapy become more common, an ever-expanding number of individuals become privy to the innermost thoughts of their fellow clients. The therapist can make an effort to protect the shared information, but cannot guarantee absolute privacy. However, the therapist must take steps to protect group members as much as possible.

Answers to Frequently Asked Questions about:

Alleged misconduct by another therapist

What constitutes misconduct

Duty to report "alleged" misconduct

Statements made in group or family therapy

? Question

I saw a patient who, in the course of therapy, most of it in a group setting, said she "felt uncomfortable" with a previous therapist's behavior. She refused to specify what the therapist did, but she did say she had dinner with the therapist and claimed the therapist "set her up" with a physician, but "nothing happened." She shared this with her group, which she attended every Wednesday night and which I facilitated. The members of the group could identify the prior therapist; at least some smiled broadly when she mentioned his name, but no further details were offered and the other members of the group seemed to respect her wish for further privacy. She identified the person but would not identify the specific discipline. I knew him professionally. She refused to say more, other than it happened five years ago.

Should I have tried to report this? When I suggested the possibility, she said, "No!" She wished, no, demanded, personal anonymity. (Personal anonymity is authorized under the state reporting statute.) She stated she mentioned the episode as a matter she had to work through in her own therapy, not something she wished discussed for the purpose of disciplining the former therapist.

! Answer

Your facts do not state that the client alleged a sexual relationship with a prior therapist. The facts do set out improper conduct (boundary violation) that would be of concern and interest to the licensing board of the prior therapist. However, unless your state has a mandatory reporting statute for unethical, nonsexual conduct by a mental health professional, you can report only with the client's consent. In this case, the adult client has emphatically said "no" so your "tongue is tied."

♀ Additional Thoughts

- A client reporting a situation such as this probably wants you to be aware of her feelings. She does not want to be involved in pursuing a complaint with the licensing board. This might cause more harm or damage to her.

- If, as a factual matter, she was married at the time, she may not want her current husband to know she saw a therapist, had dinner with him, and went out with a physician, and would prefer that the episode not be a public incident.
- Check the mandatory reporting requirements of your licensing board. Be attuned should she complain further about her "dinner" with the therapist. She is intentionally vague. Perhaps the information is necessary for the therapy you offer, and she wants it to be part of the clinical record, for your information. Perhaps she has a hidden agenda that she wants the group to know about.
- Since you don't know what *really* took place, let it go at that.

Legal Lightbulb

- There is no absolute confidentiality in individual, family, or group sessions.

- Participants must be informed of this concept at the start of the group sessions and reminded periodically.

- A carefully designed, lawyer-drafted intake and consent form will offer a front-line modicum of protection in the event there is a breach in the confidentiality of a group or family session.

- Remember that group therapy is not excluded from HIPAA's Privacy and Security Rules.

- Do *not,* in a moment of weakness, promise confidentiality in group sessions: No therapist can *promise* or legally represent that another person in a group will not hear information and repeat it. The most the group leader can do is periodically repeat the admonition concerning confidentiality, have everyone sign a carefully drafted form, and extol the virtues of confidentiality.

- The legal exceptions to confidentiality are determined by case law, statute, and the HIPAA Privacy Rule. Although the Privacy Rule creates a minimal level of privacy, confidentiality exceptions vary from state to state and are situational.

Sample Form

GROUP CONFIDENTIALITY

As evidenced by my signature below, I agree to participate in group therapy with the undersigned therapist. I acknowledge that, with group therapy, there is risk of disclosure of confidential information by persons in the group to individuals outside the group. I agree that I will not disclose information learned by me during the course of any group session and will protect each participant's right to confidentiality. I agree to hold the undersigned therapist harmless from any claims or liability resulting from my disclosure of confidential information to a third party outside a group session. I further agree not to hold the undersigned therapist responsible and release her/him from same, for/from any claims or liability that I could assert as a result of disclosure of my confidential information by coparticipants in my group therapy sessions.

I understand I may choose to discontinue group therapy at any time.

_____   _____

Client   Date

_____   _____

Therapist   Date

Should be used in conjunction with a Notice of Privacy Practices as required by HIPAA Privacy Rule—see Chapter 44.

10

Insider Information

Susan was explaining her troubles to her therapist, Dr. Pick, during a regularly scheduled therapy session. She had just heard from a very reliable corporate source that her company, a large publicly traded corporation, was going broke. Only her accountant friend was privy to this secret information. Susan told Dr. Pick about it in a therapy session while discussing her work-related stress. Dr. Pick, unknown to Susan, had personal investments in Susan's company. Shortly thereafter, he sold all his stocks short and garnered substantial profits when the stock plummeted.

~

Jack, a client, was explaining his troubles to Dr. O'Reilly. In the course of conversation, he mentioned that he had made a unique technological discovery, which, when made public, would guarantee a stock rise. After hearing this news, Dr. O'Reilly bought a substantial stock position. When the discovery became public, the stock rose dramatically and Dr. O'Reilly's investment more than tripled. Later, during an investigation, Jack was asked if he told anyone about the discovery. Jack's reply: "Only my therapist!"

A few weeks later, a representative of the Securities and Exchange Commission arrived with a subpoena for Dr. O'Reilly.

Are these instances of securities fraud? Prohibited insider trading? The wrongful use of confidential information?

These therapists didn't seek the data. The developments were revealed to them in a therapy session, and neither therapist told anyone the source of the information. In their orientation, not only is client information confidential, but so is the identity of the confidant. Can all information shared in a therapy session be guarded? When challenged, can it remain confidential?

The Paper Trail

A therapist has to keep in mind that there is a trail of paperwork in every transaction. There are notes of each session, billing information, reimbursement

The purpose of therapy is to help the client.

submissions, long-distance phone logs, and, if a buy or sell order is issued, records of the transaction. Few activities of life go on without some written objective evidence.

Clients share business information freely in most therapeutic situations, and some of these data might be potentially lucrative to an astute therapist. You must keep in mind: *The purpose of therapy is to help the client.* The client assumes that information shared with the therapist is confidential and private. There is a real probability that clients never, in their wildest imagination, consider that the therapist might use the information for personal gain.

Making a One-Time Killing

Every so often, a client confides news that is potentially lucrative—developments that can make big bucks for the therapist. The event might involve real estate (a rezoning); the stock market (a new discovery); litigation (who is being sued and the potential outcome); a rare painting coming to the market from a seller who is not knowledgeable about art or aware of the value of this particular work; or supposedly "worthless" land, bonds, stock, stamps, or currency that is actually valuable. Regardless of the particular circumstances, the therapist has insider knowledge not available in the public arena and can be tempted to use this information to make money on the transaction.

Don't!

"A *California therapist pleaded guilty to insider trading* after using information obtained during a counseling session to make a *stock market killing . . .*" [Source: *Psychotherapy Finances, 21:12* (December 1995).] Although this case has not been specifically followed to conclusion, the fact that it was reported is sufficient to raise a concern. The danger is obvious.

Don't take advantage of any information garnered in a therapy session. In the case previously cited, the therapist made $177,235. You might make more, or less, but how much is your license worth? Possibly, over a lifetime, more than this amount.

The use of insider information is prohibited and is a breach of confidentiality.

Resist the temptation to make a business killing by using information gained in a therapy session. Information garnered confidentially often has implications in areas other than therapy. The use of this information is prohibited and is a clear breach of confidentiality.

Even if a client suggests that the therapist should act on insider information or trade secrets for personal gain, the use of this information may be illegal or, possibly, unethical, and creates a dual relationship. After the therapist has netted large sums of money, the client may ask for a share of the profits, or else. . . . Legal and ethical nightmares can result.

Although there may be no obligation to report most crimes a client may have committed (call a lawyer for particulars), a therapist who offers advice concerning a crime (e.g., stealing trade secrets) can become an accomplice.

Insider information might include:

- When to buy or sell a stock.
- A zoning change that will affect the value of a property that is for sale.
- A commodity that will become scarce because of events not yet known to the public.

Ethical Requirements

General ethical requirements are contained in the codes of ethics of many jurisdictions. Although the wording may differ from state to state or from one mental health discipline to another, the principles might be stated as follows:

- The therapist shall not engage in activities that seek to meet the professional's personal or business needs at the expense of a client without full disclosure and informed consent of the client.
- The therapist shall not provide counseling to business associates.
- The therapist shall not have or engage in a dual relationship with a client.
- Boundary violations are to be avoided at all costs. Sometimes they are conceptually cloudy. When in doubt, *don't.*
- The therapist shall not use relationships with clients to promote, for personal gain or profit, commercial enterprises or transactions of any kind.

The purpose of conservative practice is not only to avoid a trial, but also to avoid even the appearance of an unethical or illegal act.

Answers to Frequently Asked Questions about:

Clients who talk about deals

The promoter client

Good deals

? Question

I have a client who is always talking about his new "deal." Most of the time I dismiss it out of hand because he is always chasing rainbows and business clouds, and part of his need for therapy is that most of his promotions go bankrupt or are just not worth pursuing. This time he is on to something and a huge profit is possible. I have some money that I could invest, and I have a friend who is a more substantial investor. It would be possible to speculate in this venture without the client's knowledge. The

Legal Lightbulb

- Clients may indicate information that could be financially beneficial to the therapist. If used by the therapist, it is used at his or her peril.

- Remember this basic rule: The purpose of therapy is to help the client, not the therapist.

- The paper trail in therapy—as well as billing and third-party reporting procedures—makes information difficult to conceal if challenged. Surrounding circumstances often indicate the sequence of clandestine personal and business transactions.

- In most major litigation, depositions may be taken of the parties or the witnesses. Each person is sworn, and the opposing attorney asks questions that must be answered under oath. A court reporter takes down the answers and later transcribes them. Depositions may also be recorded by audio or audiovisual equipment. When under oath, a lie (a false statement made under oath) is perjury and a serious offense. Thus, once an event occurs, it is difficult to conceal if it becomes involved in the civil or criminal justice system. Therapists cannot assume anonymity or ignorance, nor can they claim to have a faulty memory, the "oops" theory.

- Therapists are vulnerable. An appearance of impropriety in a transaction can be unethical, illegal, or, at the very least, embarrassing, especially if it becomes a media event.

- The purpose of conservative practice is not only to avoid a trial, but also to avoid even the appearance of an unethical or illegal act.

client has no need to know my investments or those of my friends. A few phone calls to a third party, and we (my friend and I) could be in on the money-making venture. I have been looking for something such as this because I am a therapist and earn income only when I am seeing clients. Perhaps there is an easier way to make money because I could have investment income and money making money for me without my having to work hourly.

 Answer

Don't even think about it.

💡 Additional Thoughts

- Anyone treating stockbrokers, real estate investors or salespeople, speculators, venture capitalists, and so on will get tips concerning "good deals" once in a while. Resist the temptation.
- No one can act with immunity in our paper trail, recorded phone conversation, and electronic world. There is a record of almost every human transaction. In a case such as this, there will be a record of any order, purchase, option, settlement and, perhaps, phone conversations.
- Insider information cannot be used for personal gain or the gain of friends.
- There are multilevel governmental agencies whose job it is to prosecute individuals who profit from insider trading. (Let Martha Stewart's case serve as an example.)
- Somehow, in our experience, this type of transaction always boomerangs around and haunts the therapist.

11

Third-Party Payers

Dr. Anthony Kindheart, a licensed psychologist in private practice, agreed to accept assignment from his client's insurance benefits for payment of services. Dr. Kindheart's secretary completed the insurance claim form with assignment provisions furnished by the client and forwarded it to the claims office of the insurance company. In response, the claims office requested backup data, including the psychological testing and session notes. The information in the psychological testing and session notes would be embarrassing to the client and, if disclosed to his employer, could jeopardize his position with his company. In addition, his file contained proprietary tests that require permission for release. (Some testing tools cannot be shared because they belong to the test owner and/or may be copyrighted.)

Can Dr. Kindheart provide the claims examiner with the requested documents? What information can the claims office legitimately request in order to review the claim?

An insurance policy, a contract between an insurer and the insured, may include specific provisions concerning information that must be supplied by the insured in support of a claim. By law, federal and state agencies regulate insurance company contracts with clients and often provide guidelines and regulations for claims information and the processing of claims. An insurance company will have the right to all information reasonably necessary to determine the validity of the claim and the extent of any benefits to which the claimant is entitled. Under most circumstances, this would not include therapy notes and psychological testing or raw data but would include dates of treatment, test results, diagnosis, and prognosis. Problems result when the insurer challenges the claim and requests additional information beyond the submitted claim form.

Insurance companies are required to keep confidential the information received in support of a claim.

Insurance companies are required to keep confidential the information received in support of a claim. Federal and state laws prohibit disclosure of the information to the insured's employer, even if the employer provides the insurance as a benefit of employment. That does not mean information never "leaks" out; for example, representatives of the insurance company may play golf with a client's employer. Great concern must always be directed to records or information of a client that are shared with a third party, even an insurance company.

Requests for Additional Information

When additional information beyond the claim form is requested by an insurance company, the therapist is caught between the desire and need to be paid for services rendered and the client's right to privacy and confidentiality. The therapist has a duty to protect the client's right to confidentiality, and even the disclosure of a client's name can constitute a breach of confidentiality. Client consent must be secured, in most cases, before information can be revealed to a third party. If the client asks that assignment of benefits be accepted in payment of services rendered and the therapist agrees, you could safely argue that the client has consented to disclosure of the information requested on the insurer's claim form. The HIPAA Privacy Rule discussed in Chapter 38 provides specific authority for submission of protected health care information for billing purposes without specific authorization from the client. Submitting the completed claim form would not be a breach of confidentiality.

Client consent must be secured before information can be revealed to a third party.

But what happens when additional information, beyond the claim form, is requested? Has the client consented to submission of information beyond the claim form? HIPAA's Privacy Rule requires that a mental health provider release only the minimum amount of information necessary to accomplish the stated purpose or need of the potential recipient of the information. Psychotherapy notes require a specific authorization from the client before disclosure can be made. A practitioner should secure the client's written consent before the release of any information or records requested in support of the submitted claim form. A safe practice policy is to have clients sign a HIPAA Privacy Rule-compliant authorization form at the time the therapist accepts assignment of insurance benefits. This is especially true if the therapist anticipates the necessity of providing psychotherapy notes consistent with the Privacy Rule's reasonably minimum necessary disclosure rule.

HIPAA's Privacy Rule requires that a mental health provider release only the minimum amount of information necessary to accomplish the stated purpose or need of the potential recipient of the information.

In some areas, public policy arguments have been raised by consumer protection advocates against "any and all" release forms. If any question exists in the therapist's mind about the release of a particularly sensitive document or piece of information, the client should be asked to sign a consent for release of that specific document or information. A good practice is to attach a copy of the document or information itself as an exhibit to the signed release.

Have clients sign a HIPAA Privacy Rule-compliant authorization form at the time the therapist accepts assignment of insurance benefits.

Caveats about Insurance Claims

What if there is *no* assignment of insurance benefits, but the therapist agrees to process an insurance claim form for a client as an accommodation? The same

Avoid getting involved with billing insurance companies. Instead, take direct pay for services rendered and provide the client with completed claim forms and information.

considerations come into play, and providing no information to the insurance company without the specific written consent of the client is a safe practice.

The easiest solution for the therapist is to avoid getting involved with billing insurance companies. Instead, take direct pay for services rendered, and provide the client with completed claim forms and information, which the client can choose to forward to an insurance company directly.

There are a few key points for the therapist to keep in mind when dealing with a request for information from an insurance company:

- Disclosure of any information, including a client's name, can constitute a breach of confidentiality.
- Secure the client's written consent (consistent with Privacy Rule requirements) to the release of any information to an insurance company.
- If possible, let the client deal directly with the insurance company; supply the client with completed claim forms and requested information to deliver to the insurance company.

Don't ever run the risk of forwarding a client's records or information without the client's written consent. If you choose to accept insurance assignment of benefits, be sure to have the client sign a consent for release of information at the very moment you make that agreement with the client. Getting the client to sign at a later date could prove to be difficult or even impossible if the relationship with the client has deteriorated.

Answers to Frequently Asked Questions about:

Insurance
Third-party payers and managed care
No shows
Copayments

❓ Question

Many of my clients are covered by either third-party payers or managed care companies. Recently, I have been plagued by clients who make appointments and then don't keep them. They don't cancel; they just don't show up. Can I bill the third-party payer or the insurance company when I have to kill an hour? Usually I wait about 15 minutes before I realize the person will not appear for the appointment. When I tell the client he owes me for failing to cancel the appointment, he is usually angry and hostile, as if cancellation were not his responsibility. A 24-hour cancellation notice requirement is in my intake and consent form, which all clients sign before therapy commences.

Sample Form

CONSENT FOR RELEASE OF INFORMATION UPON INSURANCE ASSIGNMENT

I, the undersigned, on this date have requested that Anthony Kindheart, LPC, accept assignment of my insurance benefits for charges for mental health services rendered to me by Mr. Kindheart. Mr. Kindheart has agreed to accept assignment of my insurance benefits. I agree to sign any and all forms necessary for the submission of a claim for payment of benefits to Mr. Kindheart by my insurance company. I hereby consent and authorize Mr. Kindheart to provide my insurance company with any and all reasonably necessary information, including but not limited to his psychotherapy notes, requested by my insurance company in connection with its review and consideration of the claim for payment of benefits. I acknowledge and understand that I am waiving my right to confidentiality with respect to the records and information requested by my insurance company, and I hereby release Mr. Kindheart and his agents and employees from any and all liability arising from release of the information and records requested.

This information is to be provided at my request for use by my insurance provider only in connection with the claims for payment by Mr. Kindheart for mental health services he provides to me. This authorization shall expire upon termination of therapy and thereafter upon payment to Mr. Kindheart for all services rendered by him to me.

I acknowledge that I have the right to revoke this authorization in writing at any time to the extent Mr. Kindheart has not taken action in reliance on this authorization. I further acknowledge that even if I revoke this authorization, the use and disclosure of my protected health information could possibly still be permitted or compelled by law as indicated in the copy of the Notice of Privacy Practices of Mr. Kindheart that I have received and reviewed.

I acknowledge that I have been advised by Mr. Kindheart of the potential of the redisclosure of my protected health information by the authorized recipients and that it will no longer be protected by the federal Privacy Rule.

I further acknowledge that the treatment provided to me by Dr. Kindheart was not conditioned on my signing this authorization and that I was provided with the option to pay for his services personally. However, I have chosen to access my insurance benefits and requested Mr. Kindheart to bill my insurance provider directly.

SIGNED this _____ day of _____, 20__ .

_____
Client

(continued)

Sample Form
(continued)

WITNESSED BY:

_____
Address

_____
Anthony Kindheart, LPC

_____
City and State

_____
Telephone Number

_____
Social Security Number

_____
Date of Birth

I acknowledge that I received a copy of this signed authorization from Mr. Kindheart on this _____ day of _____, 20_____

_____
Client

Sample Form

CONSENT FOR RELEASE OF INFORMATION TO INSURANCE COMPANY

A request for records or information has been received by my therapist, Mr. Anthony Kindheart, LPC. I hereby consent and authorize Mr. Kindheart to provide XYZ Insurance Company with the document or information attached to this consent as Exhibit A, consisting of _____ pages.

I acknowledge and understand that I am waiving my right to confidentiality with respect to the records and information requested by my insurance company and hereby release Mr. Kindheart and his staff from any and all liability arising from release of the information and records requested.

This information is to be provided at my request for use by my insurance provider only in connection with the claims for payment by Mr. Kindheart for mental health services he provides to me. This authorization shall expire upon termination of therapy and thereafter upon payment to Mr. Kindheart for all services rendered by him to me.

I acknowledge that I have the right to revoke this authorization in writing at any time to the extent Mr. Kindheart has not taken action in reliance on this authorization. I further acknowledge that even if I revoke this authorization, the use and disclosure of my protected health information could possibly still be permitted or compelled by law as indicated in the copy of the Notice of Privacy Practices of Mr. Kindheart that I have received and reviewed.

I acknowledge that I have been advised by Mr. Kindheart of the potential of the redisclosure of my protected health information by the authorized recipients and that it will no longer be protected by the federal Privacy Rule.

I further acknowledge that the treatment provided to me by Dr. Kindheart was not conditioned on my signing this authorization and that I was provided with the option to pay for his services personally. However, I have chosen to access my insurance benefits and requested Mr. Kindheart to bill my insurance provider directly.

SIGNED this _____ day of _____, 20___ .

WITNESSED BY:

_____
Anthony Kindheart, LPC

_____
Client

_____
Address

_____
City and State

_____
Telephone Number

_____
Social Security Number

_____
Date of Birth

❗ Answer

A therapist in private practice can legitimately require that clients pay for a session when they fail to cancel within a certain time period. This would become a contractual obligation. However, when third-party payers are involved, there might be a contractual agreement that a no-show does not have to pay the therapist. And there is no obligation to pay for a no-show appointment if there is no contractual obligation in the intake and consent to treat form. Many third-party payer contracts forbid charging clients for not showing up, and no third-party payers or insurance companies or managed care companies will pay for the time the therapist waits for the no-show to not show. Likewise, copayments are forfeited.

Thus, if a client does not show up, try gently to coax the client into showing responsibility by paying, but if the client refuses, forget it and write it off to experience.

💡 Additional Thoughts

- Have a no-show clause in the initial consent to treat form signed by you and the client. Make sure this is discussed with the client at the time of the first session and clearly understood by the client. State that payment for the missed appointment must be made at the next session. (See Chapter 6 for discussion of fees.)
- If there is a series of inconsiderate no-shows, arrange to terminate the client, offering options for therapy with other individuals or entities. Make sure there is no abandonment.
- Check with the third-party payers and see their policy. They might have a strongly worded letter that they send to clients encouraging prompt appearances and no-show notification. It is possible they will notify their insureds that the insured is personally liable and obligated for not showing up for a definite appointment. This *might* do the trick.
- Insist on copayments and no-show payments at the time of the next session. *Don't let the bill accumulate.* Arrange a payout if needed. But stress that the responsibility is the client's and the therapist's policy is universal.
- Whatever you do, don't sue or turn over past due bills to a collection agency. The repercussions can be very dramatic, such as a licensing board complaint or a suit for malpractice. We never recommend harsh collection efforts to recover a past due account. Collections are a business risk and, as in all businesses, there are business losses.
- A therapist who depends on third-party payers has to depend on the third parties and must make sure that public relations are in place and working. That means eliminating matters that will irritate the payer, such as complaining about no-shows.

Legal Lightbulb

- Something to discuss with a client: Some clients might prefer to pay cash rather than depend on a third-party payer or insurance company. As soon as anyone other than the client pays the bill, there is a record of that service in a data bank somewhere. We have had many clients who pay cash directly to the provider rather than have any record created. Thus, they can be assured of more, but not complete, confidentiality. (Some clients even see a therapist under an assumed or fictitious name, just to add another layer of secrecy.) The provider has clinical or progress notes in accordance with all ethical standards, but that record remains in the clinician's office.

- Be aware that clients assume absolute confidentiality as a beginning point. You have to explain the exceptions to confidentiality.

- When there is to be a sharing of information, make sure the provider/therapist has the written consent (consistent with HIPAA's Privacy Rule) of the client to give out any information.

- If the information requested may endanger or embarrass the client, discuss the request with the client and obtain written, informed consent to share the data. If, in the professional opinion of the therapist, the information should not be shared under any circumstances, discuss it with the client and, if needed, seek a protective order from a court.

- Keep the client informed. Remember, under certain circumstances, it is better to forgo payment for services than to allow confidential information to be disclosed.

- Insurance companies and third-party payers are staffed by ordinary humans, and there is no absolute guarantee that they will not share information that should remain private and confidential.

- The purpose of a lawyer-drafted or lawyer-reviewed consent to release information form is to prevent a complaint of inappropriate release of information. Each jurisdiction has its own particularities.

SECTION THREE

CONTRACTS

12

Capitation Agreements

ABC Professional Health Care consists of six associated mental heath professionals: a psychiatrist, two psychologists, a social worker, and two licensed professional counselors. They share office space and have worked out a formula for sharing income and expenses. DEF Manufacturing, Inc., employs 3,000 men and women in their community and would like to establish a plan whereby ABC provides mental health services to DEF employees at a reasonable cost to DEF employees. DEF realizes that job performance is enhanced if family problems are minimized and mental health treatment is available to its workforce at an affordable price. How can ABC and DEF arrive at a fair and reasonable cost basis per capita, that is, per employee, for mental health services?

A capitation agreement covers a specific population group and provides that a fixed fee per member will be paid to a provider for specified mental health services. The current trend in capitation agreements is toward lower fees. Competition among providers of behavioral health services continues to escalate, and purchasers are becoming more knowledgeable and sophisticated about available plans and services. This means that providers will be assuming a greater financial risk.

Under a capitation agreement, mental health care services are provided during a set time period to a group of potential clients, and a flat fixed fee is charged for each client.

Under a capitation agreement, mental health care services are provided during a set time period to a group of potential clients, and a flat fixed fee is charged for each client. If there are 1,000 clients in the population group and the contract rate is $3.50 per member per month, a provider must service the mental health needs of this group for one year for $42,000.

Because employers and insurance companies want to be able to predict with greater certainty their behavioral health care costs, capitation agreements are becoming increasingly attractive. With more provider groups competing for capitation contracts, the bid prices are dropping.

It is very unusual for a capitation contract to be considered by a single mental health provider or a small group of providers. However, as the trend continues, it may become increasingly common for employers to turn to smaller integrated groups that may be able to provide a higher quality of care at a cheaper rate.

How the Trend toward Capitation Affects the Average Practitioner

As the capitation rates that employers are willing to pay to a managed care company fall, so will the rates paid to the individual providers who contract with the managed care company. Everyone in the chain of behavioral health care delivery services will be impacted.

An inadequate bid results in financial losses when demand for services exceeds projected rates.

Capitation involves tremendous risk. An inadequate bid results in financial losses when demand for services exceeds projected rates. These types of contracts require a tremendous amount of sophistication and should not be approached without counsel from skillful and experienced legal advisors and industry consultants.

Before any consideration can be given to entering into a capitation agreement, a provider group must have a thorough knowledge of its own operating costs. Capitation agreements involve calculated risk assessment. Assumptions and projections must be made, and they should be based on solid and verified information and statistics.

Population Data

After operating costs are determined, it is important to identify the size and the nature of the population to be covered by the contract. The number of persons is easy to obtain, but, beyond a simple count, there should be a thorough investigation of the nature of the population: its history of mental health needs, number and nature of past claims, and utilization rates. The mental health provider should be patient and persistent to maximize its own investigation and the accuracy of the data from the fiduciary who is representing the population group. A capitated provider wants to avoid having to provide mental health services without compensation because utilization has exceeded projected rates.

Carefully examine the records indicating the mental health needs of the population over a period of time.

Carefully examine the records indicating the mental health needs of the population over a period of time. Do you or your group of practitioners have the expertise, training, or experience to provide the kinds of services this identified group has needed in the past? If not, additional providers must be placed under contract.

Provider's Concerns

A provider group considering a capitation contract should have a nucleus of mental health practitioners who excel in brief solution-focused therapy and have good case management skills.

Generally, a summary plan description is prepared and made available for study by anyone interested in bidding on a capitation contract. Its provisions define covered services or conditions, exclusions, definitions of medical necessity, and descriptions of employee contributions (i.e., copayments, deductibles, and maximums). Plan descriptions vary widely. Providers must examine each one closely and compare its requirements with their own practice standards.

Any managed care contract, whether it is capitated or simply a provider agreement, does not supersede the individual therapist's ethical and legal responsibility to a client. If a plan excludes mental health services that are normally provided by you and you determine that a client needs those services, you could be forced to provide them for free. The contract should include a definition of medical necessity that every party understands and agrees to and a statement concerning *who* makes the determination of necessity.

Any managed care contract does not supersede the individual therapist's ethical and legal responsibility to a client.

The contract should also provide that, if the capitated contract is terminated for any reason, the provider has no further obligation to the client. Both client and employers assume the responsibility for further services, if needed, at their own or a negotiated expense. If appropriate, the current provider will supply the parties with the names of other competent professionals but has no further ethical or legal obligation to the client. Treatment terminates automatically with the termination of the provider agreement.

Here is a typical provision:

[Medically necessary] means services or supplies that are determined by _____ to be: (i) appropriate for the symptoms, diagnosis, or treatment of the medical condition; (ii) within acceptable mental health practice standards in the organized mental health community; (iii) not primarily for the convenience of the covered individual or any provider providing covered services to the covered individual; (iv) among only those services determined by _____ criteria and/or _____ as adequate and essential for the treatment of mental disorders or substance-abuse-related disorders, as defined by the standard nomenclature and the current version of the *Diagnostic and Statistical Manual of Mental Disorders* (DSM-IV-TR; American Psychiatric Association, 2000) or any of its later amendments.

A key consideration of the mental health professional providing the mental health services should be: Who will determine when mental health services are medically necessary, and what criteria will be used to make the determination? Would the employer who is paying a fixed fee per employee care if services were overused under a capitation agreement? Would the provider want an employee or agent of the employer making that determination? Would the employer care whether the criteria used to determine the obligation to provide services were weak? Careful consideration of these questions is critical. Overuse could cause substantial financial losses under the contract and place professional licenses in jeopardy if needed services were denied. In addition, the denial of services could lead to allegations of abandonment, both a cause of action for negligence and an ethical violation.

Underutilization—caused when a very stringent "medically necessary" provision is rigidly applied—could cause even more serious problems for the provider. A low and inadequate contract rate could present the provider with a dilemma: refuse to provide services or lose money. Any denial of access to services could easily lead to a malpractice claim and a complaint lodged with a state licensing board.

The names or information that go into the blanks in the definition of "medically necessary" are critical to the financial success of the provider as well as to his or her professional future.

Study the list of covered services. Does it align well with the providers who will be servicing the population group? Do they have the ability and experience to profitably provide quality services? If not, what will it cost to bring the necessary providers on board?

Make sure the contract carves out and excepts risk for medical treatment interventions. It is not uncommon for mental health clients to experience either real, sophisticated, or imagined medical needs while receiving mental health treatment (e.g., a therapy client might attempt suicide and be hospitalized). The cost of the medical services should not be borne by the provider who contracted to provide mental health services only.

Answers to Frequently Asked Questions about:

    Level of competence

    Employee therapist versus employer

    Abandonment of client

❓ Question

I recently graduated from a graduate program and have less than two years' experience in psychotherapy. Presently, I work for a community mental health center. I was recently assigned to treat a client with factitious disorder by proxy. I reviewed this person's clinical records and knew immediately I was unqualified to treat this individual. I am having difficulty convincing my employer to refer this client to a more experienced clinician and feel it is unethical to have her in my caseload. Do you have any suggestions about how I can navigate this situation with my employer?

❗ Answer

Exceeding an individual's level of competence is an ethical violation at both the national and state level for every mental health discipline. On occasion, simply showing your employer the national and state ethical canons on *exceeding one's level of competence* might be sufficient to encourage the employer to refer this client to another more trained professional. It is also malpractice and can lead to disastrous legal consequences. A wrongful diagnosis and, poof: malpractice! A therapist's ethical obligation to a client exceeds and supersedes the therapist's obligation to an employer. *Your* license is the license in jeopardy. When an employer insists that a therapist treat a client the therapist knows he or she is not capable of treating effectively, it is time to take a stand. The therapist must terminate with the client and make an appropriate referral, hopefully, with employer approval.

Preferably, the client should be referred to at least three sources for continuing care that the therapist personally knows can provide effective treatment to the client for his or her problems. If the employer retaliates with termination, an employment lawyer should be consulted about a possible wrongful termination lawsuit. If the employer does not terminate, consideration should be given to resigning anyway. A mental health professional should be very reluctant to provide services where client care is not the entity's primary interest. A person facing this situation might wish to share this response with the employer or a supervisor and advise that any further attempts to compromise his or her professional judgment and client care would be reported to the licensing board of the rigid supervisor or employer. Perhaps this would circumvent the need for a resignation or a firing.

One commonly used technique in matters of this type is to show a copy of your state and national ethics code of conduct, together with a copy of the licensing law, to your employer or supervisor. Codes that provide penalties for treating people beyond your competence are generally clearly defined in these codes of ethics and is often sufficient to inspire the employer or supervisor to find another option.

Additional Thoughts

- Every therapist is ultimately responsible to and for his or her client.
- This is true even if an employer, agency, or supervisor is *also* responsible.
- A complaint filed with a licensing board will involve anyone and everyone on the treatment team, as will litigation.
- Every client is entitled to treatment from a competent professional.
- Complaining to an employer, agency, or supervisor and documenting the complaint does not exonerate the treating therapist from responsibility if the therapist continues to treat the client.
- You might call a lawyer anonymously and get an advisory opinion indicating the employer's ultimate responsibility. The employer might be more flexible once responsibility is ascertained.

Legal Lightbulb

- Capitation involves tremendous risk. An inadequate bid will result in financial losses when demand for services exceeds projected rates.

- A therapist's ethical and legal responsibility to a client supersedes any provision of a capitated contract. Services that are not covered but are needed may have to be provided without additional charges.

- Retain control over, or at least maintain input into, the decision as to whether mental health services are "necessary."

- Be sure the contract carves out and excepts risk for medical treatment interventions.

- Negotiate for a sharing of profits (or losses) over (or under) certain amounts.

- Capitation is all about risk and the risk-reward ratio. Information is essential in assessing, weighing, and accepting the risk. At least know what risk is being assumed.

- Beware the fiduciary who refuses to provide specific requested information, and avoid bidding on the contract such a source offers.

- Never approach a managed care contract, *least of all a capitation agreement,* without the input of skillful and experienced legal advisors and industry consultants.

- The contract between the provider and the employer and employee-client, as well as the contract between the employer and employees, should provide that services will be rendered to the client as long as the original contract for capitated services is in force. In addition, on termination of the contract or termination of employment, the obligation to offer and render services expires also and the only obligation the provider has is to make an appropriate referral.

- While the obligation of an employer may be easily handled by contract, because of the ethical obligations of mental health professionals, termination must be effected by the ethics and practices of the profession.

Changes in Population and Term of the Agreement

Two other areas of the contract should be carefully considered:

1. The eligibility of members of the population pool.
2. The term of the agreement.

Is the population highly fluid, increasing and decreasing with the hiring and firing of employees? If so, will there be financial adjustments to the contract as new members are enrolled or terminated? If an employer lays off a substantial portion of its covered labor force, will the employer be entitled to a refund of part of the capitated amount paid? If prosperity suddenly requires the addition of a substantial number of employees, will the provider be compensated for the addition to the population pool? If so, at what rate? Agreements negotiated in January may seem inadequate in November. And what about a traumatic work-place death, homicide, or suicide, which necessitates emergency action and in-creased consultation and therapy?

Two other areas of the contract should be carefully considered: (1) the eligibility of members of the population pool and (2) the term of the agreement.

Should you enter into a one-year capitated agreement to avoid the losses a longer term could generate if the bid rate proves to be too low? Or, is a longer term a sounder financial consideration because another provider may submit a lower bid after the one-year contract is up?

These are difficult questions, and they cannot be answered quickly or gener-ally. Even with an abundance of information and caution, these considerations, like all aspects of capitated agreements, are difficult to address. Appreciating, weighing, balancing, and, in the final analysis, *accepting* risk is what capitation agreements are all about.

A true balance of the risk to the employer and the provider might be arranged as a sharing in any profit or loss realized by the employer or the provider. Consideration might be given to establishing a profit (or loss) figure over (or under) which each party might share. Such an agreement would re-duce the risk of financial loss for the provider and allow the employer to recover overpayment if the contract rate proved to be too high.

Capitation agreements are here to stay and apparently will be increasing in number, at least in the near future. The risk associated with these agreements and the complicated nature of the provisions they contain make it imperative that competent advice be obtained from legal and industry sources and consultants.

Capitation agreements are here to stay.

13

"Gag Rules"

A group practice was formed to provide integrated behavioral health services by a psychiatrist, a psychologist, two social workers, a substance abuse counselor, and two licensed professional counselors. All were experienced mental health practitioners who wanted to pursue managed care contracts. One of the first managed care contracts they signed as a group and, individually, provided that in the event a referral was necessary, the treating therapist and the group would refer the client only to the managed care company. Over a period of several months, one of the social workers, in conjunction with the psychiatrist who prescribed and monitored medication, provided services to a young woman who was having serious difficulty both functioning on her job and getting along with family members and coworkers. The social worker, suspecting that the woman suffered from dissociative identity disorder, consulted with the other members of the group. None of them was experienced in treating persons with this disorder, and the group was unanimous in recommending termination and referral back to the managed care company. The client was instructed at a termination session to ask the managed care company for referral to a specialist who was experienced in working with multiple personality clients. The managed care company was advised of the perceived problem and needs of this client.

Unfortunately, the managed care company did not have a provider under contract who was experienced with this disorder. Instead, the client was referred to another social worker who had recently attended a dissociative disorder workshop. After two visits with the social worker, the young woman committed suicide. Her family hired an attorney, who asserted that the group, the social worker, the psychiatrist, and the managed care company had had a duty to make a referral to the best possible source for care of dissociative identity disorder. The managed care company, the group, the social worker, and the psychiatrist were all facing a suit for professional negligence.

Failure to review and understand a contract presented by a managed care company can lead to serious consequences for a provider.

Very few practitioners are able to sustain a private practice without entering into managed care provider agreements. "Private pay only" practices are vanishing in today's era of highly competitive behavioral health services. Therapists often join as many panels as possible without taking the time to review and carefully consider a proposed contract or a proposed managed care company. They adhere to a faulty philosophy that, because managed care is a necessity of successful practice, the more provider panels you can contract to join, the better. More is not always better, however, and the failure to review and understand a contract presented by a managed care company can lead to serious consequences for a provider.

Managed care contracts are prepared by the attorneys for the managed care company. They have the company's interests and protection in mind, and provisions of the agreement may conflict with the interests of the therapist. A therapist cannot abrogate his or her professional and ethical responsibilities when they conflict with a contractual obligation in a provider agreement. It is imperative to review all contracts before executing them and to consult a legal specialist who can advise on any terms or conditions that are unclear. The provider may finally elect to sign the contract as presented, but at least the terms of the agreement have been understood in all their ramifications.

Provisions That Deserve Careful Attention

There are certain provisions that typically appear in contracts promulgated by managed care entities. These clauses are written in a way that are very protective of the managed care entity's interests but are adverse to those of the mental health provider.

Gag Clauses

Gag clauses, commonly included in provider contracts, attempt to preclude the therapist from discussing with third parties or clients any disagreements with care standards, procedures, management, sharing rate, or referral information. Many states have moved to ban these types of clauses. If you practice in a jurisdiction where they are permitted, negotiate the elimination of that particular clause before you sign the agreement, or limit the clause to defamatory statements. An issue may arise on which you will have a moral or legal obligation to speak out.

Hold Harmless Clause

Another common provision, the hold harmless clause, imposes a financial obligation on the therapist to reimburse the managed care company if the company becomes a defendant in a lawsuit or must pay damages for any negligent or fraudulent acts of the therapist. The following is a typical—but very broad and risk-laden—hold harmless provision:

> Provider shall indemnify and save harmless ABC, Inc., and its officers, agents, and employees from all suits, actions, losses, damages, claims, or liability of any character,

Gag clauses attempt to preclude the therapist from discussing disagreements with care standards, procedures, management, sharing rate, or referral information.

Negotiate the elimination of a gag clause before you sign the agreement, or limit the clause to defamatory statements.

The hold harmless clause imposes a financial obligation on the therapist to reimburse the managed care company if the company becomes a defendant in a lawsuit or must pay damages for any negligent or fraudulent acts of the therapist.

type, or description, including, without limiting the generality of the foregoing, all expenses of litigation, court costs, and attorney fees for injury or death to any person or persons or property, arising out of, or occasioned by, the acts of Provider or Provider's agents or employees.

If the managed care company is named in a suit, the hold harmless clause shifts the responsibility for defense and damages to the provider.

This clause means just what it says, and it goes to an extreme in providing protection for the managed care company. If the provider performs *any* act, justifiable or not, or is sued for *any* reason (also justifiable or not) and the managed care entity is named in the suit as a party defendant, the provider pays all costs of defense and any judgment that is entered. It doesn't matter whether the provider was wrongfully accused and sued or whether the suit is successfully defended by the provider and the managed care company. It simply says, "If we get sued, you pay."

As a practical matter, if the managed care entity is named in a suit involving the provider, receives a letter of complaint, or has to negotiate a settlement, the provider will ultimately be financially involved. The details vary from case to case, but, in general, the responsibility for defense and damages shifts to the provider.

Unless endorsed on the malpractice policy of the provider, the provider's personal malpractice or professional liability policy usually does not cover expenses of the managed care entity's defense. The contractual "save harmless" agreement does not extend obligations of the malpractice carrier without endorsement.

It is virtually impossible to negotiate the elimination of a hold harmless clause in its entirety, but it is possible to negotiate a narrower and fairer provision and to make it mutual. If you must indemnify the managed care company for your mistakes, they should be obligated to indemnify you for its mistakes. Suits are now being filed for wrongful *denial of care*. These suits have a short history, but managed care entities are becoming sensitive to their vulnerability.

Options

- Cross out the clause entirely. Delete the paragraph by lining it out, and initial the change. It doesn't hurt to try. For example:

  ~~Provider shall indemnify and save harmless ABC, Inc., and its officers, agents, and employees from all suits, actions, losses, damages, claims, or liability of any character, type, or description, including . . . .~~

- Make the clause reciprocal or mutual; place the managed care company under a similar indemnity agreement:

  ABC, Inc. shall indemnify and save harmless Provider and its officers, agents, and employees from all suits, actions, losses, damages, claims, or liability of any character, type, or description, including, without limiting the generality of the foregoing, all expenses of litigation, court costs, and attorney fees for injury or death to any person or persons or property, arising out of, or occasioned by the acts of ABC, Inc. or ABC, Inc.'s agents or employees.

- Negotiate a narrower scope for the clause. Limit the indemnity obligations to a situation where the provider is found guilty of or liable for negligence or fraudulent conduct. Consider adding the following language:

Provider shall indemnify and save harmless ABC, Inc. and its officers, agents, and employees from all suits, actions, losses, damages, claims, or liability of any character, type, or description, including, without limiting the generality of the foregoing, all expenses of litigation, court costs, and attorney fees for injury or death to any person or persons or property, arising out of, or occasioned by, the acts of Provider or Provider's agents or employees, **but only to the extent that Provider or Provider's agents or employees are found judicially liable for such losses.**

- Call the malpractice carrier and negotiate for coverage of a possible indemnity risk. For a premium, the carrier may be willing to extend its coverage.
- Ask the managed care company to extend its policy to cover you, as provider, and your group and to unify protection in one policy. Offer to pay the additional premium if there is one.

Coverage and Payment

When reviewing a contract, examine the specific benefits and exclusions of the plan for mental health services. Learn the copays and deductibles, and study the demographics of the covered population to determine whether you and your practice are a reasonable match.

The most important consideration for therapists is usually the amount of compensation for the services provided. Look for a fixed payment schedule, but don't stop there. Be sure the contract contains provisions for payment within a fixed and short time period. Try to impose penalties and interest on the managed care company if payment is not made within the prescribed time period.

Find out whether the managed care company publishes a list of providers and, if so, what information you can include with your listing and what specialty listings are available. Be sure to review a proof of the listings before they are published.

Referral Restrictions

Referral agreements and restrictions should be carefully considered. Many contracts require referral back to the managed care company or only to another panel member. Some require the client to repeat the utilization review process for an alternate referral. A few contracts impose the assumption of financial responsibility on any referring therapist who makes a referral to a provider outside

Learn the copays and deductibles, and study the demographics of the covered population to determine whether you and your practice are a reasonable match.

When reviewing a contract, examine the specific benefits and exclusions of the plan for mental health services.

Negotiate for the right to make a referral to a provider outside the plan.

the plan. A therapist cannot contract away the ethical and legal duty to refer a client to the best possible source for care.

Negotiate for the right to make a referral to a provider outside the plan if you believe that such a referral is the best option for a client.

Confidentiality and Reviews

The contract should provide for confidentiality of client records. Any access by the managed care company or the employer should occur only with the consent of the client. Try to impose the most protection possible for the client. Learn who will be viewing client information and what their qualifications are. Narrow the scope of any provisions that compel access to information by the managed care company.

Know what types of reviews (i.e., prior, concurrent, retrospective) are required by the plan and what rules are in place with respect to reviews. Ask about the appeal processes and determine whether they are reasonable and fair. If they are too onerous or appear to be unfair, you should probably decline the provider agreement presented by that company. If the client has a problem with the managed care company, you, as the treating therapist, will be drawn into the legal fray.

Consult your colleagues concerning company or contract issues.

Providing services through a bad managed care company is just inviting unwanted involvement in legal proceedings. Get as much information as possible about the company and its plan while contemplating the terms of a contract. Other providers and colleagues are a wonderful source of information and should be routinely consulted concerning company or contract issues.

Continuity of Care

Examine carefully what the plan contractually provides for continuity of care. Try to ascertain what happens when a client's insurance coverage—or care—is terminated. Your responsibility to a client is not as easily severed. You are taking on a client, not a managed care company, and your professional and ethical responsibilities to the client are independent of and supersede your managed care contractual obligations and duties. If the company won't pay for coverage and you feel the services are necessary, you may have to decide how to deliver those services to the client or make a proper referral.

Be sure that the term of the contract is consistent with your professional goals and needs.

Some managed care contracts forbid the provider to charge the client for noncovered services, even if the client agrees to pay for them. If the client has a need for noncovered services, you may have a legal and ethical obligation to provide them or to refer the client to a private-pay therapist, if permissible under the managed care contract. Negotiate to have this clause stricken from the contract.

Be sure that the term of the contract is consistent with your professional goals and needs. A long-term contract may appear to provide security and stability, but you may want the flexibility to get out of a contract quickly if it doesn't meet your expectations.

Not every provider contract is the same. Never assume that all provider agreements have the same standards. Contracts vary from company to company, and you must carefully review each provider agreement before signing. Consult with a lawyer and peers and, at the very least, put yourself in a position to make an intelligent risk assessment.

Rarely does a provider present a managed care contract to a managed care company. Uniformly, the contract is drafted by a managed care company's lawyers for the benefit and protection of the company (the lawyer's client) and delivered to the provider for acceptance. Some clauses can be negotiated and others eliminated. The potential mischief in gag and hold harmless clauses is enormous. A potential provider might finally agree to these clauses, but it is important to first view all their implications. Many managed care companies have some flexibility built into their contracts; with tact and persistence, some of these provisions might be amendable. Negotiation is always worth some effort. Once the contract is signed and operating, changes are almost impossible.

Answers to Frequently Asked Questions about:

Assessment: Fitness for duty

Who owns the data

Rights of person or company who pays for evaluation or data

Right to refer and to whom

❓ Question

An employer refers an employee to a managed care provider for a fitness for duty evaluation. The assessment was brought about by workplace violence following a verbal threat. The first psychologist, Dr. Smith, sees the employee and conducts an evaluation that is adverse to the employee. The employee then seeks a second opinion from a second psychologist, Dr. Brown. Dr. Brown requests "all raw test data, reports, and notes" from Dr. Smith and has an express release signed by the employee for the same. Dr. Smith refuses to release the data, stating that it is owned by the company who paid for the evaluation, not the employee. Hence, the managed care contractor reasons, the confidentiality of the data belongs to the employer, and they have discouraged the employer and Dr. Smith from releasing these data. Who owns the data? What is the status of confidentiality? What is the employee's recourse? Is Dr. Smith ethically bound to release this information to Dr. Brown? How controlling is the contract between: (1) employer and managed care provider, (2) the managed care provider and the client, and (3) the managed care company and the ultimate provider of services, usually a licensed person?

❗ *Answer*

The questions raised should have been worked out before the evaluation of the employee was completed. The fact that raw data was not going to be shared with the employee should have been disclosed to him upfront, and he should have been asked to consent to this arrangement in a written consent to treatment form. He should have been made aware that Dr. Smith was working for the employer under a contract with a managed care company. He could then make an informed decision to submit or not to submit to the evaluation.

Because there could be an issue of informed consent under these facts, we believe that the data should be shared with Dr. Brown. It would seem that fundamental fairness would also dictate this result. Who pays for therapy, assessment, evaluation, and treatment is not relevant. If a woman pays for her significant other's therapy, is she entitled to view the record? Of course not. If the significant other consented to her receiving a copy of the report and supporting data,

Legal Lightbulb

- Carefully review each provider agreement and consult with a knowledgeable attorney before signing one.

- You are taking care of clients, not managed care companies. Your professional and ethical responsibilities to a client are independent of and supersede your managed care contractual obligations and duties.

- Carefully evaluate a company's offer to list you on its provider panel.

- Proof your listing and all information disseminated about you by the managed care company.

- Thoroughly inspect each term and provision of the provider contract.

- If the client is angry at and dissatisfied with the managed care company, you may be caught in a legal fray and named as a codefendant in any lawsuit filed. Note well: The employer and managed care entity can lose money whereas the licensed person can lose a professional license, making that professional *unemployable.*

- Consult peers about a company's reputation and contract issues.

- It is always worth the effort to negotiate important clauses.

can she keep it from the client? Of course not. Patient/clients have a right to demand and receive copies of their files.

💡 Additional Thoughts

- Therapists who deny clients access to a copy of their file do so at their peril in absence of a court-ordered protective order limiting the availability of the file or a contractual restriction.
- The demand for the file should be made by the client/patient.
- If a complaint is filed, it will be against the client's psychologist, the service provider, not against the managed care company or the employer.

14

Office Leases

After working 10 years for a nonprofit church counseling center, Susan James, LPC, searched for the perfect space where she could establish her new private practice and locate her first individual office. Locating a small, well-maintained, commercial office building, Susan quickly signed a five-year lease and commenced business on February 1. For the remainder of that year, Susan struggled valiantly to make a go of the practice; and although she was late with her rent on one occasion, she managed to keep current with the payments provided in her lease. On the one-year anniversary date of her lease, Susan received a bill from her landlord for several thousand dollars for pass-through expense increases she could not afford. Sixty days later, the landlord locked her out of her space, asserting a statutory landlord's lien securing, for unpaid expenses, all the contents of her office including her professional client files.

~

Dr. Richard Kindheart practiced psychology from the cozy confines of his two-room office suite for more than 15 years, annually extending his lease with only occasional modest increases in rent. When new building management informed him his rent would be increased by 25 percent for the upcoming year, Dr. Kindheart elected to give 30 days' notice of his intent to vacate the premises as required under his original lease. Two weeks later, Dr. Kindheart was in the middle of a therapy session with a well-known local sports celebrity when in popped the building manager with a prospective new tenant. Dr. Kindheart was alarmed, but his client was furious because the prospective new tenant immediately recognized the client and asked for an autograph. When Dr. Kindheart confronted the building manager over this outrageous interruption, the building manager quickly referred Dr. Kindheart to his lease. A clause provided that once Dr. Kindheart gave notice of intention to vacate, the building manager was allowed to show the space to prospective tenants during normal business hours.

A mental health professional must give careful consideration to ordinary financial and business issues when leasing office space but must also keep in mind the ethical duties and responsibilities owed to clients and the records of clients maintained in the normal course of the practice. Leases are legal instruments, carefully crafted over time *to protect the landlord's rights and interests,* often to the detriment of the tenant. In negotiating with the landlord, the mental health professional must be vigilant in protecting his or her own interests and those of the practice's clients as well; that is, clients have individual rights that must be protected under the terms of the lease. If they are not protected, the tenant/professional might be liable to the client for infractions. These rights include confidentiality, which was breached in the celebrity case.

Space Considerations

In selecting and designing office space, confidentiality and client safety are key. The HIPAA Privacy and Security Rules seek to enhance and protect the confidentiality and physical integrity of protected health information. A well thought out and designed office environment can go a long way toward ensuring confidentiality and physical integrity and compliance with these privacy and security rules.

Confidentiality and client safety are key.

If possible and affordable, a mental health professional's office should have a separate entrance and exit for clients to eliminate the possibility that clients will pass one another as they arrive and leave from therapy sessions. If this arrangement is impossible, a therapist should consider staggering appointment times to lessen the possibility of client confrontations.

Consider staggering appointment times to lessen the possibility of client confrontations.

Consider designing the space to contain a separate room to house client files. This should be a room that can be locked to keep out prying or curious eyes. Negotiate a lease provision with the landlord to the effect that no one but you and the landlord would have a key to this secured interior space and janitorial staff would not be allowed access except under your direct supervision. The physical space itself must be clean, insect and rodent free, dry, and safe. Client files must be preserved for specific time periods in many jurisdictions; therefore, they must be protected from mildew, mice, bugs, and all other forms of record deterioration.

Clients are the business invitees of the mental health professional and are owed a duty to be kept free from harm if, as, and when they access the premises. For example, if the building has water leaks and stained, damp ceiling tiles eventually give way and strike a client in the head, the therapist will have legal responsibility for the harm caused to the client. This is true even if written complaints and requests for repairs were given to the landlord.

Common areas of the building as well as the parking lot should be closely examined. Inspect the restrooms for cleanliness and maintenance. If client appointments are scheduled at night, be sure the parking lot is well lighted. Check with the local police department about incidents or problems they may be familiar with at this location. Ask what can be done about those problems to keep clients protected.

*Soundproofing
may be required.*

Check to see how soundproof your office is and will be. If you share a common wall with another tenant, there must be no possibility that conversations can be overheard outside your office. This is true even if your office is located on an outside wall. Have someone stand in the next office or outside the building and test whether sounds are audible from your space. If so, soundproofing may be required or an auditory device that disguises or masks sounds and voices must be installed.

Check to see what kind of signs or other evidence of your presence in the building will be permitted by the landlord. Ask about the building directory and how your name and location will be listed. If you want your name on the exterior of the building, negotiate for the right to display it. You want your office to promote you and your services as much as possible; therefore, you may have to negotiate to have your name listed on a directory, an illuminated sign outside the building near the street, a plaque near the entrance, or a neon sign on the roof.

Dr. Love leased space in a quiet strip shopping mall, which seemed very convenient to his clients at first. After he developed a broader clientele, the landlord rented the adjacent space to a dance studio. The thumping beat of dance music made quiet therapy impossible. When clients requested evening sessions, Dr. Love realized his lease did not provide for therapeutic quiet enjoyment of the office space. He was obligated under the lease and had no recourse against the landlord.

*It is wise to have
comprehensive
insurance coverage.*

Last, be sure to maintain your own private, individual premises liability insurance policy. Despite all precautions, accidents do happen and it is wise to have comprehensive insurance coverage. In addition, obtain content insurance to protect against loss of your personal property due to fire, water, theft, or other unforeseen causes. Negotiating both kinds of coverages with the same carrier may result in lower overall insurance rates.

General Business and Financial Considerations

If you are unfamiliar with commercial lease agreements, consider hiring a leasing agent to scout for suitable space and to negotiate the lease for you, on *your* behalf, with the landlord. Be sure to educate the leasing agent about the special considerations you have as a mental health professional. Remember, however, that the leasing agent's fee is ordinarily paid by the landlord, who will want to pass this cost on to you in some manner. It may be subtle such as not offering you as large a "finish out" allowance as the landlord otherwise might ordinarily have done. All things considered, a leasing agent is a professional with specialized knowledge in an area where most mental health professionals are naive greenhorns. The leasing agent, if properly prepared by the mental health professional, should be able to provide valuable assistance.

Give careful consideration to the length of the lease term that makes sense for you. Although a longer term may result in a lower monthly rate, it may be an unfortunate decision. In our first example, Susan James optimistically opted for a five-year term with substantially reduced monthly payments, not understanding the landlord's right to assess and pass through to her annual cost increases over which neither she nor the landlord had any control, that is, tax, insurance, and utility raises, for example. She finally signed a lease that her practice income could not support. If you do not have an established practice, consider a shorter term lease in the event you are not as successful as hoped and include an option to renew for periodic one-year terms at the same, slightly higher, or negotiated terms, such as current market price.

Give careful consideration to the length of the lease term that makes sense for you.

If you anticipate growth, or even if growth is just wished for, negotiate for an option to lease additional adjoining space or the ability to relocate within the building to larger space during your lease term at the same rental rate. Growth and income possibilities are often missed because of space and lease constraints.

Moving is not always an attractive proposition for professionals. Location sometimes is critical to maintaining a client base. Clients who spend 10 minutes driving to your office may be reluctant to drive 20 minutes or through traffic if you are forced to relocate. Even with a long-term lease, numerous possibilities could prevent you from obtaining a new lease and the right to maintain the space. Build space guarantees into your lease renewal options if possible.

Research your landlord. Ask for credit references or a financial statement. An insolvent landlord can result in foreclosures or new owners with a different vision for the building use and management, that is, one large corporate tenant instead of 30 separate leaseholders. It can also lead to the failure to adequately maintain the building, creating dangerous conditions for you and your clients. Ask to review the landlord's general liability insurance policy to see that it is in force and, further, that there is coverage to compensate you or your clients for damages caused by or due to the negligence of the landlord or staff.

Research your landlord.

If you practice in an entity other than a sole proprietorship, negotiate to sign the lease in your entity capacity rather than individually to prevent having individual responsibility for the lease payments. Although this is the optimum situation, it is probable that the landlord would insist on a personal guarantee from you anyway. If market conditions favor the tenant, that is, a glut of office space, avoiding the personal guarantee may be possible.

Be wary of escalation clauses and pass-through expense increases. It is not uncommon in commercial leases for landlords to pass on increased expenses such as taxes to its tenants. The lease will establish a base year expense, and if certain fixed expenses increase in a given year, the landlord is given the right to collect additional rent from the tenant based on the tenant's proportionate share of the overall building space. Susan James did not understand these clauses in her lease and suffered the consequences. Get the professional assistance of a leasing agent or attorney to explain what you are getting into. Network with real estate agent friends for informal professional guidance.

Rarely, in our experience, do mental health professionals have undergraduate or graduate degrees in business or finance. Indeed, it is often difficult to conduct a conversation wherein investments, finances, or technical clauses in leases are the focus of the conversation. The calling of the mental professional is to help people, rarely to check out legal jargon, negotiate fine legal points in a lease, or use technical phraseology.

Check with the companies providing utility services to the building. Ask about utility service interruptions or problems and the number of service calls to the building in prior years. If you work evenings, weekends, and holidays, be sure there will be adequate utility service to make your space comfortable for yourself and tenants. Some buildings provide for energy conservation after normal business hours, and tenants must request and pay extra for normal utility service if they work late or on weekends and holidays.

The same is true for building security. There may be reduced security staff after normal working hours, on weekends, or on holidays. If so, be careful in scheduling appointments when security is not present and available if needed. Ask if security personnel could be made available to escort you or your clients to the parking lot.

Consider negotiating a rent abatement if there is a disruption in utility service or access to your space is limited because of fire, water, or other unforeseen causes, including elevator malfunctions. If you can't use your space, through no fault of your own, you cannot make money. It seems fair to request that you not have to pay rent for the time period you cannot use your office. You may also wish to consider business interruption insurance that will pay for lost income under such circumstances.

Talk to other tenants and ask questions to gauge their level of satisfaction with the landlord or management company, their space, and the common areas.

Talk to other tenants and ask questions to gauge their level of satisfaction with the landlord or management company, their space, and the common areas. Request that they show you their lease and even give you a copy to examine. Other tenants can share a wealth of information that impact your negotiations and decision to practice at that particular location, perhaps possibly including the benefit of other tenants as referral sources.

Learn what other kinds of businesses are located at the same location.

Learn what other kinds of businesses are located at the same location. There may be businesses, even therapy practices, that would make the location inappropriate for your practice. For example, if you treat pedophiles, you would not want to locate near a child psychologist or day care operation.

If you intend to sublease some of your space, be sure to negotiate for the right to rent portions of your space to other professionals. Many form leases contain provisions that prohibit subleases and require that only the tenant has the right to occupy the premises. The right to sublease is generally not a deal breaker with the landlord and, assuming prior notice, use of the subleased space consistent with the overall use of the space will be permitted.

If you intend to sublease from an existing tenant, be sure to review the prime lease for the right to sublease and any restrictions. Read the entire lease and understand its terms. Your right to occupy the space is limited to the tenant's right under the prime lease. You should follow all the suggestions in this chapter as if you were negotiating a prime lease. A sublease can offer no greater rights than the prime lease. If possible, ask the prime landlord to endorse the sublease, signifying the landlord's consent.

Read the entire lease and understand its terms.

Ethical Considerations

Susan James was locked out of her space for nonpayment of rent, and the landlord asserted a lien against all the personal property belonging to Susan in the leased space. Her lease and the law in her state contractually bestowed these rights. Susan should have negotiated into her lease a provision that excepted her client files and gave her the right to access and remove the files no matter what the circumstances. It took a court order and some fancy and expensive legal footwork for Susan to get access to her client files. Fortunately, she was able to do so before any clients requested copies from her. A lease cannot circumvent your obligation to safeguard client files and to allow clients to access their protected health information.

Dr. Kindheart had a therapy session interrupted by a horribly inconsiderate building manager, and confidentiality was breached. Because the client had a long-term therapeutic relationship with Dr. Kindheart and wished to continue therapy with him, he chose not to file a complaint with the state licensing board. The possibility still exists, however, that he could do so in the future. Every commercial lease has access provisions whereby the landlord has the right to access the space for maintenance and repairs and, oftentimes, to show it to prospective tenants. A right to inspect at all times is also not uncommon. These kinds of provisions must be negotiated to ensure the privacy of your clients. Consider negotiating terms that permit access on reasonable prior notice and not during times clients are scheduled.

Avoid arrangements either as a tenant or sublessee that require you to pay rent based on a portion of your fees. This arrangement is often looked on as an illegal fee-sharing agreement. If you are dealing with a kind landlord who is sympathetic to your uncertainty about your practice income, it is better to negotiate a very short-term lease, that is, three to six months, with a fixed rental payment. As you become more certain about your practice income, a longer lease or sublease can be negotiated.

The most important contracts you will enter into are the ones you enter into with clients to provide professional services and the one you enter into with your landlord. Consider clients as third-party beneficiaries to your lease, and preserve and protect their rights in all your negotiations with the landlord.

Answers to Frequently Asked Questions about:

Liability on a lease
Agreements between colleagues sharing space
Death, disability, and abandonment
Joint and several liability

? Question

Several of my licensed and professional friends and colleagues and I have decided to rent office space. Our intention is to share space and contribute equally to expenses, but run and operate our own practices. Several questions have been discussed, such as: Are we liable for all the lease obligations or just our one-fourth share of the lease? Do we need an agreement among ourselves that outlines our understandings and what happens if one of us dies, is permanently disabled, or, for whatever reason, simply abandons the project? Is each one of us legally responsible for the whole lease term?

! Answer

These are relevant and important questions. Yes, everyone who signs a lease is responsible and liable for the entire lease and all obligations under the lease, unless the lease *specifically provides* that each is responsible for only his or her proportion of the lease responsibilities. This includes rent, pass-through tax, insurance or utility payments, damages caused in the space by other tenants, and other commitments as are provided in the lease agreement. Each is responsible and is legally liable for all the small print responsibilities contained in the lease and any attachments to the lease. A litigious landlord who wished to file suit could name all the lessees or just one of them in any default litigation. Often, to simplify a legal action, the plaintiff names as a party defendant only the individual with the deepest pockets. But all signatories are liable, and they are liable jointly and severally. All can be sued or just a selected few may be sued.

The individual colleagues must have their collective association agreement, which provides for their obligations to one another in unambiguous terms. This agreement might provide for insurance in the event of the death or disability of a colleague or co-lessee and specific or liquidated damages should any lessee abandon the lease, withdraw from the leased space before the end of the lease term, lose his or her professional license so that continued practice is impossible, seek early retirement, or leave because of transfer of a spouse or simply the chance of a better opportunity. The agreement of the colleagues must provide for all foreseeable contingencies so that should a contingency occur, the procedures are in place for orderly dissolution of the rental agreement and termination of obligations.

Legal Lightbulb

- Client rights and interests must be considered when negotiating a lease.

- Particular attention should be given to privacy issues in connection with the space itself and the lease.

- Leased space must be soundproofed in some manner, and, if possible, a separate entrance and exit should be provided.

- The premises and common areas must be clean and safe for clients to access.

- Be sure the parking areas are secure and well lighted.

- Client records must be secured from landlords and their staff, including janitorial personnel.

- Do not allow landlords or their staff unbridled right to access your space.

- Appropriately insure your practice and premises.

- Consider hiring a leasing agent to help locate and secure appropriate space on terms favorable to you.

- Know your landlord and fellow tenants *before* you sign the lease.

- Never base rent on a percentage of your fees.

- Client files, computer access, daily logs, and accounting journals must be secured whenever professional staff is not present.

- All file cabinets should be locked every night.

- Leases are generally drafted by the lawyer for the landlord, and each time they are amended, another landlord-protecting clause is inserted. The tenant must have these instruments inspected, reviewed, and altered to fit the clients' needs.

- Any written instrument can be changed by simply lining out, dating, and signing or initialing.

- Remember, you can negotiate anything.

- The fact that a form lease is printed does not indicate the terms are fixed in concrete.

- Know, in advance, the special requirements of mental health office leases.

The terms of the lease are binding. They are obligations of the estate in the event of the death of a colleague and continue even if a lessee is disabled or loses a license and cannot continue practice. Insurance can provide some comfort in the event either of these actions takes place.

💡 Additional Thoughts

- Leases are serious contractual obligations. Their terms bind and obligate all signatories.
- Each person who signs is fully liable.
- Individuals who agree to share office space and obligations should have a written agreement, reviewed by a lawyer, that clearly sets forth the rights, duties, obligations, and responsibilities of all parties.
- Careful thought has to be given concerning the legal entity, such as individual practitioners, independent contractors, partnerships, limited partnerships, professional corporations, and so on, so that the entity is clear to the consuming public.
- Oral agreements are not worth the paper they are written on.
- Most leases are created with general business tenants in mind. They do not include the special requirements (e.g., confidentiality) of a mental health professional.
- Because of the HIPAA requirements, some construction modifications have to be made to ensure the privacy and security requirements. Before opening the doors to establish a practice, a complete set of HIPAA-compliant forms should be in place.

SECTION FOUR

FEES

15

Sliding Fee Scales

A therapist received a call from her minister asking if she would see a member of the congregation whose husband had run off with another woman and taken all the couple's money. The minister informed the therapist that the congregant was extremely distraught, had four young children, no insurance, and limited financial resources. The therapist agreed to see the woman in therapy and charitably reduced her normal hourly rate by 50 percent.

~

A managed care referral wished to continue in therapy after all authorized, covered benefits had been exhausted. But he was unable to pay the therapist's full fee in cash. The therapist agreed to see the client at a publicly published reduced rate.

~

A managed care referral, a widow with eight minor children and limited financial resources, struggled to pay her $20 copay for each session. The therapist, aware of the problem, waived the copay for future sessions.

These are examples of sliding or variable fees. To kindhearted therapists, they present a serious risk of civil and criminal fraud and possible claims for breach of contract.

All states prohibit a health care provider from charging a higher fee to a client who has insurance coverage than to one without insurance, when insurance (or the lack of it) is the only differentiating criterion applied. Many statutes, such as Article 21.79 E of the Texas Insurance Code, criminalize the charging of different fees for the same service, where the higher price is based on the fact that an insurer pays all or part of the fee.

The altruistic reasoning behind sliding fee scales is easy to grasp, but, in practice, flexible fee policies present a dangerous legal trap for the unwary mental health professional. Giving an uninsured client a break and charging a lower

Flexible fee policies present a dangerous legal trap for the unwary mental health professional.

rate than would be billed to an insurance company could result in a criminal conviction. Fines and imprisonment are possible penalties, even for the best intentioned therapist.

Contract Restrictions

Insurance companies and managed care payers look very closely at the fee arrangements of their providers and take a hard stand on seemingly insignificant acts, such as waiving copays. If the therapist contracts with a managed care company for an hourly rate of $85 per hour with a $10 copay and then waives the copay, the rate is really $75 per hour. The therapist should be receiving only $65 per hour from the managed care company and $10 from the client. Several therapists who waived copays have been sued for refunds on fraud grounds. **Never waive a copay.**

Never waive a copay.

Most therapists, when asked about their rate for services, respond with an amount and a time period (e.g., $75 per 50-minute session or $150 per 45-minute session). That is the information they circulate when asked by inquiring clients, insurance carriers, and managed care companies. Their rates might also be published in brochures and stated or implied when answering questions in public. When the therapist contracts to provide services at that rate with one client and subsequently charges another client a lower rate, misrepresentation of the fee can be argued and used to establish a basis for a civil or criminal fraud complaint.

Suppose the $75 rate is disclosed to a managed care company and the therapist ultimately agrees to a provider contract for reimbursement by the managed care company at $60 per hour. Can the managed care company complain if the therapist sees a few private-pay clients at $65 or even $50 per hour? Yes! The managed care company could argue that if it had known that the therapist charged some clients less than $75 per session (the quoted rate), it would have negotiated to pay the provider an amount less than $65 per hour.

Some managed care companies have a negotiating strategy of compensating therapists at a fixed percentage of the therapists' quoted rate. Suppose a company typically contracts to pay a therapist 80 percent of the stated rate of $75, or $75 × 80 percent = $60. If the therapist then charges some clients $65 per session, the managed care company could assert "material misrepresentation" and sue to recover the excess fees paid. If lack of insurance was the only differentiating criterion used by the therapist to determine who paid $65 per session instead of $75, a criminal prosecution could also result.

Rates quoted for the purpose of third-party payments should be rates actually charged and received.

The therapist could be held responsible if the reduced rate structure is published, especially if the actual charges are substantially reduced and an audit indicates that hardly anyone pays the rate quoted to the insurance company or third-party payer. Rates quoted for the purpose of third-party payments should be rates actually charged and received.

Insurance Restrictions

These fee issues are being monitored nationwide by payers and governmental agencies, as reported by *Practice Strategies* (April 1997): "Therapists should, however, avoid routinely reducing fees or routinely waiving copayments for clients while billing insurance for the full fee. Where the full fee is routinely reduced, it may appear that the reduced fee is in actuality the full fee—and the therapist is charging a premium for services billed to insurance. In this case, insurance and government fraud units may charge the private practitioner with misrepresenting the actual fee."

Many provider agreements restrict the fees that can be charged to a client when benefits under the client's managed care plan have been exhausted or "when needed" services are not covered by the plan. It is imperative to read benefit summaries and provider contracts carefully before offering additional services to clients at reduced prices. Be careful when switching from a covered service in a plan to a private pay client. Make sure it is permissible under the terms of the plan.

Read benefit summaries and provider contracts carefully before offering additional services to clients at reduced prices.

Can a mental health practitioner have a sliding fee scale? Yes. If insurance or lack thereof is not the *only* factor considered in determining the rate, a therapist can have a sliding fee scale. Some state laws require a county hospital to look at the following factors in determining eligibility for free medical care:

- Number of persons in the applicant's household.
- Existence of insurance coverage.
- Transfer of real property within prior 24 months.
- Applicant's household or other income.
- Applicant's fixed and liquid assets and liabilities: fixed and flexible or discretionary expenses.
- Work-related and child-care expenses.

Incorporating these and other factors into a sliding fee scale should prevent the therapist's violating a statute that prohibits charging a higher fee to persons with insurance coverage when insurance is the only criterion. An intake form soliciting this information would have to be completed and signed by each client seeking a sliding fee scale and maintained as part of the client's permanent record. Some therapists have a form on hand, similar to a bank loan application that is offered to clients who seek sliding fees. The form is completed by the client before any reduction in the standard fee and is submitted to the therapist at the time a sliding fee determination is requested.

Answers to Frequently Asked Questions about:

Copay
Writing off charges

▣ Question

Is it illegal to write off copays and/or remaining charges after an insurance/managed care company has paid its bills?

▣ Answer

Waiving a copay upfront or during therapy should never be done. It would be inappropriate, with a wink and a nod, to tell a client that the therapist will accept insurance payments only in full for all services rendered.

Once therapy has terminated, however, you can discontinue collection efforts if a client fails or refuses to pay. The same can be said for client balances. Send two or three bills, and if you believe the client is not going to pay, write it off. Harsh or offensive collection efforts, in the opinion of most lawyers, bring about complaints to the licensing boards and automatic cross-actions for negligence. Writing off an unpaid copay is simply a business risk.

▣ Additional Thoughts

- The practitioner is not obligated to make extraordinary collection efforts, nor is the practitioner obligated to refer an unpaid bill to a collection agency or an attorney for collection. Indeed, writing off an unpaid bill is usually better then creating an unresponsive, angry, and hostile client.
- You do not *waive* the copay. It is simply uncollectable.
- The practice of therapy has its business ramifications. Few businesses can exist without some bills that remain unpaid. Unpaid bills are a business risk and are absorbed as a part of the cost of doing business.

Pros and Cons

If a therapist is going to have a sliding fee scale, it must be announced to each prospective client, insurer, or managed care company, and it must be consistently applied.

If a therapist is going to have a sliding fee scale, it must be announced to each prospective client, insurer, or managed care company, and it must be consistently applied. If the therapist has existing managed care contracts in which an hourly rate has been disclosed but he or she wishes to switch to a sliding fee scale, each managed care company must be informed of the change in the fee structure, schedule, and policy. You must be *very* careful about prior rate disclosures to, and contracts with, insurers and managed care companies.

Most managed care contracts contain an *audit* clause. The managed care entity has a right to audit the fees of the therapist to determine the actual fees charged and to ascertain whether the therapist is in compliance with the managed care contract.

Can a therapist have a fee policy whereby a reasonable fee is negotiated with each client? Yes, but this must be the therapist's stated fee policy and it must be universally applied. Most state licensing laws require fees only to be reasonable and consistent with law. It would be acceptable if a therapist chose not to establish a fixed session rate but had an announced policy of negotiating a reasonable fee with each client, insurer, or managed care company on a case-by-case basis. However, because such a policy would consume considerable time and negotiating a fee would imply revealing personal financial status, many clients would opt not to come in. Looking for certainty on cost, the client calls the next name on his or her list of potential providers. People want to know what they will be charged before they take time out of their busy day to come to a therapist's office. Therapists are also concerned about time, a resource most would like to conserve and use efficiently.

A sliding fee scale can be implemented, but the criteria must be documented; and this type of inquiry and documentation presents another layer of paperwork and complexity in the mental health practice. Any fee schedule except a stated fixed rate will result in great difficulties in billing. A variable fee schedule causes additional complexity and consumption of time and makes it an unattractive choice for even the most altruistic therapist.

To therapists who want to help out the less fortunate and don't want the headache of implementing a sliding fee scale, we suggest charging everyone the same rate but offering flexible payment plans when an insurer or managed care company is not providing payment. An increase in delinquent accounts may result, but the therapist will face much less risk for having a kindhearted attitude toward unpaid invoices than for reducing fees.

We suggest charging everyone the same rate but offering flexible payment plans when an insurer or managed care company is not providing payment.

Questions continue to arise concerning sliding fee scales, reduced fees, waiving copayments, the percentage of the full fee that is payable by insurance companies, the amount communicated to insurance companies as being the full fee, third-party payments, discounts, charitable or pro bono therapy offered to clients who cannot afford the full amount, and any number of arrangements that alter a fixed fee and create a flexible market price.

This is truly a case-by-case situation. Before establishing a sliding fee scale, reducing fees, devising methods of reducing fees for noninsured clients, or indulging in partial pro bono billing, it is advisable to call a specialist or lawyer for expert input. Insurance fraud is a very serious matter. In cases where insurance fraud has been proven, providers have faced jail time. Some providers, months or years after the treatment was completed, have received letters demanding reimbursement of all or part of the fee paid.

Careless billing practices can also be grounds for a complaint to the licensing board and may result in an investigation by a professional organization.

When dealing with managed care or third-party payments in any form, the payer has the right to audit the records of the provider.

Legal Lightbulb

- Altruism with respect to fee setting can subject an unwitting or naive therapist to claims of criminal and civil fraud and return of fees paid.

- Fraudulent fee practices can result in the suspension or revocation of a professional license.

- Avoid the appearance of charging lower fees simply because the client does not have insurance.

- If a variable fee structure is to be used, base the fee on a number of financial and personal factors, not solely on insurance coverage or the lack thereof. Document the fee considerations and apply them uniformly. Create a paper trail.

- Whatever fee policy is adopted, apply it universally to each managed care organization, insurance company, and client.

- It is imperative to read benefit summaries and provider contracts carefully before offering additional services to clients at reduced prices.

- Review carefully each plan summary and provider contract. What fee restrictions are stated?

- Never waive a co-pay.

- If a sliding or variable fee scale is being considered, consult carefully with knowledgeable legal and industry advisors.

- A sliding fee scale must be announced to each prospective client, insurer, or managed care company, and it must be consistently applied.

- A set fee, consistently applied but allowing for flexible or easy payment terms, may be the easiest policy to implement.

- Take insurance audits seriously. When dealing with managed care or third-party payments in any form, the payer has the right to audit the records of the provider.

Debate continues in this volatile and often delicate area. Caution, careful planning, and a meticulous paper trail are advisable. Remember, when dealing with managed care or third-party payments in any form, the payer has the right to audit the records of the provider. When audits are conducted by payers, they are seeking to uncover fraudulent practices and recovery of payments made.

16

Recovering Unpaid Fees

Jack and Susan saw Ms. Love, LMSW (Licensed Master Social Worker), for family therapy. At the end of each month, Ms. Love sent them a bill, which they promptly paid in accordance with the original agreement. After a few months, Susan indicated that a family financial problem had occurred and asked to have payment delayed a month or two while the couple put their resources in order. Not wanting to put added pressure on them, Ms. Love agreed. The couple continued in therapy for another six weeks, then separated and filed for divorce. Neither would pay Ms. Love for the last few sessions. Instead, each told her to seek payment from the other. The total unpaid bill was $530. Although they were satisfied with the treatment, both refused to pay. Three months after their last visit, Ms. Love had still not been paid.

~

Lynne was married to Bob, a long-term employee of a major company with excellent mental health insurance benefits. She felt depressed and sought long-term therapy with Dr. Wise, who was on the preferred provider panel for her husband's employer's insurance program. Dr. Wise called the insurance carrier, and the treatment was approved. For about two years, Dr. Wise treated Lynne. Finally, after excellent care from Dr. Wise, Lynne recovered and was discharged. During the two-year period, Dr. Wise submitted his monthly bills and was paid promptly.

Six months after Lynn's discharge, an internal insurance company audit conducted by the insurance company that paid Dr. Wise revealed that Lynne and Bob had been divorced about five months after Lynne's therapy began. Lynne had not revealed the divorce to Dr. Wise nor had she informed Bob's employer or the insurance company. The insurer had made payments for the benefit of a former wife who was not entitled to coverage. The auditor wrote a letter to Dr. Wise, indicating that Lynne was not covered after the date of the divorce and demanded reimbursement. The amount involved was thousands of dollars.

What are the options for both of these therapists?

Both the social worker and the psychologist had in their clients' files a carefully drafted, lawyer-reviewed intake and consent form, signed by the respective clients, which stated that the client was primarily responsible for the therapist's fees. Third-party reimbursement of any amount would be credited toward the bill, but the form clearly indicated a personal contractual obligation. Payment for the therapeutic services was the obligation of the client if sums were not forthcoming from any third-party payer.

Ms. Love's Options

1. Forget the fee; write off the $530 as a loss.
2. Make numerous calls to the former clients, offering terms, a payout, a settlement for less than the amount due (half or three-fourths, for example), or let Jack and/or Susan suggest percentages.
3. Turn over the unpaid bill to a collection agency, which will charge 40 to 50 percent of the billable amount for collection services.
4. File a suit in small claims court and be her own advocate, as is permitted in most small claims courts.
5. Turn over the unpaid bill to a lawyer for collection. Most lawyers consider a $500 to $1,000 collection a favor, not a business venture.
6. Have a lawyer draft some collection letters for her to send; then pursue a small claims court action.

The best option? Ms. Love should drop the whole payment issue. True, the bill is owed. True, the client, jointly or severally (either or both of them) ought to pay the amount incurred as a legitimate debt. However, the payment is not worth pursuing.

An uncollected bill cannot be written off as a business loss, especially if taxes are computed on a cash basis.

Small bills involve aggravating phone calls, collection agencies' fees, and collection letters sent personally or through an agency or an attorney. Therapists earn a living by offering therapy, not collecting bills. Better to write off a bad debt than to pursue collection efforts that annoy everyone, including the therapist. The bad news: An uncollected bill cannot be written off as a business loss, especially if taxes are computed on a cash basis.

In our litigious society, a disturbed client is apt to file a complaint with the licensing board or seek some sort of malpractice relief if strong collection efforts are pursued. As an almost knee-jerk reaction, when a suit for collection is filed, the client consults with an attorney and files a cross-action or counterclaim for malpractice. The usual outcome: The therapist drops the collection claim, and the client drops the malpractice suit. The parties are back to where they were in the beginning, but only after time and money have been wasted, and tempers have flared.

There are business losses in every business. A relatively small, unpaid bill is just another business risk and should be written off. The goodwill of the client (and possible future referrals) is more important when measured against the difficulties of collecting. There is no nice way to pursue collection efforts.

Dr. Wise's Options

In this scenario, everyone may have acted in good faith. Lynne may not have known that her divorce affected her eligibility, nor realized that her benefits would be terminated at the same time as the marriage. With hindsight, she understood the concept of coverage, but she was so happy with Dr. Wise she just continued working on her own problems. She was not paying, so she did not give much thought to payment.

Dr. Wise was unaware of the divorce or the fact that eligibility was terminated on the date of the divorce. For all sessions after that date, he was not entitled to reimbursement. He received authorization and payments in good faith, and he relied on the representations of the payer that coverage was appropriate and continuing.

The insurance company fulfilled its contract beyond the agreed-on limit (the divorce) and asked for reimbursement when it was discovered that the facts had changed and the employee's wife was no longer entitled to coverage. Should the company "be a sport" and not pursue a just claim against Dr. Wise? What is the value of the contract, compared to the amount to be recovered?

Dr. Wise is responsible for reimbursing the insurance company for all payments made to him after the date of the divorce (i.e., when Lynne lost her eligibility). In the contract Dr. Wise signed with the insurance carrier, all authorizations were contingent and temporary, and, in the event a client was later found to be ineligible, the company was entitled to reimbursement. All contracts provided by insurance companies and drafted by insurance company lawyers favor the company. In a clause read but not necessarily understood by Dr. Wise, he had a contractual obligation to refund the amounts paid to him after the divorce.

All contracts provided by insurance companies and drafted by insurance company lawyers favor the company.

Dr. Wise also had a lawyer-drafted and lawyer-approved contract with Lynne, which makes her responsible for reimbursing him for the sum he had to return to the insurance company. Although Dr. Wise was clearly entitled to be paid by Lynne, as soon as he pursued the matter, she reminded him that she had divorced during the therapy, and, as a psychologist, he should have sensed the trauma she was going through and been aware of her increased stressors. She insinuated that his diagnosis was incomplete and the treatment plan was inaccurate, although the results were satisfactory and the present prognosis was excellent. Not wishing to be faced with a counterclaim or a complaint to the licensing board, Dr. Wise, sadder and wiser, closed Lynne's file.

Unpaid Bills and Reimbursement for Insurance Claims: Considerations

- There is no nice way to collect an unpaid bill.
- Suing a client for failing to pay a bill can have adverse consequences for the therapist, including:
  —The client might file a cross action or counterclaim.
  —The client might file a complaint with the therapist's licensing board.
  —The client might report the therapist to the Chamber of Commerce, the Better Business Bureau, or a local or national professional organization.
  —The dispute might come to the attention of the hospital where the therapist has privileges, the provider group where the therapist is on the panel, or professional colleagues who might be anxious about having in their midst a therapist who is vulnerable to media coverage.
- The justness of a claim for payment has little effect on the aggressiveness and creativity of an upset, angry, hostile, or borderline client.

Answers to Frequently Asked Questions about:

Collection agencies

Consent to treatment forms

Past due bills

Theory: The best defense is a good offense

? Question

Should I use a collection agency? In my consent for treatment form, I do advise patients that I will use a collection agency if reasonable monthly payments are not made toward past-due balances. I did comprehensive psych testing on a child, and the parents have repeatedly ignored my $750 bill. In writing, I've offered them arrangements for gradual payment and also asked them to begin making systematic monthly payments, if not full payment. What else can/should I do before referring them to a collection agency? Is there any way to reduce the possibility that they will respond with a lawsuit threat, or is there any way to protect myself in advance should that occur? I've done nothing either unethical or unprofessional but am aware that sending people to a collection agency or even reporting the past due claim to a credit reporting agency can sometimes result in retaliatory actions. Would it matter if I referred it to a lawyer for collection?

▐ Answer

We are unaware of a state that does not provide for an exception to confidentiality for the collection of legitimate fees by a mental health professional. The HIPAA Privacy Rule allows disclosure of protected health information for collection of fees by a therapist. There may be specific state prohibitions, however, against the use of collection agencies although HIPAA does not prohibit their use. Always remember that more protective state statutes will not be preempted by HIPAA. Be sure to check with your licensing board for any specific statutes or rules. The exception concerning confidentiality may apply only to you as the treating therapist trying to collect and not to a collection agency or attorney.

Section 1.25 (f) of the American Psychological Association Ethical Principles of Psychologists and Code of Conduct states: "If the patient, client, or other recipient of services does not pay for services as agreed, and if the psychologist wishes to use collection agencies or legal measures to collect the fees, the psychologist first informs the person that such measures will be taken and provides that person an opportunity to make prompt payment."

We suggest that you go one step further than this provision and create in your intake/consent form language that clearly demonstrates that the client is agreeing, in writing and in advance to the assignment of his or her account, if delinquent, to a collection agency or attorney for collection. We refer to client consent as the number one exception to confidentiality and urge therapists to build into their intake and consent form as much client consent as possible. (See Chapter 6.)

Be aware that you could be liable for misconduct by the collection agency that acts as your agent. There are federal and state fair debt collection practices acts that provide stiff sanctions for violations. Be sure you choose a reputable collector. If collection agencies are licensed in your state, make sure this agency has a proper, current license and a *liability insurance policy* in the event one of their collectors exceeds reasonable collection efforts.

Mental health professionals are generally required to avoid conduct that harms or has the potential to harm a client. Seemingly unsavory calls from a collection agency may be very harmful to a particularly sensitive client. Chose not only your collection agency carefully but also the client accounts you wish to assign. We receive numerous calls concerning collection procedures. Rarely do we suggest or imply using a collection agency or an attorney. Usually, clients who do not pay either have (in their mind) a legitimate complaint or financial worries. Either way, should they contact a lawyer, you can be assured the lawyer will threaten a counterclaim, which will make the original amount in controversy seem inconsequential.

We have practiced collectively more than 50 years. We have never sued a client for an unpaid fee nor turned a client over to an agency for collection. Our theory: We make our living practicing law and don't want to waste our time and emotional energy collecting bad debts from recalcitrant debtors.

💡 Additional Thoughts

- Should any client be unhappy with collection efforts either by a collection agency or a lawyer and, should they consult a lawyer, the unpaid and unhappy professional can anticipate a threatening letter from the lawyer. A counterclaim will be the best defense, whether justified or not.
- Every practitioner should have a *credit policy*, which is more critical than a collection policy. For example: (1) most clients should pay on the date of the service, (2) clients who fall more than $100 to $200 behind should be warned and terminated (every professional should have a list of local, free, or reduced fee agencies available for continuing counseling and therapy so that a terminated client has no excuse for not continuing treatment), and (3) when there is a one-time service such as comprehensive psychological testing or forensic testimony in the courtroom setting, an account should be set up whereby the client deposits the money with the therapist equal to an estimate of the service to be rendered. Should the service cost less than the sum deposited, the overage is immediately refunded to the client. Any additional amount is billed. This policy is carefully stated in the consent to treatment form so the client, in writing, knows the financial obligation and consents to it.
- Telling a client your policy for charges is not the same as having the client agree to the policy in advance, in writing, and giving the client a copy of the consent contract.
- Usually, the failure to receive payment is the result of bad credit policies rather than bad service.
- The professional is always vulnerable if a collection effort is harassing, too harsh, or vigorous. The recipient client is immune except to the extent of the amount sought to be collected. In addition, the client, in need of mental health services to begin with, can claim astronomical damages for the zealous use of inappropriate, harsh, or illegal collection efforts.
- Good, tough language in a consent form is helpful, but there is no language that offers absolute immunity from a cross-action for negligence or creative litigation such as a lawyer can initiate.
- A few gentle calls about past due bills is about all that can and should be done.
- If you still don't receive payment, go on to the next client, and arrange for timely future payments.

Answers to Frequently Asked Questions about:

Retainer fees for therapy

Trust accounts

Therapy on retainer

❓ Question

My colleagues, who offer forensic services, often work on a retainer, which certainly makes sense given the nature of their work. I've begun to think about working on a retainer basis for psychotherapy services as a means of improving cash flow, avoiding collection problems, and so on. Are there any ethical or legal considerations in providing psychotherapy when the fee is handled as a deposit for future services to be rendered or a retainer?

❗ Answer

Ethically, fees charged to clients for mental health services must be reasonable and consistent with fees charged by similarly licensed and experienced practitioners in your area. Other than provider contracts with managed care entities, we know of no prohibition for charging retainer fees as long as they are reasonable. It would be difficult to argue that a retainer fee equal to your normal session rate (which is reasonable in your location) multiplied by an estimated number of sessions is unreasonable. The unreasonableness could creep in if you charge and collect a nonrefundable retainer and the client's therapy terminates before the time all of the retainer has been earned. It would be best to agree that unearned retainers will be refunded to the client. This would require you to set up a trust account and move funds from the trust or deposit account to an operating account as they are earned.

💡 Additional Thoughts

- A trust account is simple to establish. Almost every lawyer has one. Check with your accountant and banker for details and procedures.
- Insert the accounting details into your billing procedures.
- Consider an *evergreen* account, whereby the client agrees that the retainer/trust account will never fall below an agreed-on sum. For example, if the agreed-on sum is $1,000, whenever the retainer falls below $200, the client will make a deposit to bring the account up to the agreed-on $1,000. Failure to do so is permission, in advance, to terminate with an appropriate referral, if needed.

- Be prepared to refund, cheerfully, any unearned fees.
- A client who deposits a substantial retainer and then quits therapy for any reason is sure to want the unearned portion refunded and will almost certainly complain to the licensing board if the refund is not received in a timely manner.

Answers to Frequently Asked Questions about:

Depositions

Location

Compensation

Subpoenas (We get more calls from therapists with questions about subpoenas than any other subject. Unfortunately, the time and income lost responding to a subpoena is usually a nonreimbursed cost of doing business.)

❓ Question

A colleague of mine received a notice for a deposition concerning a former patient who is litigating for disability. The lawyer for the insurance company issued the deposition request stating that the deposition was to be held at the offices of the insurance company lawyers.

Who determines the location and/or time of a deposition? Could my colleague request/demand that they come to her office rather than have her go to their offices?

She also suspects that she will not be paid for her time. Can she bill either the lawyers or the insurance company for her time, or is this just a nonreimbursable cost of doing business? What rights do therapists (she is a social worker) have concerning requests for depositions?

What consequences would likely occur if she simply refused to appear or ignored the subpoena?

❗ Answer

There are subtle differences in deposition procedures and rules from state to state, but we will share some general information with you in response to your questions. It is always a good idea to consult with an attorney in your own area for specific advice. Ordinarily, *the attorney issuing the deposition notice or subpoena sets the time and place* for a deposition. It is common for the lawyer to take the deposition in his or her own office. A witness has the right to file a motion for a protective order to seek a court ruling that could possibly *change the date or location for good cause.*

Mental health professionals who are hired specifically for a lawsuit negotiate a fee and are paid by whoever retains them. Most of the time, however, a mental health professional is a prelawsuit provider of mental health services and is dragged (sometimes kicking and screaming) into a client's lawsuit. In Texas, where we practice law, the client's prelawsuit provider has no basis to collect a fee for testifying unless an attorney or client agrees to pay a fee. We recommend that mental health professionals contract with a client (via an intake and consent form) *prior to* providing any services, specifying that the client will be obligated to pay a fee for the therapist's time in preparing for and responding to subpoenas for deposition or courtroom testimony regardless of who issues the subpoena. (Chapter 6 contains a sample contract, the Client Information and Consent form, that provides for fees for responding to record production requests or testimony requests.) With such an agreement, the therapist at least can send someone a bill.

Assuming you do not have a signed intake or consent form that provides your client will pay you a fee for records and/or testimony, it doesn't hurt to try to get the lawyer, firm, or client to commit to paying your fee after you receive the subpoena. You can't condition your appearance in response to a subpoena on payment of a fee, however, even if you have a signed contract. If you wish to avoid a subpoena once it has been served, a motion to quash or for a protective order must be filed with the court.

Refusing or failing to appear is not an option, but we have encountered in our practices more than one cagey therapist who refused to open the office door to be served until a check (preferably, a cashier's check) was received. Until service of the subpoena, there is no obligation to appear.

If you get a commitment to be paid from someone involved in the case, but are not paid in advance, it is *best to get confirmation of the agreement in writing.* This confirmation should include the amount of the anticipated sum due plus the date it will be paid. If that is not possible, at least get the party to agree to acknowledge this fact in the deposition or court record.

💡 Additional Thoughts

- A subpoena can be issued for any person, and the individual must appear without compensation unless compensation is agreed to in advance.
- Even if an intake and consent form provides for compensation to the mental health provider in the event of litigation, we do not recommend filing suit or referring a bill for testimony or records to a collection agency.
- If a lawyer promises reimbursement for a deposition or a court appearance, get it in writing.
- *The best time to get paid is in advance.*
- Don't make a fuss over location unless it is truly inconvenient.
- Review your intake and consent form. It is the best protection you have if you wish to be compensated for involvement in the judicial process.

Legal Lightbulb

- Read your malpractice policy carefully. Some policies state that the malpractice carrier will not defend against a malpractice suit filed as a defensive measure against a collection effort.

- Generally, lawsuits for the collection of fees are not cost effective.

- Handle every unpaid bill as a "problem," and don't let your accounts receivable accumulate.

- Read managed care contracts carefully. Therapists are bound by the contract terms, which are usually drafted by the managed care company's lawyer for the benefit of his or her employer.

- Most clients pay, eventually. When they do not, accept the loss as a business risk.

- When a bill is unpaid, negotiate, mediate, compromise, or settle. Don't sue, unless you are so advised by a knowledgeable attorney who is willing to take the case to conclusion. In that event, compare the unpaid bill to the legal fees you will incur.

- In a dispute between a therapist and a consumer, the therapist is more vulnerable, especially if the case gains media attention.

- Before taking any legal action, talk to *your* therapist, your lawyer, your minister, and your colleagues.

SECTION FIVE

FORENSIC ISSUES

17

Abuse Allegations

"A volunteer baby sitter at a Sunday school who was jailed without bail for two and a half years before being cleared of inflicting satanic ritual abuse on children is now suing **child therapists,** *prosecutors and the church where he worked. . . . [He was] acquitted . . . of . . . sexually abusing nine children, . . . therapists . . . had prodded children into fabricating fantastic accounts of ritual abuse. . . . [The children] testified that he had killed a baby . . . slaughtered an elephant and a giraffe . . . [the plaintiff] alleges slander, libel, false imprisonment, professional negligence, civil rights violations and infliction of emotional distress [and] accuses the prosecutors of selecting therapists who they knew were inclined to find evidence of abuse. . . ." [Source:* Mental Health Law Reporter *(November 1994, Vol. 12, No. 11, p. 81).]*

Every state has a child abuse reporting statute that requires mental health professionals—and, in most jurisdictions, every citizen—to report suspected child abuse to legal authorities. These reporting statutes generally grant immunity, civil and criminal, to anyone who makes a *good faith* report of abuse or reports a reasonable suspicion that abuse has occurred.

A therapist who reports child abuse has a certain amount of protection under the law, although, if a suit were filed, the protection of the statute would have to be invoked. A fact issue could exist for a judge or jury: Was the report made in good faith and was it reasonable to suspect abuse had occurred?

Liability for False Allegation

In light of litigated cases filed against therapists, mental health providers are often concerned about being sued for a false allegation and may be reluctant to make a child abuse report. Many statutes make it a criminal act *not* to report child abuse, so declining to report should not be considered an option. In all jurisdictions, the potential risks and harm from reporting a case that may be

Many statutes make it a criminal act not to report child abuse, so declining to report should not be considered an option.

invalid should be weighed against the potential risks from failing to report a case. A child may subsequently be abused, killed, or seriously injured. Making the report is definitely the lesser of two potentially bad options. Most judges charged with the responsibility of addressing custody or visitation issues admit that, when in doubt, they prefer to err on the side of the safety of the child. There should be only one rule of thumb for therapists: **The best interest of a child or the safety of a child is always paramount.**

All therapists know (or should know) that child abuse must be reported. The therapist should have some clinical reason or justification for reporting the abuse and be aware of the danger of encouraging children to speak up: The words and images of the therapist may become the words and images of the child.

The accusation of abuse may come from a spouse who is seeking custody of a child and who quotes the supposed words of the child to a lawyer. On investigation, the lawyer may discover that the words are those of the spouse, not the child. Or, the words of the child are taken out of context and are so exaggerated that they are meaningless.

The uncorroborated statements of a child whose parents are involved in custody litigation have to be reviewed and evaluated carefully.

A child, wishing to please a parent, especially an aggressive or controlling individual, may tell the parent what he or she wishes to hear. The child often has no inkling of the ramifications of the words or how the information will be used. In this situation, the therapist must tread carefully. The uncorroborated statements of a child whose parents are involved in custody litigation have to be reviewed and evaluated carefully. Don't dismiss them; just scrutinize them cautiously.

Any case involving abuse carries a clear warning: Child abuse is serious and must be reported. However, there are situations when the evidence must be weighed carefully to determine whether the allegations or evidence received truly come from the child reporting the abuse or from an overreacting therapist. Or, are the allegations the words that an angry or hostile parent put into the mind and mouth of the child? Has the parent, now an embittered divorcing spouse, made suggestions to a child that, after a period of time and constant repetition, the child now thinks are his or her own?

A clinical and defensible basis should be established for making the report in the event that the good faith or reasonableness of the report is called into question.

A clinical and defensible basis should be established for making the report in the event that the good faith or reasonableness of the report is called into question.

Therapists receive some clinical training to determine abuse, but an allegation cannot exceed the individual mental health professional's level of competence. To do so would be an ethical violation. If a therapist suspects abuse, the statute in that jurisdiction will require reporting the suspicion to appropriate legal authorities. If a therapist does not have the expertise or experience to properly evaluate a suspected abuse case, a referral should be made to a therapist who possesses the requisite learning, training, education, and experience to evaluate the situation. This may be accomplished after the initial report is made.

Answers to Frequently Asked Questions about:

Duty to report child abuse

Remoteness of the abuse

Immunity from civil or criminal liability

? Question

A child I'm seeing in individual therapy has described being made by her father to view what sounds like pornographic videos several years ago. The parents are divorced and a protective services complaint was recently made against the father for physical abuse of the child. In light of the remote nature of the alleged video incident, do I still have a duty to report? If I do make a good faith report, am I protected from retaliatory litigation on the father's part? (He is a personal injury attorney!)

! Answer

The child abuse reporting statutes we have reviewed over the years would obligate you to make a report to the proper authority if a child were forced to watch pornographic videos by an adult. These statutes often specifically provide for immunity from civil and criminal prosecution for persons making good faith reports pursuant to the statute.

Generally, these statutes *do not provide for a statute of limitations* on reports. Even if the alleged abuse occurred several years previously and the child is still a minor, a report should be made. Decisions concerning how or whether to proceed depend on the local protective agency.

We are not aware of the specific statute in your state. Consult with an attorney in your area if you are not familiar with your reporting statute or do not have access to a copy. It is not your job to determine if, in fact, the abuse occurred. That is up to the authorities. *Your job is to make timely reports in good faith.* Generally, good faith will protect you from any potential retaliatory actions by Attorney Dad. We are not promising you will not be sued, but if you acted in good faith you ordinarily will not be found liable for any damages.

💡 Additional Thoughts

- Whenever child abuse has been or may have been committed, the suspicion should be reported to authorities that take the case to the next step.
- You, as a concerned citizen, are not responsible to make a *determination* whether the abuse occurred, only to report your good faith suspicions.
- Failing to report is far more serious than reporting erroneously.
- In many states, failing to report is a crime, with criminal penalties and civil liabilities.

- *Caveat:* If you are in the middle of an ex-wife versus ex-husband continuing conflict, have an attorney orchestrate each step of the way to guarantee self-protection, as well as protection for the child.
- *Document everything said to you* by any involved individual, including your report to authorities.
- Even if the incident is remote, report it and let the authorities decide. This may be a deeper pattern than you are aware of, and other information they have received may make the incident more meaningful to the authorities than it appears to you at first glance.

Children's Truthfulness

Can a child make things up? Can a child allege child abuse, convince a psychiatrist that such abuse occurred, observe his or her parents being arrested, and then recant and sue the mental health professional who reported the alleged abuse?

> "A jury . . . awarded more than $272,000 to a couple and their teenage daughter, who had joined in a suit charging a psychiatrist with failure to properly evaluate the girl's accusations of parental sex abuse. . . . [The] psychiatrist diagnosed her patient's condition as posttraumatic stress disorder brought on by sexual abuse . . . some of the girl's claims were immediately discounted: She said that her grandmother flew about on a broom, that she had been tortured with a medieval thumbscrew device, that she had borne three children. . . . The family reconciled after their daughter told a judge in 1992 that she had made the whole thing up. . . ." Allegations against the psychiatrist included considering the daughter's statements as a certainty, not checking out anything else, failing to challenge claims, not considering that some of the claims were immediately discounted. [Source: *Mental Health Law Reporter* (January 1995, Vol. 13, No. 1, p. 2).]

This case offers lessons on the continued procedures after abuse has been reported (i.e., what takes place in treatment after the child abuse is reported as required by statute). If there is to be continued treatment by a therapist, whether in a public, private, or school setting, efforts should be made to establish corroborating evidence that verifies the allegations. If parts of the story are discounted (the grandmother flew about on a broom, torture with a medieval thumbscrew, and so on), it may be time to question the abuse itself and revise the diagnosis, treatment plan, and prognosis.

If corroboration is not attempted or corroborating evidence cannot be discovered, the evaluating or treating therapist should document this fact and qualify any report or findings accordingly.

Diagnosis and treatment of child abuse are difficult because, very often, there is no physical evidence to substantiate the allegations. The onus is on the professional to record and support each evaluation and treatment plan with, ideally, verifiable evidence. The purpose here is not to intimidate the therapist, but to raise a flag of caution. When abuse is alleged, it must be reported. When continuing treatment is indicated, there is an additional need to look beyond the client's words for corroboration or some other meaningful input.

Children sometimes make allegations that they later discount or deny. If litigation results, they might then join in the suit with their parents and pursue damage claims against the therapist.

In the case cited earlier in this section, a child made up a story that was accepted initially at face value by authorities. It was repeated to the psychiatrist, who visited with the child more than 100 times in therapy sessions. Apparently, at no time did the authorities *discount or disbelieve* the child, nor did the psychiatrist, who seems to have taken the story at face value and did not determine independently whether parental sex abuse actually took place.

Later, the parents were reconciled and the child recanted and resides once again with the parents in an affluent suburb; the mental health professional was forced to pay $272,000.

This type of dilemma can be faced by any mental health professional who treats sexually abused children. Child abuse may be revealed as incidental to family or marital therapy, play therapy, or even in a marriage enrichment seminar, and the same dilemma is present: Is the story true?

If the child is doubted, the therapist can be challenged as being unprofessional. If the child is believed and proves later to be unworthy of belief, the therapist can be sued. *If a complaint of this type is alleged, keep copious notes, document everything said and alleged, and, if possible, videotape the sessions.* Videotaped sessions can be very effective in refuting allegations of implanted memories. If a lawsuit is brought for a misdiagnosis by the therapist, the clinical notes and taped sessions can be offered to support the diagnosis and treatment plan.

Documentation—followed by consultation, referral for specialized treatment, and testing—is the best procedure. You cannot, in the light of current research and litigation, assume a child's allegations to be true and devise a treatment plan based solely on the assumed truth of the allegations, especially if part of the story has already been discounted. When appropriate, qualify reports and opinions, and be wary of children who tell lies, exaggerate, or carry their imagination so far that they cannot distinguish fantasy from reality.

The onus is on the professional to record and support each evaluation and treatment plan with, ideally, verifiable evidence.

If a complaint of this type is alleged, keep copious notes, document everything said and alleged, and, if possible, videotape the sessions.

Documentation is the best procedure.

Answers to Frequently Asked Questions about:

Physical abuse

Court orders

Written agreements that are voluntarily *inconsistent* with court orders.

? *Question*

I am serving as the therapist for a boy who alleged his father physically abused him. The allegations were made before the start of therapy with me and were reported to protective services and the police. The family court judge has issued an order of non-contact between the child and the father, pending completion of a forensic evaluation of all parties, and that evaluation is underway.

Recently, both mother and father agreed that there could be contact between father and son if it were to occur in my office with me present. I indicated I would be happy to facilitate such a reunion; however, I would not be able to supervise contact on an ongoing basis, and alternative arrangements would have to be made if supervision were necessary on an extended basis.

Two questions: (1) If both parents are in agreement (in writing) with this plan for me to facilitate a meeting between father and child, can we proceed or does the judge first need to vacate the order of noncontact; and (2) do I incur any liability for being the facilitator of this one meeting, should something bad (e.g., further abuse) take place in the future after I am no longer supervising the contacts? If there is liability, can you suggest any language I might include in a written consent for this meeting to address the issue?

! *Answer*

We advise you to tread carefully in this matter. Without reviewing the actual court order, it is not possible to say whether the parents, by agreement, can supercede the order. To be safe, insist on a revised court order allowing you to supervise a session in your office with the child; that is, get a court order *allowing you* to do what you intend to do and what the parents want you to do. Remember, court or child protective services may choose to have some input into any changes in the court order. Indeed, they may insist on participation in any court-ordered changes.

We also suggest that you have the parents sign a document consenting to the visit with the child in your office and releasing you from all liability for any and all claims or damages that might arise from the visit. You have no way of predicting what the dad will do and how the child will react. Again, tread carefully.

♀ *Additional Thoughts*

- Don't ever offer to perform a service that does not agree with a court order without first calling a lawyer.
- If the arrangement does not work, both parties, or at least one of them, could easily turn on you.
- The parties to the suit are probably the mother, the father, child protective services, the judge, and the lawyers for all sides. *The agreement of all these parties and the court are necessary to make any changes.*

- At a minimum, have the parents sign an agreement, and then get the approval of protective services and the court.
- You might also require a statement that, in the event of future conflict, you will *not* be available to either party as a witness, or, if you are called as a witness, provide for a method of *payment* for your services.
- Whatever you do, make sure you recommend, in writing, that therapy continue for the child and the parents following all the courtroom litigation.

Legal Lightbulb

- Suspected child abuse requires reporting to legal authorities.

- Civil and criminal immunity exists in most jurisdictions for good faith reports or reports made on the basis of reasonable suspicion.

- Case precedent imposes a duty to attempt corroboration and independent verification of allegations made by a child. Beware of the imaginative child.

- A therapist who lacks the experience and training to provide quality mental health services to an abuse victim should consult with another expert professional and make a referral to a therapist who has experience and training in treating victims of abuse. The suspected abuse must be reported, in good faith, to the proper legal authorities.

- Try to look beyond the words of a child, but if corroboration of the abuse victim's story is not possible, qualify any report or opinion to reflect this fact.

- Copious documentation, including, but not limited to, a videotape of the interview with the child, is critical. Videotaped sessions can be very effective in refuting allegations of implanted memories.

- Take care not to influence the abuse victim's story and allegations.

- Avoid leading questions when interviewing the child.

- If in doubt about reporting abuse, err on the side of the safety of the child.

- Read the local child abuse statute. It's rarely more than a few pages.

- If corroboration is not attempted or corroborating evidence cannot be discovered, the evaluating and treating therapist should document this fact and qualify any report or findings accordingly.

Each parent should have his or her own therapist and the child a third. Get the approval of the court-appointed evaluator.

- Ask the parents to write a note to the court-appointed evaluator, and you can do the same. If the evaluator suggests that type of visitation and it makes sense to the court, the court will sign the order.
- Have a lawyer draft a mutually satisfactory agreement that exonerates you from as much liability as possible.

18

Child Custody and
Consent-to-Treat Issues

Sam, age 7, was brought into Dr. Kline's office by a couple who introduced themselves as Sam's "father and mother" and was presented for play therapy. The office
manager asked Sam's parents to fill out the usual intake form and discovered that
Sam's "mother" was actually his stepmother. Does this present a special situation?

⁓

Edgar, age 10, was reared by his grandparents since birth. Edgar's father deserted
his mother before Edgar was born. His mother, unable to handle the child, left him
with her parents, moved away, and married someone else. Edgar's grandparents
have cared for the boy and have provided for his daily needs, but no custody papers
have ever changed hands, and there were no court orders concerning legal custody.
Edgar's grandparents decided to take Edgar to Dr. Johnson for therapy. They agreed
to sign Dr. Johnson's standard consent form. Do the grandparents have the authorization to consent for Edgar? Is their signed consent form valid?

⁓

Five years ago, when Jennie was 7 years old, she went to Dr. Howard's office with
her parents for family therapy. Each family member met with Dr. Howard individually as well as in the family group setting. Each session was documented, and Jennie's parents signed the standard intake and consent form. Therapy lasted a year or
so and was terminated by agreement of all parties. Six years later, Jennie's parents
were involved in a disputed divorce, and each wanted sole custody of Jennie. Jennie's
mother requested a copy of the complete therapy record. Her father, however, sent a
certified letter demanding that Dr. Howard not release any of the family's records.

Background

Children are often brought to therapy by a parent, a divorced parent with custody, a divorced noncustodial parent, a stepparent, a sibling, or a more remote

Informed consent by a person without the authority to give consent is no consent at all.

relative—a grandparent. Depending on the circumstances, the therapist may or may not be able to obtain informed consent to treat the child from the *legally appropriate person*. Informed consent by a person without the authority to give consent is no consent at all. This rule holds true in almost all nonemergency situations. The person presenting the child must have the legal authority to do so, and the therapist must determine who has this authority before taking on the child as a client.

Most states have statutes that define the rights and duties of the custodial parent, but statutes have to be examined on a state-by-state basis. In Texas, the general rights and duties of the custodial parent are:

1. The right to establish the primary residence of the child.
2. The right to consent to medical, dental, and surgical treatment involving invasive procedures and to consent to psychiatric and psychological treatment.
3. The right to receive and give receipt for periodic payments for the support of the child and to hold or disburse these funds for the benefit of the child.
4. The right to represent the child in a legal action and to make other decisions of substantial legal significance concerning the child.
5. The right to consent to the child's marriage and to his or her enlistment in the armed forces of the United States.
6. The right to make decisions concerning the child's education.
7. The right to the services and earnings of the child.
8. The right to act as an agent of the child in relation to the child's estate, if the child's action is required by a state, the United States, or a foreign government, except when a guardian of the child's estate or a *guardian* or *attorney ad litem* (appointed for purposes of a particular suit or action) has been appointed for the child.

In many jurisdictions, these rights of the custodial parent are shared by both parents as *joint custodians* or, in some states, *joint managing conservators*. The joint control may come about either by order of the court or by agreement of the parties as approved by the court.

In some cases, when a divorce decree is granted, these rights are divided between the parties. For example, if one parent is a physician, the right concerning medical treatment may be assigned to the physician parent; or, if one parent is an attorney, the right to represent the child in a legal action may be awarded to the parent who is a lawyer.

In almost all cases, the right to determine the child's primary residence is allocated to one parent to provide the child with stability and to comply with school residence requirements.

Medical, dental, and surgical care, as well as psychiatric and psychological treatment, may be divided between the divorcing parents.

Answers to Frequently Asked Questions about:

Minor's records

Parental records as part of minor's records

Protecting a record

Release of records to noncustodial parents

? Question

1. A noncustodial parent requests his minor daughter's mental health records. The noncustodial parent has a court order entitling him to all psychological records concerning the child and is requesting all of the records. The request for records includes the clinical assessment report, which documents the mom's mental health history, as well as that of several other close family members. It is not legally necessary that the mom consent to the release of the records because his right to the records was granted in his divorce decree. Can the record be redacted, eliminating references to anyone other than the child?

2. A mother is reporting that her child has been sexually abused. The mom fully cooperates with the child abuse assessment center at a big city hospital, and the dad (alleged abuser) absolutely refuses to cooperate. His attorney then requests the records, and the dad is able to use the mom's sexual abuse history against her. Could the records have been redacted, or did legal stuff, such as discovery, kick in here?

! Answer

1. If the child's records contain a history of mental or physical disorders or treatment of family members, that information is part of the child's file and should be included when a copy is delivered to the requesting parent. You indicated that the court order entitles the father to "all" psychological records.

2. It is a dangerous practice to redact records or alter or edit them after a request or subpoena has been issued. If there are issues in a lawsuit that give rise to an exception to confidentiality and a person is entitled to the records, the complete file is what they are entitled to—in their entirety. An attorney does not have the right to review a person's mental health records without a written release or authorization from the client/patient or a court order. Do not send any records to a lawyer or even acknowledge the person in question is or was a patient without written authorization or a court order.

💡 Additional Thoughts

- In general, parents have a right to review the medical, psychological, and educational records of their children, whether they are custodial parents or not.

- Although in some states, court orders and agreements between the parties restrict these rights, any restrictions would be a part of state law, a written court order, or some written and binding agreement between the parties, usually in writing and signed and often filed as part of a court order.
- If there is a restriction, read it carefully.
- Redacting or editing (there are established procedures for amending or correcting clinical files and progress notes) is not usually possible after a subpoena has been issued, a court order signed, or a request for documents filed. If there is any residual question, file a motion and seek the guidance of an attorney and the court. Ultimate protection of the file is the ultimate duty and obligation of the court.
- Where a party seeks to limit accessibility to a file, the limitation should be contained in a motion for a protective order filed with the court. After motion and hearing, the court will outline, in writing, the restrictions.
- Clinicians should avoid the tendency for self-help. If any part of a file or all of a child's file is to be protected, it should be protected by the court. The clinician can give the court the rationale for protecting all or any part of a child's file, but it is the court that makes the final ruling. The attorney, on behalf of the child or the provider, files a motion, there is a hearing or an agreement, and the court issues an order. The court order binds all the parties.

Legal Ramifications

Before treating a child, the therapist must determine whether the couple representing themselves as the child's parents are the biological parents and are married to each other. If so, either parent can consent to the treatment of the child. If the parents disagree and the therapist is caught in the middle, **the child should not be treated without a court order.**

If the parents are not presently, or have never been, married to each other, the mother usually has the right to consent to therapeutic treatment for the child. The biological father has no right to consent to treatment for the child until his paternity is established via a decree of paternity signed by the court. Request a copy of the paternity decree to determine whether the presenting parent is named as the legal father in the document. Make sure the nonmarried (to the mother) biological father has the right to consent to treatment if he is the presenting parent.

If the parents are divorced, the rights of each parent are usually stated in the divorce decree in clear and unambiguous language.

If the parents are divorced, the rights of each parent are usually stated in the divorce decree in clear and unambiguous language. Read the decree and ask whether there have been any modifications since the decree was entered. If so, read the modifications; they sometimes change the rights of each parent in a significant manner. The latest modification will indicate parental rights. Divorce decrees can be modified until the child reaches majority.

All legal divorces have a written decree; a divorce cannot occur without one. Whenever a child of divorced parents is presented, demand a copy of the divorce decree and all modifications, and make a notation of your demand in the file. If the decree is not produced, do not commence treatment. Divorce and paternity decrees are public documents. They can often be ordered by fax and paid for by check. A lost decree can be replaced in a short time.

If an out-of-state decree is presented, contact a lawyer in the state where the decree was issued, and make sure you have the correct nomenclature and interpretation of the decree. Words and their meanings may differ from state to state. The same is true for out-of-country decrees and court orders. Seek and obtain a certified translation and legal opinion before proceeding.

A court order also exists when a party claims to be the guardian of the person of a minor child or an attorney ad litem or guardian ad litem. Demand to see, and take time to examine, the papers presented with the child. Court appointments usually state, specifically and clearly, the limits and responsibilities of the guardian or attorney. If you have a question, ask an attorney to examine the papers.

If you have a question, ask an attorney to examine the papers presented with the child.

Children are often presented to therapists in real emergencies, when it is important to give them immediate help to improve their condition. They are also presented at times when the word *emergency* is a judgment call. A therapist who is asked to treat a child in an emergency should determine whether treatment is appropriate, document the emergency with a recitation of the facts leading to the conclusion, and state the conclusion, "Emergency," and the rationale for the conclusion.

Remember, documentation *at the time of treatment* is critical. Should a suit be contemplated, the potential plaintiff/client may wait two years before filing. The court may take another few years before it brings the case to trial. At the time of trial, the therapist might not truly remember details of the incident, but a judge or jury will consider notes made at the time credible evidence of an emergency. A restored memory some years later, with no substantiating data to support the actions of the therapist, would be subject to question.

Documentation at the time of treatment is critical.

In rare instances, parents, acting on behalf of their children, have the right to sue a therapist for malpractice and to complain to the licensing board. Be careful. Although the child is technically the client, *everyone* is, in family systems therapy. The rights and obligations of the therapist should be carefully stated in the intake and consent form. The statute of limitations, which controls when a child can sue, generally extends to two years *beyond majority*. The child's records must be retained at least until this time period expires or until the time required by a state licensing board. Majority is generally reached when a child becomes 18 years of age; however, in some states, children reach majority when they marry or when they have their disabilities of minority removed (emancipation).

Majority is generally reached when a child becomes 18 years of age.

Some states have *mature minor* statutes that give minors, at ages 16 and 17, the right to receive therapeutic treatment without the consent of their parents in the areas of drug and alcohol abuse, birth control, sexually transmitted diseases, and some other specific areas. When considering treatment for a mature minor, it is best to read the current statute. Mature minor statutes tend to be in a constant state of flux, depending on the opinions of state legislators and the interpretations of the law in court decisions. Mature minors are in a litigious area. Be very careful before you consult with the minor and before you inform or fail to inform the parents.

Although statutes vary, many states give the noncustodial parent the right to *consult with* a psychologist who is treating a child. Consultation is different from authorization to consent to the treatment of the child. Read the relevant documents carefully and ask a lawyer for advice. One of the most difficult dilemmas a therapist can experience is being caught between the positions of two battling parents.

When children are presented by siblings, grandparents, friends in possession, or others, a genuine effort should be made to obtain the consent of the parent or other person authorized in the paperwork to consent to treatment of the child. If consent is unobtainable, have the presenting party sign a hold harmless agreement wherein he or she agrees to take responsibility for the child and for the consent being offered. Make a note in the file that you demanded the presenting person to obtain a court order giving authorization for consent to treatment on behalf of the child. In a technical sense, a stepparent is a legal stranger to the child. The fact that the stepparent and the child have the same name does not confer any legal authority on the stepparent. Have the stepparent obtain consent from the proper person.

When families are in therapy together, keep a separate record for each person in the family system.

When families are in therapy together, keep a separate record for each person in the family system. Each person can then receive, if requested, a copy of his or her record only, without the necessity of removing or concealing a portion of the record that pertains to another. The general rule is that each client has a right to a copy of his or her record only—not the record of a spouse or relative. Culling a multiple file is a nightmare. Avoid it by establishing separate records.

Usually, either parent has a right to a copy of a child's file. Where there are serious conflicts—for example, when one parent demands that a child's file be delivered and the other demands privacy, confidentiality, and secrecy—seek a court order. Compliance with a court order removes from the custodian of the records the responsibility for sharing a file—or the possibility of serving jail time for contempt of court in preserving the secrecy of a file. When a judge rules, the file may be delivered or held confidential, depending on the judgment of the court.

One major exception to confidentiality is the mandatory reporting of child abuse. Every state requires that child abuse be reported. All clients must be told of this exception to confidentiality upon intake, and the intake form

Legal Lightbulb

- Each state has different statutes concerning minors. Consult your state's statutes before treating a minor child.

- Obtain the protection of a court order before treating a minor child if the parents are in positions of conflict.

- Guardianships, the appointment of attorneys and guardians ad litem, and paternity and divorce decrees (with modifications) are court orders that control the authority to consent to a child's treatment. Read them carefully and obtain the latest court order.

- In most divorce decrees, the statements concerning a child are subject to modification as long as the child is a minor. Any modification is as important as the decree itself.

- Minors can be emancipated by court decree or marriage.

- Minor children who are parents of children have the authority to consent to the treatment of their children.

- Generally, parents always have a right to be informed of the treatment of their minor children under 15. Only the mature minor provisions are exceptions.

- Before treating a child, the therapist must determine whether the couple representing themselves as the child's parents are the biological parents and are married to each other. If so, either parent can consent to the treatment of the child.

- If the parents are not presently, or have never been, married to each other, the mother usually has the right to consent to therapeutic treatment for the child.

- Some states have mature minor statutes that give minors, at ages 16 and 17, the right to receive therapeutic treatment without the consent of their parents in the areas of drug and alcohol abuse, birth control, sexually transmitted diseases, and some other specific areas.

- When families are in therapy together, keep a separate record for each person in the family system.

should indicate that child abuse will be reported. Although most statutes provide that the person reporting abuse has civil and criminal immunity from suit, the client should nevertheless be notified to allow some discretion concerning the information shared with the therapist. This concept does not debate whether notice should be given; it only suggests that clients who believe that confidentiality will be maintained must be told that any abuse disclosed during a session must be reported to authorities.

Minors are indeed a special population. They have certain rights because of their status as children, but for the most part, the rights of children are controlled by parents, guardians, or other persons whose authority is contained in a court order.

When dealing with a child, it is imperative to review all legal documents that refer to the child in any way. Call a lawyer if you have any questions. Be aware that parents or guardians who are in conflict may place the child, and the therapist, in the middle of the dispute. When treatment for a minor is being contested, obtain a court order. Stay current on all the statutes that affect minors.

19

Children as Witnesses

Janie, age 4, was crying when her mother returned home from the supermarket. She pointed between her legs and said she hurt. Her mother examined her vagina and discovered bruises and abrasions. Janie's mother's boyfriend, Sam, was home at the time babysitting Janie. Janie could describe some details but was hazy when trying to explain exactly what happened while her mother was away.

~

Joshua, age 5, lived with his parents and was present when an altercation took place in the living room. He saw and heard the whole conflict and observed his mother hitting his father over the head with a frying pan. His father suffered permanent damage, sued for divorce, and sought custody of his son. Joshua, having remembered the incident, was afraid of his mother and cringed every time she entered the room. Joshua was able to narrate the incident clearly and with animated language.

~

Julie was looking out a window as she waited for guests to arrive to celebrate her third birthday. She saw a big truck careen out of control and strike a friend's automobile just as the passengers were stepping onto the sidewalk. Three people were seriously hurt. The route of the truck and the location of the auto and passengers were at issue. Julie's testimony was critical for her friends to win their case.

Can a Child Be a Witness and Testify in Court?

Often, children are the only witnesses to a crime, an event, or their own neglect or sexual abuse. Before attorneys allow a child to testify, they confirm that the following characteristics are present in their young witness:

- The child has adequate mental maturity, intelligence, and articulation to testify about a case—what he or she saw, heard, smelled, felt, or otherwise experienced.

- The child feels a duty to tell the truth because *to tell a lie is wrong,* and the child can separate truth from falsehood.
- The child can separate fact from fantasy, knows the difference, and can narrate the "facts."
- The child observed, can recollect, and is able to narrate the facts in a meaningful way that provides to the judge and/or the jury valuable information that is not elsewhere available. The testimony of the child will yield truly significant input.

The View from the Bench

Any party to a suit can offer a child to the court as a witness.

These characteristics describe the capacity of a child to testify. Any party to a suit can offer a child to the court as a witness. The child can be sworn and is under the same rules as an adult although, as a practical matter, children are handled more gingerly by cross-examining attorneys. If the judge, after talking to the child from the bench or in chambers, determines the child has reasonable maturity, intelligence, and capacity; knows it is wrong to tell a lie; can separate fact from fantasy; and can provide a narrative, the judge will allow the child to testify. Any thoughts concerning the child's testimony will then affect weight and credibility, not admissibility.

The Lawyer's View

Children are less manageable, more volatile, and subject to more influences than adult witnesses.

There are some questions a lawyer must ponder, with the input of the mental health professional, before offering a child as a witness. A child is not just another witness. Children are less manageable, more volatile, and subject to more influences than adult witnesses. In addition, children must be handled more gently, and they cannot be prepared for trial with the same intensity as adults. Thus, the lawyer must review a bigger picture before calling a child as a witness, preparing the child for trial, or, especially, submitting the child to cross-examination by opposing counsel. When offering a child as a witness, lawyers should consider the following:

- Children are vulnerable to having their memories and testimony distorted.
- Children are suggestible.
- Children can be led to get peripheral details wrong.
- Children can be led to distort the central gist of events they experienced.
- Children might distort or inaccurately recall events affecting their bodies—what something felt like, whether it hurt, and where.
- The drama of the courtroom can affect a child long after the trial ends and the legal issues are settled or determined.

- A child should not be sworn as a witness if the primary evidence, or corroborating evidence, is available elsewhere.

In criminal or family law cases involving child abuse (sexual, physical, or emotional), the testimony of a child can be critical to the eventual outcome. The decision on whether to call a child as a witness is made by adults—parents, district attorneys, the contesting parties' attorneys, or the judge. When considering a child as a witness, these adults must carefully weigh the possible outcomes of the trial, the effect on the child, the effect on future relationships between the child and any adult family members involved in the case, and whether the child's perception of events constitutes an accurate narrative.

The Therapist's View

When consulted by an attorney, a parent, a party to litigation, or a judge as to whether to put a child on the witness stand, the therapist must consider many factors, including the anticipated duration of the trial and, because months or even years may pass between the event itself and the trial date, the anxieties produced in the interim. The therapist also needs to evaluate the personal, family, and posttrial therapeutic resources that are available to the child as well as a therapist who might be responsible for and available to offer future therapy.

The ultimate consideration is: What is in the best interest of the child? If two adults have a conflict and the child has been a bystander, should the child, usually a reluctant witness, be brought before the court, sworn, and subjected to examination and cross-examination? Once the child takes the stand, the child can be protected only by the judge and remains as a witness until dismissed. When consulted about the possibility of making a child a witness in a courtroom drama, a therapist must consider:

- When is the case set for trial and can a series of postponements be expected?
- Is there a real possibility that the case will go to trial, or is an out-of-court-settlement being considered?
- If the therapist is engaged solely (or primarily) to prepare the child for trial, will this same therapist be available to the child for posttrial therapy? (Third-party payers and managed care companies rarely, if ever, pay for trial preparation or posttrial treatment if the client's difficulties were caused by the trial itself.)
- Will informed consent for the child to testify and to be prepared to testify be available from appropriate parties? If the child's parents are divorced, the therapist must read the divorce decree and determine from the decree who has the right to seek and consent to therapy for the child.

- Is funding or insurance available for posttrial therapy for the child and perhaps for other parties involved? What are the limits?
- Will the parents (or significant others) participate in the child's therapy, if needed?
- Will a child witness be treated fairly or is the child a pawn in a bigger picture, and, if so, will the therapist be informed of the scope of the global machinations?
- Should an attorney ad litem (appointed for purposes of a particular suit or action) be requested and appointed to protect the child's rights?
- Is the child willing to testify? Does the child know what processes and people are involved—a judge, the lawyers, and the contesting parties?
- Does the child have any idea of the ramifications of the outcome of the case?
- Can the therapist prepare the child for cross-examination and will the attorneys have protective orders in place to reduce the stress on the child?
- Can a possible conflict in loyalties be reconciled by the child? Will testifying in court make the child feel guilty? Can this feeling of guilt be handled in therapy in a manner that serves the best interest of the child?
- Will the child be available, before and after the trial, to role-play with parents, the therapist, and/or others?
- Is there an alternative to a court appearance to obtain the testimony of the child: audiotape or videotape; talking to a mental health professional and having the professional report to the court; or submitting written questions to the therapist, who then asks the child the questions in a private setting with a court reporter present?
- How obsessed are the parents (or significant others) and the lawyer with the testimony of the child and the circumstances that are reported to have occurred? Before, after, and during the trial, are they going to pump the child for information or cajole the child into narrating certain testimony? How many times will the child have to tell the story to different people who may be interested and involved or who may be just plain curious? If the trial turns into a media circus, can the child handle reporters, with or without therapy?
- Will the child's testimony be transcribed and become part of a public record?
- Is the risk to the child as a witness greater than the risk to the parties if the child does not testify?
- If child sexual abuse or some other intimate circumstance is the presenting problem and if the case is lost, will the court return the child to the alleged perpetrator or abuser?
- What will the posttrial reaction be in school, in church, in the neighborhood, and in relations with siblings, friends, family or extended family, or other important support groups?
- What will the effect of delay be on the child?
- How can the therapist ensure the payment of a bill for services rendered if, after all is completed and done correctly, the party who engaged the therapist refuses to pay?

Terminology differs in each jurisdiction. When a child is presented, demand a copy of the latest court decree and any amendments or changes. If the decree is not clear, seek a lawyer's advice to determine its meaning. If the decree is from a different jurisdiction (another state or nation), ask a local lawyer to engage a lawyer in that jurisdiction to educate the therapist about the meaning of unfamiliar legal jargon.

If the decree is not clear, seek a lawyer's advice to determine its meaning.

Children as witnesses present unique problems to the therapist, the judge, and the lawyers. Calling a child to be a witness because the child knows some simple fact is naive and unfair. Judges and lawyers ponder children's testimony seriously before deciding whether to call the child and then whether to admit the testimony.

The mental health professional's duty involves more ponderable alternatives and circumstances and transcends that of the lawyer, the judge, and the contesting parties. The therapist asks two questions: What will the child say? What will be the consequences to the child after the testimony is given?

Answers to Frequently Asked Questions about:

Father

Child witness

Competence to testify

❓ Question

The mother and stepfather of a 5-year-old complain about visits with his biological father who, in the past, has been arrested and convicted of several charges (assault, drugs, stalking, phone harassment). He currently has standard visitation. According to the mother and stepfather, the child returns home wearing the same clothes, often smelling of beer, exhausted, and hungry; and he wakes up several times screaming the first night. The latest event is that the child wakes up Monday mornings with a fever and cough, flu-like symptoms. The mother takes him to a doctor, who treats the symptoms. In spite of all this, the magistrate involved will not even allow a hearing. I and several other professionals have made numerous attempts to meet with the father, but he does not answer any requests. Any suggestions of where we could go from here?

Suppose the child was 7 to 10 years old. Could the child be a witness in court as to dad's conduct?

❗ Answer

It appears from your facts that the mother and stepfather have pursued the appropriate motions with the judge who has continuing jurisdiction over the child in question. If the judge has in fact *refused* to set the matter for a hearing, we would suggest three options:

1. If the child is being either abused or neglected during the father's possession time, a report to law enforcement or the state agency charged with investigating child abuse or neglect should be made. If state officials believe abuse or neglect has occurred, they could precipitate a hearing.

2. If the parties believe the judge is incompetent, a complaint can be filed with the state agency that is responsible for investigating and sanctioning judges. (Be careful; if you lose, you and your client will not be courthouse favorites.)

3. Contact your local state congressman and senator and explain the predicament. They may be influential in prompting the judge directly to schedule a hearing or in pressuring the appropriate state agencies to take action against the father or the judge.

Legal Lightbulb

- Children of all ages, if they have the required characteristics as set out previously, can testify as witnesses.

- A judge determines whether a child is competent to testify. If a court finds a child competent, opinions about the information elicited go to weight and credibility.

- In forensic work, conventional wisdom would dictate that one therapist should be engaged for trial work and another for ongoing assessment and treatment. A conflict of interest might be charged if one therapist performs all tasks.

- Be cautious. Many losing parties blame the therapist, unjustly, for their loss. Some clients will not accept blame or responsibility for their actions. When their expectations concerning testimony or a trial outcome are not met, they may blame someone else—usually, the therapist.

- Judges try to protect children from overaggressive lawyers. Having an attorney ad litem and filing protective orders are often appropriate strategies, especially if the testimony is expected to be very damaging to one party. Cross-examination of a child, even when presented gently, can be brutal.

- Preparing a child for court testimony is not the job of an amateur. If the problem arises, the therapist must gain competence by learning, training, education, or experience.

Additional Thoughts

- Do not be too proactive in a case like this. The mother should *engage her own lawyer,* and the *lawyer can orchestrate a family/legal game plan.*
- You, as a treating therapist, can be a supportive witness. But remember, you are primarily a clinically objective practitioner, not an advocate. That is the role of the lawyer.
- Be careful before you suggest that the child be called as a witness regardless of the age of the child. The effect on the child may be subject to "the law of unforeseen consequences." If the child is called, try to obtain a commitment from the mother that the child will receive continued therapy following the testimony, at least until the therapist clinically feels the consequences of the trial have been ameliorated.
- A child can be a witness at any age. The test is the maturity of the child as stated in this chapter where it answers the question: Can a child be a witness and testify in court?
- Trying to move an immovable judge can be difficult. Good luck.

20

Expert Witness

Six years ago, Dr. Jones saw a couple for marital therapy. He met with the father, the mother, and, on one occasion, their children. In family therapy, the daughter told Dr. Jones privately that she was apprehensive about her father, but gave no details. Dr. Jones recorded the remark in the file, but the remark was never clarified. Shortly thereafter, the couple stopped seeing Dr. Jones. Dr. Jones documented the file and, in accordance with state law, stored the file for the required maintenance period. Years later, the couple decided to divorce and each sought custody of their daughter. In light of the custody litigation, the daughter's remark, noted in the file, had taken on more meaning. Dr. Jones was served a subpoena duces tecum (his records were required as well as his person) for the custody hearing.

~

Dr. McCann, a therapist for child protective services, visited a child who alluded to child sexual abuse. Dr. McCann met with the child and concluded that no abuse had occurred. He reported his findings to the agent at child protective services. The agent dismissed the case and closed the file. Later, the mother and father were battling over termination of the father's parental rights after allegations of sexual abuse resurfaced. Dr. McCann received a subpoena to testify in court. Will Dr. McCann have to defend his conclusion in light of subsequent allegations of abuse?

The Big Picture

For many mental health professionals, the least attractive aspect of a therapeutic practice is responding to subpoenas or requests (actually, demands) to participate in litigation. A very small percentage of the mental health community makes a living offering forensic evaluation and testimony.

Most therapists get pulled into a lawsuit because they happened to have treated a client who is subsequently involved in litigation: A parent is divorcing a mate and is seeking custody of a child, or a defense attorney is attempting to reduce the damages (emotional distress, posttraumatic stress disorder) claimed by a former client after an accident. In many more scenarios, a therapist may be asked to donate time to an individual's quest for justice.

Anyone involved in litigation knows it can be a very intrusive, time-consuming, unpleasant, and costly experience. The process can also be extremely intimidating for a mental health professional who ordinarily does not have contact with the legal system. There is no substitute for knowledge, preparation, and experience in alleviating the panic and fright that can set in upon receipt of a subpoena. This chapter provides information that can help reduce the anxiety of first-time recipients, as well as seasoned forensic experts, when an unwanted and unanticipated subpoena is served.

Litigation is a stressful process. Lawyers are often stretched too thin to give adequate time and resources to processing a case. Occasionally, lawyers are ill prepared and make bumbling attempts at direct and cross-examination. They do not have time to master the techniques and jargon of therapy, yet they must ask intelligible questions and seem knowledgeable. (Lawyers are constantly aware they are grandstanding for their clients—making a lasting impression.) However, most attorneys are bright, conscientious, and concerned about doing a good job for their clients. To match their skills, the mental health practitioner needs to be ready and fully prepared for the task of testifying in court.

There is no substitute for knowledge, preparation, and experience in alleviating the panic and fright that can set in upon receipt of a subpoena.

Depositions and Courtroom Testimony: Any Differences?

There are generally two forums for offering testimony: an out-of-court deposition or courtroom testimony.

A deposition is a tool used by attorneys to discover any evidence that might be used at trial or to preserve testimony to be introduced during a trial. Depositions generally take place in the office of one of the attorneys or the office of the witness being deposed. A witness is sworn in by a court reporter, who records the proceedings and produces a typewritten transcript for review and signature by the witness. The transcript is then filed with the court. Depositions are often called "fishing expeditions." The attorneys have wide latitude for the types and number of questions that can be asked of the witness. Virtually all questions, no matter how ludicrous, are permissible.

Discovery, in a civil case, is defined as "the gathering of information that is relevant or likely to lead to relevant information." Thus, unlike courtroom testimony in front of a judge or jury, the witness may be asked to express opinions, speculate, relate hearsay, or reveal rumors. Lawyers control depositions. There is no judge present, and the witness does not have the protection afforded by a knowledgeable judge.

If you feel a question is vague, calls for speculation, or asks for hearsay, qualify your answer in those terms. In many respects, a deposition is a feeling-out process by all parties and counsel. Everybody is sizing up everyone else's

A deposition is a tool used by attorneys to discover any evidence that might be used at trial or to preserve testimony to be introduced during a trial.

If you feel a question is vague, calls for speculation, or asks for hearsay, qualify your answer in those terms.

strengths and weaknesses, and good lawyers will use the information learned in a deposition to their advantage.

Confidentiality is only a word used in a deposition. In view of all its exceptions, the concept has been reduced to the status of myth. Before you even open your mouth to answer a question about a client, you must be sure that an exception to the client's right to confidentiality exists. Before a deposition, you should seek the client's written consent to be deposed. If you do not have the client's written consent or are not sure that an exception to confidentiality exists, do not answer until you see a court order authorizing or ordering you to do so.

Before a deposition, you should seek the client's written consent to be deposed.

A court order can be obtained only by filing a motion. Usually, a hearing is held; then an order is issued by the court and signed by the judge. An attorney must be engaged to process the paperwork.

Do you, as a therapist, have a right to privacy/confidentiality? Unfortunately, in a deposition, your personal and professional background is fair game. One of the purposes of a deposition is to learn about you and to establish or attack your credibility.

Who will be your audience? All parties, as well as their attorneys and the attorneys' assistants, may attend a deposition. If people unrelated to the case are present (e.g., newspaper reporters), insist on a ruling from the court before proceeding. A deposition transcript is part of the official court record—a public record that can be viewed by anyone.

In court, you can assume the world is your audience. In high-profile, media-worthy cases, expect that every public document will be reviewed, and reporters will be camping on your doorstep. Before saying a public word, consult your lawyer.

Helpful Hints for Testifying in Court

1. Tell the truth: You have absolutely nothing to gain by lying. Lying can cost you your job, your license, your reputation, your right to vote (if convicted of perjury), and your freedom.

2. Testify from your own personal knowledge or observation, unless asked otherwise: Testify about what you know and avoid using the word *we* (i.e., "We always do it this way," "We were told to . . ."). This usage tends to confuse jurors and could cause them to disregard your testimony because it sounds as if you are making it up or trying to shift blame.

3. Listen to the question: Not listening is, without doubt, the biggest mistake witnesses make. Unless you listen carefully to each question you will fall into verbal traps and give poor testimony. Focus your attention exclusively on the person asking the question and try to block out your anxiety and other fears. Make sure you fully understand a question before answering it.

4. Answer only the question asked of you; if you do not understand it, ask that the question be rephrased: It is permissible to advise the questioner/attorney that you do not understand the question that is being asked. Ask for an explanation or rephrasing. Clarity is even more critical in a deposition because there is no judge present to rule on objections. You have a duty to be sure that you understand each and every question before you answer. Many lawyers preface depositions by stating to the witness that giving an answer to a question implies that the question was understood.

5. If you don't know an answer, say so: After their many years of undergraduate schooling, graduate and perhaps doctoral programs, professional licensing exams, and licensing renewal, many mental health professionals have difficulty in saying, "I don't know." Trials are all about truth, and if "I don't know" is the truthful answer, it should be given. Your ego may be more severely bruised if you attempt to answer a question when you don't know the answer. Faking, overstating a position, bluffing, and getting caught in defending an indefensible position can be embarrassing and humiliating. Lawyers can ask interminable questions. A witness is not excused from the stand until the judge gives permission, and this usually occurs when the lawyers are finished with all of their questions.

6. Don't exceed your level of competence, experience, or training and qualify your testimony when necessary: If you are not qualified or do not have the experience and training to answer a question or give an opinion, do not offer one. Do not let yourself be badgered and forced into responding, no matter how much ridicule the lawyer directs at you. If you do not have sufficient information, or if there are extraneous or contingent facts or events that could influence your opinion, qualify your answer or opinion. You will be called on to defend every opinion you express.

7. Avoid being specific about dates, times, and empirical statistics unless you personally recorded them and are certain they are correct: Use phrases such as "on or about" or "estimated to be" when testifying. Mistakes about dates and numbers invite heavy cross-examination. If you are not absolutely positive about a date, time, or empirical data, do not be specific. There is often a long lag time between a deposition and a trial. If you testified in your deposition that a client made a statement to you on March 3, 1995, and two years later, at trial, you testify that the statement was made May 13, 1995, you would certainly be challenged on cross-examination. By using the phrase "on or about" each time, a small discrepancy is much easier to handle. Never guess; if you are approximating, be sure to say so. Use the phrase "I would estimate. . . ."

If there are dates to be introduced into evidence and the sequence of the dates or the events is important, make sure they are documented in a chronological list either or both as to date and to time of day. *One easy way to be flustered in the courtroom is to mix up what happened when and then have to correct the misstep. Make a list and take it to the stand.*

If an error is made, the next question is foreseeable: "Are you as sure of the rest of your testimony as you are sure that the event took place on January 3, at exactly 2:00 P.M.?"

8. Be prepared, and never testify without reviewing your records and any prior depositions you have given in the case: Sometimes, the only favorable evidence an attorney has is the inadequacy or inconsistency of records or reports in the files that were furnished to him or her by potential witnesses or that were buried deep in a client file. If you are unable to recall details of your own records or your prior testimony, you will make a terrible impression on the judge or jury. Look over your records very carefully; if necessary, memorize them. If you are aligned with an attorney in the case, ask him or her to review your records with you beforehand. Look for problem areas, weaknesses, inconsistencies, and points of direct and cross-examination.

Ask the attorney whether other documents have been delivered about which you could be asked to comment. Review those documents as well to avoid surprises.

Be sure to review the transcript of any deposition you have given. You may be asked whether you reviewed any documents, pictures, or files in preparation for the deposition. If you did, the questioning lawyer is entitled to review them and to question you about them.

If you are providing documents as the basis of your testimony, make sure they are marked for the record and refer to them as "marked exhibits." This designation will prevent confusion later on, when memory of the deposition has faded.

Prepare a chronology of significant dates so that you can testify crisply about when events took place. Prepare an index and table of contents so that, during interrogation, you can find specific notes more easily. The client file should be in a loose-leaf notebook or a securely fastened file. (The only thing more disconcerting than having a witness shuffle pages frantically, looking for a notation in a file, is having the whole file spill on the floor.)

Visit a courtroom; observe and sit through a trial. A wise man once said, "The learned are educated by the experience of others; a fool learns only by the fool's own experience."

The Bottom Line

1. Remember the four c's—be cool, calm, courteous, and consistent in your demeanor: The best witnesses are those who respond in the same manner to each attorney asking the questions and are equally helpful and concerned when questioned by the opposing attorney as when questioned by their own attorney. Before giving a deposition, ask for the identity of each person in the room. Know which lawyer represents which party in the case. This will help you understand where an attorney may be coming from in framing and directing questions.

A deposition is an opportunity to preview a witness for testimony at trial. Attorneys probe to see what upsets, angers, or frightens a witness.

An attorney may try to wear you down by prolonging the length of the deposition. Check local court rules. They often determine breaks, length of the deposition, ability to visit your attorney, time to begin and end the questioning, and so on. Depositions are scheduled to continue from the time they are set to begin until they are finished, excluding holidays, weekends, and non-business hours. Many individual judges have established procedures to protect the witness from being badgered. An attorney can ask you the same question several times. "Asked and answered" objections are generally waived, and no judge is there to rule against repetition.

Avoid sarcasm and argumentative responses. They will generally only invite tougher and more numerous questions from the attorney and greatly reduce your effectiveness as a witness.

2. Do not volunteer unnecessary information: Respond with "Yes" or "No" to a question whenever appropriate, and do not expound on your answer unless specifically asked to do so. Volunteering information has been the downfall of many witnesses, especially during cross-examination. If you absolutely feel the need to explain your answer, make the explanation brief, thoughtful, and responsive to the question.

In a deposition, there is absolutely no reason to volunteer information. Often, at the end of a deposition, an attorney will ask whether a witness would like to add anything for the record. In trial, this question would be met with an objection ("Calling for a narrative"); in depositions, objections are generally waived and there is no judge. You should respond by advising the attorney that, to the best of your ability at this time, you have answered all the questions propounded to you.

3. If in court, seek help from the judge when needed: If an attorney bombards you with a series of quick questions and you feel you are not being given ample opportunity to consider and respond appropriately to each question, turn to the judge and let him or her know you are having trouble with the questioning.

If you don't understand a question and the attorney is causing you difficulty, advise the judge that you really don't understand the question, and ask whether you still must respond. Most judges will assist you under these circumstances.

4. Rely on your attorney for help in a deposition: During a deposition, breaks may be taken at any time. (In a courtroom, the judge schedules them.) If you are having difficulty with a line of questioning, plead the necessity of a restroom break or the need to respond to a page signal, and then consult with your attorney outside the deposition room. Local rules may govern how many times or how often you can excuse yourself to consult with the lawyer. Remember, the examining attorney is entitled to *your* testimony, not that of your attorney. Try to avoid stopping the record merely to consult with your attorney. But if it is unavoidable, it is better to stop the record and discuss the matter with your attorney than stumble into a trap.

If your attorney instructs you not to answer a question, do not answer it. If opposing counsel is particularly aggressive, he or she may try to pressure you into responding by saying that if you don't answer, you will be brought before a judge who could not only compel you to answer but also make you pay attorneys' fees and court costs. It would be appropriate for you to advise the opposing lawyer that any further attempts to get you to respond to the question will be considered unethical interference with your attorney-client relationship and will be reported to the bar association.

5. Don't assume your attorney knows anything about you or the subject matter of your testimony: Not all attorneys are well prepared or knowledgeable about the subject matter at issue. Force your attorney to take the time to visit with you about matters or evidence you would like to be asked about and what you view to be significant problem areas. You may have to educate your attorney. Remember, you will generally know more about the subject matter in the case than the attorneys will.

In evaluating witness testimony, the law allows certain criteria to be used to weigh credibility. It is helpful for you to know the basis on which you will be reviewed and judged when testifying.

You should understand the general goals of the attorneys in both direct and cross-examination and the legal criteria and goals used by the judge and jury. Knowing and understanding them can better prepare you for offering testimony.

Being prepared—understanding attorneys' goals and the criteria on which the therapist's testimony will be judged—should be helpful in alleviating anxiety when testifying. Take the time to review the helpful hints in this chapter every time you are subpoenaed. Having your memory refreshed can help to reduce your anxiety.

Answers to Frequently Asked Questions about:

Expert witnesses

❓ Question

What guidelines do you recommend for mental health professionals asked to appear in court as an expert witness? I first testified for my patient as his treating psychologist concerning work-related stress. He won his case. There was a technical or procedural error and many complications, none concerning my testimony. His current, new attorney is reopening the case, and I am again asked to testify, only this time as an expert witness as contrasted to or opposed to last time as his treating psychologist. What do you recommend I do?

! *Answer*

It is difficult to give you the comprehensive advice your inquiry requires in the limited time and space afforded. There are many books in print about courtroom testimony, and you may wish to consider purchasing such a resource if you anticipate doing much courtroom work. Our *Portable Ethicist* (Wiley, 2000) offers some suggestions. Another is *Social Work and the Courts: A Casebook,* second edition, by Daniel Pollack, March, 2003, Brunner-Routledge.

We will offer a few practical pointers, however. Since you have previously testified, be sure to get a copy of the transcript of your prior testimony and review it very carefully now and again before you testify in the second trial. The defense attorneys will be looking for inconsistencies, sometimes referred to as "prior inconsistent statements."

Force the client's lawyer to take time with you to rehearse your direct testimony and to role-play cross-examination, anticipating questions you may be asked by the defense attorney or opposing counsel. Cross-examination is the tough part. Make sure you are never surprised.

Do not let yourself be forced or tricked into stating an opinion for which you do not have a sound basis in fact or professional theory. Do your homework. Do not speculate and do not go out on a limb for the client. If you have no opinion, say so. Qualify statements and opinions when necessary. Don't ramble, and answer only the specific question that is asked.

Avoid giving definite time, date, or empirical testimony unless you are absolutely certain of the number. Use phrases such as "to the best of my ability to recall" or "approximately."

If you have no current data on the client, you may wish to spend time with the client getting current. Know what has happened to the client since the last therapy session. Often, new experiences of the client change the diagnosis, prognosis, or treatment plan.

Consult with the client's lawyer first, however, because the lawyer may not want you to be current, especially if the client has dramatically improved, deteriorated, or changed since you last saw the client. You can testify only as to the client's condition as of the last visit and examination.

♀ *Additional Thoughts*

- Testifying in court as an expert witness is not for the faint at heart.
- Remember, you may be attacked personally by opposing counsel, and your credentials and personal history may be challenged as will your diagnosis, prognosis, and treatment plan.

Legal Lightbulb

Criteria Used by Judge and Jury to Evaluate Witness Testimony

- Conduct, attitude, demeanor, and manner while testifying.
- Ability to recollect, remember, and clearly relate the facts about which the witness is testifying.
- Prior/subsequent consistent or inconsistent statements.
- Consistent or inconsistent testimony, compared with other witnesses' statements.
- Bias, interest, motive not to tell the truth.
- Character or community reputation: honesty and veracity or dishonesty.
- Admission that the witness did not tell the truth.
- Prior conviction of a felony.

Additional Criteria for Evaluating Experts' Testimony

- Education, training, and experience.
- Truth of the basis of the expert's opinions. Is the foundation for the opinion of the expert witness sound?
- Are opinions supported by sound scientific criteria?

Goals of the Attorney

Direct Examination

- To establish the witness's credibility via credentials, objectivity, reliability, and training.
- To discredit the opposing witnesses (or party) by attacking their credentials; lack of objectivity, reliability, and training; and their actions, conditions, and motives.
- To elicit favorable testimony.

Cross-Examination

- To attack the opposing witnesses' credibility by casting doubt on their credentials, objectivity, reliability, and training.

Legal Lightbulb
(continued)

- To discredit the opposing witnesses' testimony by attacking their actions, conditions, and motives.

- To elicit favorable testimony.

- To show that the expert's opinion is not based on sound scientific criteria.

- If you are not qualified or do not have the experience and training to answer a question or give an opinion, do not offer one.

- Look over your records very carefully; if necessary, memorize them.

- Prepare a chronology of significant dates so that you can testify crisply about when events took place.

- Avoid sarcasm and argumentative responses. They will generally only invite tougher and more numerous questions from the attorney and greatly reduce your effectiveness as a witness.

- Respond with "Yes" or "No" to a question whenever appropriate, and do not expound on your answer unless specifically asked to do so.

- Make sure you can defend and have documented your diagnosis, prognosis, and treatment plan.
- If you are going to become a forensic expert, read the literature concerning procedures on the witness stand. There are abundant books in every bookstore and on the Internet.
- Role-play every court appearance with the lawyer who has engaged you.
- Make sure you know *who* is responsible to pay you for your expert witness services and *when* you can expect to be paid. If possible, *establish a trust fund in advance.*
- When you finish, insist on a critique, so you will do better next time.
- Become an expert on the condition in the case (e.g., work-related stress). Conversational platitudes that work in professional conversations will not suffice on the witness stand.

21

Forensic Evaluation

Kate, a social worker, was appointed by the court to prepare a custody evaluation in a divorce case. At the trial, she offered testimony adverse to the father. As a result, the mother was awarded custody of the two children. The father, unhappy with the outcome of the trial, was upset with Kate. He filed a complaint with the licensing board alleging gross incompetence. His comments included the fact that his ex-wife suffered from a manic depressive disorder, but no home visits were ever made and his ex-wife's psychiatrist was not consulted. Furthermore, he alleged Kate was biased against him because, in contested divorce proceedings, Kate had just lost custody of her own teenage son to her husband.

~

Eric, a divorced father of a 2-year-old girl, was convicted of sexual abuse, due in large part to the testimony of Dr. Schmidt. Dr. Schmidt testified that, in his opinion, the girl had been sexually abused. His conclusions were based on two interviews with the child, four interviews with the ex-wife, and one half-hour session with Eric. No psychological testing of Eric was performed. Six months after Eric was sent to the state penitentiary, his ex-wife recanted and admitted she contrived the whole case because she was upset that Eric had been having an affair. On release from prison, Eric filed a complaint against Dr. Schmidt.

Crucial to the proper administration of justice are mental health forensic experts, who, by virtue of their education, training, and experience, testify and offer to the judge or jury in a lawsuit opinions concerning ultimate issues of fact: mental competency, mental health or condition, best interest of a child, sanity, competency to perform certain acts, capacity to make a will, characteristics of date rape, propensity to violence, or psychological profiles of mass murderers. In any courtroom on any given day, a mental health professional is assisting in a court case.

Criteria and Guidelines

Mental health practice is as much an art as a science. Many opinions and diagnoses are based on subjective interpretation of (sometimes limited) objective criteria. The education, training, and experience of mental health forensic experts are of vital concern to the courts, the contesting parties, and the attorneys who rely on their opinions, analysis, and testimony.

Many mental health experts have had problems because they offered forensic opinions even when they lacked sufficient training and experience with the issues. Each state has established criteria for professionals who are qualified to offer forensic mental health testimony. In addition, national and state mental health organizations publish guidelines for giving forensic testimony. In Texas (40 Administrative Code, Chapter 725), the minimum qualifications for a person who wishes to conduct a court-ordered social study in a custody case are:

> Licensed or certified in an appropriate professional field, and possess a master's degree from an accredited college and have 2 years of professionally supervised full-time experience that includes evaluating physical, intellectual, social, and psychological functioning and needs and the potential of the social and physical environment (present and/or prospective) to meet those needs; or, at least 10 court-ordered social studies under the supervision of a person meeting the minimum qualifications, or, possess a bachelor's degree from an accredited university or college and five years of professionally supervised experience or at least 20 court-ordered social studies under the supervision of a person meeting the minimum qualifications.

The person conducting the study must meet the following requirements:

- If the investigator has a conflict of interest with any party or may be biased by previous knowledge, he or she must disqualify himself or herself.
- If the investigator needs to discuss substantive issues about a case with an attorney representing a party, he or she must communicate with all attorneys in the case.
- The investigator must verify, to the extent possible, all statements of fact pertinent to the study. Sources of information and verification must be noted in the report.
- The basis for the investigator's conclusions must be stated in the report. If only one side of the case has been investigated, the investigator must refrain from making a custody determination but may state if the party investigated appears to be suitable for custody.

The Texas statute goes on to require that, unless the court directs otherwise, the social study must be conducted according to the "Guidelines for

Each state has established criteria for professionals who are qualified to offer forensic mental health testimony.

Court-Conducted Child Custody Evaluation," published by the Association of Family and Conciliation Courts. Many other similar guidelines are published by national mental health associations.

The American Psychological Association, in its *Guidelines for Child Custody Evaluations in Divorce Proceedings* [*American Psychologist, 49,* 677–680 (1994)], requires in part:

- The psychologist gains specialized competence.
- The psychologist is aware of personal and societal biases and engages in nondiscriminatory practice.
- The psychologist avoids multiple relationships.
- The psychologist obtains informed consent from all participants.
- The psychologist informs participants about the limits of confidentiality.
- The psychologist uses multiple methods of data gathering. (Important facts and opinions are documented from at least two sources whenever their reliability is questioned.)
- The psychologist does not give an opinion about the psychological functioning of any individual who has not been personally evaluated.
- The psychologist clarifies financial arrangements before commencement of the evaluation.
- The psychologist maintains written records.

Failure to follow such published guidelines can result in suits for professional negligence (malpractice), licensing board complaints, and expulsion from professional associations.

Answers to Frequently Asked Questions about:

Conflict of interest

Bias and prejudice

Forensic evaluation

Conflicting psychological or mental health opinions

❓ Question

I am treating a mother who has lost her children to Child Protection Services (CPS) for depression. CPS, in their effort to permanently revoke the mother's rights, sent my patient to a psychologist for an independent evaluation as required by law. The evaluation came back exaggerated, slanted, and full of misrepresentations, concluding that the mother was unfit to care for her children. (In some states, this might be called permanent termination of parental rights, *in that continuing to honor these parental rights would not be in the best interest of the children.) I, in response, suggested to the mother that she hire her own psychologist and get a second opinion. She saw another psychologist, who has a sterling reputation. The second psychologist's report favored the mother and was in stark contrast to the first. Now, I learn through our small town gossip that the referring CPS worker and the "independent" psychologist are gay lovers. Where should I go from here? I fear that if I report my findings, I could be sued for slander. And, in this conservative community, a hint of homosexuality would impact the psychologist's ability to continue to practice. On the other hand, if I don't expose this conflict of interest, a family could be severed for life. What do you think?*

❗ Answer

I assume the mother has an attorney. If not, she should retain one. Because the matter is before the court, I would suggest you let her attorney explore and present the alleged conflict of interest in the context of the legal proceedings. As an outsider, you are not in a position to judge the evaluation of the first psychologist and to render an opinion as to whether the report furnished the court is inaccurate and a reflection of bias. *Professionally, you are not permitted to render an opinion concerning this problem without first interviewing all the parties and conducting appropriate evaluative tests.* Furthermore, your information about the relationship between the CPS worker and the psychologist is only "small town gossip." You should stay out of it. However, have the mom discuss this matter with her lawyer, who will most certainly want to explore it further in the hopes of discrediting a key witness in the case. If the judge perceives the report to be biased, he or she can report all findings and opinions to the appropriate licensing boards and professional associations.

💡 Additional Thoughts

- Two competent psychologists can evaluate the same person and/or family and come to different conclusions, both of which are defensible.
- The fact there is a personal relationship between the CPS worker and the psychologist does not, of itself, make the report inaccurate; rather, it only makes it subject to question.
- Lawyers know that each party to almost any litigation can hire a professional expert witness who will favor their case. This is known as the battle of the experts.
- Custody, termination of parental rights, and the concept of the "unfit mother" are usually determined by judges and juries.
- Remember, the psychologist is only a witness. The determination was or will be made by a judge or jury.
- Always bear in mind your role as treating therapist. Remember, you are neither an advocate nor adversary. You are a mental health service provider and may lose your clinical objectivity if you get too involved in the technical aspects of the case itself.

- Resist the temptation to get personally involved or incensed by the conduct of another professional. If the referral to the first psychologist was negligent, there is a cause of action for negligent referral. However, if the professional is competent, the sexual orientation of the individual making the evaluation is of no consequence.
- If you want to express your views, meet with the patient and the lawyer. Have them orchestrate the scenario. A judge or jury will listen to the testimony and decide who is the most persuasive.
- Look over the negative report. Perhaps assist the lawyer in preparing for cross-examination.

Suggestions to Consider

A review of the requirements and guidelines embodied in state statutes or found in association guidelines bring to light certain basic concepts about forensic testimony:

1. Do not give forensic testimony without first acquiring the appropriate knowledge, skill, training, and experience: Just because Dr. X has a Ph.D. in psychology and 15 years' experience, he is not necessarily qualified to offer forensic testimony in a particular case. If a seasoned therapist who has little experience in evaluating sexual abuse cases stumbles into sexual abuse allegations while involved in a custody evaluation, he or she would be required to defer to another professional who has sufficient experience in that specific area.

It is important to know your own level of competence and not reach beyond it. Learn the criteria required by your jurisdiction with respect to becoming qualified to testify and how evaluations are to be conducted. Find out what particular judges want and how the expert can best serve the court as well as the parties.

The opportunity to earn a fee has clouded the judgment of therapists who, when asked to make an evaluation they really are not competent to render, accept the offer. Know your limits and professional levels of competence in different areas. Can your testimony withstand rigorous cross-examination?

2. Do not do an evaluation if there is any possibility of bias, dual relationship, or conflict of interest: We all have biases or prejudices, however slight they may be. The court and the parties deserve as objective an evaluation as possible. Failure to disclose a prior relationship with a party, a personal prejudice, or an experience that could cloud judgment invites fertile cross-examination when uncovered by an attorney or other party; it can be the basis of a complaint for malpractice or disciplinary action. Attorneys probe for even the slightest hint of bias, prejudice, or conflict and usually discover facts that impair clinical objectivity.

3. Do not be the treating therapist *and* the forensic evaluator: This dual relationship poses a problem. Many therapists have contracts with governmental agencies to perform evaluations and offer treatment to sex offenders or other criminals. The treating therapist should always have the client's best interest in mind, but having to be an objective and impartial evaluator can create conflict. A treating therapist may also be put in the position of breaching confidentiality. The therapist should clarify the relationship with the client and then wear only one hat throughout the professional relationship with that client.

If the therapist chooses to provide treatment and court-ordered evaluations, this dual role should be carefully and clearly disclosed to the client. Informed consent should be given to the therapist. It is imperative to clearly document both the disclosure and the consent. Licensing boards are becoming ever more sensitive to the "informed" part of informed consent.

4. Do a thorough evaluation and verify important facts and information: Get as much verified information as is required to allow you to render a meaningful opinion. Verify from more than one source the critical facts or information in the case. Do independent investigation. In therapy, a mental health professional can accept a client's view of the universe, but this is definitely not the case with forensic evaluations. Do not accept at face value all the information provided by participants. If you are unable to satisfactorily verify important facts, state so in your report. A major question: If one fact proves to be incorrect, how reliable is the rest of the information?

5. Qualify the report when in doubt, when information is not received or verified, or if a participant was not evaluated: Lawyers and litigants want you to offer information and opinions that will advance their side of the case. They may even be paying you with the expectation of favorable testimony. The mental health expert is obligated, however, to be scrupulously honest and must avoid misleading courts and parties with their reports and testimony. It is better to admit a weak area in the evaluation report than to have it forcefully (and often sarcastically) drawn out during cross-examination.

6. Keep thorough records of all that transpires during the evaluation process, including all information gathered, a list of all sources, a list of all records used to attempt verification of information, a list of all recommendations and requests made, and a list of all the relevant times and dates of the material: Document as if a complaint was going to be filed against you.

7. No matter what the circumstances, do not be pressured into stating an opinion if you are not qualified and do not have the backup data to give one: Every opinion must be defensible.

8. Stay current and well informed concerning developments and changes in the mental health field: What is common and acceptable in one year may very well be obsolete the next.

9. Clarify any fee arrangements upfront, and disclose fee arrangements readily: Lawyers often question an expert witness about his or her fee in lieu

Legal Lightbulb

- Courtroom testimony is a specialty. It is different from treatment in which only the professional and the client are involved.

- When participating in the justice system, the mental health professional can expect to be questioned concerning every phase of the evaluation or assessment.

- All points about which the professional testifies are proper for the withering crossfire of cross-examination.

- Judges offer wide latitude to lawyers when they vigorously question the education, learning, training, or experience of professional witnesses or their conclusions or the rationale or basis for their conclusions.

- Fees, relationships, or anything that might affect the clinical objectivity of the witness should be stated in advance.

- All actual or potential conflicts of interest must be disclosed.

- Factual materials and their sources that are assumed but not verified must be acknowledged.

- Forensic witnesses who have an inclination about how a case should be determined, in their opinion, must refrain from displaying bias or prejudice and retain the posture of clinical objectivity. Let the lawyer do his or her job.

- Be acutely aware of your level of competence and remain within that level when stating an opinion.

- Wear only one hat when participating in forensic evaluations and offering treatment before or after a trial.

- Prepare for trial and understand that everything you say will be seriously questioned by a knowledgeable professional. Another professional with your background may help and assist the opposing attorney in framing the questions.

- Try to be paid in advance or at least have a written agreement for prompt payment. Experience has reminded professionals that if a case is lost, in the opinion of the client or the client's lawyer, payment is not graciously forthcoming.

of "expertise." State the fee arrangement at the inception of the report, for example:

> I, Dr. Q, was engaged by Party Y to perform an evaluation of the parties and their children and to render an opinion concerning which parent should be named the primary caretaker of the children. The fee agreed upon was $125.00 per hour with a $2,500.00 retainer fee paid in advance. . . .

10. Consult with judges and lawyers in your jurisdiction concerning expectations of forensic mental health experts and testimony in their courts: Knowing what is expected can help you do a better job of evaluating and rendering your opinions.

11. Nothing can absolutely eliminate the unsavory experience of vigorous cross-examination by an attorney for the party against whom you have rendered an unfavorable opinion: However, by following these suggestions, you can eliminate the possibility of a personally adverse decision being rendered against you in a malpractice case or in a licensing board investigation.

12. Each state has established criteria for professionals who are qualified to offer forensic mental health testimony.

13. Failure to follow such published guidelines can result in suits for professional negligence (malpractice), licensing board complaints, and expulsion from professional associations.

14. Consult with judges and lawyers in your jurisdiction concerning expectations of forensic mental health experts and testimony in their courts.

22

Involuntary Commitment

A psychologist, Dr. Anthony, had seen a patient, Justin, in therapy for six months. The patient had been diagnosed several years earlier as schizophrenic and was living alone. Justin was also seeing a psychiatrist, Dr. Barnett, who monitored his medication.

When it became apparent that Justin was not taking his medication, Dr. Anthony consulted with Dr. Barnett about the symptoms he was observing. Justin was hearing voices again and was threatening to "blow away" the voices as soon as he identified where they were coming from and whom they belonged to. Drs. Anthony and Barnett agreed that inpatient care was required to stabilize Justin. Dr. Anthony signed an affidavit and submitted a mental health warrant to the County Mental Health Department so a 48-hour commitment order could be entered by the probate court.

Justin was subsequently taken into custody by the county sheriff and transported to County Hospital for observation and evaluation. He was released after 48 hours; the County Hospital psychiatric staff determined that Justin was not a danger to himself or others. Justin filed a licensing board complaint and a lawsuit alleging wrongful diagnosis by Dr. Anthony and false imprisonment.

〜

A family applied to the probate court for an involuntary commitment order for their daughter, Jennifer. Jennifer's psychiatrist recommended admission to a local facility where she had staff privileges. The court issued a commitment order confining Jennifer to the recommended hospital. While hospitalized, Jennifer was sexually abused by two attendants. Unknown to the family, the hospital had been investigated twice by state authorities within the past year. Complaints by prior patients or their families cited sexual abuse and neglect. The investigations were closed when the families and the patients allegedly refused to cooperate. Jennifer's psychiatrist had been aware of the allegations but assumed, when the investigation was closed, that the complaints were meritless. Does Jennifer's psychiatrist have anything to worry about?

〜

Susan, a licensed professional counselor, provided postdivorce therapy. One of Susan's patients, June, a divorced mother with one daughter, was having a difficult *time dealing with her divorce. She was depressed and occasionally mentioned the difficulties of raising a child alone. She said she wished that her daughter would just disappear so that she would be spared the pain of child rearing. June met with Susan irregularly; she canceled appointments at the last minute or forgot about them entirely. One day, Susan received a phone call from June's sister. She described to Susan her concerns about June, who was exhibiting strange behavior patterns; she felt that June's behavior was so extreme that June's daughter might need some protection. Susan offered her services to facilitate an inpatient admission at an excellent facility. After a few more calls to discuss inpatient admission, June's sister stopped calling. No action was taken to admit June to a mental health facility. A few weeks later, Susan picked up a newspaper and read that June had stabbed her daughter to death and then had killed herself.*

The problems presented by an involuntary admission of an angry, unstable, or borderline patient can create havoc for a mental health professional's peace of mind. A therapist could face a "damned if you do and damned if you don't" situation. A balancing of risks must take place. You could correctly assume that the damages that could be awarded in a suit for improper diagnosis and a brief involuntary admission would be far less than the damages assessed for inaction, no admission, or police investigation, and then a resulting suicide or homicide.

Legal Mandates and Safeguards

Every state has an involuntary commitment law that details the steps and criteria to be followed and applied before a person can be involuntarily admitted for inpatient mental health care. Most require a legal finding of mental illness plus "imminent physical danger to self or others" before a court can deprive a person of his or her liberty and order confinement to a mental health facility. (You must keep in mind that no crime has been committed, and deprivation of liberty is usually associated with criminal acts and criminal law.) State statutes stagger the length of confinement for an initial evaluation period from 24 hours to 76 hours. Lengthier commitment terms apply upon appropriate legal, medical, and/or psychiatric findings.

Every state has an involuntary commitment law that details the steps and criteria to be followed and applied before a person can be involuntarily admitted for inpatient mental health care.

Consumer activism in all parts of the country has resulted in tremendous changes in the law concerning commitment for mental illness. The federal government has mandated that each state establish a protection and advocacy system for mentally ill persons to safeguard against abuses. Many states specifically set out by statute the rights of an inpatient when committed (involuntarily or voluntarily) to a mental health facility. Usually, a finding of "danger to self or others," by itself, will not constitute a finding of mental incompetency. The patient must be consulted on all aspects of his or her diagnosis and treatment, and an informed consent must be obtained. Until a guardian or conservator is appointed by a court, the therapist must provide services only with the consent of the patient or by court order directing the treatment.

Patients' Rights

A person who is confined to a mental hospital but has not been declared incompetent can bring a suit for habeas corpus and obtain release.

The patient, until adjudged by the appropriate court to be mentally incompetent to manage his or her own affairs and personal health, retains all constitutional and civil rights, including the right to sue. A person who is confined to a mental hospital but has not been declared incompetent can bring a suit for habeas corpus and obtain release. Of even greater concern, the person can sue his or her "captors" (mental health professionals) for negligence and false imprisonment.

Specific state statutes often set out a precise list of additional rights a person has while an inpatient at a mental health facility. These specific rights may include:

- Right to receive visitors.
- Right to communicate with a person outside the facility.
- Right to communicate by uncensored and sealed mail with legal counsel, courts, or the state attorney general.
- Right to be notified, upon admission, of the existence, purpose, address, and telephone number of the protection and advocacy system for mentally ill persons, as required by federal law.
- Right to appropriate treatment for the mental illness, in the least restrictive setting that is available and appropriate.
- Right to obtain an independent medical or psychiatric examination or evaluation.
- Right to an individualized treatment plan and to participation in developing the plan.
- Right to humane treatment and reasonable protection from harm.
- Right not to receive unnecessary or excessive medication.
- Right to be informed of these rights upon admission. (In some states, communication in a language understood by the patient is required.)

With the nationwide concern for patients' rights and protection from abuse, the deck seems to be stacked against the mental health professional. Compared to even a decade ago, it is much more difficult to involuntarily commit mentally ill persons and keep them in an inpatient facility. What can a therapist do when a client does not clearly present an imminent physical danger to self or another party, but is knowingly or unwittingly not taking necessary medication or following treatment recommendations? What can a therapist do when a client refuses to stay in treatment or counseling when, in the therapist's opinion, it is badly needed?

In most instances, all the therapist can do is provide the client, or significant third parties, with warnings as permitted by law. The therapist can also give the client, in writing, treatment recommendations and potential resources. The client's file should clearly document, with date and time of day, all information provided directly to the client or sent to the client's authorized mailing address. Certified mail is not always recommended since a client may refuse a certified letter whereas regular mail is delivered. Until legislation is passed that will allow for court-ordered outpatient treatment for a mentally ill person before the person or another party is in imminent physical danger, not much else can be done. *Patients have a right not to act in their own best interest.*

Clinical Records as Documentation

Before seeking or supporting an involuntary commitment, a therapist must be sure the clinical record reflects findings consistent with the state's burden of proof for involuntary commitment. If, as in most states, the standard applied by the court is the "imminent physical danger test," the file should reflect adequate evidence to support the therapist's conclusion that someone (a third party) is in imminent physical danger from the client or that the client is personally in imminent physical danger. If in doubt, consult often with colleagues using deidentifiable information about all observations and concerns. Document all consultations and the advice or conclusions received from colleagues. Colleagues need not identify the client, only the problem.

Contact a lawyer and become familiar with commitment procedures and law in your jurisdiction. Learn what the burden of proof will be and what findings a court must make before ordering commitment. Create a record that leaves no doubt about the reasonableness of your conclusion and proves the imminent physical danger existed. Consider whether your clinical record will hold up in court and under close scrutiny by other experts.

If the client has authorized you to contact family members, recommend, to each person contacted, that involuntary commitment proceedings be pursued. (Do not initiate this action yourself.) Provide the family with information on how to secure a commitment order. An angry client is less likely to sue a family member than a therapist.

Before contacting family members, however, urge the client to voluntarily commit to inpatient care. You can then either arrange the admission or provide the client with written information concerning the steps to take for admission. Document your concerns and your recommendations to the client.

Contact a lawyer and become familiar with commitment procedures and law in your jurisdiction.

The duty to warn issue is discussed in Chapter 23, but the issue to consider here is whether it is enough to warn as permitted by law. Does a therapist have a further obligation to seek involuntary commitment when inpatient care is indicated? To date, statutory and case law does not impose on the therapist the duty to seek involuntary commitment of a client. However, a therapist does have the duty to advise the client of all treatments that the therapist believes are needed. If the therapist cannot provide the type or quality of care needed, an appropriate referral must be made. Beyond recommending inpatient care and quality sources and resources, no further action is required of the mental health professional at this time.

To date, statutory and case law does not impose on the therapist the duty to seek involuntary commitment of a client.

Clients Who Live Alone

A client who lives alone, without family or friends who can be identified, poses a unique concern for the therapist. The person may present a situation in which, after balancing the risk and reward, a therapist chooses to initiate and secure a mental health commitment order for the client. This action may be taken even though the therapist recognizes there is no legal duty to do more than provide mandated warnings or recommendations as to needed care and sources of care and other resources. As with other challenges in professional mental health practice, a thoroughly documented file can help reduce and manage risk. At a minimum, it provides some comforting backup when taking on a duty you are currently not obligated to assume.

If a therapist plans to recommend a treatment facility or to secure commitment of a client to a particular facility, the therapist is obligated to have that facility thoroughly checked out and to know the quality of mental health treatment available. Not only must the facility be of high quality, but it must also be able to serve this specific patient adequately. Negligent referral to another therapist or to a treatment facility can be the basis of a lawsuit and an award of damages. Know your referral sources. Do some detailed homework. Call the state board or appropriate state agencies and inquire about complaints and the licensing status of the facility. Consult with colleagues and document all findings.

Negligent referral to another therapist or to a treatment facility can be the basis of a lawsuit and an award of damages.

Answers to Frequently Asked Questions about:

Dementias

Commitment

Timing

Testimony

? *Question*

An elderly client was brought to me by her worried family members. The client was deteriorating on a monthly basis and, in my opinion, would require either voluntary or involuntary commitment or guardianship within a short time. The family members asked what they might do to prepare for this eventuality.

! *Answer*

Whether voluntary or involuntary commitment should be the case or best alternative, there are certain preparatory activities. Many are coordinated with the lawyer and others with the accountant, banker, insurance expert, and estate or financial planner. In summary:

- Make sure the will and estate plan are updated.
- Have a current list of all assets and liabilities. Some properties might have to be sold, repaired, or handled differently now that the active person can no longer control the work personally.
- Inventory the legal documents: durable powers of attorney, durable powers of attorney for health care, right to die a natural death, living will.
- Prepare for a guardianship if that is a better option.
- Consult with the lawyer, banker, insurance expert, financial planner, accountant, and all those concerned who affect or control the client. Secure their input so there is no contest as actions are gradually taken.
- Document carefully the mental status on a regular basis, so that if you ever have to testify concerning competence, you are prepared and professional. Make sure your clinical notes or progress case notes are always up-to-date and current.
- Emphasize the importance of a lawyer at this point because certain documents can be executed only when the individual is competent to sign the instrument.
- Handle only the mental health of the client. Let the other professionals do the rest.

♀ *Additional Thoughts*

- Dementias are gradual. But they are reasonably medically predictable. It is a wise family who, recognizing the future problem, prepares for it. A good resource is Chapter 10 in *Dementias, Diagnosis, Treatment and Research*, third edition, edited by M. F. Weiner and A. M. Lipton (Arlington, VA: American Psychiatric Publishing, 2003).
- If you refer to a facility, make sure *this* facility can care for *this* patient/client. You don't want to make a negligent referral.

Legal Lightbulb

- All states have legislatively advanced the protection and rights of mentally ill persons, and protection and advocacy systems are in place.

- Contact a lawyer and learn about the commitment process and laws in your jurisdiction. Know where the burden of proof rests and what findings a court must make before ordering commitment.

- As a first effort, try to get the client to self-commit to inpatient care.

- If the contact is authorized by the client, involve family members and urge them to pursue involuntary commitment.

- Document all your recommendations, findings, and observations. When seeking or assisting in involuntary commitment, your clinical record should leave no doubt as to the reasonableness of your conclusion that the client, or another person, is in *imminent physical danger*.

- Consult early and often with colleagues if you are unsure about a client's condition or about what action you should take. Document each consultation. The right to consult with colleagues should be in the initial intake form.

- Keep a current list of referral sources, individual mental health professionals, and reputable mental health facilities. Contact licensing boards, state agencies, and colleagues and document your inquiries and findings. Recommend only excellent-quality care providers.

- Make sure every person or entity to whom you make a referral has adequate, current, and appropriate mental health liability (malpractice) insurance.

- You may have no legal duty to directly seek commitment of a client. However, there may be a duty to warn in your jurisdiction. There also may be a duty to refer a client to the best available source of care if you cannot provide it. Check your local statutes concerning commitment.

- If circumstances and conscience compel you to directly seek involuntary commitment of a client, do so only if you are sure it is absolutely necessary to protect the client or another party. Get competent legal and professional mental health advice before seeking involuntary commitment.

- Act gingerly and remember, the deteriorating client today can rebound to-morrow and be in remission. He or she might want to undo everything. Have in your possession a copy of the health care power of attorney giving you the authority to treat the elderly client.
- If there is a danger to self and/or others, make sure documentation appears in the file.
- Voluntary commitment is preferred because the client initiates the action or at least acquiesces to it.
- Involuntary commitment is a judicial process. Become familiar with this process before entering into the judicial system.

23

Threats of Violence

Mark, a junior varsity star athlete, was scheduled to meet with his school counselor to discuss possible college opportunities. But instead of discussing college options, Mark was enraged by a minor confrontation he had had with his general manager at his workplace the previous day. He was absolutely furious with her and told his counselor he was going to "blow her away." The general manager, who had already dismissed the confrontation from her mind, did not know of Mark's anger and was unaware of any possible danger.

~

Beth, in the midst of a hotly and bitterly contested divorce, met with her therapist frequently and displayed inordinate and inappropriate anger toward her lawyer. In each session, she became irate over what she considered her lawyer's incompetence and lack of understanding. She complained, with ever increasing hostility, that her lawyer might cause her to lose her children in the ongoing custody fight. In one conversation with her therapist, Beth was so agitated and angry, she blurted out she would do "something" to her lawyer if she did not gain custody. Her lawyer, aware of the tension but not realizing the depth of Beth's hostility toward him, continued representation in the case, with no change of approach or strategy.

~

What should the counselor and the therapist do—notify the general manager and the lawyer? Should the lawyer and the general manager dismiss the verbal threats as part of the normal risk of their job or take serious precautions?

Determining whether an upset person is potentially dangerous is a clinical quagmire, and what to do about it is a complex dilemma that presents a real challenge in the area of clinical judgment. Unfortunately, there is no clear-cut method for evaluating verbal threats, but there are guidelines.

A serious threat is not to be taken lightly, without complete documentation explaining why the threat has been discounted. Correct treatment for a client who is belligerent or who threatens violence is not the aim of this chapter. The purpose here is to encourage every mental health professional to take even the slightest threat seriously.

A serious threat is not to be taken lightly, without complete documentation explaining why the threat has been discounted.

As a precaution, check your local statute. Some statutes (and related case law) indicate that a therapist can warn an identifiable intended victim. Other statutes (and case law) indicate that the therapist *may* call only police or medical authorities. In some states, laws are not definitive, and the legal future of the duty to warn is yet to be determined. Local statutes (and case law) are supplemented by rules of licensing boards, which often contain conflicting requirements, rights, and duties when a client or identifiable potential victim is threatened (i.e., there is danger to self or others). Typically, the rules state that the therapist shall use "reasonable steps and procedures" to prevent harm.

The HIPAA Privacy Rule (see Chapter 38) allows for disclosure of protected health information, *consistent with applicable law and standards of ethical conduct,* to prevent or lessen a serious and imminent threat to the health or safety of a person or the public. Disclosure under these circumstances can be made to person(s) reasonably able to prevent or lessen the threat, including the target of the threat. It is important to remember that this federal rule does not preempt existing state law in this area but gives additional support for a therapist's ability to notify any person in a position to prevent harm to the client or the public, including the identified victim, if permitted to do so pursuant to state law.

Duty to Warn

The duty to warn potential victims of a possible attack or homicide so they can take steps to protect themselves or the duty to warn family members that a client has threatened suicide remains one of the developing areas of law and varies from state to state. Here are some conflicting examples from different jurisdictions:

- In one, there is an affirmative duty to warn an identifiable potential victim of a plausible or threatened homicide.
- In another, there is no duty to notify anyone. Therapy is not such a science that the danger to self or others is so clear-cut as to impose a duty on the therapist to recognize potential homicide or suicide and then to warn the victim (homicide) or the family (suicide).
- In another, a professional *may* disclose confidential information only to medical or law enforcement personnel if the professional determines that there is a probability of imminent physical injury by the client to the client or to others or that there is a probability of immediate mental or emotional injury to the client.
- In another, when the therapist feels the client presents a danger to self or others, the therapist shall take "reasonable steps" to prevent the anticipated harm. (This is the wording in the guidelines of most ethical canons.)

Some state statutes imply that because a therapist can rarely determine, with a reasonable degree of certainty, whether a client is a danger to self or others, there is no duty to warn family, friends, or potential victims. Whatever is done must be documented thoroughly to protect the therapist.

When danger to self or others becomes part of the therapeutic facts, a warning signal should appear. Doing nothing is not acceptable; it is actually acting by inaction. The therapist must make an immediate investigation to determine the best course of action. Several sources of information should be contacted:

1. A lawyer.
2. The malpractice insurance carrier. Give notice of a potential homicide or suicide and ask for information concerning the problem. (An insurer would rather prevent a lawsuit than defend one, even successfully.)
3. The licensing board. Ask whether a knowledgeable person on staff or a competent staff attorney is available to share information. Some boards are very helpful and offer the latest law, the current board rules, and suggestions concerning the best solution to the problem. Other boards just bounce the problem back to the therapist. They declare the problem "legal in nature" and say a lawyer must be consulted.
4. A colleague who is knowledgeable in therapeutic ethics or a professor who teaches such a course at a local university.

Wording on the Intake Form

State law and the HIPAA Privacy Rule require the therapist to notify each client concerning the limits of confidentiality.

Review your intake and consent form before any incident happens. Most confidentiality statutes provide that the client can *waive confidentiality in writing.* State law and the HIPAA Privacy Rule require therapists to notify each client concerning the limits of confidentiality. These limits apply if the state requires the therapist to warn potential victims of harm or to notify families in the event of a potential suicide. On the intake form, the client should authorize the therapist in advance to breach confidentiality if there is a reasonable danger to self or others and if there is a possible way to protect the life of the client or some other person who is assumed to be in danger. The therapist customarily uses the same form when releasing any information to a third party.

The therapist has some protection if, on the intake and consent form, there is a specific, written waiver of confidentiality when the client or another person is in danger. A defensive intake form provides that if, in the therapist's opinion, the client presents an imminent danger to self or others, the therapist may breach confidentiality by notifying persons who, in the therapist's opinion, might be in a position to prevent the harm. Confidential information is released only when the client waives the right to privacy in writing. The therapist is then permitted to share information with third parties.

A waiver contained in the intake and consent form, which is signed when therapy commences, does not allow the therapist to share information inappropriately, but it does grant permission to breach confidentiality when danger to self or others is a reasonable therapeutic possibility, and then only on a "need to know" basis.

The Homicide or Suicide Scenario

Kathy had been seeing a therapist for about six months. Accurate records were maintained for each session in accordance with the legal and ethical guidelines of the profession. They were completed and up-to-date. Suddenly, Kathy committed suicide. Her family demanded all the records and, as part of the litigation, desired a deposition by the therapist, complete with a subpoena duces tecum (in person, with all the case records).

A subpoena, in these circumstances, is the nightmare of every therapist. Review the potential allegations that might be filed in the complaint or the petition for damages. Each of these as yet unproven allegations is filed in court papers, made a part of the public record, and accessible to reporters, the licensing board, or any curious citizen. Charges might include:

- Deficient or negligent diagnosis, assessment, or evaluation.
- Deficient or negligent treatment, history or file review, or prognosis.
- Negligent deviation from accepted standards.
- Failure to formulate a comprehensive and interdisciplinary treatment plan.
- Failure to have the client undergo a physical examination.
- Failure or inappropriate reluctance to refer for further treatment or for psychotropic medication.
- Exceeding personal level of competence.

These allegations will be made, with some modification, in most malpractice suits when a suicide or homicide has occurred and a therapist is named as a defendant. Therapists, armed with the knowledge of what can go wrong, have the opportunity to protect against the problem by documenting, during therapy, that none of the allegations is true. These are the recommended practices in dealing with every client:

Therapists, armed with the knowledge of what can go wrong, have the opportunity to protect against the problem by documenting during therapy.

- Thoroughly document every diagnosis, assessment, or evaluation.
- Document the reason for a treatment, review the file often, and change the treatment plan and prognosis (when indicated) by updating your evaluations and assessments.

- If a past therapeutic history is available, review it. Insights concerning the client may have been uncovered and recorded by previous therapists.
- When deviating from accepted or common standards, document (as substantiation for the deviation) the recommendation of some legitimate mental health authority to depart from common treatment modalities.
- Consult with other professionals and document the consultations. Other therapists, rehabilitation counselors, lawyers, physicians, and other specialists can be very helpful.
- Adopt the sensible procedure of requesting that the client take a full physical exam to rule out physical illnesses that can be treated with medication or the need for a prosthesis such as a hearing aid.

Homicide or Suicide: The Aftermath

At the first inkling of the suicide of a client or at the first notice that a client has hurt another person (or self) or has killed someone, the therapist should call his or her malpractice insurance carrier.

At the first inkling of the suicide of a client or at the first notice that a client has hurt another person (or self) or has killed someone, the therapist should call his or her malpractice insurance carrier. Every therapist in private or public practice has some exposure to a malpractice suit, and the best self-protection is a substantial malpractice policy, which can be obtained privately or through a national organization at reasonable cost. Malpractice insurance carriers have risk management experts who can guide a therapist through the steps suitable for self-protection. Keep in mind that each policy contains directions in the event an actual or perceived loss occurs, and, to remain protected under the policy, the terms of the policy must be scrupulously honored.

This is also the time to consult with a private attorney who is knowledgeable in mental health law. Generally, the interests of the malpractice insurance carrier and the therapist are identical, but, in some cases, especially if the claim exceeds a policy's limits, their interests may conflict. Collect all the client records and make copies for the lawyer, the insurance carrier, and, perhaps, a learned colleague. Review the paperwork and all client documentation. Should there be litigation, the clinical record will be the first item reviewed. Study the record, make any corrections in the appropriate manner (see Chapter 3), and be sure the file is ready for review by third parties, if necessary.

Advisable Actions

1. Make sure clinical notes and records are current and reflect recognition of all presenting problems via a diagnosis, a treatment plan, and a prognosis.
2. Make a referral when a problem exceeds your level of competence. Recommend a physical exam where warranted, and note the recommendation in

the record. Coordinate with other health care providers as an interdisciplinary team. Note when a client fails or refuses to follow your suggestions, and quote the reason the client gives for such failure or refusal. Has the client assumed a risk of any damage by failing or refusing to follow legitimate suggestions such as attending certain classes, obtaining a physical exam, or other recommended helpful actions?

3. Indicate in the records that the facts and notes support the treatment plan and are not recorded for insurance reimbursement purposes.

4. Follow all protocols where an agency, entity, organization, or school has published procedures concerning the danger to self or others. Document your compliance.

5. Consult with a colleague(s) whenever a suicide or homicide is a possibility. Make sure no preventive stone is left unturned.

6. If a suicide or homicide occurs, consult at once with your malpractice insurance carrier. Say and do nothing unless the insurer advises you to do so. A slip at this time might waive the protection offered by the insurance policy.

7. Take every threat of suicide seriously, even if it is constant and repetitious. If possible and authorized, involve family members. Have a waiver of confidentiality in the intake and consent form in the event of a threat of harm to self or others.

8. Establish office protocols for suicide or violence prevention.

When danger to self or others is a possibility, notify the police if permitted in your jurisdiction. Calls to 911 are recorded, providing good evidence that a preventive call was made. A report on the call must be entered in the clinical record.

Should the problem of homicide or suicide arise, review the latest state mental health code and the latest ethical canons of your licensing board. Notify your malpractice insurance carrier and your lawyer. Homicide and suicide are serious and tragic events, and input from all sources is critical to a sensible assessment of the problem and future decision making.

An angry client who makes threatening remarks should be taken seriously at all times. The client may mean it. Although the duty to warn cases and statutes vary from state to state, the risk of having a possible suicidal or homicidal client is significant enough to take the necessary precautions. Violent threats of homicide or suicide expose the therapist to many issues, including malpractice, ethical complaints, pecuniary damages, public scrutiny, and/or queries of competency.

An angry client who makes threatening remarks should be taken seriously at all times.

The guidelines in this chapter will be helpful when the unthinkable occurs. A therapist can't look for a rule of thumb or a set of procedures to be followed in all cases, but case-by-case awareness will minimize risk.

Answers to Frequently Asked Questions about:

Duty to warn

❓ Question

I live in Maryland. I know there have been some recent developments surrounding duty to warn identifiable nonclient possible victims of potential danger posed by a client. Can you review the law for me? One of my current clients implied a threat to a former girlfriend, which was handled as part of the therapy, but I am concerned in case a future client comes into the office, angry, armed, and with a plan and the stated intention of harming another person or perhaps committing suicide. What are some options and where do I go to keep current concerning the status of the law in my state?

❗ Answer

The duty to warn issue is handled differently from state to state. The federal HIPAA Privacy Rule allows a therapist to warn the victim if the applicable law in the therapist's location of practice permits such a warning. We are not specifically aware of the law in each state although every professional liability carrier has this information available in its legal department. It is an evolving area of law. Check with an attorney in your state, your state licensing board, or your malpractice insurance carrier for the particulars. In addition, check with your malpractice carrier's legal staff and review your state licensing law for references to clients who are a danger to self or others. Every ethics seminar in every state includes this ethics component. Duty to warn of potential violence to self or others will always be covered.

💡 Additional Thoughts

- Legislatures and case decisions constantly affect the duty to warn obligation.
- HIPAA's Privacy Rule permits a therapist to warn identifiable third parties or any person in a position to prevent or lessen harm if state law permits the therapist to do so.
- Some states impose a duty to warn identifiable third parties that they are in danger or there is civil liability.
- Other states impose no duty at all. The clinician can hear about a threat, believe it is realistic and possible, and *do absolutely nothing except, perhaps, recommend an anger management course.*
- Other states have statutes that indicate you *may* contact medical or law enforcement personnel.

Legal Lightbulb

- States have statutes or ethical canons or case precedents that control the duty to warn intended victims of danger or to warn others about a client's own safety. Check the current state requirements each time there is a potential problem.

- There is no definitive legal yardstick indicating exactly when a therapist has a duty to warn of potential homicide or suicide.

- Whether the therapist elects to warn or to not warn, clinical notes should document the rationale for the decision.

- A threat to commit violence in the future is not always an indication that violence will occur.

- Every graduate therapist knows the *Tarasoff* case,* a California decision with duty to warn implications. Is *Tarasoff* the law in your jurisdiction? Fifty independent determinations have to be made—one in each state—and even then, nothing will be really known until the first state supreme court case is decided in each jurisdiction. There is no federal case.

- Call the state chapter of your professional organization. Most national organizations have taken a stand on the duty to warn situation, but the positions change occasionally. Get a current reading.

- Ethical canons and guidelines, as well as published materials, are admissible evidence to show the minimum standards of conduct required by therapists' duty to warn.

- In almost every homicide or suicide case, a lawyer is consulted to determine therapeutic liability.

- Take threats seriously. If you hear of a client homicide or suicide, take immediate steps toward damage control.

- Document every potentially harmful comment and how it was handled.

---

* *Tarasoff v. Regents of the University of California,* 551 P.2d 334 (Cal. 1976).

- Other states have case law that indicates that if confidentiality is breached and the therapist warns a third person, the therapist who breaches confidentiality without a waiver from the client may be liable for damages.
- National and state organizations as well as many licensing boards have promulgated rules and regulations that state that the professional should take *reasonable precautions* to see that no harm comes to either a client or a third party.
- The right to call the potential identifiable victim and authorizing the clinician to call family members or *designated others* in the event of a potential suicide may be included in your intake and consent form (a waiver of confidentiality authorizing the therapist to call or warn the victim). *The greatest, most common exception to confidentiality is an express, written waiver of confidentiality.*
- When in doubt or when a crises occurs, follow the recommended route:
  —Call a lawyer familiar with the rules and regulations.
  —Call the professional liability (malpractice insurance) carrier.
  —Call the state licensing board.
  —Make sure the file is documented in all respects.
  —Consult with a learned colleague.
  —Pray!
  —Let us know if your prayers were answered.

SECTION SIX

PRACTICE MODELS

24

Groups

The prospects for the average mental health practitioner in today's competitive and cost-containment environment are threefold:

1. Continue in solo practice with a shrinking client base.
2. Become a contract panel provider and accept increasingly reduced fees for services.
3. Become entrepreneurial by enlisting the support of a group of other like-minded professionals and becoming a "Group without Walls."

Too often, solo practitioners settle for an expense-sharing or office-sharing arrangement. They share office space, employees, supplies, billing, and scheduling. They may even share publicity, public speaking engagements, advertising, stationery, business cards, and other common expenses. Such arrangements have always been attractive for key reasons—the ability to maintain individual practices, reduce overhead, and gain vacation and emergency coverage and cross referrals of clients and patients.

The principal disadvantages in today's mental health care market are the inability to contract independently for group managed care and the potential for joint liability if clients perceive the suitemates as partners. In addition, the members may face antitrust issues if they implement a common fee structure.

Group without Walls

An attractive and increasingly popular way to eliminate these disadvantages is by formalizing a Group without Walls—a single legal entity, usually a professional corporation (PC), in which participants share a common license; for example, all members are licensed professional counselors (LPCs). If the group consists of a mix of LPCs, social workers, and psychologists, a general business corporation or partnership can be established. This model differs

When a group creates a legal entity, each member may continue to maintain his or her individual practice at a different location.

from a preferred provider organization (PPO), which is usually established by a single investor corporation or group of corporations rather than a group of individual practitioners.

When a group creates a legal entity, each member may continue to maintain his or her individual practice at a different location. By combining specialties and offering a broad range of services of multiple providers at different locations, the group is more attractive to employers, hospitals, health maintenance organizations (HMOs), insurers, and payers. Operating as a single entity, the members are in a better position to negotiate financially rewarding managed care contracts.

The legal entity created by the group acts as a centralized vehicle for contracting, billing, purchasing, scheduling, marketing, and quality assurance. The entity is responsible for developing the practice standards, quality controls, and outcome studies that are critical when applying for managed care contracts.

The greater the degree of integration, the lower the potential for antitrust violations.

However, the concept of multiple independently operated offices raises price-fixing issues. It is crucial to retain the services of an attorney and an accountant who have experience with issues faced by the health professions to avoid potential antitrust and federal regulation violations and typical management issues. The group must resolve compensation issues, conflicts between participants, the potential for inefficiency, and the loss of economies of scale due to multiple locations. Generally, the greater the degree of integration, the lower the potential for antitrust violations.

Alternative Group Arrangements

Some groups have preferred complete integration, with all sites owned and operated by the group and all revenues and expenses flowing through the common legal entity. Others, preferring partial integration, have followed the independent practice association (IPA) model, in which participants maintain independent practices and compete against one another for all non-IPA business. The group shares the risk associated with (1) the managed care contracts negotiated by the IPA and (2) the individual participants who have entered into provider agreements with the IPA. (A complete set of bylaws for an IPA is reproduced in Appendix A.)

Providers in independent practices are prohibited from establishing a common fee schedule.

Partially integrated groups are generally not as efficient as fully integrated entities; the expense sharing is not as complete, and they face antitrust issues. They can negotiate capitated rates and fees-for-service rates with the payer, but cannot maintain a common fee schedule for discounted fee-for-service work among the participants. In theory, the IPA must negotiate the fee that will be paid to each provider for services to enrollees under the managed care contract. The IPA profits when providers are paid less than the amount the IPA will receive from the payer. Providers in independent practices are prohibited from establishing a common fee schedule. This practice, called *price fixing*, is illegal.

Pros and Cons

Before deciding on whether to participate in a group or a Group without Walls, a practitioner should answer these questions:

- Who are the other participants? Can I trust them? Are they competent and ethical practitioners? Can we work together? Are they solvent?
- What are my objectives? Do they align with those of the other participants?
- Does the group as a whole have enough management experience and business acumen to successfully operate the entity and negotiate favorable contracts?
- Do I want to completely integrate my practice with the group, or do I want to maintain an independent practice and share only clients, revenues, and losses flowing from the managed care contracts the group negotiates?
- Am I willing to devote, each week, the extra hours necessary to the successful operation of the group entity? (Often, individual practitioners lose sight of the time necessary to manage, control, and operate a group. Meetings can drive some practitioners nuts.)
- What is the condition of my practice? Am I comfortable with my income and workload, and should I risk capital and independence for participation in a group entity?
- How far can I peek into the future of the "business" of providing mental health services?
- Does everyone understand that the practice of mental health is also a business and has to be run and handled as such and that it must acquire clients, treat clients, and also manage income and expenses in a businesslike, efficient, and cost-effective manner?
- Will the group be able to raise enough capital for start-up? Prudent capitalization requires sufficient capital to meet costs for the first two, or perhaps three, years.
- Am I prepared to share management and decision-making authority?
- Am I willing to abide by decisions made by others when they affect my income and my future?

Answers to Frequently Asked Questions about:

Marketing

Liability in associations

Collective liabilities

? Question

I am working with several licensed colleagues in full-time private practice to form a marketing guild. We will advertise through print media and have a web site with published articles and biographies of each of us. We are not a partnership and don't share office space, income, expenses, and so on, except for the expense of advertising as stated here. What precautions does the guild need to take to protect itself from liability exposure? Is a disclaimer enough, or do we need to form a legal partnership for this purpose?

! Answer

To protect yourself from liability claims for the negligent acts of your guild mates, be sure that all promotional materials identify each of you *as independent health care practitioners* **not associated** in any partnership, corporation, or other entity or with any other practitioner(s). This same message should again be *delivered by each of you to each client* at his or her first therapy session before therapy begins. It is important to *never give even the appearance* of an association through a partnership, corporation, or other entity. Include the disclaimer mentioned in the question.

There are legal theories often referred to as "ostensible partnership or agency" that have been asserted successfully against persons who were careless in how they represented themselves to clients and the general public. Although we do not know what you have in writing to date, you are probably collectively responsible for the costs of advertising, including the web site, in addition to common legal and accounting fees and/or other collective purchases, if any.

Consultation with a local business, corporate, or entity attorney on this issue would be a good idea.

♀ Additional Thoughts

- Each intake or consent to treatment form should clearly state that you are *sole or independent practitioners (independent contractors)*—not partners, corporate members, or shareholders and not associated in practice with one another.
- Each client is to look *only to his or her own personal therapist* for redress should any problem occur. A local attorney can draft the correct language. The client should sign this document on or before the commencement of treatment. Should any change occur, a new document should be signed.
- *Each practitioner should have professional liability insurance* (malpractice insurance policy), and the carrier or insurer should be aware of the guild concept and see that you are all protected. The guild concept may be unique in some

jurisdictions. Make sure it applies where you practice and have it cleared with the licensing board.

- Normally, the insured (you) are not protected should another person perform an improper or negligent act and you are somehow named as a codefendant in a suit. The usual professional liability insurance policy covers and protects only the named insured for the named risks. There are numerous exclusions.

- After you have roughed out the interprofessional contract and the consent to treatment form (also a contract), run it by a local lawyer for review. Good practice is to have a lawyer review the contract among the guild members as well as the clinician-client contract.

- Have your lawyer determine if the guild approach is the proper choice for what you have in mind. Is there a better local approach? Could a guild approach in your state indicate some collective liability?

- Marketing collectively is a cost-effective approach as long as it does not give the impression that the providers are intertwined legally. Remember, in the event of litigation, lawyers take a shotgun approach and sue everyone they can attach to liability. Later, they eliminate those who are not liable or able to respond in damages. Should the case result in a trial, generally only those liable and with deep pockets remain in the litigation.

- If there are advertising literature, common advertisements, plaques on walls, signs in the foyer or in front of a building, yellow page advertising, announcements of business openings, posters, letterheads, a web site, cards, or other publications, run them by your lawyer. Make sure there is no collective liability language in the pamphlets. Remember . . . all are independent contractors, practicing independently and not associated with one another in the professional practice.

The Professional Corporation

After a group has decided to establish a legal entity to promote managed care contracting, the participants must select the most effective type of entity to form. (Subsequent chapters in this section describe the various entities.) As previously stated, the most common entity is the professional or general business corporation. Once the articles of incorporation have been approved by the state and the corporation's charter is issued (both steps are the responsibility of the corporate attorney), careful thought must be given to day-to-day management and operation of the entity. This phase begins with the drafting and adoption of the corporation's bylaws—the rules by which the corporation must operate.

A common method of operation uses an executive committee, of which all participants are members. Regular meetings are usually scheduled. Meetings may be more frequent during the initial start-up period and become less frequent as the entity becomes established. Contracts can be reviewed, adopted, rejected, or modified at these meetings. Duties can be delegated and offices rotated.

Credentialing should be a process in which all participants are involved. The bylaws can provide for the establishment of a credentialing committee, of which all participants are members.

The company bylaws are the most critical document prepared during an entity's formation. They should be reviewed carefully and must be clearly understood by all participants in the group. Considerable time and money can be saved if the participants review and consider the bylaws before visiting with an agreed-on attorney. If each issue has to be discussed and decided with an attorney present, the hourly charges will be very high. (*Lawyers charge $200+ per hour.* It adds up quickly. The money you save can be critical and substantial.) The final draft of all legal instruments must be prepared by an attorney, who will coordinate business, legal, and professional requirements into the final legal vehicle.

Many groups flounder under the weight of disputes over (1) unexpected or higher than anticipated costs and expenses and (2) real or perceived inequitable workload distribution. It might be prudent for the entity to consider leasing equipment for greater flexibility and cost savings in light of the fast pace at which technology is advancing. Tasks requiring outsourcing, such as marketing and utilization review could also lead to time savings, flexibility, and long-run cost savings.

Internal conflicts can usually be avoided by thoughtful communication and planning. An inherent risk in any group activity, however, is an unpleasant association with people who prove to be problematic because of disposition, temperament, character, and ability. The entity will be only as strong or as successful as the people behind it, so choose fellow participants well. At a minimum, check references, community reputations, and professional histories. Check with all available former associates. Then check to determine whether there is malpractice insurance in force and no pending complaints before the licensing board.

Negotiating a managed care contract with a health plan or an employer is almost an impossibility for a solo practitioner.

Choose advisors well, also. As with any legal entity, it is imperative to obtain competent legal advice on structuring and operating the company and on statutory and regulatory issues. Given the right participants and the right structure, there can be greater success in numbers and participants than you might achieve as a solo practitioner. One thing is certain: Negotiating a managed care contract with a health plan or an employer is almost an impossibility for a solo practitioner.

Legal Lightbulb

- To be a player in the game for managed care contracts, group formation is necessary.

- Improperly established groups can lead to liability for negligence, faulty contracts, and antitrust and regulatory violations.

- The group will be only as strong and as successful as the people who comprise the group.

- Competent legal advice should be obtained by each participant before formation and by the group upon formation.

- The articles of incorporation, bylaws, contracts (leases, purchase documents, debt instruments), and other documents are all legally enforceable instruments. They are to be drafted by a professional, but not signed without careful review and detailed explanation as needed.

- The sample bylaws in Appendix A are only a sample and are not to be copied or used verbatim. They will be most helpful if used as an agenda for discussion before consulting with the lawyer who will draft the final documents.

25

Partnerships

Kevin and Don, two marginally successful mental health professionals practicing in the same building, decided to combine their practices and talents and form a partnership. They agreed to cosign a lease for new space in the same building where they had maintained their individual practices for several years. They agreed to share all profits and losses fifty-fifty, and they even created a new name: "The Healing Behavioral Health Center." However, they never got around to putting together a written partnership agreement. Twelve months later, in the midst of an afternoon of bickering over teaching income, vacation time, and disproportionate revenue generation, Kevin was served with a citation in connection with a lawsuit filed against him by an unhappy client with whom he had had an inappropriate sexual relationship. Don was stunned. He immediately went to his lawyer and asked if it was too late to back out of a verbally agreed on partnership. Or was he also liable?

For decades, a partnership has been the most common and preferred business entity for two or more professionals. There is presumed safety in numbers, and it is comforting to have someone with whom to share risks and losses and who can cover a practice when an illness occurs or a well-deserved vacation takes place.

Each partner in a partnership must know all his or her rights and obligations.

When properly conceived, drafted with the appropriate and necessary detail, signed, and implemented, the traditional partnership is a sensible and useful legal entity. When improperly conceived and structured or when too casual or imprecise, a partnership can be fraught with peril. Each partner in a partnership must know all his or her rights and obligations.

A Handshake Is Enough

A partnership is a basic legal entity that simply requires an agreement, which can be expressed or implied, between two or more persons, to carry on a business for profit. It does not require a formal, written partnership agreement. Two professionals, by their conduct and course of dealing, can create a partnership by implication. Many partnerships and individual business ventures began with a handshake and still are in existence today.

Once a partnership is established, each partner has a fiduciary duty to the partnership and has the right to use partnership property for conducting partnership business. Unless specifically negated in a partnership agreement, each partner has an equal right to participate in the management of the partnership, including the hiring, firing, and supervising of employees and staff.

The attraction of a partnership entity has always been the simplicity of its creation and operation. Partnerships have fewer legal requirements for their operation and management than corporations. There are usually no state filing fees for general partnerships. They have unlimited flexibility, and partners are free to structure compensation, allocate contributed assets and liabilities, and control management, ownership, operations, dissolution, and responsibilities any way they wish.

Partnerships, like sole proprietorships, result in only one level of taxation. All income and expenses flow through the partnership to individual partners in accordance with the percentages established in their partnership agreement. For federal tax filing, each partner would receive a K-1 form from the partnership, reflecting his or her share of partnership income and expenses. Partnerships are generally not subject to state franchise taxes.

Partnerships have fewer legal requirements for their operation and management than corporations.

Disadvantages of Partnerships

As with any entity, there are disadvantages to partnerships, as Don found out when he finally sought legal advice concerning his partnership with Kevin. Partnerships feature shared responsibility and authority, and, unless limited by the partnership agreement, each partner has an equal voice in the management of and liability for the partnership.

In a general partnership, each partner has joint and several liability for the obligations of the partnership and for each partner's malpractice, as well as for negligent acts of agents, servants, employees, and staff members. When Kevin was sued for inappropriate acts with a client, Don could be held personally liable, as Kevin's partner. By registering the partnership as a limited liability partnership under appropriate state law, Don could have avoided personal liability for the negligent acts of the other partner (Kevin) or of representatives of the partnership, unless he was directly involved in the activity or had notice of the wrongful activity at the time of the occurrence.

In one case, an intern was under the supervision of a licensed therapist. The intern, unknown to the supervisor, had carried on an inappropriate sexual relationship with two clients. The supervisor's clinical notes did not reflect that the subject of sexual relationships was ever discussed, although the intern did pass an offhand remark that each of his clients was very "sexy" and he had fantasized about them at different times.

The supervisor was disciplined by the licensing board and liable in a malpractice suit. Had the supervisor been a partner, and had the partner acted as the intern did, there would have been partnership liability and partnership responsibility.

Limited Liability Partnerships

States allow partnerships to register as limited liability partnerships by filing an application with the Secretary of State.

Generally, states allow partnerships to register as limited liability partnerships by filing an application with the Secretary of State. A partnership is required to carry a minimum amount of liability insurance or provide minimum funds designated and segregated for the satisfaction of judgments against the partnership. Because these insurance or fund requirements are generally much lower than policy limits on the average malpractice insurance policy carried by mental health professionals, they are not a prohibitive financial burden when securing limited liability registration. A partnership is also required to include the phrase "registered limited liability partnership" or the initials "LLP" in the partnership name.

Partnership laws vary from state to state. A therapist contemplating a partnership entity should seek competent legal advice well before any agreement is reached or action is taken.

Many diverse factors need to be weighed carefully before entering a partnership agreement, but, with careful consideration and good legal advice, a partnership agreement can be crafted to eliminate most problems before they occur. A brainstorming session to discuss possible areas of conflict is always helpful. Remember, never enter into a partnership agreement that is not well thought out, reduced to writing, reviewed by a lawyer and an accountant, and signed by each partner.

An example of an application for registration of a limited liability partnership is shown in this chapter. The format in your jurisdiction will vary. Familiarize yourself with the basic content; then take your comparable data to a competent attorney for review, preparation, and filing.

An example of a complete partnership agreement appears as Appendix B.

Answers to Frequently Asked Questions about:

Vacation

Checking voice mail

Relief but not referral

Appropriate referrals while on vacation—partner's coverage

Issues of abandonment

Confidentiality

❓ Question

I am planning a first vacation from my (fledgling) solo private practice and have several questions about coverage for patients/clients in case of urgent/emergency situations . . . or, perhaps, in case a client is upset and just wants to "visit" for reasons of his or her own. I have considered a partnership for situations such as this, but can never seem to find the workable mix of practice, person, and therapeutic philosophy. My questions are:

1. *Is it okay for me not to check my voice mail at all while I'm gone, as long as I've made appropriate arrangements for coverage?*
2. *I'm weighing giving patients the name and phone number of an equally licensed colleague who will provide coverage versus giving them the number of a 24-hour mental health crisis hotline. On the one hand, the colleague is known by my patients to have some (presumably reassuring) connection to me and is someone I know and trust. Yet he is not available to the same extent that a 24-hour hotline would be. Do you have any thoughts on the relative merit of one option versus the other?*
3. *Should I actively seek a partner? Is that a problem or a problem solver?*

❗ Answer

Revise your phone's recorded message to alert clients about your unavailability, provide them with the number of your colleague who can be reached during normal business hours, and the number of the 24-hour mental health crisis hotline for emergencies when the colleague is unavailable; that is, give all callers both numbers. Include the date of your departure and the date of your return to the office. You may also wish to provide this information in writing to your active clients before departure.

Have a great time, but don't consider a rush partnership just to have vacation coverage. Most partnerships are formed by friends, professional colleagues, associates, or others who know each other either in person or by reputation and who are drawn together by common financial and professional interests. Organizing a partnership is not a hasty process. Take your time. Partnerships usually are intended to last a long time.

💡 Additional Thoughts

- Make sure the relieving colleague has at least the same or greater technical credentials as you have. Make sure he explains that the treatment during your absence is temporary and you will resume consultations on your return.
- If you are making your files available to your colleague, have a waiver of confidentiality form signed by the client before you depart on your vacation so the colleague has access to the files.

Legal Lightbulb

- **Liability:** Limit liability by registering as a limited liability partnership.

- **The number of partners:** Having just two partners almost always guarantees deadlock when a genuine disagreement occurs. Two competent individuals can reasonably disagree with each other, but some disputes can be profound (i.e., each can feel deeply about his or her point of view).

- **Ownership percentages:** When deciding income and expense allocations, what income should be considered partnership income as opposed to separate income of each partner (book royalties, honoraria, lecture fees, teaching income)?

- **Partnership management:** Should the partners alternate titles and terms such as *managing partner*? What issues should be submitted for majority vote of the partners? All? Should the agreement provide for "alternative dispute resolution" methods such as arbitration, mediation, conciliation, and negotiation? Under whose auspices? How often, or seldom, should meetings be held?

- **Operational expenses:** Should a partner's right to obligate the partnership for operational expenses be limited? Should any expense in excess of $150 require approval of a majority of partners? If there is a monetary limit, what should the limit be?

- **Maintenance of client files and records:** How should the files be maintained, distributed, destroyed, or preserved when a partner withdraws from the partnership or if the partnership is dissolved by law, consent, death, or termination? Who is allowed access to the files and records? (Each partnership requires a comprehensive plan for disposition of a file if either the therapist or the client dies.)

- **Office hours:** How much time should each partner be expected to devote to the partnership?

- **Vacation days:** How many vacation and sick days should each partner be allowed?

- **Insurance policies:** How much insurance (life, major medical, income disability, malpractice, personal property) should the partnership carry for the partnership and for each partner?

Legal Lightbulb

(continued)

- **Signature authorization:** Should all partners have signatory authority on bank accounts, or should more than one signature be required for checks or withdrawals? Who should sign contracts with managed care or insurance companies, sign as lessors of equipment, distributors of tests, purveyors of personal property, or subcontractors?

- **Storage of records:** Where will financial records of the partnership be maintained, and what financial records will the partnership generate? Who will retain the CPA, lawyer, banker, insurance advisor, or other service providers, if appropriate?

- **Background check of partners:** Learn who your partners are. Call the licensing board and inquire about complaints or disciplinary actions. Require each potential partner to submit a credit report for review by the other potential partners. Consider mandating instant termination for any partner whose malpractice insurance is terminated or denied.

- **Legal counsel:** Secure your own independent legal advisor. Conflicting views and interests may exist among partners, and one lawyer cannot appropriately advise and represent each partner when conflicts arise.

- **Financial losses:** If there are financial losses, can each partner pay a fair share? For example, suppose a partner dies or the partnership terminates and the partnership has outstanding obligations, such as yellow page ads, telephone listings that require long-term payments, long-term insurance policies, utility expenses, leases, purchase agreements, or long- and short-term debt. Should each partner place a sum in escrow to ensure the fulfillment of partnership financial obligations?

- **Debt:** Can any partner guarantee the debt of any third party for any reason? Or is this a prohibited act?

- **Termination:** Detail the procedures for terminating the partnership for any reason.

Sample Form

APPLICATION FOR LIMITED LIABILITY PARTNERSHIP

The following named partnership applies to become a registered limited liability partnership pursuant to the Texas Uniform Partnership Act.

1. The name of the partnership is 3P Wellness Center, LLP.

2. The federal tax identification number of the partnership is 04-123568.

3. The street address of the principal office of the partnership in Texas is 4635 Main Street, Richardson, Texas 75064.

4. The number of partners in the partnership at the time the application is submitted is three.

5. The partnership engages in the following type of business: mental health counseling.

6. The undersigned partner has been authorized by a majority in interest of the partners in the partnership to execute this application.

   Signed this 30th day of February, 20__

3P Wellness Center, LLP

By: _____
James Hathaway, Managing Partner and Attorney-in-Fact, authorized to execute this application for a majority in interest of the partners

- If the client cannot afford the colleague or is on a sliding fee arrangement, make sure you have some additional community resources available and notify the client of these resources with names, addresses, and telephone numbers.
- Give clients as much notice as possible. Provide a quasi-termination interview and make sure the client is comfortable with your back-up clinician.
- When you return, check on each client and provide for the orderly transfer of the client back to you. Review any files handled by the colleague and verify client satisfaction.
- Review your intake and consent form. It should provide for your vacations and authorize, in writing and in advance, that the client understands you will take vacations and have a qualified colleague available for continuing treatment. Incidentally, your form should also provide for a plan in the event of your disability or death.
- If the relief therapist is in a partnership or shareholder in a professional corporation, make this information available to the client so that the client knows the nature of the relationship between you, your relief colleague, and the colleague's associates. On rare occasion, a colleague may be in an association with partners with whom the client is not comfortable, and that situation is not known to the treating therapist.
- A partnership is a special arrangement that ties people together for a long time. Be as careful with the people you choose as they were in selecting you as a potential partner.

26

Solo Practitioner: Incorporate or Not?

Henry James, Ph.D., a newly licensed psychologist, moved to a small community to enter private practice. He expected referrals from two local physicians and the local school district. He located a small commercial building in the central business area that was available for lease and was perfect for his needs. He anticipated hiring a part-time clerical person to help with billing, correspondence, filing, and scheduling. His brother-in-law, an in-house accountant for a small manufacturing company, advised him to incorporate right away. Should he?

The vast majority of mental health practitioners in private practice are solo practitioners who operate their practices as sole proprietorships. Operating out of one or more leased offices, a solo practitioner enjoys complete autonomy and is responsible for all decision making. The success of the practice rises and falls on his or her talents and efforts. Having a small support staff often allows for improved cohesiveness, loyalty, and congeniality in the workplace. The solo practitioner has absolute personal responsibility for compliance with all local, state, and federal regulatory requirements, as well as for his or her own acts, negligent or otherwise, and those of the support staff.

Advantages of a Solo Practice

- Complete **autonomy:** perfect for the self-reliant, independent practitioner.
- **Flexibility** on hours, working conditions, operational practices, services, and so on.
- **Easy to start:** can be owned and operated with no formal or burdensome structure.

- **Single layer of taxation:** all income and expenses reported on Schedule C of the federal income tax form.
- **Responsible only to** the licensing board; to national, state, and local organizations; and to persons with whom a contract exists.
- **Minimal or no start-up legal fees.**

Disadvantages of a Solo Practice

- **Personal liability:** All of the practitioner's nonexempt assets, personal or practice-related, are at risk for negligent or wrongful acts of the practitioner and staff members and are subject to both general and professional liability claims.
- **Complete financial responsibility:** No one else shares in the risk and losses or covers during downtime for illness or vacations. Liability for all signed contracts with suppliers of services or supplies.
- **Limited financial and professional resources:** All capital and income are dependent on one person.
- **Limited professional support:** The work week has longer hours, especially at night and on weekends, and the practitioner is on call all the time.
- **Limited staff support:** A small number of employees must fill a variety of roles.
- **Divided duties:** The practitioner handles business and management responsibilities as well as the practice of mental health. The *business* of a practice is as important as the *practice* of a practice.
- **Reduced competitiveness:** There is little possibility of securing major managed care contracts.
- **Limited cost sharing:** No scale economies for library, common waiting room, receptionist, if needed, stationery, and networking.
- **Limited expertise:** The practitioner's own competence in mental health limits the scope of the practice. There is no broad opportunity for different specializations.
- **Bragging rights:** A partner, joint venturer, or shareholder can praise others in the practice and steer business their way, while a solo practitioner finds it difficult to talk well about himself or herself.

A serious drawback to the sole practitioner model is the risk of personal liability for negligent or wrongful acts and contracts. Many mental health practitioners incorporate to protect themselves from malpractice claims. A common, but false, belief is that if a practitioner incorporates a practice and later is sued for malpractice, his or her personal assets will be protected from a successful litigant's reach.

Comparison with a Corporation

*A corporation does
not shield a
practitioner and
his or her personal
assets from a claim
of personal
negligence.*

A corporation does *not* shield a practitioner and his or her personal assets from a claim of personal negligence. A professional person is always personally liable for his or her own acts of negligence. If Dr. James negligently breaches a client's right to confidentiality and is sued, it does not matter whether he is an employee of a corporation that he may or may not own or whether he is associated with a corporation. He will be sued in his individual professional capacity and, if found to be negligent, will be individually liable for the damages assessed. His personal assets would then be at risk to satisfy the court judgment.

A corporation can shield a practitioner from liability for the negligent or wrongful acts of other employees of the corporation only if the mental health professional is free from personal negligence or wrongdoing. If a staff worker's negligent acts were committed in the course and scope of his or her employment, the corporate employer and the staff worker would be named as defendants in the lawsuit. When an incorporated small office is the defendant, however, it is unrealistic to think that the plaintiff's attorney will not assert a theory of negligence (i.e., failure to properly supervise or control) in an attempt to impose personal liability on the shareholder professional.

Dr. James was notified that his regular part-time office helper was involved in a motor vehicle accident and would be out for six weeks. Desperate for assistance, Dr. James called a local temporary-employment agency. The agency sent Shirley to Dr. James, but she arrived 45 minutes late. Dr. James had a full schedule that day and little time to acquaint Shirley with office procedures. Later in the day, Shirley took a break to use the restroom and left a client's file on the counter. While she was away from the front desk, a client's husband came in unannounced to discuss with Dr. James his concerns over his wife's depression. He noticed that the file on the counter was his wife's file. She had had an appointment earlier in the day with Dr. James. When she left, Dr. James gave Shirley the file and instructed her to put it in the file cabinet in the adjoining room and lock the cabinet. The husband opened the file and read several pages of notes before Shirley returned. The notes revealed that the wife had had a two-year affair with a coworker. The affair had ended a while back, but the wife was depressed and guilty over the episode. The husband confronted the wife and filed for divorce.

If a lawsuit is filed, Dr. James would face accusations of negligent supervision and training of Shirley concerning confidentiality because he did not personally ensure that the file would be secured from prying eyes. Even if Dr. James had incorporated his practice, that fact would not shield him from personal liability. His corporate and personal assets would be at risk. Professionals are always responsible for their own professional negligence. And failure to adequately train and supervise temporary employees is negligence. The full schedule of the practice and staff errors are not legal excuses.

By incorporating, a therapist could create the possibility of contracting for services, space, loans, and other practice needs in the corporate name. When a legal instrument is signed—for example, "Dr. Henry James, President, ABC Behavioral Health Center, Inc."—a corporate obligation is created, as opposed to a personal obligation. If the practice is unable to generate enough revenue to make loan or lease payments, the lender and landlord could sue only the corporation. The personal assets of Dr. James could not be garnished or attached (subject to reach) by the creditors. Should the corporation default on a debt, such default would not become part of Dr. James' personal credit history.

As a practical matter, most landlords and lenders require personal guarantees from the principal shareholders in a corporation. If the business falters and money is owed, they can then look to the guarantors, as well as the business and its assets, to recover funds due. If possible, it is wise to contract only as "President [or other title] of _____ Corporation."

Advantages of Incorporating

There are certain tax advantages to incorporating, but, in recent years, these advantages have been tremendously diminished. In theory, a corporation establishes multiple layers of taxation. Both the corporation and the individual employees are subject to federal income taxes. If a corporation makes a profit after all expenses, including salaries, are paid, it must pay corporate income tax. Employees pay taxes on the salaries paid to them. After corporate taxes are paid, some portion of any excess profit may be distributed as dividends to shareholders, who must pay federal income tax on the dividends. By electing Subchapter S status, however, a corporation can avoid the multiple tax layer problem. All income will flow out, and only the recipients will be taxed. To elect Subchapter S status, the shareholders—and their spouses—must file IRS Form 2553. There are eligibility restrictions, so competent legal tax advice should be sought.

The cost of incorporating a practice may run from $500 to several thousand dollars, depending on the state of incorporation. Over the course of a career, these incorporating expenses may be trivial, but they are often very significant to a practitioner who is just starting out. Incorporation costs include legal fees, seal, minute book, incorporation fees, and state franchise taxes.

Faced with the cost of establishing a corporation, the lack of a shield for a practitioner's own personal acts of negligence, and the multiple tax layers, why would a practitioner choose to incorporate? Three reasons are often cited:

If a corporation makes a profit after all expenses, including salaries, are paid, it must pay corporate income tax. Usually, financial planning within the corporation eliminates double taxation.

1. Limited liability (a shield from employees' negligence and corporate debts) is better than total liability.
2. A corporation has continuity of life; it will survive the death, incompetency, retirement, withdrawal, termination, or resignation of any officer or employee because it is a separate legal entity.
3. The transfer or issuance of stock makes it easier to transfer ownership or to allow others to participate in ownership.

When a solo practitioner dies, so does his or her practice. It is much easier to pass on a practice that is incorporated; the corporation itself owns the assets, including the location, telephone number, and goodwill (reputation). The heirs of the shareholder/practitioner who passes away can negotiate to sell the practice in one neat package: They sell all their inherited stock in the corporation.

If an incorporated practitioner wants to bring in a partner, it is not necessary to establish a new legal entity. Only one event would have to occur: The issuance of additional shares of stock to the "partner," now a shareholder. Special kinds of corporations can be created in each state, but most states allow for *like kind* licensed professionals to incorporate under professional association or professional corporation statutes. These statutes allow people who hold the same professional license to establish a corporation in which ownership will always be limited to holders of that same professional license. These special corporate vehicles are not available for integrated mental health group practices, where practitioners hold different licenses and are involved in different mental health disciplines.

In any arrangement to practice with other professionals, it is critical to limit liability for another professional's negligence through incorporation or another limited liability vehicle (i.e., limited liability professional partnership or limited liability company). The corporate shield can prevent personal liability if another therapist is sued and you have had no contact with the suing client (plaintiff, complainant, or petitioner) and no responsibility for training or supervising the responsible, guilty, or liable therapist.

The corporate shield can prevent personal liability if another therapist is sued and you have had no contact with the suing client and no responsibility for training or supervising the responsible, guilty, or liable therapist.

Disadvantages of Incorporating

- **Possibility of ownership restrictions:** For licensed professional corporations, Subchapter S status requires 35 or fewer shareholders for special tax treatment.
- **Possibility of corporate and dividend taxation:** Unless Subchapter S status is secured, multiple layers of taxation can occur, and the sale or dissolution of the corporation can trigger capital gains tax liability.

- **Corporate formalities:** Board/shareholder meetings, payment of annual state franchise taxes, and maintaining the corporate minute book are only some of the protocols that must be observed.

For most individuals who practice alone, with limited or no support staff, incorporation does not make much sense. If continuing the life of the practice, attracting additional ownership or capital, or fulfilling some compelling state tax requirement is not a relevant consideration, the additional cost of establishing and maintaining a corporation and the additional burden of observing corporate formalities would convince a sole practitioner to remain unincorporated. If any of these reasons do exist or if a group practice is anticipated, incorporation certainly should be considered, but only after careful consideration of advice from legal and financial advisors, usually including an accountant, a banker, an insurance representative, and, if possible, a financial planner.

Examples of articles of incorporation for a professional corporation and a general corporation are presented in Appendixes C and D, respectively. Because incorporation statutes and requirements vary from state to state, these models from our home state should not be used without competent legal advice from an attorney in your jurisdiction. They serve as an agenda for discussion and consideration during the decision-making process.

Answers to Frequently Asked Questions about:

Incorporation

? Question

My accountant has explained the various advantages and downsides to becoming a professional corporation (PC). Could you describe the legal upsides and downsides to this practice structure for a mental health professional?

! Answer

Incorporating under a professional corporation (PC) statute allows like-licensed professionals to establish a corporate entity and structure. The two main reasons behind incorporation are: (1) limiting liability for the negligence of *other professionals* or employees of the business and (2) the ease of *transferring ownership*. (Convey stock via stock certificates instead of scheduled assets and debts or liabilities.)

We generally do not recommend incorporation for sole practitioners. Creating a corporate entity *will not* shield a person from his or her own acts of negligence.

Legal Lightbulb

- There is no shield from liability for your own personal acts of negligence or misconduct, but a corporation can shield you from the negligence and malpractice of others.

- Having employees or other professionals in the practice usually is sufficient reason to incorporate.

- Corporations have continuity of life. If you wish to pass on your life's work or sell out and live comfortably in retirement, incorporating makes sense. You won't have to sell files and furniture, only a stock certificate.

- If a corporation makes a profit after all expenses, including salaries, are paid, it must pay corporate income tax. Usually, financial planning within the corporation eliminates double taxation.

- Corporations can result in multiple layers of taxation (without Subchapter S election).

- Incorporating makes it possible to enter into contracts in a corporate, as opposed to a personal, capacity, creating corporate, rather than personal, liability. This can be critical when escaping from long-term obligations due to unforeseen circumstances.

- Incorporating requires start-up money for attorney and accounting fees, state incorporation fees, and first-year state franchise taxes.

- Incorporating requires adherence to corporate formalities—meetings, maintenance of a minute book, payment of annual franchise taxes.

- Secure competent legal and financial advice before deciding to incorporate in your jurisdiction.

All professional people have certain risks when dealing with the public as they practice their profession (e.g., malpractice). Incorporation does not insulate the professional from these personal and professional risks. There is also the cost of creating and maintaining the corporation to consider. Once established, the legal formalities of a corporation must be adhered to, that is, annual meetings, corporate minute books, corporate tax return, annual state franchise taxes, and so on. The cons in our opinion outweigh the pros for the sole practitioner. Check with your accountant and then with your attorney. Review last year's earnings and make a projection for next year. Give the numbers to an accountant. Would you be better off as a solo practitioner or a corporate shareholder in terms of how much you would take home or how much you might save in taxes? Incorporation is really a numbers game.

Additional Thoughts

- Professional corporations offer some legal protection when there are employees and partners. There are also some additional tax and retirement advantages available.
- PCs do not insulate or protect the professional from personal professional liability.
- The professional is always responsible for his or her own negligence.
- To incorporate or not to incorporate is usually an accounting problem, not a legal problem. The question: Will the process cost or save money? The accountant will have to push a pencil and come up with the answer.

SECTION SEVEN

HOW TO AVOID MALPRACTICE CHARGES

27

Acts of Commission

Dr. Smith, a psychologist, primarily worked with couples in therapy. One particular couple, thankful for Dr. Smith's help and inspiration in therapy, wanted to create a foundation focusing on widowhood and remarriage. They approached Dr. Smith and asked if he would be the clinical director, as well as business manager and chief operating officer, of this foundation. Can Dr. Smith take this job?

~

Susan, a social worker employed by a church foundation in Los Angeles, helped the child of a minister and his wife with play therapy. After a year, therapy concluded satisfactorily, and Susan had no more contact with the family. One day, Susan unexpectedly met the minister again. He was now divorced, and he invited Susan to visit, and perhaps join, his congregation. Later, Susan began taking lessons from the minister in an effort to integrate social work with religious values. Gradually, their relationship became intimate. One evening, they were kissing and were seen by a friend of the minister's former wife, who reported the incident to Susan's agency. Is Susan's conduct a violation of professional boundaries?

~

Seven years ago, John, a professional counselor in private practice, terminated therapy with a client, Samantha, by mutual agreement. John did not see or hear from Samantha for years afterward. He had relocated from San Francisco and was practicing in Massachusetts. Samantha also had relocated to Massachusetts and happened to discover that John was practicing in the area. She called to make an appointment for therapy. When she came for her appointment, both decided they would rather date than become involved professionally as patient and therapist. John referred her to another therapist, and they began dating. Can John date Samantha?

What Is a Malpractice Action?

A malpractice action is a civil action that seeks monetary damages. A civil action is distinguished from a criminal action, where conviction results in a fine or a jail sentence, and from an ethical violation, where the therapist's license is jeopardized.

A malpractice action is a civil action that seeks monetary damages.

In a malpractice action, the plaintiff is usually a client and the defendant is the therapist. The suit is filed in the civil justice system, and the decision, if won by the plaintiff, results in money damages. The money damages are paid by the defendant therapist or the therapist's malpractice insurance company to the plaintiff.

Most therapists have malpractice insurance. Most insurance carriers will provide the therapist with a defense attorney; make experts available; pay damages if assessed by the judge or jury; pay for a transcript of the trial, if needed; appeal, if necessary, and pay the premium on an appeal bond; and settle and pay the settlement costs if appropriate. (For the limits and benefits of your malpractice insurance, read your policy carefully.)

Elements of Malpractice

To recover damages in any malpractice action, the client/plaintiff must prove four historical elements:

1. The therapist owed the client a *duty to conform to a particular standard of conduct* (i.e., what a reasonable therapist would have done under the same or similar circumstances).
2. The therapist was derelict because the therapist *breached the said duty* by some act of commission or omission.
3. Because of the dereliction or negligence, the *client/patient suffered actual damage*.
4. The *therapist's conduct was the direct or proximate cause* of the damage.

A breach of duty forms the basis of malpractice suits.

A breach of duty forms the basis of malpractice suits. The therapist must keep duty, standard of care, and negligence in mind at all times. In determining the appropriate standard of care, there is a "battle of the experts." Each side calls expert witnesses to testify, and each side, in testimony, offers an opinion concerning the appropriate standard of conduct. The jury then renders a verdict. Some prohibited acts are such obvious violations of the standard of care that experts may not have to be called. Among these prohibited acts are having sexual relations with a client and marrying a client.

The next section warns of situations to avoid. In each situation, the therapist is likely to be sued and must settle out of court or face losing at trial. In some situations, a plaintiff/client elects not to pursue a case to conclusion and either drops the charges or refers the matter to the licensing board for further action. The consequences for the therapist can be severe and might affect his or her entire professional career and family life. When *any* of these occurrences arises, beware! In our consumer-oriented society, even the appearance of impropriety can give rise to a lawsuit.

Even the appearance of impropriety can give rise to a lawsuit.

Activities to Avoid

1. Entering into a dual relationship of any type with a client: A relationship, as defined here, might include serving on a committee together; going to each other's homes for school, church, or political functions; attending cultural events; or any other activity wherein the client-therapist boundary might be made fuzzy. When in doubt, avoid the circumstance. Become a master of aversion.

In small communities, some contact with clients is difficult to avoid, and there have been few cases when a simple "Howdy" in a supermarket has led to litigation. However, an effusive public hug or having coffee or lunch together can cause, in the mind of the client, an impression that the therapeutic connection is now one of friendship. And that creates a dual relationship.

Historically, dual relationship situations start off very innocently. Soon, they are difficult to control or terminate. Better to stop the possibility before it begins.

2. Blurring the boundaries between therapist and client: Therapists hear many of a client's intimate thoughts. Socially, a therapist can share intimacies with friends, colleagues, and business associates, but not clients. The roles of the therapist and client are clear and well defined. There is a boundary between the two, and the boundary is obvious and apparent at the moment therapy begins. As time and therapy proceed, the tendency is to become more casual and informal. Be careful. Informality, if misconstrued by the client, can have serious consequences.

3. Doing business with a client: There might be a time when it seems appropriate to sell or buy something—a used car, for example. Can you sell to or buy from a client? Doing business of any type is frowned on. Possibilities include buying or selling merchandise; using the client as a broker; having the child of a client mow the lawn or baby-sit; hiring the client as a secretary, typist, bookkeeper, public relations person, business manager, accountant, auto mechanic, plumber, lawyer, physician, and so on. Business opportunities may arise in the therapeutic relationship on occasion. Such activities are off limits to therapists.

Dr. Helen Mitchell visited with Bob and Susan in marital therapy. After about one year, the couple terminated therapy and obtained a divorce. Susan received custody of their child. Following termination, Bob, who was in the television production business and had been impressed with Dr. Mitchell, approached her about producing a one-hour tape describing her particular type of therapy. He would put up the financial investment, and she would invest her expertise. She was flattered, and the project began. It failed. Bob would have been happier if the tapes had sold and there had been a profit to be divided, but he was willing to accept the business loss.

Susan, two years later, was a law student at a state university and wished to receive more child support. When investigating her former husband, she was appalled to discover that, one year after therapy ended, he had gone into business with her therapist and had formed a corporation that she assumed (incorrectly) had made money. She was even more furious when, as a result of another court action, she discovered that there would be no increase in child support because her former husband made less money than before and had suffered a substantial business loss. Susan was poorer by almost $200 in court costs and $1,500 in attorneys' fees. Where could she vent her anger? She complained to the licensing board.

Dr. Mitchell spent some $3,000 for lawyers' fees to represent her, but she won the case before the licensing board and retained her license. She received only an educational letter as an admonishment.

What had started as a simple business venture became an ethical nightmare with malpractice implications. In addition, Dr. Mitchell has to explain the whole event every year when she renews her malpractice insurance and again when she requested inclusion on a managed care list of preferred providers.

4. Establishing a friendship with a client, or accepting the client's invitations to family or social events: Clients often want to show friendship or express appreciation to their therapist by inviting him or her to weddings, graduations, confirmations, bar mitzvahs, engagement parties, anniversaries, or other family events. The therapist, prior to the beginning of therapy, should set the boundaries and indicate to a prospective client that the connection between client and therapist precludes social contacts. If such a discussion takes place during intake, the client will not be insulted when there is a refusal.

5. Marrying a former client: After therapy ends, many clients and therapists date, court, get engaged, and ultimately marry. *This is to be avoided.* In one state, the quarterly newsletter published by the licensing board contained the names of three therapists who were former residents of that state, all of whom had lost their licenses after marrying their former clients. And who filed the complaints? Either the former spouse of the client or the former spouse of the therapist. Marrying does not legitimate an inappropriate client-therapist relationship.

6. Accepting substantial gifts: A small gift of a few dollars' value, presented for the end-of-year holidays, *may* be acceptable. A huge or expensive gift is clearly not acceptable; it could easily cause the therapist to lose clinical objectivity. Children in play therapy are often anxious to please and give drawings, decorated boxes, and small objects to the therapist. We are unaware of any cases wherein a child's gift led to legal action of any type, so such a token is presumed acceptable. But beware. Small gifts of antiques and heirlooms have a tendency to increase in value. If a conflict arises between the client and the therapist, a question of exploitation may develop.

7. Trading or exchanging for services: Therapists must work for cash and be paid for their services in accordance with their customary, and perhaps published, schedule. Again, the problem is one of potential exploitation.

Dr. Franklin was an amateur musician who practiced therapy as a profession and piano as a hobby. His client, Julie, owned a beautiful, old, out-of-tune piano that she never played. She was moving and wanted to get rid of it because it took up too much space. She offered it to Dr. Franklin in exchange for 25 therapy sessions, estimating that the piano and the professional fee would be of about equal value.

Dr. Franklin accepted the offer and had the piano tuned, resurfaced, and refurbished at his expense. At the end of 25 sessions, Julie continued to require individual therapy but had no money. She, with her lawyer, stated that Dr. Franklin had initiated the "trade" and had exploited her. She had the piano appraised. In its refurbished condition, it was worth much more than 25 sessions.

Was this exploitation? Not really. Was the trade a prohibited act? Yes. Trading items of value for services is to be avoided.

8. Making a misdiagnosis or exceeding your level of competence: Therapists are not expected to be correct all the time. They are expected to use usual therapeutic standards in making each diagnosis and to be able to back up the diagnosis with legitimate documentation. When a diagnosis is questionable, therapists should refer or consult rather than make a decision that might, in hindsight, be inappropriate. The best manner to reconcile differences is to consult with a colleague (or several colleagues) and to document the result of the consultation and how the consultants responded to the case. If a case is too difficult to handle or exceeds the competence of a treating therapist, making a referral to another competent professional is better than failing to recognize the limits of your own level of competence.

9. Accepting illegal or unethical remunerations: Such payments are violations of both the law and the ethical canons. A therapist cannot be paid a fee for referring clients to another therapist. Decisions to refer are founded on the best interest of the client, without any thought of remuneration for the referral. Kickbacks are inappropriate. It is possible to sell a practice and the files in a practice, but only after permission is first obtained from the clients involved. Cross-referrals are acceptable if they are in the best interest of the client. Clients can be referred when a therapist retires.

10. Failing to make arrangements that accommodate the death of a client or a therapist: Death does not end responsibility. The therapist must make provisions in his or her estate plan for the disposition of client files in the event of the therapist's death. The intake form should state that, in the event of the death of the therapist, (1) another therapist of similar competence can take possession of a file and continue therapy if the client wishes, or (2) the client has a right to request a copy of his or her file to take to another therapist. The executor, although technically the successor to the deceased therapist, should not be privy to the contents of clients' files, especially if the successor is not a trained professional specializing in mental health.

The estate of the therapist owns the file, but the client or the client's executor is entitled to a copy at reasonable cost. However, in the event of the death of a client, the surviving therapist would be wise to petition a court for a ruling concerning the release of a client file to an executor or administrator, stressing the possibility that the client might not have wanted the file to lose its confidentiality. A court order will indicate whether the file is to be copied or delivered.

When a therapist's death is unexpected, the task for a colleague who volunteers or has been designated to resolve paperwork, insurance forms, closure of the practice, and so on can be a nightmare. With some foresight and advance protection against chaos following an untimely death, the task can be less difficult. The death of the therapist or the client is always a possibility, and it should be acknowledged in the intake form and the therapist's estate plan.

11. Having sex with a client: Sex with a client is prohibited. Sex with a former client may violate the canons of ethics, depending on the time interval between the date of the last client contact and the date a social relationship begins. In general, *sex with a former client is a bad idea,* as is hugging, touching, sexy conversations, or dialogue concerning sexual topics that are not appropriate for a particular client's treatment plan. Remember: Once a client, always a client.

12. Having sex with a client's relative: Therapists will be led into temptation in many situations. For example, children will be brought to therapy by single, eligible parents who find the therapist attractive. A therapist who knows a lot about a client's spouse might meet that spouse in a social circumstance after therapy has terminated—and after a divorce has been granted to the couple. A pastoral counselor may deal with families who have attractive relatives. School counselors often have consultations with children who are delivered to the counseling session by aunts, uncles, or cousins who are single and eligible. The list could go on and on. Relationships with any relatives of a client are to be avoided. In some case verdicts, therapists have been disciplined or sued for such social contact. Do not have sex with individuals related to the client.

13. Revealing a client's identity in published works: When writing books, journal articles, mass media presentations, or lectures, use examples that present no potential breaches of confidentiality. If a real case is the basis of an example, change the sex, name, location, age, religion, and any other identifying data of any persons described in the printed text. In a book such as this one, all the names and parts of all circumstances are fictitious, but if a client's situation can be easily identified and damage befalls the client, the client has a right to be upset. When an article or any other source is published, no one connected with the real person should be able to identify the circumstances and connect the person and the event described. If the person described can identify himself or herself and chooses to tell everyone, the therapist is not at fault.

14. Revealing any private record: Carefully maintain the security of records. Each current file, whether in a manila folder or on a computer disk, must be secured within a total security system. File drawers must be locked. Files stored in cardboard containers must be in a secure space, under lock and key. Computer access codes should require unique knowledge. Wherever there is a file, there is a confidentiality issue. The client is entitled to the security that every entry in a client file deserves. It is up to the professional to establish a protective system.

There is no way to practice a profession and be free from all possible risk. Some circumstances have proved to be riskier than others. Readers should seriously consider the list of prohibited activities and avoid them at all cost. A risk-free practice is not possible; however, with some caution and conservative responses, most risks can be minimized, and some can be eliminated.

Answers to Frequently Asked Questions about:

Phone referrals

Negligent referral

Limits of referral in general

Doing what you *should not* have done

? *Question*

I am the referral coordinator for a private, nonprofit outpatient clinic. One service we offer allows individuals seeking treatment to call us to receive referrals to outside clinicians in private practice and to other clinics and agencies. We offer free referrals when our own schedule is full, when we do not have the expertise to handle a particular problem, when the client calling cannot afford our minimum fee (we have a sliding scale), or when, geographically, we are not convenient. These referrals often take place over the phone if the caller cannot or will not come in.

I understand the need to avoid negligent referral. I wonder what our responsibility, legally and ethically, is to the caller, beyond offering reputable referrals. Are we liable if the person does not follow through and has some untoward outcome? Are we liable if we cannot find a referral that meets the client's perceived criteria in terms of fee structure, expertise, and location?

❗ Answer

We assume from your description of services that you do not offer crisis or hot line services. As long as you do not attempt to treat callers over the phone, you should be able to avoid liability for anything other than a negligent referral. It would be a good idea to attempt to document each call and the referral advice given. A follow-up letter to a caller who discloses an address and consents to the written communication would be a great way to document the information given. If that is not possible, a permanent log should be maintained that records, for each call, the time, date, caller identity, request for services made, and the referral advice given. Refer to all callers as *callers* until such time as they come into your offices and *engage a therapist*. Never refer to callers as *clients*. Train your phone operators to explain the referral system and say that a referral is not the beginning of therapy but only a referral accommodation.

If you do nothing but give referral information, we do not believe you have an obligation to follow up with the caller to see if treatment was obtained. Make sure you are clear in your conversation with the caller. Responsibility for follow-up *is with the caller*.

We doubt that you guarantee a provider or suitable referral for every caller. Therefore, there should not be a concern about the caller for whom you cannot find a qualified provider within the caller's price and location preferences. An honest reply to this particular caller that you are unaware of a source of care that meets the caller's criteria is the best you can do. It is up to the caller to then search individually for help or alter his or her criteria.

💡 Additional Thoughts

- *Reputable referral* is an art form. Every individual, agency, or entity on your referral list should be checked out individually or as an agency. If the referral really went badly (e.g., a child was referred to an agency who just fired the child therapist, the adult was referred for alcohol or drug addiction and the agency did not have an addiction therapist, a lonely woman was referred to a known womanizer, or the client needed a facility that furnished geriatric care and the facility had just been investigated and lost its license) and the reason for the inappropriate referral was due to the negligence of the referring agency in failure to make an investigation, the referring agency and the person making the referral would be liable.
- At a minimum, make sure any referral, whether to an individual or agency, is properly licensed and has professional liability or malpractice insurance. In some situations, it is wise to make a site visit every so often to see that the referral is continuing its services in a professional manner and is current in staffing and physical facilities.

- When compiling the list, insist that a certificate be furnished to you annually that indicates that the malpractice insurance premium has been paid and the insurance is in force for the following year.
- Always, if possible, offer at least three referrals.
- Advise each caller to interview the therapist or agency at their location *before* engaging in a therapeutic relationship. There are many matters the therapist has to discuss *before* therapy commences.

Legal Lightbulb

- There are traditional areas in which therapists have been sued for malpractice. This chapter lists some of the principal circumstances in which a vulnerable therapist has been held liable.

- The therapist, before the beginning of therapy, should set the boundaries and indicate to a prospective client that the connection between client and therapist precludes social contacts.

- When a diagnosis is questionable, therapists should refer or consult rather than make a decision that might, in hindsight, be inappropriate.

- A therapist cannot be paid a fee for referring clients to another therapist.

- Even if a therapist wins a case, the fallout is awesome because of the effects on subsequent malpractice policies, accountability to the licensing board, hospital privileges, and explanations to friends and professional colleagues or to managed care company panels.

- When an article or any other source is published, no one connected with the real person should be able to identify the circumstances and connect the person and the event described.

- Litigation is public and open. Anyone can read the verdict and all the documents filed in a malpractice case.

- Malpractice premiums often rise when a case is filed. Sometimes, future professional liability policies are denied by the insurer.

- If damages exceed the policy limits, the therapist is personally responsible for the overage.

- Review your printed material. Be sure it does not make guarantees or warranties concerning referrals, but specifies that you will try to make a referral if you can't handle the call. In addition, state in your materials that you recommend a potential client-therapist interview before actual therapy commences. Shift, if possible, the responsibility of making a good match to the caller.

28

Acts of Omission

Dr. Goshen, a successful therapist in private practice, had treated patients for nearly 30 years and was well respected and admired. Dr. Goshen had treated a relatively new client, Patrick, for five sessions. One day when Patrick appeared for an appointment, he smelled of alcohol and had slurred speech. Dr. Goshen tried to continue with the session anyway. They talked for a while, but Dr. Goshen finally acknowledged that the session was fruitless. He asked Patrick to make another appointment. Patrick left, got into his car, and hit another car just as he left the parking lot. He seriously injured himself and the passenger in the other vehicle. Is Dr. Goshen liable? Should Dr. Goshen have made a referral to Alcoholics Anonymous or called in another therapist to consult immediately while Patrick was in the office? Should he have detained Patrick until a ride home could be arranged or reserved a hotel room where Patrick could sober up? What would have been good practice?

The previous chapter defined malpractice and the elements that have to be alleged and proved in a malpractice action. The chapter also pointed out activities that, if carried out by a mental health professional, would or could be considered malpractice—acts of *commission*, for which a therapist might be vulnerable or liable. However, malpractice also includes acts of *omission*; if a therapist *fails to take a particular action*, he or she may also be liable. How might a therapist be obligated to offer a certain treatment plan and, by failing to act, be liable or vulnerable? What acts of omission can lead to a malpractice suit?

Malpractice includes acts of omission; if a therapist fails to take a particular action, he or she may be liable.

Answers to Frequently Asked Questions about:

Liability jitters, acts of omission

The statistics

Settlements

Complaints to the licensing board: Another vulnerability

❓ Question

*Seeing a friend who is a therapist go through the anguish of being sued for malprac-
tice—and believing that he does competent and conscientious work—I've become
anxious about the likelihood of a professional liability suit. How frequently are non-
medical therapists (psychologists, social workers, marriage and family therapists,
counselors) sued for malpractice, and what are the most common allegations in those
actions? How often are those cases settled or decided in favor of the defendant? Having the facts would help me put my worries in a rational perspective. What should we
do and not do?*

❗ Answer

The bad news about suits against mental health professionals is that they seem
to be on the rise, and the amounts recovered are often huge. The good news is
that very few of the estimated 730,000-plus mental health professionals are
sued for malpractice.

Although we are not aware of national statistical data (insurance companies are reluctant to share this data), our experience indicates that much
less than 1 percent of all therapists are sued for malpractice. The figure for licensing board complaints filed is larger, but even that figure is probably less
than 2 percent nationwide. Ethics complaints to a licensing board indicate
possible misconduct by a therapist, but they seldom involve damages that are
sufficient to interest an attorney in taking on a malpractice case for a contingent fee (typically 33⅓ percent to 40 percent).

Although we made a conscious decision years ago to work with therapists
and not file suits against them, we are personally acquainted with attorneys
who do. The plaintiffs' malpractice lawyers whom we know will not take on a
case unless they are certain the damages exceed $100,000 and they know there
are financial resources (assets or insurance benefits) from which a judgment or
settlement can be paid. Malpractice cases are expensive suits to prepare and
present to a jury. No lawyer wants to take on a case if reasonable probability indicates recovery will not cover costs involved and compensation for time spent
on the case.

What kinds of cases result in lawsuits? First, any case in which there are substantial damages. Suicides and homicides often result in an investigation into
the feasibility of a malpractice case. Sexual exploitation cases, especially when
coupled with more general malpractice claims (to ensure recovery under a professional liability insurance policy) are, sometimes, attractive lawsuits for attorneys. Not only are there damages, but also attractive media exposure. In the
past 10 years, many "repressed memory" suits have been filed, some resulting in
multimillion-dollar judgments and settlements. In 1999, two different law firms
placed advertisements in the *Dallas Morning News* to solicit clients who had

been treated for repressed memories or dissociative identity disorder. These kinds of cases involve diagnoses and therapies for which the mental health profession has conflicting theories and the profession and professional literature contain conflicting concepts. When a case is controversial, it is easier for the plaintiff's lawyers to find mental health experts to be critical of the defendant therapist's opinions and services, diagnosis, treatment plan, and prognosis.

In summary, what generally drives plaintiff lawyers to tackle malpractice cases against therapists includes the possibility of recovering substantial damages; the ability to secure expert testimony that the mental health professional erred, that is, was negligent; and deep pockets, that is, the ability to respond in money damages. Suicides, homicides, sexual misconduct, and repressed memory cases fit these criteria.

According to research by Roxanna Gorham and Melissa Burgess (Spring 2003 graduate students at the University of Texas at Arlington, Graduate School of Social Work), guidelines most often violated are:

- Sexual exploitation.
- Dual relationships.
- Boundary violations.
- Breach of confidentiality/refusal to provide records.
- Fraudulent billing.
- Financial exploitation of a client.
- Provision of services while impaired.
- Violation of reporting statutes.

💡 Additional Thoughts

- When you think of the total number of hours individuals are in therapy, few suits are filed and few complaints are made.
- There is no sure-fire way to avoid a malpractice suit from being filed.
- Competent practice is the obvious method to guard against a suit, backed up by serious and complete documentation.
- Always have a professional liability policy that provides for reimbursement for your lawyer if you are required to appear before a licensing board.
- Many cases are screened out by the lawyers for complaining potential clients because the actual provable damages are usually difficult to define and ascertain.
- If there is a hint of a complaint, even a minor dissatisfaction, handle it gingerly and sensitively. Think damage control. In a swearing match between a professional and a client, the client has the advantage because the client always takes the self-righteous position of the wounded victim.
- Most cases are settled for nominal damages.
- Only media-attractive cases acquire enormous damages.

- Many suits for malpractice could have been avoided by an aware therapist acting sensitively.
- Don't let even the smallest problem escalate.

Activities to Be Pursued

1. Entering into a client-therapist contract, upon intake or during the initial interview, that protects the therapist: Throughout this book are numerous items that should be included in a comprehensive intake, consent, and waiver of rights form. The form should *include, but not be limited to,* provisions for fees and no-show charges; purposes, goals, and techniques of treatment; supervision (if any); exceptions to confidentiality; what to do with the file when the therapist or client dies; permission to refer when needed; names, addresses, and phone numbers of people to contact in the event the client presents a danger to self or others; written permission to call these individuals if the therapist believes it would be clinically helpful to do so; and perhaps a mediation or arbitration clause. (See Chapters 2 and 6 for examples.) Review your own intake and consent form. Does it protect you adequately while coordinating with the latest legal and ethical requirements?

Keep in mind that therapeutic modalities change. After a person has been in individual therapy for a while, a family systems approach may be indicated. Obtain a new consent, stating that members of the family will now be included in the therapeutic process and that the technique and perhaps the goal of the therapy may be changing. Whenever the treatment plan changes from the terms originally consented to, a new form should be signed, or at least the record must reflect that a change was suggested, a discussion took place, and the client consented to the change.

2. Making a referral, or at least seeking a consultation, when a problem exceeds the therapist's qualifications and experience: Few therapists can handle all problems of all clients. Situations arise wherein the learning, training, education, or experience of the therapist is not adequate to help the client cope with presenting problems. It is then appropriate to *refer* or *consult* with another therapist about the diagnosis, treatment plan, or psychological mix. Can this therapist treat this client? Is the treatment comfortable for both the client and the therapist?

The only time the question of referral is truly put to the test is when a complaint is filed with a licensing board or a suit is threatened. Then the question arises: Should the therapist have made a referral or consulted with another therapist who has more expertise in the field? It is a question each therapist must ask himself or herself. When the therapist is not qualified or does not have enough experience to treat a problem, it is better to make a referral or bring in a consultant than to keep the client and hope for the best. Terminate treatment and refer or consult with someone more qualified whenever there is any feeling of discomfort. Each therapist must establish his or her own guidelines.

3. Using psychological tests when needed: Many therapists use available psychological tests on a routine basis; others use them sparingly or not at all. When they are helpful, the tools of the trade should be used. When the client refuses or cannot afford the test or when managed care will not permit testing, this fact should be noted in the file. Informed consent would dictate that available and appropriate tests be disclosed and discussed. Whether they are used or not, the reason for the choice made should be noted in the file. Testing is a clinical choice. A thorough record would include a note concerning a test's usefulness and the rationale for the decision.

4. Answering the answering service: Many therapists have printed in their literature, on promotional folders, or on cards that they have a 24-hour answering service, which implies that a client who calls will be called back within a reasonable time—usually, that business day or the next morning. It does not mean, literally, that there *is* an answering service. A client in crisis who calls the therapist is entitled to a return call within a reasonable time, even on weekends or when the therapist is on vacation and a relief therapist is on duty. Apply the usual yardstick. If you were a client in crisis or had a problem so personal that it could be discussed only with the therapist, when would you like to receive the return contact? The sooner the better.

A frantic client who cannot reach the therapist could easily feel abandoned, which is grounds for a malpractice action.

5. Checking every facility and individual to whom you give a referral, and making sure the resource you select can properly handle the client: Therapists refer to other therapists, hospitals, agencies, crisis centers, adoption agencies, AA, ALANON, Tough Love, and other community groups too numerous to mention. Some are general service providers with excellent supervision and credentials; others are highly specialized self-help groups. Each has excellence in a field, but a selection must be reviewed carefully before a referral is made. Calls, visits, and interviews with an agency would meet the minimum requirements, although a heavy investigation would be helpful when serious problems must be resolved.

If you refer to an individual, make sure he or she has malpractice insurance. Next, call the malpractice carrier named to check on the claims made, and call the licensing board to see whether any (or how many) complaints have been filed. Make no referral without checking references. A cause of action called "negligent referral" can be brought when a referral is made without properly checking credentials. Negligent referral can be easily avoided by establishing a method to systematically investigate before passing along the name of any other professional person, group, or agency.

Steve had been a therapist for about five years. Preferring not to handle clients who were a serious danger to themselves or others, he had the Crisis Hot Line number printed on his card. His answering machine also carried the message: "If there is an emergency, call the Crisis Hot Line, 972-123-4567."

In five years, only two clients had called the hot line. They were well satisfied with the results. Last week, another client called. The hot line had a recording: "We are temporarily out of service. We should again be online on the _____ day of _____ 20____. Sorry."

The client was devastated. Steve was unavailable, and the client knew no one else to call.

Giving out-of-date information is worse than giving out no information at all.

6. Taking homicide and suicide threats seriously: Proper intake and consent forms should give the therapist the right to call certain designated persons when a client clinically indicates to the therapist that the client might present an immediate threat to self and/or others. Those designated should be persons who, in the therapist's clinical judgment, might be in a position to prevent a homicide or suicide. In some jurisdictions, the police or a medical facility can be informed; in others, family members or the potential victim can be notified.

Family members, relatives, or other third parties involved with the patient usually look for someone to blame and seek financial compensation if a patient in therapy commits suicide or kills or hurts another person. In almost every case of homicide or suicide, the friends or relatives will consult a lawyer. The case might not be filed against the therapist, or it may be screened out by the lawyer if he or she does not feel there is a fair possibility of substantial recovery. But litigation will be discussed, and a therapist must always be on guard.

If the therapist hears a client has killed, injured, or hurt someone or has committed suicide, the therapist should review the file immediately, call the malpractice carrier, and call a lawyer. The therapist can then, armed with legal advice, *offer sympathy to the family without admitting liability.* This is the time for damage control. Seek counsel. If nothing else, losing a client in this manner is traumatic for the therapist, and a procedure to grieve should be established.

7. Establishing a continuing education curriculum for self and staff: Therapists are charged with knowledge of the latest treatment possibilities and options and must update their knowledge base periodically to ensure that the modalities being used have current validity. A therapist could easily be challenged as being negligent if a technique were available but unknown to the therapist. Some states have continuing education courses that offer the minimum requirements for preserving a license.

In addition, staff must be trained.

*Ted told a local college placement bureau that he needed a student to replace his sec-
retary during her summer vacation. The replacement was a pleasant, bright, and
competent young man whose functions over the summer were to answer the phone
and to book appointments. After several days, Ted happened to walk by the front desk
and heard the hiree talking to his mother about a new client, who happened to be a
neighbor. Ted insisted he immediately terminate the conversation and began to repri-
mand him for breaching the confidentiality so necessary in a counselor's office. The
young man replied: "I used to work in an ice cream shop and we gossiped about customers all the time. You mean a therapist's office is different? No one told me."*

Staff must be trained concerning the confidentiality of client information
and files, the way to answer inquiries about clients and potential clients, what
to say or not say to a process server, how to secure all paper and computer
records, what can and cannot be said to colleagues and friends, how to camou-
flage and deidentify clients and clients' files, and all other items that a new employee must know before becoming qualified to work in a therapist's office.
Keep in mind that the negligence of the employ*ee* is the negligence of the employ*er*, when acting in the course and scope of employment. Train employees;
assign a person to be responsible for their training. Have a manual and insist
that it be read and initialed by all new employees. Failing to train a new or temporary employee because of stresses, pressures, or time constraints is no excuse.

8. Keeping parental rights in mind when treating a child: In general,
either parent can give consent to the therapeutic treatment of a child if the parents are married to each other. When parents are divorced, the rights, powers,
and duties that confer parental rights are divided between the two parents.
Often, the custodial parent has the normal rights of a parent, and the noncustodial or visiting parent has only the right to seek emergency treatment. In
nonemergencies where assessment and treatment are needed, the consent of the
custodial parent must be obtained. (Thus, all divorce decrees and modifications
of divorce decrees must be read and reviewed.) In some states, there is a presumption that all parents are joint custodians of all children and have equal
rights to consent to treatment. Texas and some other states call parents, following divorce, "sole or joint managing conservators" when the court divides the
duties of parents. Other states use different terminology. Each jurisdiction has
its own vocabulary. Before accepting a child as a client, a therapist must understand the local rules and terminology and know who has the right to do what.

Children are often presented to therapists by divorced parents or guardians.
If the parent has been divorced, *ask for and read the divorce decree and all modifications. If the parties were divorced in another jurisdiction and different legal jargon is used there, ask a lawyer in the state that granted the divorce to interpret the
decree for you.* Only the custodial parent (usually, the parent designated in the
decree), a legally appointed guardian, or a foster parent has the right to give
informed consent for the therapeutic treatment of a minor child. Ask for and

obtain a certified translation if the parties were divorced in a foreign country. (See Chapters 8 and 18 for more information.)

9. Contacting the police when necessary, especially if authorized by statute, and keeping this option open in consent forms: There is no better organization to have involved in homicide, suicide, or threat of harm than the local police. They respond quickly, can generally take a difficult situation in hand, and can, when they take charge, remove the therapist from liability. Check the state statute and determine when it is or is not appropriate to call a law enforcement agency. Dr. Goshen, in the earlier example, should include the right to call law enforcement agencies if he believes his client is a danger to self or others. They can take charge, arrange transportation, and protect Patrick from himself and from hurting others. This advanced consent should be included in the intake and consent to treat forms.

10. Taking a lawyer to lunch: In the history of the legal profession, no lawyer is known to have ever refused a free lunch. The idea of taking a lawyer to lunch is advanced to suggest that lawyers and therapists are colleagues and should, on a regular basis, discuss common problems in an informal manner. Each therapist should have a lawyer who can be enlisted to bounce around ideas, make cross-referrals, and check out small problems before they escalate into major violations. With a few inquiries, a lawyer knowledgeable in mental health law can be located. *This networking can bring enormous benefits to members of both professions.* As the relationship develops, the information exchanged can be very helpful.

A malpractice suit is a legitimate concern in our litigious society, but should not be viewed as an ogre on the horizon. Instead, the possibility of malpractice is a constant wakeup call. To avoid personal charges, the first step is to understand where you are vulnerable. With the information presented in this chapter and Chapter 27, you can more easily avoid or eliminate malpractice suits from your central concerns.

Answers to Frequently Asked Questions about:

> Seeking an attorney
>
> Retainer fees
>
> Ongoing relationships with attorneys

❓ *Question*

I noticed that many of your responses recommend consultation with an attorney or having an attorney file a motion, for example, concerning a subpoena. I was just wondering what recommendations/advice you have about finding an attorney with whom to consult. Is it a good idea to have someone on a retainer all the time? It would seem to me that having an ongoing relationship would be much easier.

❗ Answer

We have found that mental health professionals have not learned how to effectively network in the same manner as lawyers and other professionals. In most cities with a bar association, a person can walk into the association's dining room any day of the week and find lawyers having lunch with bankers, insurance executives, financial planners, physicians, accountants, and so on, not just their clients or potential clients. We suggest therapists try to establish a relationship with an attorney in their community whom they can call on for quick advice over the phone without fear of being billed.

Start out by inviting a lawyer to lunch. Ask your questions and make it clear that you are always available to answer mental health-related questions that the lawyer may have. Get a list of lawyers who have offered satisfactory service to your colleagues or who have offered workshops or seminars in the community. Call them for lunch or meet for coffee after work or breakfast before the workday begins. Lawyers are usually responsive to casual meetings, and the lawyer knows, instinctively, that when a call is received, there is more to it than a friendly breaking of bread. Don't worry about taking advantage; in a few months, you will likely receive a call from the lawyer asking you for a friendly chat. (The lawyer may even invite *you* to lunch.) The lawyer will have a problem in the office that requires some expertise the lawyer does not possess. This lifetime trade-off usually ends up being mutually rewarding and beneficial to all parties (including clients who are rewarded with the benefit of input from both learned professions).

A retainer fee is customary only if there is an ongoing need, such as sizable business ventures or recurring legal input. For the average private practitioner, it is better to have a friendly lawyer on call for sporadic problems; arrange a more formal engagement when a substantial legal, ethical, or business problem exists.

💡 Additional Thoughts

- A mental health professional needs a *special* or *specialized* lawyer: one who is conversant with the law and the licensing rules of the professional's discipline, the national rules of the national organization, and the law that pertains to this particular field of practice and specialty.
- A lawyer in general practice can acquire the knowledge, but the lawyer must be willing to seek out and learn this particular field of interest.
- Lawyers will learn about mental health law if there is the possibility of *reward.*

- Lawyers and mental health professionals are often referral sources for each other if each is qualified to provide the service for which the referral is made.
- Retainer fees are not customary in this kind of arrangement.
- All family disputes, many probate (will or estate) matters, and some business ventures involve more than just the legal issues. Mental health input can be very helpful. The lawyer may not be aware of mental health overtones. The professional can be an advocate for and deal with the mental health of the party while the lawyer takes care of the legal ramifications.

Legal Lightbulb

- Acts of omission are as serious as acts of commission.

- When a therapist is on the witness stand as a defendant in a malpractice action, any review of any file will reveal omissions in treatment plans that "might have" been appropriate.

- Include in the treatment plan as many options as are reasonable, and tell why they were utilized or eliminated from consideration. Whenever the treatment plan changes from the terms originally consented to, a new form should be signed.

- Acts of omission and commission have shades of gray. The dark grays are to be avoided. When subtler issues arise, call the malpractice insurance carrier, a colleague, or a lawyer.

- When the therapist is not qualified or does not have enough experience to treat a problem, it is better to make a referral or bring in a consultant than to keep the client and hope for the best.

- Good news: Statistically, very few suits are filed.

29

What to Do If You Are Sued

Dr. Hansen received a letter from an attorney containing allegations that suggested a possible abandonment of her client. Enclosed was a properly signed consent form asking Dr. Hansen to release all her client's records to the lawyer. What should she do?

~

At 8:00 A.M. one day, just as the first client was scheduled to come in, a stranger walked into Dr. Frank's office and handed him a legal process that turned out to be notice of a malpractice suit. The allegations were awesome and, in Dr. Frank's opinion, ridiculous. But the suit had been filed, and he was named as defendant. He had to respond on or before the first Monday 20 days from the date the process was served.

~

What should both therapists do?

There is no possibility of practicing therapy in a totally risk-free atmosphere. You can follow the suggestions in this book and minimize risks, but, in every profession, there are built-in risks that affect the practitioner. When the risk becomes a reality, a therapist can be sued.

Avoiding Litigation

Suits can often be curtailed if they are handled long before they reach a court-house. Some of these suggestions may help:

- Treat every mild threat as an attempt to get attention. Give the attention needed, provided it is in good taste and professional.
- Listen to every complaint, no matter how trivial or small. If a short conference can ameliorate the situation, offer a free conference; if not, offer a free session. Clients seek the attention of the professional and wish to be heard. If appropriate, offer a complete session and discuss all the areas of discomfort. Most complaints can be eliminated in this manner.

Listen to every complaint, no matter how trivial or small.

*Include a
mediation and/or
arbitration clause
in the intake
contract.*

- Include a mediation and/or arbitration clause in the intake contract. Differences can often be worked out with the help of an understanding and objective, trained third person. Options that avoid confrontation and conflict may lead to a result that satisfies all parties. If advised by your attorney, provide that mediation and/or arbitration are conditions that precede litigation. No mediation . . . no suit. No binding arbitration . . . no suit.
- When a hint of a suit appears, call the malpractice insurance carrier at once. Insurance companies are fonts of information. They can suggest alternative methods for dealing with unhappy clients and will often role-play the conversation. Malpractice insurance carriers are happier avoiding suits than winning in court. They are usually delighted to develop a scenario that avoids litigation.
- Sometimes, a carefully worded apology (without admitting liability), is all a client wants. Write one, but have your insurance carrier and lawyer review it before you send it out.
- Some suits simply cannot be avoided.

Answers to Frequently Asked Questions about:

A threatened lawsuit

A filed and served lawsuit

Bad vibrations

⁇ Question

A resistant client just left the office. Her last words were, "I will see you in court." This person has made threats to her husband, her children, numerous friends, and countless business associates over the past few years. Nothing has ever materialized, and I have, so far, always treated it as blowing off steam. Somehow, this time seemed different. I am concerned that she will find some excuse to create nasty litigation, not because she thinks she will win a lawsuit, but because after blustering several times in the past, she has been offered and has accepted tax-free settlements. What should I do?

❗ Answer

What to Do When Served with a Lawsuit

1. Call your malpractice insurance carrier at once: If, for some reason, there is no malpractice insurance, engage a lawyer immediately.

2. Assemble the entire client file, index it, and prepare a summary and chronology: Examine all corrections and make sure they can be explained. If some clarification is needed, make notes. *Do not* make any erasures or introduce any opaquing or changes into the original file unless the changes are properly inserted by lining out, initialing, dating, and making sure the initial entry remains readable.

3. Make three copies of the original file: Be prepared to mail one copy to the malpractice insurance carrier, which will undoubtedly want a copy of the file. Take another copy to a colleague to review. (Consent for collegial review should be contained in your intake and consent form.) Take the third copy to your lawyer.

4. Read your malpractice insurance policy very carefully: Remember the maxim: "The big print giveth; the small print taketh away." Review the policy with your personal lawyer. Remember, the policy as written sets out the obligations of the insurance carrier. *Make sure you conform to every requirement of the malpractice policy. If you do not cooperate 100 percent, some of the rights under the policy may be forfeited.*

5. Do nothing without the advice and consent of the malpractice carrier: When you receive advice or direction from the insurance company's lawyer or claims manager, make a note of the instructions and follow them to the letter. Open a notebook and record *every contact* with insurance company personnel. Keep a log of every item or event that affects the suit. Don't discuss the litigation with anyone except the insurance company and your lawyer—and, perhaps, a trusted colleague. Offer meaningful input; other than that, put yourself in the hands of the insurance carrier's specialists. They will handle and process the claim; they have done it before. Insist that your representative in the insurance company keep you informed of all activities in the file, including settlement negotiations.

6. Participate with the lawyer in your defense against the charges: This is the time for personal involvement. Don't be afraid to ask questions and make suggestions. Lawyers aren't always knowledgeable when therapeutic problems are at issue. You may find yourself educating your lawyer, and that's fine. Consider retaining your own personal lawyer to consult with as the malpractice case progresses. Conflicts can arise between you and the insurance carrier, and the attorney retained by the insurance carrier will be caught in the middle. The insurance carrier may wish to settle a suit for $15,000 to avoid the higher cost of litigation. You, however, will want your name cleared. In some states, information concerning malpractice judgments and settlements must be sent to the therapist's licensing board. A practical settlement could cause serious licensing problems for the therapist, not to mention the loss of reputation and of future business and income.

7. Be prepared to answer a licensing board complaint: If your insurance carrier will not provide you with a licensing board defense through the same attorney, you should retain counsel. Make sure that you and your board-defense attorney coordinate with the malpractice case attorney. Admissions before the board and findings by the board can be introduced into evidence and can have a profound impact on a malpractice case. A board finding of unethical conduct can often lead to a quick settlement by your malpractice carrier and is dynamite in settlement negotiations.

Additional Thoughts

- Handle this client gingerly and try to make a referral to a competent therapist who specializes in resistant, threatening, unpleasant, and blustering clients. Perhaps think of the colleague you want to help out.
- Make sure your notes are consistent. If there are inconsistencies, clarify them by correcting them in the manner suggested in this book. Correct errors as needed.
- Consult with your private lawyer to make sure your interests are protected together with those of the insurer. Orchestrate, with your lawyer, the best approach with this client.
- Try to determine if your client wants a free session or some token agreement. If so, placate and appease her. It's better than litigation or answering a complaint to the licensing board.
- Research the diagnosis, treatment plan, and prognosis. Make sure the current literature substantiates what you have done. If so, excellent. If there are deviations, make an effort to protect yourself by being able to defend the path of treatment you offered.
- If there are any changes to be made in a record, they should be made before any litigation commences or before a subpoena is issued or served.
- Once a client says, "See you in court," the next step is self-protection and damage control. Worry more about yourself and less about the client. What you do at this critical point is very important.

Your Personal Well-Being

This may be the time to engage a personal therapist who will shepherd you through the litigation ahead. Insurance companies are not in a hurry to part with their money, and courts are so notoriously crowded that bringing a case to trial often takes years. Litigation has traditional delays and constant dilatory actions. Its pressure is well known. There should be someone available to comfort you during these months of stress and anxiety.

Consult an attorney to protect your personal assets and estate.

Most policies have limits, and beyond those limits, the insured (therapist) is personally or individually liable. In most cases, the limits are not a problem; but in high-dollar cases, they must be considered. If you must deal with a homicide or a suicide, it would be wise to consult an attorney to protect your personal assets and estate. Some maneuvering might be appropriate. Asset preservation requires careful planning and should not be undertaken without the help of an accountant and an attorney.

Legal Lightbulb

- Malpractice insurance is essential for any therapist.

- Malpractice insurance policies must be read and understood. Questions should be asked if anything is unclear.

- Agency, university, counseling center, or practice group insurance policies do not always cover all providers.

- Malpractice insurance policies, without endorsement, do not usually cover suits against managed care, wherein the therapist is a reluctant defendant.

- When a malpractice insurance policy covers a therapist, the carrier has the right to control the case. Let the carrier represent you unless there is an excellent reason *not* to give the case to the carrier's experienced legal staff. If conflicts arise, retain your own attorney to advise you.

- Make sure you conform to every requirement of the malpractice policy. If you do not cooperate 100 percent, some of the rights under the policy may be forfeited.

- If you have no coverage (i.e., no insurance to indemnify you as a provider), contact a lawyer at once to provide a defense. Having adequate coverage deserves careful attention. A judgment against a therapist can ruin his or her credit for a period of years.

- Coordination between your malpractice defense and the licensing board's defense is critical. Each will impact the outcome of the other.

- Cooperate fully with the attorneys representing you, and be sure to tell them *everything.* Your lawyers will not welcome courtroom surprises and cannot adequately defend you if they are not prepared.

- Include a mediation and/or arbitration clause in the intake contract.

- When a hint of a suit appears, call your personal attorney and the malpractice insurance carrier at once.

Why Few Suits Are Filed against Therapists

Once a suit is filed, the entire mental health record of the client becomes a matter of public record and is subject to examination by inquisitive strangers and the media.

- Most therapists care about and respond to their clients.
- Proving a causal relationship or proximate cause between the actions of a therapist and damage to a client is difficult.
- Damages themselves, in dollar amounts, are difficult to quantify. In many cases, damages are minimal and lawyers refuse to become involved.
- Once a suit is filed, the entire mental health record of the client becomes a matter of public record and is subject to examination by inquisitive strangers and the media.
- Therapy is still considered somewhat of an art form, and proving acts of negligence, commission, or omission is difficult. No two therapists would treat the same client the same way, and a judge or jury is aware of clinical differences. For these reasons, thorough documentation is critical.
- For a client who sues a therapist, future therapy is difficult to obtain. All therapists are litigation-shy.
- Mediation and arbitration (alternative dispute resolution options) have become popular alternatives to lawsuits and often lead to settlements that preclude litigation. A settlement may include a secrecy clause or an *admission of no liability*.
- A client who files a suit may have to wait years before the case comes to trial. Moving on with life while the problem is still open may be difficult. Plaintiffs may not see closure for years.

This chapter has dealt with responding to a suit filed against a therapist for *malpractice*, which is a civil action for money damages. Ethical complaints filed with the various licensing boards are handled differently. Each board has its own rules and procedures. In some policies, the therapist who engages a lawyer for representation before the licensing board is entitled to reimbursement up to $5,000. This reimbursement policy is not uniform, however.

Whether the problem is *civil*, as in malpractice; *administrative*, as in a complaint to the licensing board; or *criminal*, as in a charge against a therapist for assault, battery, sexual acts (in some states), or false imprisonment, a lawyer must be consulted.

SECTION EIGHT

MANAGED CARE

30

Confidentiality Issues

Jim, a 42-year-old department head for a medium-size manufacturing company, sought assistance for a cocaine problem and used his company's health care benefits. Jim worked for a company that was self-insured for the medical and mental health claims of its employees, but retained an outside company to administer the plan and claims. Information concerning claims, limited to the name of the employee and the amount of benefits paid to providers of health care, was forwarded to Jim's employer's human resources department, which was responsible for monitoring the claim fund.

Evelyn, the secretary in the human resources office, processed the information that payments had been made on Jim's behalf to a well-known local drug treatment facility. Jim had been admitted there for a 10-day inpatient treatment. At lunch with Jim's boss's secretary, Evelyn shared what she had seen: Funds had been paid to the drug rehab facility on Jim's behalf. When Jim's boss's secretary returned to work, she passed the information on to Jim's boss.

When Jim returned to work, he found that he had been reassigned to an undesirable nonsupervisory position.

Unauthorized Disclosures

The flow of information concerning mental health care claims is fraught with the danger of unauthorized disclosures. The more eyes that view confidential information, the greater the risk of a breach of confidentiality. A therapist is required by managed care provider agreements to communicate confidential information about clients to managed care companies and payers of the clients' health care benefits. At a minimum, a therapist has to provide the identification of the client, a diagnosis, a treatment plan, the techniques used, the goals set, and an estimate of the required length of treatment.

Many payers require much more initial information; they may even request a detailed description of the client's reported problems. Others require access to all client information, including the therapist's progress notes. The type and quality of information vary from payer to payer. A federal district court decision

The more eyes that view confidential information, the greater the risk of a breach of confidentiality.

The HIPAA Privacy Rule imposes the duty on mental health professionals to disclose only the protected health information that is the minimum necessary for the managed care entity to determine coverage, benefits, and payment.

[*Grijalva v. Shalala*, 1997 Westlaw 155392 (D. Ariz., March 3, 1997)] set out the components of a Medicare managed care appeals system and made clear that both the agency (or other party) reviewing the claim and the claimant were entitled to all information in the claimant's file. These guidelines for appeal systems are carefully reviewed and evaluated by private payers. In connection with an appeal of a managed care decision, all information in a client's file, including the therapist's progress and case notes, could be subject to disclosure and review by the managed care company.

The HIPAA Privacy Rule (see Chapter 38) imposes the duty on mental health professionals to disclose only the protected health information that is the minimum necessary for the managed care entity to determine coverage, benefits, and payment. Conversely, the Privacy Rule imposes the duty on the managed care entity to request only such protected health information that is the minimum necessary for it to fulfill its health care functions.

The Client's Consent

Under the Privacy Rule, a covered entity is permitted to use or disclose protected health information for treatment, payment, or other health care operations and pursuant to a client's authorization. To guard against claims of breach of confidentiality when information is furnished to managed care companies or payers, a mental health practitioner should secure from the client at the first session a consent to have the therapist provide to the managed care company, or other payer of the client's health care benefits, any and all information requested. A therapist should discuss and advise each client that, in these circumstances, information must be shared with the payer; and in the event of an appeal for denial of payment for services, all information in the client's file may have to be disclosed.

The client has the option of not seeking benefits under his or her health care plan and, instead, paying for services directly and personally.

The client has the option of not seeking benefits under his or her health care plan and, instead, paying for services directly and personally. The majority of clients, however, opt to seek payment through their health care plan and should then be required to sign a consent for release of *all* information required by the payer or plan.

If Jim, the cocaine-addicted employee mentioned earlier, had known that information about his problem was going to be shared with other employees, he might have considered taking vacation time and paying out-of-pocket for his 10-day stay at the rehab clinic. The human resources office received information only that $5,000 was paid to Hospital X on his behalf, but the hospital was well known in the community for treating drug dependency. It wasn't difficult for the secretary or Jim's boss to correctly guess Jim's problem. Jim's chemical dependency counselor, who undertook Jim's treatment upon admission, was not responsible for the breach of confidentiality by the secretary. But he was

Sample Form

CONSENT TO DISCLOSURE OF CONFIDENTIAL INFORMATION TO MANAGED CARE COMPANY

As a provider under contract with the managed care company providing my mental health care benefits, I acknowledge that Susan A. Jones, LPC, must necessarily disclose information regarding my care to this company. Once the information is submitted, I have been advised and understand that Susan A. Jones, LPC, will have no control over it and cannot guarantee it will be appropriately safeguarded by the company, nor can she control how the information will be used. I understand that she may be asked to share with the company *all* information in my file, including her personal case and progress notes.

I hereby consent for Susan A. Jones, LPC, and members of her staff to disclose any and all information regarding my mental health care treatment, including but not limited to her case and progress notes, requested by the managed care company that provides my mental health care benefits, upon request by that company.

This information is to be provided at my request for use by my managed care company for determining coverage, benefits, and payment of mental health services. This authorization shall expire upon the termination of my therapeutic relationship with Susan A. Jones, LPC, and payment to her by the managed care company of all fees charged for the services she provides to me. I acknowledge that I have the right to revoke this authorization in writing at any time to the extent Susan A. Jones, LPC, has not taken action in reliance on this authorization. I further acknowledge that even if I revoke this authorization, the use and disclosure of my protected health information could possibly still be disclosed under law to secure payment for the services provided as indicated in the copy of the Notice of Privacy Practices of Susan A. Jones, LPC, that I have received and reviewed.

I acknowledge that I have been advised by Susan A. Jones, LPC, of the potential of the redisclosure of my protected health information by the authorized recipients and that it will no longer be protected by the federal Privacy Rule.

I further acknowledge that the treatment provided to me by Susan A. Jones, LPC, was conditioned on my signing this authorization and my choice not to personally pay for the services provided to her.

I acknowledge that I received a copy of this signed authorization from Susan A. Jones, LPC, on this _____ day of _____, 20___

_____

Harold Cross

Birth Date: _____   Social Security Number _____

charged with the responsibility to advise Jim about confidentiality and its exceptions and to inform Jim that the health care plan requires the counselor to provide information to the plan's administrator—Jim's company.

The Therapist's Concerns

Before signing a provider agreement, a therapist should inquire about the kind of information a managed care company will require. Who will be reviewing the forwarded information? What training and experience will the reviewer have? What safeguards or procedures are in place to ensure that only necessary disclosure or review of confidential information will be made (i.e., Who needs to know what)? If procedures are lax, training is poor, or inexperienced people will be receiving the information, it is wise for the therapist to refuse to serve on the provider panel for that company.

Many provider agreements prohibit a therapist from billing a client directly for anything other than the client's copay.

After a provider agreement is signed, the therapist should assume, and should so advise a client, that all information may have to be disclosed to the managed care company. The therapist should then obtain the client's consent to disclosure of *all* information requested by the managed care company. If the client refuses to sign such a consent, the therapist should refuse to provide therapy unless the client agrees to pay directly and the provider agreement does not prohibit the therapist from taking direct pay for services from a client. Many provider agreements prohibit a therapist from billing a client directly for anything other than the client's copay. Under these circumstances, the therapist will have to decline to provide services and recommend the client seek referral to another therapist on the list of approved providers.

What if the client will consent to only partial disclosure of his or her file? A therapist who undertakes therapy with only a partial consent runs the risk of a claim being denied with no way to document an appeal in order to be paid. If the provider agreement prohibits direct billing of a client, the therapist is not going to be paid. A therapist should pass on or reject any client who refuses to consent to disclosure of *all* information required by the managed care company.

The consent form shown on page 261 can be used as a separate document or included in a more comprehensive intake and consent form.

Answers to Frequently Asked Questions about:

Confidentiality issues

Destruction of files

Preservation concerns

Therapists' concerns when closing a practice

? Question

In my early education, I understood that everything said to a therapist was confidential. Now I understand that what is said to a clinician can be subject to discovery in many circumstances. Is absolute confidentiality, as I understood it, a myth? In addition, how do I protect my files when I retire? What do I do with them?

! Answer

Clients must be informed concerning the exceptions to confidentiality. Many of these exceptions are contained in our recommended Client Information and Consent form in Chapter 6. The duty to warn statutes in different jurisdictions clarify what can and cannot be disclosed to third parties who might be in danger or who might be in a position to protect an identifiable, intended victim. If all the exceptions to confidentiality are listed in the intake and consent form as well as permission for the provider to contact third parties when deemed necessary by the provider, the clinician has a written waiver of confidentiality and is somewhat protected. Make sure each client is told to read the consent form, and give the client a copy to take home. It is then the client's responsibility to read and understand the form and ask questions if anything is vague or questionable.

Confidentiality concerns when closing a practice include:

- Preserving the file for the requisite number of years required in the local ethical canons, usually from 5 to 10 years from last contact with the client, or 5 to 10 years past majority if the therapist treated minors.
- Ultimately destroying the files in a safe and secure manner by shredding or burning them beyond recognition. There are professional companies that destroy confidential records.
- If the therapeutic files are maintained on a computer, make sure the clinical files (and all backup medium) are deleted beyond recovery if, as, and when the file is destroyed. There can be real, serious liability if a computer is sold, donated to a charity, given away or otherwise made available to third parties, or traded and the computer contains confidential clinical information. Even the names of your clients are confidential. Have a professional delete the files beyond retrieval if it is to be donated to any other person or entity. Deleted files have a habit of resurfacing where a good hacker sets his or her mind to it.
- When closing a practice, the complete destruction of all memoranda concerning clients must likewise be destroyed. Our recommendation is that a summary sheet be maintained forever, just in case a complaint arises at a later date and a memory has to be jogged.
- Make sure there is a plan in place in the event of the death or disability of either the therapist or the client. Confidentiality survives the death of

either. The death of either does not lessen the responsibility for confidentiality; rather, the responsibility continues, binding the estate of the clinician and subject to some control by the executor or administrator of the estate of the client.

 Additional Thoughts

- Every state has a statute(s) that sets out the confidentiality of mental health information and the exceptions to that confidentiality statute.
- HIPAA Privacy Rule establishes a national floor for the privacy of health care information.

Legal Lightbulb

- Although payers initially require only general information about diagnosis and treatment, they may require substantially more information later on, especially during appeal of a decision denying benefits or payment.

- Before signing a managed care provider agreement, find out what information you will be required to provide. Ask about the training and experience of the people who will be reviewing the information. Make sure you also know their procedures for safeguarding client information.

- Before beginning therapy, a therapist has a duty to discuss *confidentiality* and its *exceptions and limitations,* including the information to be shared with a payer or managed care company.

- Let the client make the informed choice to consent or not to consent to disclose information to payers and managed care companies. Obtain the consent in writing before treatment commences.

- If a client refuses to consent or will consent to only a partial disclosure of information, a therapist should consider *not* providing services to that client.

- Always carefully review your provider contracts to learn whether direct billing of, and payment by, the client is an option.

- Document what is professionally appropriate. Keep in mind that the documentation might have to be shared with the managed care company.

- Usually, there are more exceptions to the statute than there are confidential communications.
- The statute and privacy rights, both in general and under HIPAA, have to be understood to protect clients as well as therapists.
- A carefully drafted, lawyer-approved intake and consent form is the first line of protection needed by a mental health professional. The form must be drafted with protection of the professional in mind. These forms must be tightly drawn because they are interpreted by the court in favor of the client. Caveat: Managed care contracts delivered to clinicians for signature are drafted by attorneys for managed care with the safety of the managed care company in mind.
- The client must understand that once you furnish information to any third party payer, you lose a great deal of control over the information and the re-publication of the information.

31

Duty to Appeal

Suzanne, seeking counseling for stress and depression, called her managed care company for referral to a counselor. She was referred to Karen, a licensed counselor, and three visits were authorized. After three visits, Karen and Suzanne both called the managed care company to obtain authorization for additional sessions. The managed care company "gatekeeper" declined to authorize any additional sessions, and Karen discontinued therapy with Suzanne.

Two weeks later, Suzanne committed suicide. Her outraged family consulted a lawyer concerning a lawsuit against Karen and the managed care company. Karen consulted with her lawyer and was stunned to learn that she had cause for concern because she had made no attempt to pressure the managed care company to authorize additional sessions. Her single phone call may not be considered enough effort.

Therapists' Role as Patients' Advocates

Mental health professionals have a responsibility to their client that supercedes any limitations of an insurance contract or managed health care plan.

Mental health care professionals have an obligation to be patients' advocates when managed care decisions impact the quality or quantity of care provided for their clients. Their professional responsibility to their clients supersedes any limitations of an insurance contract or managed care health plan. The therapist is obligated to provide the client with treatment that is consistent with the standard of care the client would normally receive from the therapist. The ethical duties and responsibilities imposed by a licensing and statutory authority do not cease when the managed care company says "No."

Managed care companies are increasingly being held accountable when they make inappropriate decisions to save money—and so are providers who quietly go along with the managed care companies' decisions. Health care professional organizations are adopting principles requiring patient advocacy of their members on behalf of patients. The ethical standards shown later in this chapter were adopted by the Massachusetts Medical Society on November 8, 1996. They originated from or were adaptations of opinions of the American Medical Association.

Scope of Managed Care Companies' Contracts

It is important to remember that managed care contracts deal primarily with payment issues and not with a therapist's professional and ethical responsibilities to the client. With the emphasis that courts, consumers, professional organizations, and state licensing authorities are placing on patient advocacy and consumer rights, it is critical for mental health professionals to be prepared to document and ardently process the appeal of an inappropriate managed care decision.

The first step to take in preparing to meet this responsibility should be a thorough review and understanding of the provider's contract with the managed care company and the client's contract for benefits with the managed care company.

Ask for and review all written information disseminated by the managed care company with respect to benefits, procedures, claims, and appeals. Seek clarification in writing if you are unsure about or unfamiliar with anything in the materials you review. Learn the identities of the people you will be dealing with in the event of an appeal, and particularly note the documentation that may be required to support an appeal. Appeal processes vary with each company. If you are on *several panels, it will be necessary to acquaint yourself with the policies and procedures of each company.* Inroads are being made toward making companies more effective and providing honest systems of review and appeal, but the profession is a long way from mandated uniformity on the state or federal level.

After you have a good grasp of each managed care company's benefits, policies, and appeal procedures, you are ready to assume the referral of a client from that company. At the first session with the client, you should discuss the limitations imposed on you and the client by the managed care company and the steps each of you will need to take if benefits, services, or payments of fees are denied. Anticipate denial, and decide in advance how it will be dealt with.

Ask for and review all written information disseminated by the managed care company with respect to benefits, procedures, claims, and appeals.

The Appeal Process

After therapy has commenced, keep detailed and accurate records that can be presented in the event of an appeal. Consider what information may be persuasive to a reviewer and decision maker during an appeal, and document all needed data in the client's file.

When a denial is announced and the appeal process begins, be sure to document, in detail, all phone calls, written requests, and information communicated to the managed care company. Carefully log the time, date, and identity of each person you contact by phone at the managed care company. You want to be able to look at jurors, eye to eye, and advise them that you did everything

Carefully log the time, date, and identity of each person you contact at the managed care company.

you possibly could do to secure the services or care you believed the client required. In effect, you are asking not to be blamed for damages the managed care company may have inflicted.

Provide the managed care company with support and documentation for your position, including, but not limited to, therapy and progress notes, test results, relevant research, learned treatises, and confirming opinions of colleagues. Be sure to have the client's informed consent before sharing any information from the client's file. Make sure you have meticulously followed the published appeal process.

Fight for your client's rights outside the managed care appeal system.

Fight for your client's rights outside the managed care appeal system if necessary. Write to your state's insurance commissioner or to local or state mental health organizations. Let your local officials and state representatives and senators know the difficulties you and your client are encountering with a particular company. If your client is insured through employment and the client consents, contact the benefits manager for the employer and explain the problems you and the employee are experiencing with the managed care company. Urge your client to contact these same potential sources of assistance. The client should also call and pressure the managed care company directly for a favorable decision. Clients who participate in a process are less likely to blame others (the therapist) if the process fails.

Last, be persistent and insistent. Squeaky wheels get attention; sometimes, it is helpful to have the person reviewing the appeal know just how concerned you are about the outcome. With your firm resolve and the client's active involvement, the chances of a favorable decision are improved.

The Appeal Letter

An appeal letter will vary from managed care contract to managed care contract. However, after the agreement is reached, certain procedures should be established to ensure that the appellate process is pursued in accordance with the guidelines set out in the signed contract between the actual provider and the managed care company—that is, all written information disseminated by the managed care company or the employer with respect to benefits, policies, procedures, claims, and appeals.

Seek clarification in writing if you are unsure about or unfamiliar with any terms or concepts in the published materials.

Seek clarification in writing if you are unsure about or unfamiliar with any terms or concepts in the published materials. If possible, consult with another provider who has been involved in the appellate process, and learn from your colleague's experience.

Discuss the provisions in the managed care contract before or at the time treatment commences. Should a claim be denied for any reason, the client should not be shocked or surprised by the action of the gatekeeper representing the managed care company. (The client must understand that the days have passed when the client and the therapist/provider were the sole determiners of the length of time services are to be rendered or of the total nature and extent of managed care benefits.)

The following steps, taken in the sequence given, will prove helpful:

1. Outline the necessary actions as a time line:
   a. Make the telephone call seeking additional authorization.
   b. Organize and then forward the necessary documentation and file to the company for review.
   c. Write a letter supporting the documentation and requesting additional sessions and send a copy to the client.
   d. Request a written evaluation and explanation of the refusal to pay for further treatment.
   e. Write a letter seeking third-party review or peer review and re-evaluation.
   f. Take any additional steps required in the contract. Read very carefully.
   g. Request the specific reasons for denial of continued services.
2. Insert the time line for each transaction. Mark on a calendar the date on which each step is to be taken so that a claim is not denied for technical reasons. Avoid a reply stating, for example: "You did not notify us of your dissatisfaction within 10 days as provided in the contract; therefore, you have forfeited your right to appeal."
3. Review the file and contract to ensure that all data required for an appeal have been timely furnished to the managed care company.
4. Document every contact with the managed care company's authorizing agent (the gatekeeper), and follow up each contact with a written memorandum.
5. Keep the client informed of your efforts to seek additional services. Let the client know you are his or her advocate.
6. Seek mediation or arbitration if provided in the contract, or advise the client to seek legal advice if necessary. Your advocacy is toward the appeal process, not toward representing the client in litigation.
7. Establish a checklist that coordinates with the appellate process and monitors:
   a. Necessary documentation.
   b. Specific times appeal actions are to be taken.
   c. Processing of all the needed technical steps.
8. Keep a list of community resources to offer to the client in the event the appeal is denied. Regardless of the reason for the denial, be able to offer substitute options if your therapeutic services to the client have to be terminated. You can continue to provide services, *if permitted by the contract*, at a reduced fee or free, but if you cannot, or choose not to, continue treatment, community resources on a free or sliding fee scale basis should

Sample Form

ETHICAL STANDARDS IN MANAGED CARE

1. Patient Advocacy Is Fundamental

The duty of patient advocacy is a fundamental element of the physician–patient relationship that should not be altered by the system of health care delivery in which physicians practice. Physicians must continue to place the interests of their patients first. [American Medical Association Committee on Ethical and Judicial Affairs (AMA CEJA), Opinion 8.13(1), Managed Care; AMA Policy 285.982(1), Ethical Issues in Managed Care.]

2. Advocacy for Patient Benefit

Regardless of any allocation guidelines or gatekeeper directives, physicians must advocate for care they believe will materially benefit their patients. [Adapted from AMA CEJA, Opinion 8.13(1), Managed Care; AMA Policy 285.982(2)(b), Ethical Issues in Managed Care.]

3. Appeals from Denials of Care

Adequate appellate mechanisms for both patients and physicians should be in place to address disputes regarding medically necessary care. In some circumstances, physicians have an obligation to initiate appeals on behalf of their patients. Cases may arise in which a health plan has an allocation guideline that is generally fair but in particular circumstances results in denial of care that, in the physician's judgment, would materially benefit the patient. In such cases, the physician's duty as patient advocate requires that the physician challenge the denial and argue for the provision of treatment in the specific case. Cases may also arise when a health plan has an allocation guideline that is generally unfair in its operation. In such cases, the physician's duty as patient advocate requires not only a challenge to any denials of treatment from the guideline but also advocacy at the health plan's policy-making level to seek an elimination or modification of the guideline. [Adapted from AMA CEJA, Opinion 8.13(2)(d), Managed Care; AMA Policy 285.982(2)(d), Ethical Issues in Managed Care.]

A physician should assist patients who wish to seek additional, appropriate care outside the plan when the physician believes the care is in the patient's best interests. [Adapted from AMA CEJA, Opinion 8.13(2)(d), Managed Care; AMA Policy 285.982(2)(d), Ethical Issues in Managed Care.]

be offered to the client to avoid, as much as possible, claims or feelings of abandonment.

9. Make sure your file contains letters that support the client's condition and your professional opinion. Should the claim still be denied, accept the decision gracefully and inform the client that you have been his or her advocate

Legal Lightbulb

- Therapists have a duty to advocate for clients with managed care companies.

- A therapist's professional and ethical responsibility to a client exceeds and supersedes any managed care contract. The managed care contract may limit a therapist's options, however, to provide additional services for free or for a regular or reduced fee on denial of additional benefits.

- A thorough knowledge of the client's benefit contract with the managed care company is essential for client advocacy.

- Learn all you can about the appeal process and the people who will decide the appeal before you meet with the client for the first time. Who are the players and what are their jobs and powers?

- Plan, from the first session, what to do if a denial occurs. Have an established in-office procedure. If possible, explain the appeal process to the client and what you can and cannot do on appeal, that is, the limitations on your authority and effectiveness.

- Detailed documentation of therapy and of efforts in the appeal process is critical for successful appeal to the managed care company as well as for defense at trial.

- Document your appeal (if the client consents) with therapy and progress notes, test results, research or learned treatises, a colleague's confirming opinion, and so on.

- Failure to be an advocate and to vigorously pursue an appeal may be grounds for a malpractice action.

- If necessary, go outside the managed care system by contacting state insurance commissioners, politicians, and, with the client's consent, the employer.

- Communicate your resolve and seriousness about the care you believe your client needs, and urge the client to do likewise.

in good faith and in accordance with the managed care guidelines and the contracts in force. Remember, you, the clinician or provider, are not responsible for the terms of the managed care contract or health plan with the employer.

Answers to Frequently Asked Questions

In the numerous seminars, lectures, and classes we have offered to clinicians, no question has ever been asked concerning the appeal process. We can only conclude that either few, if any, clinicians appeal cases because they are afraid to be removed from the managed care panel, or managed care companies are inherently fair and do not deny care without careful consideration. Or, it might be possible that the time and effort necessary to appeal a decision is not cost effective and other methods are worked out between the provider and the clinician.

SECTION NINE

TEAMWORK

32

Legal Aspects of Delegating

Dr. Birdwell is the clinical director of a university counseling center. He has three Ph.D. licensed therapists working at the center, and they supervise six additional interns who are either future psychologists or future pastoral counselors.

One of the pastoral counseling interns was not suitably impressed with the early in-house lectures concerning the impropriety of dating clients and asked a client, a female undergraduate, for a date. They went out for one unpleasant evening. The student's mother learned of the date and was incensed. This was a violation of pastoral counseling ethics, university rules, and therapeutic boundaries. The client now says she will never trust a therapist again.

Dr. Birdwell interviewed the student at the time of intake. He assigned her to a supervisor, who in turn introduced her to the intern. Who is responsible for any rule infraction?

In every organization and in every profession, there comes a time when it is necessary to delegate professional services to staff, technicians, other professionals, or specialists due to work load disparity, a conflict of interest, a lack of interest, or an excessive burden of responsibilities. When delegation is required, there are some questions to ask of yourself and others.

We rely here on an article titled: "Patient Care Management Skills: Delegation and Supervision—Professional and Legal Aspects of Delegating to Staff Members: Key Questions to Ask." [Source: *Healthweek* 2:26 (December 18, 1995).] The article focuses on medical personnel, but the same guidelines can easily be applied currently to mental health professionals of all disciplines. The article raises these questions:

- Is the delegatee stable and knowledgeable enough for care delegation?
- Are the responsibilities stated in a current job description or scope-of-practice listing and authorized by policy or procedure?
- Is the delegatee competent to perform the necessary tasks?
- Have all the necessary tasks been communicated clearly and reviewed?
- What degree of direction and supervision will the delegatee receive?
- Who will judge whether the delegatee is performing tasks correctly?

- Who will judge whether the client(s) is (are) benefiting from the care?
- What criteria will be used to declare a task completed correctly and safely?
- What criteria will be used to show positive response to the care?
- Has the delegator been given feedback by the delegatee?
- Is this feedback a condition of the delegating responsibility?

Considerations When Delegating

Don't make assumptions about the knowledge of employees.

- Has there been sufficient training within the practice to guarantee that the staff person is up to the responsibility and understands the internal procedures? Busy therapists are often reluctant to take time from income-producing practices to do the necessary training.
- Don't make assumptions about the knowledge of employees. A new employee may not know that therapeutic sessions are confidential and gossip is not tolerated. Remember, every client is entitled to know what *is* confidential and *all* the exceptions to confidentiality.
- Every professional entity should issue a training manual and appoint a professional to be responsible for the education of new staff. Staff includes university or practicum interns temporarily attached to the agency or group.
- Employers are liable for the acts of employees when such acts occur in the course and scope of their employment. An employer would be held responsible if confidentiality were breached through office gossip. This gossip includes any conversations in which clients are discussed by staff, interns, students, temporary help, professionals, or others.

Negligent referral can be initiated when the delegation or referral is negligent, careless, or without proper foundation, or when the delegatee is not equipped, for any reason, to handle the client.

- When a referral is made internally or externally, is there a proper protocol for checking out the person, agency, facility, or entity to whom the referral is made? A cause of action called *negligent referral* can be initiated when the delegation or referral is negligent, careless, or without proper foundation, or when the delegatee is not equipped, for any reason, to handle the client.

Answers to Frequently Asked Questions about:

Delegating treatment to interns or practicum students

Responsibilities of the individual delegating

Damage control

❓ Question

I think I have a problem. An intern was assigned to my agency, a battered women's shelter, and placed under my supervision. I am a licensed therapist. She holds a master's degree in counseling from an out-of-state theological seminary and proceeded to offer counseling to one of the women in the shelter. After two sessions, she claims the relationship changed to that of "friends," and there were home visits, and, at one point, reinforcing hugs. Nothing more, according to the intern and the client. Now the client is complaining to the agency that there was an inappropriate implied sexual relationship. I knew nothing about the therapy sessions except that the intern was assigned to this woman and two sessions took place in our agency offices. The complaint to the agency head is pending. What is my responsibility?

❗ Answer

As a supervisor, it is your responsibility to train interns or supervisees concerning the ethical boundaries between interns and clients. Interns come to the agency for training, and one of the more sensitive fields for training is in the area of dual relationships, proper boundaries, and making sure that clinical objectivity is always preserved.

In a sense, the supervisor delegates the responsibility for direct treatment to the intern, but at the same time retains total responsibility for offering services to that client. All client contact should be reported to the supervisor, who, at any given moment, should know the status of the diagnosis, treatment plan, and prognosis. As soon as the second session was terminated and there was an inkling that the status was changing to that of "friends," the supervisor should explain in clear, unequivocal terms that clients don't become friends, and high boundaries or walls between client and clinician, whether intern or practitioner, must be maintained just for this purpose. The wall remains after treatment terminates. (Review Section Seven of this book.) Consult with your liability insurance carrier, a lawyer, and a learned colleague. Practice damage control. Proceed gingerly in this case. Since the hugging may have been bad judgment but within permissible limits, perhaps some mediation is sufficient. Check out all the options. Avoid a confrontation if possible. Apparently, in this case, in the mind of the client, the hug was more than a "hug." This has to be handled as a therapeutic problem and is probably only the tip of a psychological problem. Handle gingerly, but retain a lawyer to advise you concerning a possible lawsuit or complaint to the licensing board.

The supervisor retains responsibility for offering services to that client.

💡 Additional Thoughts

- When supervising or delegating, the license of the supervisor is always at risk.
- Interns, supervisees, and students under supervision always have to be debriefed after every session, especially in circumstances when there is an *alleged* termination and friendship is about to begin inappropriately.
- Sometimes the supervisor forgets that interns may not have been trained to keep definitive boundaries and clear separation in dealing with clients. While every practicing therapist knows the dangers of the friendly client,

interns are in training to learn these rules. They must be told that under no circumstances are they to have any relationship with a client other than clinician-client. No hugs, no friendship, and no worshiping together except at a distance.

- Clients who need therapy should receive *therapy only*.
- Delegating is permissible. It does not relieve the licensed person from clinical responsibility.
- Delegating does not indicate that involvement in the situation is over. Rather, it continues. Probing inquiry must follow any hint of impropriety.

Final Thoughts on Delegating Responsibility

A school counselor may refer or delegate to a specialist. A licensed marriage and family therapist (LMFT) may refer to an alcohol counselor, if needed, or send children to a play therapist. A licensed professional counselor (LPC) may refer to a psychologist for extensive testing and a psychological workup. A psychologist may delegate a social worker to do a home study. Mental health professionals of all disciplines refer to one another or cross-refer when a client will benefit from additional expertise. Although delegation is to another professional, the responsibility of the delegator or referrer does not end. The

Legal Lightbulb

- Give adequate training to each person you delegate to.

- Verify the person's malpractice insurance coverage.

- If you are delegating to a licensed person, call the licensing board to see whether any complaints are pending.

- Make sure the person performing the task has had adequate learning, training, experience, and education and is competent to perform the task.

- Document internal training and keep a file on classes, continuing education, correspondence courses, and other indications that efforts were made to ensure the protection of the client, including all conferences in which the clients were discussed.

- Preserve evidence of active supervision.

questions concerning the appropriateness of the delegation must be asked, answered, and, if needed, explored fully.

Once active treatment begins, it can only be terminated by an appropriate procedure in accordance with professional standards. Delegation does not terminate professional responsibility. In most cases, continued involvement is needed until a formal termination is agreed on, entered into the clinical record, and properly documented.

A proper delegation of treatment may suit both the client and the provider, but the delegation must be handled properly—and often, delicately.

33

Supervisor/Supervisee Responsibilities

Dale G. completed his master's degree in counseling and was under the supervision of Jack Hanson, Ph.D., LPC. Dale had to complete the requisite 2,000 hours of clinical, supervised practice before he could receive his license and practice independently.

Unknown to Dr. Hanson, Dale had a house with a hot tub at a nearby lake. Also unknown to Dr. Hanson was the fact that, on weekends, Dale invited "choice" clients to soak in the tub and receive a modified version of group therapy. Finally, a client complained to the licensing board, alleging sexual acts with Dale, a dual relationship, and numerous boundary violations. Dr. Hanson's first inkling of the problem occurred when he received a letter from the licensing board.

~

Cindy practiced and was being supervised in Susan's office. The two women were professional as well as social friends and often went to lunch together. During lunch, they discussed problem clients in Cindy's practice. Susan offered advice concerning treatment. Each week, after lunch, Cindy recorded in her clinical notes: "Supervision this date" for each client discussed at lunch. Is this sufficient?

~

Dr. Rose Johnson rented a substantial office and sublet space to numerous other practitioners and interns whom she supervised. The intake and consent form signed by each client contained a clause stating that, although the client was initially referred to Dr. Johnson, she may utilize the services of the other providers and interns in her office if they are competent to handle the client. She conferred with each supervisee on a weekly basis—and more often, if deemed necessary. Dr. Johnson received a call at night from an unhappy client who complained that an intern had just propositioned her. No touching, just inappropriate innuendo.

The supervisor is responsible for the acts the supervisee performs in the course and scope of the supervision relationship.

A supervisor/supervisee relationship is similar to that of an employer/employee. The supervisor is responsible for the acts the supervisee performs in the course and scope of the supervision relationship.

At one time, supervision was less formal, and the rights, obligations, and duties of the supervisor were less clearly defined.

Now, however, supervision has to be taken seriously and face-to-face supervision is required. At a minimum, each client has to be discussed periodically, and notations in the clinical record must indicate the fact that the supervision took place; the nature of the supervision; the effect of the consult between the supervisor and supervisee; and any clinical changes in the diagnosis, evaluation, assessment, or treatment plan as a result of the supervision conference. For full protection, both the supervisor and supervisee should make *independent notations in separate files concerning the consult.*

General Guidelines

Over the years, each mental health discipline has published guidelines concerning supervision. Many of these have universal application:

- When a state has published guidelines for supervision—for example, the credentials of supervisors, the hours needed, the methods to be used, or the records to be maintained—these rules have to be scrupulously honored.
- Certain requirements are stated for the supervisor. Check what those requirements are before beginning a supervised relationship.
- The supervising therapist must be trained in the area of supervision provided to the supervisee.
- Supervision of individuals within certain degrees of affinity or consanguinity is prohibited. Don't supervise a relative.
- In most jurisdictions, a percentage of clinical internship supervision must be hands-on with clients.
- Some guidelines provide that the therapist can supervise only a certain number (perhaps two to nine) of supervisees at one time.
- Supervisees must notify clients of the supervision and supply the name and credentials of the supervisor.
- Supervisors may delegate to supervisees only such responsibilities they can reasonably be expected to perform competently—given their education, training, or experience—either independently or within the level of supervision being provided.
- Supervisors must provide proper training and supervision to supervisees and take reasonable steps to see that such persons perform services responsibly, competently, and ethically.
- Supervisors must establish an appropriate process for providing feedback to supervisees.
- Supervisors are expected to evaluate supervisees on the basis of their actual performance when given relevant and established requirements.

The supervising therapist must be trained in the area of supervision provided to the supervisee.

- Supervisees must keep and maintain documentation showing that their supervisor meets technical requirements and has the credentials to be a supervisor.
- A supervisor must maintain and sign a record(s) to document the date of each supervision conference, the minimum duration of _____ hour(s) per week of face-to-face supervision in individual or group settings, and the supervisee's total number of hours of supervised experience accumulated to (and including) the date of the supervision conference.
- A supervisee may not establish an independent practice while under supervision.
- In some states, a temporary license must be obtained before official supervision can begin.
- The supervisor may not be employed by the supervisee.
- The supervisee may usually, if agreeable to both, be employed on a salary basis or be a consultant or volunteer. All supervisory settings must be structured with clearly defined job descriptions and lines of responsibility.
- The full professional responsibility for the therapeutic activities of the supervisee rests with the supervisee's official supervisor.
- The supervisor should ensure that the supervisee is aware of and adheres to the appropriate codes of ethics.
- A dual relationship between the supervisor and the supervisee may impair the supervisor's objective, professional judgment and should be avoided.
- A procedure must be established for contacting the supervisor, or an alternate person, to assist in a crisis situation.
- All supervised experience must be on a formal basis, by contract or other specific arrangement, before the period of supervision. Supervision arrangements must include all specific conditions agreed to by the supervisor and the supervisee.
- If a supervisee enters into contracts with both a supervisor and an organization with which the supervisor is employed or affiliated, the contract between the organization and the supervisee must clearly indicate:
  —Where professional therapeutic treatment intervention will be performed.
  —No payment for services will be made directly by a client to the supervisee.
  —Clients' records are not the property of the supervisee.
  —Financial arrangements with the supervisee cannot extend beyond the period of supervision.
  —All supervised experience must be in accordance with the canons of ethics of the profession.
- At any time during the supervised experience, and for any reason, if a supervisor determines that the supervisee may not have the skills or competence to practice independently, the supervisor must develop and implement a written plan for remediation.

The full professional responsibility for the therapeutic activities of the supervisee rests with the supervisee's official supervisor.

- States that require supervision for specialty recognition usually require that a plan be submitted for approval. Implementation and documentation of the plan are the responsibilities of a qualified supervisor.
- A supervisee who commits malpractice may be liable, together with his or her supervisor.
- In most cases, when a client files a complaint with the licensing board, the supervisor and the supervisee are both called to account for their activities; their acts of negligence, omission, or commission; or their failure to comply with the ethical standards of the profession.
- Don't assume the supervisee knows anything about professional ethics. In many graduate schools, the courses are theoretical and give little information concerning daily application. The supervisee must be diligently informed of ethical canons. Prepare a handout of the ethics requirements of the discipline, see that it is read, and have the supervisee initial the canons after reading the material. Have each supervisee read and initial (on each page) the code of ethics published by the designated licensing board.

The various licensing boards—for therapists, licensed professional counselors, psychiatrists, social workers, marriage and family therapists, licensed chemical or drug abuse counselors, crisis intervention therapists, psychologists, and others—have issued guidelines for supervision. Published rules encompass the qualifications and responsibilities of supervisors and the responsibilities and requirements for supervisees. Each state is different, and each specific discipline promulgates its own guidelines. There is no universal set of rules on supervision. Common understandings are set out in the previous list, but, to be truly accurate, the supervision publications of each state's licensing board must be consulted.

There is no universal set of rules for supervision.

To further complicate matters, some state and national organizations have published guidelines, the violation of which can lead to expulsion from the organization. In addition, some agencies, organizations, universities, insurance companies, and managed care panels have their own guidelines. This chapter sets out some of the rules. Active and curious therapists must review and coordinate all sources if they seek to practice in peace, free from worry and concern.

Most disciplines provide that graduates, interns, postdoctoral candidates, and future therapists undergo a period of supervision before they are prepared for independent practice. Following this active client contact and an evaluation of the input offered by the supervisor, the supervisor approves the supervision and the supervisee is authorized to practice independently. The liability of the supervisor is profound. During the period of supervision, the supervisor takes on a responsibility of immense proportions, and no legal document can exonerate the supervisor from the related obligations.

Answers to Frequently Asked Questions about:

Conflict with supervisor
Supervisor/supervisee responsibilities
Differences of opinion
License in jeopardy

❓ Question

I work in a state child protective agency. I have been in a position in the past where my supervisor ordered me to remove a child from the home, but I felt this was unethical and unlawful because there was no imminent risk. I refused to do it. I am a licensed independent clinical social worker with 10 years' experience and felt I was being torn between being insubordinate and violating the ethics of the social work profession and putting my license in jeopardy. Because of my years of experience, I did not have the excuse of saying that my boss told me to do it. Do I have any legal rights to protect my job in the future if I find myself in a similar dilemma? The state requires that all social workers in the agency be licensed.

❗ Answer

As a license holder, you always have independent obligations concerning ethical and professional conduct that supercede anything your employer does or demands of you. Reread the ethical guidelines in your licensing act. In many states, there are whistle-blower statutes and statutes that protect employment if an employee refuses to commit an illegal or unethical act and is fired. You should consult with a labor or employment attorney in your state for the best way to protect your job.

It is easy for us to say, but there are some jobs that are just not worth keeping, especially if a supervisor is repeatedly asking you to put your license on the line.

💡 Additional Thoughts

- Words and concepts such as *imminent risk* are words of art. Two individuals, even highly trained, licensed professionals, could reasonably differ. We are familiar with cases where a social worker opined that there was no imminent risk in her professional opinion and then the child died of neglect.
- Winning a whistle-blower suit is not exactly a career-enhancing experience.
- If imminent risk is the standard, why not simply ask your supervisor to indicate, in writing, the facts and circumstances that lead to this conclusion. See if you can obtain agency guidelines.

Legal Lightbulb

- The supervisor may be held responsible before the licensing board if the supervisee has violated ethical guidelines. The supervisor should, with due diligence, determine whether the supervisee is acting properly. This takes some hands-on investigation.

- Supervision consultations must be documented and should include a review of the therapy to date and any changes in the diagnosis, assessment, evaluation, treatment plan, or prognosis brought about by the consult.

- Supervision is more than casual exchanges of information over lunch, the phone, or cocktails. Ask the right questions. Document both the questions and the answers. Document all changes in the treatment plan.

- Supervision, to be objective, must be at arm's length. No family, friends, business associates, or other questionable relationships should be involved. When in doubt, don't supervise.

- Supervisors with huge clienteles cannot treat their clients wholesale and receive a kickback from supervisees. The substance, not the form, of the relationship will be reviewed if questioned by either a client or the licensing board.

- Supervision may occasionally be done over the phone, but mostly it should be face to face, with the file on the table.

- Supervision guidelines provide minimum standards. They are admissible in court to indicate what the supervisor or supervisee "should have done."

- Supervision must be disclosed to the client, together with the name and credentials of the supervisor.

- Supervision must be documented. Both parties should have independent progress notes.

- The supervisor is responsible, legally, for the supervisee.

- The supervisee is responsible, also, for his or her own actions.

- Some agencies have been burnt by the media when leaving a child in a home where risk is suggested but not proven; then, when the child or children are further injured, the failure to remove from the home has serious legal and ethical consequences.
- One thing is reasonably certain: If the child or children remain in the home and if they are further injured, your license and that of the supervisor are on the line.
- Try mediation with the supervisor if it is available.
- Remember, it is easier to remove and protect than it is to prove lack of negligence if a child remains in the home and is hurt because of failure to remove. Failure to remove situations are more difficult to defend because the children have been damaged, and the clinician has to defend an action or actions designed to protect children from exactly the type of harm that occurred.

SECTION TEN

UNUSUAL PRACTICES

34

Geriatric Clients

Bill Bigbucks, a very senior citizen, had a taxable estate. His physician believed that he was either in the early stages of Alzheimer's or dementia, conditions that were probably irreversible. Bill thought about estate planning, but each time he consulted an attorney, the price of planning seemed to increase. He remembered his dad's $15 will and did not want to pay the $1,000 plus that was now quoted to him as an estimate for a complete estate plan. He could not even tie a lawyer down to one definite price before consultations began.

Bill was a widower with three adult children, one retarded, and several grandchildren. His current wife also had children and grandchildren by previous marriages. Bill's home, owned before his latest marriage, was full of collectable and valuable antiques, many of which he promised over the years to various individuals, including children and grandchildren. After each assurance that the property would be theirs, he put a little sticker with the date and person's name on the item. There were little sticky papers on the piano, instruments, furniture, vases, glassware, and other items all over the house. He was supported by investment income automatically deposited into his money market account. His wife paid all bills from this account.

His wife and eldest child visited several assisted living communities to determine options for the future. They spoke to the intake mental health professional who would assist in Bill's mental health requirements should he choose to reside in that particular facility.

If Bill Bigbucks should die tomorrow, would there be any problems? Yes, all his survivors will face delicate moral and legal dilemmas if Bill does not, while he is of sound mind, memory, and understanding (i.e., competent to make a will and estate plan), consult with a competent professional who is engaged to draft the documents that will become effective on his death.

The geriatric client presents special problems to the mental health professional, whether the senior client is seeking mental health advice himself or herself or if the advice is sought by the adult children of elderly clients. The problems are unique because, often, they are not directly problems of the client, but problems of potential survivors. There are few cases of probable heirs suing

The geriatric client presents special problems to the mental health professional.

future testators for their budding expectancies (because the law says that no one is the heir of a living person), but there are countless suits among heirs or individuals with expectations who file suit when these expectations are not fulfilled. Sadly, these suits are between and among close family members, relatives, and friends who might have been close but are now isolated, not speaking, in litigation, bitter, and inconsolable. Perhaps the bottom line for mental health professionals is that death, senility, and dementia as well as other mentally debilitating illnesses have to be faced squarely, with the mental health professional impressing on the geriatric patient and the family that there is a need for estate planning, which, although seemingly expensive when first arranged, is cost effective financially and emotionally in the long run. Indeed, in our minds, estate planning is part of eclectic therapy, and peace of mind comes with a current, legally binding, effective estate plan that takes into consideration the wishes of the testator (Bill) together with the expectations of his wife, children, and grandchildren, and further considers ramifications of state and federal tax consequences.

Decisions can be made only when the testator is alive and has the mental capacity to make informed decisions.

Assuming the mental health professional can create a climate of discussion where the stated objective is to put the client's present needs and future wishes in perspective, what are the various topics that Bill, his wife, children, as well as intimate friends and colleagues, should discuss? A thorough discussion takes time and some headaches to generate decision making, but remember, these decisions can be made only when the testator is alive and has the mental capacity to make informed decisions and when open and frank discussion can be held with the mental health professional serving as therapist-mediator-facilitator-consensus builder.

Topics for Discussion with the Geriatric Client

1. Inventory: Every person needs a readily accessible inventory of all assets, liabilities, deeds to properties, insurance papers, brokerage reports, income and expense statements, purchase documents of expensive items, inventories furnished to insurance companies, lists of specifically insured items, income tax reports, mortgage and loan applications, places and locations of specific items such as collections of stamps, gold, silver, coins, hand-me-downs, or heirlooms. There should be several copies of the list in the possession of the testator and executor or administrator, which itemizes all properties of the geriatric client and which, when consulted, indicates a total financial profile of the estate.

2. Will or will with trust provisions: It is not the job of the mental health professional to determine the type of estate plan a client needs. The role of the professional is to alert the client that various plans exist and to recommend that the client consult with an attorney to put together a plan. The professional may have a recommended list of attorneys, financial or estate planners, trust officers, accountants, or other specialists whom the client may consult and may offer to be present at the consultations, but the final decision is always up to the client. We have seen many a client who, when the estate plan is finally put in place and executed, signs the document with a sigh of relief. There is a feeling of liberation knowing that loved ones are protected to the extent the law allows such protection. In the case of the opening vignette, the new wife and retarded child will need special protection. A carefully drafted plan can provide for future care and support and for anything remaining on the death of the wife or retarded child to vest in designated heirs. It can also provide that if any child is divorced, the money remains in the family. Carefully, legally, and meticulously drafted instruments can accommodate most, if not all, potential concerns.

3. Durable power of attorney and durable health care power of attorney: The durable power of attorney and durable health care power of attorney allow another person to step into the legal shoes of the geriatric client and control or make decisions for that person. The former concerns general financial decisions; control of property; and buying or selling of goods, real estate, or services; and the latter allows the designated attorney to make health care decisions when the individual is not able or willing to do so. Both of these documents have significant ramifications, which must be carefully considered by the client and an attorney, on the financial and medical future of the client. However, they are useful tools to use with geriatric clients. The word *durable* indicates that the instrument is signed when the individual has the capacity to execute the instrument and the legal effect will continue despite the disability or later incompetence of the client. The instrument and the powers granted by the instrument survive the incapacity of the client executing the document.

4. Guardianship: Should powers of attorney not be executed, a court-originated and supervised guardianship will be necessary to take charge of the person and estate of the geriatric client. A guardianship will be recommended when a person cannot manage his or her individual needs, estate, or property, and cannot make sensible decisions concerning his or her person. In that case, a court-appointed guardian (sometimes a family member, but not always) takes over the personal or financial estate of the client, manages it, and accounts to the court (usually on an annual basis) for income, expenses, sales of property, and other significant decisions and judgments concerning the client. Court-supervised guardianships, trusteeships, conservatorships, and other legal vehicles are available for individuals who are unable to manage their persons and property.

5. Insurance review: Insurance is always evidenced by an insurance contract. When a person dies, the insurance company does not come looking, check in hand, for the deceased. Rather, the beneficiaries, executor, administrator, or trustee sends the policy together with a death certificate to the insurer, who then verifies the death and sends the stipulated amount to the appropriate party or parties. However, insurance policies have been lost, misplaced, destroyed, or forgotten. This is the time to locate all policies, copy them, and maintain them in a safe and available location. The geriatric client may know where the papers are or possibly remembers putting them in a "safe place." The heir, on the other hand, may not have the foggiest idea where to start the paper search and then how to put the paper trail in proper sequence. In addition, if any insurance beneficiary designation changes are to be made, now is the time to make amendments as the geriatric years approach, not after senility has sapped judgment and competence is subject to question.

6. Additional considerations: Additional considerations include preparation for burial in *advance* using a cemetery or funeral home. It is easier to negotiate for the purchase of a casket, a service, a plot, cremation, and so on, when alive and before any mourning process. This is the time to put the postdeath house in order, before everyone is upset, sad, and often unable to function clearly. This is also the time to consider signing an organ donor or body donation card, which might read: "I have donated my body to the Anatomical Board of the State of Texas at the University of Texas Southwestern Medical School" or words to that effect. Then, on death, a phone call, as stipulated on the donor card, summons professionals to retrieve the body and make it available to the donee organization.

7. Veterans: This is the time to determine any veteran's benefits. Veterans are entitled to be buried free at any national cemetery. The funeral home makes arrangements with the Department of Veteran's Affairs to deliver the body following any services, and the cemetery personnel make arrangements for a dignified, military funeral with full military honors. A veteran might arrange to donate his or her body to science, after which the remains would be delivered to the Veterans Department to handle. There is no charge for either receiving or disposing of the body, and the stone is provided. All the veteran needs is the DD 214 or discharge papers to make these arrangements.

An Overview

The provider of mental health services to geriatric clients should consider the following suggestions:

1. The mental health professional should be aware of important documents that must be considered by all geriatric clients before they reach the stage when they cannot execute free will or competently sign legally binding legal documents. The mental health professional can provide the impetus that guides the client or the client's family into a lawyer's office so that the estate can be discussed and an estate plan implemented. Many diverse interests may have to be accommodated, including those of potential heirs; diverse personal needs, expectations, hopes, and fears; as well as family conflicts that may run deep and are difficult to bring to the surface and discuss openly.

2. The family members, the lawyer, the mental health professional, and other specialized individuals such as financial planners, insurance executives, bankers, and accountants may all have some input into the process. In the long run, you must serve the geriatric client as a holistic person. Assisting the client is the objective of the collective wisdom of the entire interdisciplinary team.

3. Perhaps the most meaningful service a mental health provider can offer to a geriatric client and the family is the enthusiastic and delicately forceful proposal that they seek legal counsel.

Perhaps the most meaningful service a mental health provider can offer to a geriatric client and the family is the enthusiastic and delicately forceful proposal that they seek legal counsel.

Dying without a Will (Intestate): A Possibility That Should Not Be Allowed to Happen

Professionals worthy of the title *professional* cannot allow their clients to die without a will. Dying intestate means dying without a legally drafted and executed (with the requisite formalities) instrument. The law of intestate succession determines the distribution of an estate; that is, the state writes the will for the deceased and determines where, how, and to whom the acquired personal and real property is distributed if no legally binding will were executed. It is chaotic and is not discussed here except to say that it should not happen. Individuals should make conscious choices and take the responsibility for disposing of their worldly goods and possessions. They should not take the chance that the state will understand and implement their disposition wishes. Choices are made when a will is written. Chances are taken when a person dies intestate.

Intestate means dying without a legally drafted and executed instrument.

The complexity of dying without a will can be illustrated by summarizing the problems: Real property is disposed of differently from personal property. The distribution is different depending on whether a person is married or divorced; has children, parents, or relations surviving or does not have blood relations surviving; whether there is anyone ready, willing, or able to take on the responsibility of winding down the estate and paying bills before distributing assets; and whether there are half brothers or sisters, adopted children, children who cannot be located, or unknown heirs who are known but their whereabouts are unknown. In addition, are all divorces finalized or are there unfinished bits and pieces of litigation, which were started in another jurisdiction and abandoned only to come to the surface when some money appeared to be available?

Answers to Frequently Asked Questions about:

Who owns the body of the geriatric client when the client dies?

Who owns the property of the geriatric client when the client dies?

What are some services the mental health professional can offer as time takes its inevitable toll?

How can I offer legal suggestions without practicing law?

❓ Question

I am a counselor at an assisted living community. In an interview before admission, I usually talk to the elderly person as well as some of his or her adult and in-charge children and often the older grandchildren if they are interested and involved. Although they know I am not a lawyer, they ask questions such as: What happens when their loved one dies? What happens to their property?

What are the extent and limits of my services? What general suggestions do I have to offer peace of mind to them and to their senior family member as this major transition is accommodated, that is, from independent living to a room or apartment in a home with a multitude of services provided? The question is open ended, but I want to be careful not to either overstep the limits of propriety or practice law without a license.

I think I know a lot about the legal requirements of aging, death, and dying from my educational experiences, personal familiarity, and discussions with lawyers and workshops, but I want to be careful and operate within circumscribed boundaries.

❗ Answer

The first answer to these questions is: "These are legal questions; see a lawyer." This answer will not satisfy the clients, so additional conversation must take place, which will be more acceptable. Begin each sentence with: "Of course, I am not a lawyer, but it is my understanding that . . ." Then share such information as you have with the clients.

The body belongs to the next of kin, while the real and personal property is devised by will, which appoints an executor to wind up the estate, dispose of accumulated property, and pay outstanding bills. This is a good time to emphasize some of the suggestions in this chapter. You might copy this chapter and make the copy available to inquiring clients or suggest that they purchase the book. Be emphatic when recommending that they consult a lawyer. It is true that wills and estate plans are expensive, but the cost is negligible when compared to the incredible expenses associated with the complex conflicts that arise when a person dies intestate. Family squabbles tear relationships apart and do irreparable damage for generations to come. One of the principal services a counselor can offer is to encourage a complete estate plan with all the ancillary documents set out in this chapter. The counselor does not practice law or draft anything, but the counselor does encourage and advise the family of the importance of professional preparation of these documents. If there isn't a family lawyer, suggest that the client or family interview lawyers until they have located one who connects

Legal Lightbulb

- There are numerous documents that must be considered in drafting an estate plan.

- Some issues might be considered and rejected, such as organ donations, body donations, do not resuscitate instruments, or the right to die a natural death or living wills. Others, on a selective basis, should be considered and implemented.

- Simple estates, with few assets and no complications, can be organized easily with general forms available through stationery stores and on the Internet. As assets and complexities increase, the need for a lawyer becomes clearer. The mental health professional can facilitate the selection of a lawyer and encourage the orderliness of an estate plan. Both tax and personal concerns are important.

- If a plan is accomplished using stationery or Internet standard forms, the forms should be examined for legal sufficiency by a lawyer both as to draftsmanship and execution. There are formalities to be observed so that certain instruments are legally binding.

- Some states provide for handwritten (holographic) wills, which can also be legally binding. However, lawyers do not consider such instruments to be generally in the best interest of the client.

- Most states have provisions for simple estate plans and probate, that is, estates with minimum assets and complications. Each state law has to be examined.

- Workshops, seminars, and courses are helpful, as are open informal discussions with lawyers. Networking interprofessionally is mutually advantageous to both the lawyer and the mental health professional.

- Plans have to be reviewed and updated periodically whenever a substantial financial or personal change (such as the death of a loved one) takes place.

- Wills are governed by state law; thus, when geriatric clients move or are moved, a local attorney should be consulted to see that the former plan conforms to current state law.

with their needs and personalities. There is no shortage of lawyers who are knowledgeable in the field of wills and estates. Friends can recommend competent lawyers and, failing that, so can banks, trust companies, accountants, and insurance professionals.

Decisions concerning the disposition of an individual's property can be difficult and wrenching. An empathetic counselor can shepherd the client through the decision-making process by facilitating the organization of thoughts and concepts. Final decisions are always those of the client, implemented by the lawyer. The counselor can help organize thoughts and prioritize them.

💡 Additional Thoughts

- Counselors do not and cannot practice law.
- Counselors can recommend lawyers and suggest some of the tasks and services lawyers perform.
- There are numerous documents mentioned in this chapter, which the counselor dealing with geriatric clients should understand and which could be appropriately discussed with clients in a knowledgeable manner, without offering legal advice.
- Most clients have not thought about their estate plans in detail. They are delighted to discuss these plans with an informed layperson who understands the interpersonal dynamics that are taking place during the aging process.
- Geriatric clients have many concerns peculiar to the process of aging and shifting of powers from the individual to numerous others. This is a sensitive area.
- Individuals who are used to being in charge sometimes resist even the most well-intentioned suggestions.
- Counselors are often, by both education and temperament, better suited than lawyers to deal with the emotions of geriatric clients and can offer conversations and services as trained professionals. This input is critical.

35

Nontraditional and Exotic Therapies

A therapist occasionally took clients to a petting zoo as a therapeutic tool. A petting zoo animal, a goat, had bitten the hand of one of the therapist's clients. The therapist, a licensed professional counselor with more than 15 years of professional private practice experience, received a letter from an attorney representing the client demanding to know the name and address of her professional liability insurance carrier and the limits of her policy. The attorney advised the therapist that his client had been injured during a therapy session, a portion of which was visiting the petting zoo, and sustained fractures and puncture wounds to two fingers and her left hand. Furthermore, nerves were damaged, and the client allegedly sustained permanent impairment and injury to the fingers and hand. The therapist had incorporated the use of animals into her private therapy practice with reportedly good therapeutic results over the years and without any prior incident.

Answers to (Not Too) Frequently Asked Questions about:

Nontraditional therapies

The use of animals in therapy

Responsibility for damages caused by animals

Risks when employing nontraditional therapeutic methods

❓ Question

What risks do therapists face when adopting or incorporating new, novel, innovative, or cutting-edge techniques or therapies into their practice? Does a cutting-edge technique imply or carry with it additional risks for the therapist-practitioner?

❗ Answer

The science of mental health treatment cannot advance without creative ideas and innovative approaches *and* therapists and clients who are willing to explore

A mental health professional has the obligation to safely treat clients and protect them from harm.

exotic and unusual possibilities. However, the mental health professional has the obligation to safely treat clients and protect them from harm. In addition, clients have to be fully informed of all the risks inherent with any offered treatment alternative so an informed decision can be made concerning its selection or rejection. Informed consent is one of the cornerstones of mental health treatment, and treatment does not commence in nonemergency situations unless and until informed consent is first obtained.

A quick review of the literature generates a list of therapies that could be considered nontraditional and, in varying degrees, outside the mainstream, for example:

- Aromatherapy.
- Animal-assisted therapy.
- Light therapy.
- Mind-body therapy.
- Guided imagery.
- Color therapy.
- Humor therapy.
- Meditation.
- Dance therapy.
- Sound therapy.
- Visualization.
- Neural linguistic programming.

In the past, music therapy and art therapy were considered nonmainstream, but through time and increased knowledge and application, these therapies have gained widespread recognition and acceptance. What were once unusual are now part of mainstream psychotherapy and are available in many psychiatric institutions and mental health facilities.

Any therapist practicing nontraditional therapies has greater risk of professional negligence claims than mental health professionals employing traditional and accepted therapeutic techniques.

Art therapists organized and created a national organization (American Art Therapy Association) that in turn created a national certification program (Art Therapy Credentialing Board), whose credential is recognized by the licensing boards of most states. In time, many current nonmainstream therapies may become just as accepted. They will first have to organize, create, present, and accumulate a credible and significant body of learned and acknowledged literature and generate the supportive scientific data that bestows acceptance.

Meanwhile, any therapist practicing nontraditional therapies has greater risk of professional negligence claims than mental health professionals employing traditional and accepted therapeutic techniques.

Lawsuits against mental health professionals often center on the issue of informed consent. Informed consent requires multiple disclosures to a potential client explaining the risks associated with a recommended therapy or technique and the alternative treatments available. Another risk that must be explained to the client is the risk of not obtaining the particular type of therapy offered as well as the risk of medications and the risk of not taking prescribed medications.

It is imperative that all nontraditional therapy be thoroughly discussed and explained to a client before treatment is commenced. This means providing the client with as much information as can reasonably be delivered to and digested by the client. Explanations must be given in a language the client understands. Seek an interpreter if needed. A prudent practice might be to schedule the client for an information session only, at no charge, to discuss the suggested therapy in detail. Give the client adequate time to ask questions as you explain all the potential risks and benefits of the nontraditional therapy you are recommending. Then schedule the first therapy session and send the client home with information including literature and web sites about the nonmainstream therapy or technique. If, after taking the time to consider all options and information, the client returns for the first therapy session, you will have gone a long way in eliminating a claim of lack of informed consent.

Be sure to include in your discussion with the client information about other therapies, including traditional treatment, that the client may wish to consider so there is ample time to either reject or accept the nontraditional approach. If a client is offered only one treatment option, it can be easily argued there was no informed consent given since the client assumed the therapy offered was the only available or sensible choice. In the field of therapy, there are always options, from published and recognized traditional therapies to the self-help pop psychology options that fill the bookshelves of every popular bookstore.

Include in your discussion with the client information about other therapies, including traditional treatment.

Be completely honest in selecting the information you disseminate to the client and *document* all information disclosed including reading material, web sites, and bibliographies you make available. Your written records will be your first line of defense if the client files a lawsuit against you or files a licensing board complaint. Encourage clients to read the relevant materials conscientiously, and have them sign a receipt that they have received the literature and have been advised to read the information, they understand the concept contained in the literature, and they are comfortable with the techniques that will apply to their therapy.

Document all information disclosed.

You must document why you believe the client is a candidate for the particular type of nontraditional or exotic therapy you are recommending. Be specific in identifying mental health problems or issues and explaining how the specific recommended therapy could, and should, in reasonable therapeutic probabilities, be helpful in treating them. Document the information you give the client about other therapeutic options. Document also the options rejected by you and the client and the reasons for rejecting them.

Check with your malpractice insurance provider to be certain that you will be covered for claims of professional negligence or any other claims that might be made under the policy. If you are using animals in your practice, it is wise to

Work with a knowledgeable insurance agent to be sure you are covered for the nontraditional risks.

obtain liability insurance coverage specifically for *the risk of injury caused by the animals.* A general liability or premises liability insurance policy may not cover you for this specific risk. You should work with a knowledgeable insurance agent to be sure you are covered for the nontraditional risks and know what the exceptions and exclusions are to the coverage you are offered. You may need to tailor or alter your practices to bring yourself within your insurance coverage.

Note: If using aromatherapy, the insurance policy should cover allergies that might be triggered by scent. With dance therapy, see that the client has a physical exam and has no injury that might be aggravated by the movements necessitated by the therapy. If guided imagery is proposed, see that the imagery does not reimpose harmful or dangerous flashbacks. The possibilities are endless. The alert therapist must conduct the therapy sessions in a manner that is consistent with the best interest of the client under the protection of an insurance policy that insures against the therapeutic risks for the particular type of nontraditional therapy utilized. A competent insurance consultant can provide expertise in this field.

When talking with the agent, remember the maxim: "Whatever can go wrong probably will." With proper insurance, if it does go wrong, you are protected.

🔆 Additional Thoughts

- Whenever nontraditional or exotic therapies are employed by a therapist, there is additional risk involved.
- Traditional therapy has a therapeutic and legal history and literature; nontraditional therapy has a less solid professional foundation.
- The burden can shift to the therapist to demonstrate to the court or jury that this particular therapy, with a particular client, was appropriate under all circumstances existing at the time of treatment.
- A jury, listening to exotic treatment testimony, is more likely to be skeptical.
- A licensing board, listening to exotic treatment testimony, might be inclined to defer to the therapies with which they are familiar, rather than the new and exotic.
- Demonstrating successful outcomes in a scientific manner is difficult if the particular therapy does not find general acceptance in the expert therapeutic community or in the generally accepted literature.
- Whenever deviating from the norm, a carefully drafted, lawyer-reviewed intake and consent form is required to protect the practitioner.

Other Considerations

Animal-assisted therapy has obvious unique risks, as experienced by the therapist whose client was bitten by a goat, that are not attendant with other types of

Sample Form

SPECIFIC CONSENT TO ANIMAL-ASSISTED THERAPY

I acknowledge that I have been thoroughly advised by Susan James, LPC, regarding the risks and benefits of animal-assisted therapy. Susan James, LPC, has answered every question I asked regarding this nontraditional therapy and explained other kinds of therapy that are available to me. After adequate time to consider what is best for me under my present circumstance, I knowingly and voluntarily agree to participate in *animal-assisted therapy* with Susan James, LPC. I have no known animal-related allergies. I fully understand that there is always a risk associated with contact with animals and knowingly assume such risk and hereby release Susan James, LPC, for any and all liability for injuries or damages of every kind I may sustain from contact with the animals used in my therapy.

_____   _____
Client   Date

Witnessed by:

_____   _____
Susan James, LPC   Date
Therapist

[NOTE: This form is tailored to one specific form of nontraditional therapy. It can be crafted or adopted for other forms of therapy.]

nontraditional therapies. Every nontraditional therapy, however, presents risks for the mental health professional. When a client does not benefit from treatment and has spent hard-earned dollars on therapeutic services, it is not difficult to imagine that particular client turning on the well-intentioned therapist. The client will not consider that treatment failed for reasons attributable only to the client and blames the therapist and the therapy that was recommended by the therapist.

A subsequent therapist who provides traditional therapeutic services to the client may suggest or even advocate that the client file a complaint against the previous therapist or pursue a refund of fees paid. Open-mindedness is not always a characteristic of experienced traditional health care service providers. Judges, juries, and licensing boards may look with equal disfavor on a cutting-edge, unproven, therapeutic technique. With caution and full disclosure, as well as proper insurance coverage, nontraditional therapies can be and should be implemented with an appropriate client who gives informed consent. The future of the mental health treatment and advances in available treatment options depend on it.

Stay current on nontraditional therapies.

To properly advise your clients, you must stay current on the available research, general publications, and literature with respect to nontraditional therapies or the techniques that you offer. Be alert for lawsuits or claims that are filed against other practitioners so you can avoid similar mistakes and avoid litigation or the threat or appearance of impropriety. Join the organizations that champion the specific therapy or educate and train other mental health professionals concerning this specific type of nontraditional therapy. Learn the therapy's limitations as well as its benefits. Assist these organizations or associations in their quest for recognition, licensure, or certification. Associate with other practitioners in your area and meet with them to discuss practice issues and experiences. Seek and obtain publicity to foster general acceptance in your community. The term *exotic* therapy may create certain resistance in the minds of the general and professional public. *Nontraditional* has gained limited acceptance in medicine and may gradually spill over to assist mental health practitioners.

Develop and use intake and consent forms that help to document the client's informed decision to engage your services to provide the nontraditional therapy. To limit your risk and exposure, consider incorporating language into your consent forms similar to the sample form provided in this chapter.

The history of mental health treatment is replete with breakthroughs that were initially dismissed, belittled, ridiculed, and challenged, only to be accepted, utilized, modified, and gradually incorporated into the mainstream of traditional psychotherapy. Luckily for the population in need of mental health services, innovators are bright, patient, and inspired professionals who insist on making their mark on the world and keep at it, in spite of initial opposition.

Legal Lightbulb

- Nontraditional therapies require that extra consideration be given to obtaining and documenting informed consent.

- The more information given to a prospective client about the nontraditional therapy, including its risks, and the more information given to a client about alternative treatment options, the greater the probability of establishing informed consent.

- Give the client adequate time to consider engaging your services before providing the nontraditional therapy.

- Have clients contractually acknowledge their assumption of the risk of this particular treatment and their release of liability.

- Carefully review your insurance policies to be certain you are adequately insured for the kind of therapy you want to provide and the client wants to accept.

- Be tireless in promoting the therapy with both the general public and the health care industry.

- Stay current on the research and literature with respect to the nontraditional therapies or techniques you employ in your practice.

- Be prepared to make supporting learned literature available to any professional or non-professional who requests further reading materials.

36

Internet Therapy

Late one afternoon, Susan A. James, a licensed counselor, received a call from a person who identified herself as Sarah. She said that she was given Susan's name by a friend who had been in treatment with Susan five years ago. Sarah resided in another state and asked if she could counsel with Susan via the Internet. Not having participated in Internet therapy, Susan indicated she would have to check with her licensing board to see if it were permissible. E-mail addresses were exchanged. When Susan confirmed with her board that Internet therapy was not prohibited, she launched into weekly chat sessions with Sarah via their respective e-mail accounts. After 12 weeks, Susan received a call from a man who identified himself as Kevin, Sarah's husband, and informed her that Sarah's real name was Sherry. The husband further advised Susan that Sherry had committed suicide and that he had learned of their Internet counseling sessions by accessing his wife's computer after her death. The husband informed Susan that Sherry had been in counseling with Susan five years previously when they lived in the same state as Susan and that Susan had terminated therapy with Sherry and referred her to another treatment provider when Sherry's problems proved beyond Susan's professional competency. Susan had advised Sherry in the presence of the husband of her lack of competence to effectively treat Sherry's problems and gave them several referrals.

This sad story illustrates the inherent risk of Internet therapy: the inability to positively identify the individual to whom the mental health professional is providing services. The trend with licensing boards is to permit Internet or other forms of long distance therapy to occur for two major reasons: (1) the appropriateness of distance therapy in certain circumstances and (2) the inability to effectively stop the practice if they wanted to. If a state denies its licensees the ability to provide distance therapy, it would be placing its licensees at a competitive disadvantage with therapists in other states that allow it to occur.

When we first heard of Internet therapy many years ago, it involved a missionary organization that wanted to provide mental health services to their missionaries who were stationed in remote locations. A few of their missionaries had been experiencing emotional and psychological difficulties and did not have access to mental health professionals for traditional face-to-face therapy. The need and appropriateness for distance therapy was obvious.

Guidelines for Internet Therapy

The American Counseling Association's (ACA) Governing Council approved guidelines for Internet therapy in October 1999. The guidelines established appropriate standards for the use of electronic communications over the Internet for counselors and are instructive for other disciplines as well. Mental health treatment providers must also be aware now of the HIPAA rules that most certainly apply to the use of the Internet to provide distance therapy.

The ACA's guidelines for confidentiality set out the following standards:

Mental health treatment providers must be aware of the HIPAA rules that apply to the use of the Internet to provide distance therapy.

1. Professional counselors ensure that clients are provided sufficient information to adequately address and explain the limitations of computer technology in the counseling process in general and the difficulties of ensuring complete client confidentiality of information transmitted through electronic communications over the Internet through online counseling.
2. To mitigate the risk of potential breaches of confidentiality, professional counselors provide one-on-one online counseling only through secure web sites or e-mail communications applications, which use appropriate encryption technology designed to protect the transmission of confidential information from access by unauthorized third parties.
3. To mitigate the risk of potential breaches of confidentiality, professional counselors provide only general information from nonsecure web sites or e-mail communications applications.

Professional counselors may provide general information from either secure or nonsecure web sites or through e-mail communications. General information includes non-client-specific, topical information on matters of general interest to the professional counselor's clients as a whole, third-party resource and referral information, addresses and phone numbers, and the like. Additionally, professional counselors using either secure or nonsecure web sites may provide links to third-party web sites such as licensing boards, certification bodies, and other resource information providers. Professional counselors investigate and continually update the content, accuracy, and appropriateness for the client of material contained in any links to third-party web sites.

4. To provide online counseling services only in practice areas within their expertise and not to provide online counseling services to clients located in states in which professional counselors are not licensed.

The trend is to allow online counseling to occur across state lines, but mental health professionals must review the state law specific to the jurisdiction in which they are licensed. One tactic is to provide in a client consent form a statement that the parties agree that the services provided to the client are being provided to the client in the state in which the therapist is licensed and where the therapist's computer ("office") is located. *Venue* is then defined for all purposes as the city, county, and state where the therapist is located, and the law of this same state will be applied at all times between the client and therapist.

Consider the example of the missionaries receiving distance therapy at the beginning of the chapter. It is highly unlikely that very many U.S.-based therapists are also licensed to provide mental health services in Africa, South America, Europe, or Asia, the locations the religious organization was sending its missionaries to. We doubt the ACA or any mental health discipline regulating authority would knowingly want to prohibit distance therapy to those potential worldwide clients.

5. Professional counselors inform clients of the limitations of confidentiality and identify foreseeable situations in which confidentiality must be breached in light of the law in both the state in which the client is located and the state in which the professional counselor is licensed.

See Chapter 38 for a discussion of the HIPAA Privacy Rule. Distance therapy requires the same Privacy Notice and practices.

The ACA standards require professional counselors to provide the following:

1. A readily visible notice indicating (i) that information transmitted over a web site or e-mail server may not be secure; (ii) whether the professional counselor's site is secure; (iii) whether the information transmitted between the professional counselor and the client during online counseling will be encrypted; and (iv) whether the client will need special software to access and transmit confidential information and, if so, whether the professional counselor provides the software as part of the online counseling services. The notice should be viewable from all web site and e-mail locations from which the client may send information.

Clients should be made aware of the risk of inadvertent and unintended disclosure of their confidential information.

Clients should be made aware of the risk of inadvertent and unintended disclosure of their confidential information. As an informed consumer, they then can choose to participate in the electronic therapy. This information is critical to establishing informed consent. (Uninformed consent is no consent at all.)

2. A readily visible notice advising clients of the identities of all professional counselor(s) who will have access to the information transmitted by the client and, in the event that more than one professional counselor has

access to the web site or e-mail system, the manner, if any, in which the client may direct information to a particular professional counselor. Professional counselors inform clients if any or all of the sessions are supervised. Clients are also informed if and how the supervisor preserves session transcripts. Professional counselors provide background information on all professional counselor(s) and supervisor(s) with access to the online communications, including education, licensing and certification, and practice area information.

This is consistent with practice requirements for traditional face-to-face therapy. The same ethical canons and obligations of the therapist are applied and expected.

3. A schedule of times during which the online counseling services will be available, including reasonable anticipated response times, and an alternate means of contacting the professional counselor at other times, including emergencies.
4. An alternative means of communication, such as telephone numbers or pager numbers, for back-up purposes in the event the online counseling service is unavailable for any reason.
5. The name of at least one other professional counselor who will be able to respond to the client if the professional counselor is unable to do so for any extended period of time.

In addition, the ACA's standards require professional counselors to:

1. Identify clients, verify their identities, and obtain alternative methods of contacting clients for back-up situations or in the event of an emergency.

Nothing will prohibit securing client authorization consistent with the HIPAA Privacy Rule to notify third parties to verify identities or in the event of emergencies. Request that prospective clients fax or forward a copy of their driver's license.

2. Have their clients execute client waiver agreements stating that the client (i) acknowledges the limitations inherent in ensuring client confidentiality of information transmitted through online counseling and (ii) agrees to waive the client's privilege of confidentiality with respect to any confidential information transmitted through online counseling that may be accessed by any third party without authorization of the client and despite the reasonable efforts of the professional counselor to arrange a secure online environment.
3. Develop and maintain appropriate procedures for ensuring the safety and confidentiality of client information acquired through electronic

If the client is unable or unwilling to consent to the client waiver, professional counselors are expected to refer the client to more traditional methods of counseling and should not provide online counseling services.

communications, including, but not limited to, encryption software, proprietary on-site file servers with fire walls, saving online or e-mail communications to the hard drive or file server computer systems, creating regular tape or diskette back-up copies, creating hard copies of all electronic communications, and the like. Clients must be informed about the length of time for, and method of, preserving session transcripts and warned of the possibility or frequency of technology failures and time delays in transmitting and receiving information.

HIPAA Security Rule (see Chapter 46) requires similar safeguards: Client information must be maintained for at least six years. Mental health professionals may be required to maintain the information longer if their state law dictates a longer retention period. Check local law concerning minor clients and preservation of client information after the age or circumstance of majority.

4. Electronically transfer confidential client information to authorized third-party recipients only when (i) both the professional counselor and the authorized recipient have "secure" transfer and acceptance communication capabilities, (ii) the recipient is able to effectively protect the confidentiality of the client's confidential information to be transferred; and (iii) the informed written consent of the client, acknowledging the limits of confidentiality, has been obtained.

Be sure client authorizations comply with HIPAA Privacy Rule requirements.

Develop an appropriate intake procedure and therapist-friendly form for potential clients to determine whether online counseling is appropriate for the needs of the client.

5. Develop an appropriate intake procedure and therapist-friendly form for potential clients to determine whether online counseling is *appropriate for the needs of the client.* Professional counselors warn potential clients that online counseling services may not be appropriate in certain situations and, to the extent possible, inform clients of specific limitations, potential risks, and/or potential benefits relevant to the client's anticipated use of online counseling services. Professional counselors ensure that clients are intellectually, emotionally, and physically capable of using the online counseling services and of understanding the potential risks and/or limitations of such services.

6. Once the appropriateness of online therapy has been established, develop an individual online counseling plan that is consistent with both the client's individual circumstances and the limitations of online counseling. Professional counselors shall specifically take into account the limitations, if any, on the use of any or all of the following in online counseling: initial client appraisal, diagnosis, and assessment methods employed by the professional counselor. Professional counselors who determine that online counseling is inappropriate for the client should avoid entering into or

immediately terminate the online counseling relationship and encourage the client to continue the counseling relationship through an appropriate alternative method of counseling.

7. Verify that clients are above the age of minority, are competent to enter into the counseling relationship with a professional counselor, and are able to give informed consent. If clients are minor children, incompetent, or incapable of giving informed consent, professional counselors must obtain the written consent of the parent or legal guardian or other authorized legal representative of the client prior to commencing online counseling services to the client.

8. Confirm that their liability (malpractice) insurance provides coverage for online counseling services and that the provision of such services is not prohibited by or otherwise violates any applicable (i) state or local statutes, rules, regulations, or ordinances; (ii) codes of professional membership organizations and certifying boards; and/or (iii) codes of state licensing boards.

9. Seek appropriate legal and technical assistance in the development and implementation of their online counseling services.

Many of these standards are going to be difficult to apply, but mental health professionals must make every effort to do so. Consider the scenario presented at the beginning of the chapter. How could Susan have established, with certainty, the identity of the client who sought to deceive her? One method might be to ask the client to have another health care treatment provider corroborate her identity information including name, birth date, driver's license, any special or unique characteristics, and social security information as a precondition to accepting the client for Internet therapy.

The ACA's standards are thorough and place a heavy burden on the therapist who wishes to engage in this kind of distance therapy. In light of the risks associated with distance therapies, however, they seem reasonable and practicable.

Answers to Frequently Asked Questions about:

Internet therapy

Progress or case notes—documentation

Presumption: Clinical file will also be preserved on computer

❓ Question

I practice in an area where many of my clients are transferred or relocated frequently, yet they want to continue our therapeutic relationship electronically using e-mail as

the principal method of treatment. I know them, have the proper consent forms, but am unsure what to preserve or how to preserve our computer-generated conversations, which take place either by e-mail or instant messaging. Occasionally, when the emotion of the situation or the patience of typing wears thin, we talk by phone. What type of records should I preserve, and how much do I need? Do I have to print out every client contact on the computer, in addition to noting all my phone or personal contacts? Computers were designed to save trees, not contribute to their demise!

❗ Answer

The documentation of a client file does not change because a computer is the method of communication. Review Chapters 5 and 7 for general guidelines. Whatever would normally be significant in the file should be documented regardless of the method of therapy. Our book *Portable Ethicist for Mental Health Professionals* (see chapters titled "Practice Considerations," "Record Keeping"; John Wiley & Sons, Inc., 2000) also contains information concerning the records to be established, maintained, and secured for the requisite number of statutory years. But remember, if all the documentation concerning a client is preserved on a computer, this record must be available for the 6- to 10-year requirement for the preservation of files as set forth in the HIPAA Security Rule, state statutes, and licensing laws. Not only must they be on a disk, but also the technology to retrieve from the disk must be available.

💡 Additional Thoughts

- Internet technology as a method of treatment is here to stay.
- Documentation and preservation of records remains the same in principal.
- Clients still have the right to review their records and must be provided with a copy for reasonable cost on demand. Under certain circumstances, the electronic records are subject to subpoena.
- This type of electronic therapy and record keeping is subject to the new HIPAA statute and its privacy and security rules, which will be applicable to almost all mental health professionals.
- Not seeing a client face to face has certain obvious and inherent risks. These risks have to be accommodated by occasional face-to-face or at least voice-to-voice contact if possible.
- Beware of imposters. You can be anyone on the Internet, real or fictional.
- Sorting out the real from the fictional is the job of the mental health provider.
- Offering treatment to a person who does not exist can be embarrassing, especially if you charge and are paid for the professional consultation or if a third-party payer is reimbursing for the service.

Legal Lightbulbs

- Careful review of state law and ethical canons must be conducted to learn the permissibility of Internet therapy and any applicable special duties or considerations in the home state or local jurisdiction.

- You must research and decide on the encryption software that you will use in your Internet therapy. Remember that clients will need to acquire the same software, so be conscious of price and availability before choosing. In addition, consider using nicknames with clients and e-mail addresses that will not identify either you or the client.

- Remember that compliance with HIPAA's privacy and security rules is required.

- Consider a method by which a client's true identity can be conclusively established, that is, requiring confirmation by a health care provider that treats the client in the area in which he or she lives. Get a copy of the client's drivers licence.

- Study and apply the ACA's standards in developing your online therapy procedures and practice. Be especially certain that clients understand the limitations of online therapy and the risk of unauthorized disclosure of their health care information.

- Be sure to verify with your malpractice insurance provider that online or other distance therapy will be covered by the policy. If not, add the coverage. Often, endorsements are available for a premium.

- Consider requiring *at least one face-to-face* session with each client or, as the cost decreases and the technology becomes easier to use, cameras and digital imaging for some, if not all, of the distance therapy sessions.

- On your intake form, provide that the client inform you at once if his or her e-mail address changes and keep the client informed of your current e-mail address. Seek and obtain an alternative means of contacting the client.

SECTION ELEVEN

THE HEALTH INSURANCE PORTABILITY AND ACCOUNTABILITY ACT (HIPAA)

This special, all-inclusive, far-reaching section contains information not available when *Portable Lawyer* was originally published. The comprehensive contents of the HIPAA Act will affect, in one way or another, every mental health practitioner and every mental health discipline.

The Privacy Rule will indicate how information is disseminated to clients and made available to others. There are requirements for marketing and the maintaining and securing of client records as well as the methods by which this information can be shared with other lay and professional individuals and entities. The Security Rule contains requirements for the safeguarding of client files, as well as their preservation and maintenance. In addition, there are required forms, which are provided in the appendixes. Subject to a local attorney's approval, these forms provide a good starting point for HIPAA compliance.

HIPAA implementation is mandated and, in our opinion, will apply in time to all mental health professionals in this country. This mandate is supported by serious penalties for noncompliance.

Since the Act is relatively new, there are few assessed penalties or judicial opinions to date. However, that does not indicate that in the future, enforcement of the law will be lax or nonexistent. HIPAA compliance is going to be a fundamental requirement when establishing or continuing a practice. In the following chapters, there are only a few "Frequently Asked Questions" because the law is new in its application and has little historical basis for recommending answers. Comprehensive responses, supported by case analysis or administrative rules and regulations, will be available only when there is sufficient case precedent.

We recommend that practitioners read and understand the contents of these chapters and make an effort to alert all staff and employees to HIPAA rules and regulations. Internal continuing education is a key factor and a sensible requirement. Conform all forms to the HIPAA provisions as they exist today and as they may be amended from time to time in the future. Gone are the days when a well-drafted and lawyer-approved form would last the lifetime of the practitioner or the agency. Today, every form must be legally, ethically, and HIPAA compliant at the time it is drafted and further amended as the law changes.

37

HIPAA Overview

The Health Insurance Portability and Accountability Act (HIPAA) is the federal legislation signed into law in August 1996 that imposes new duties and responsibilities on the country's health care providers. The law's primary purpose is to protect Americans with preexisting health problems from losing health insurance coverage if they change residences or jobs. In addition, the administration simplification provisions of the law attempt to simplify our national health care system by:

- Standardizing the electronic transmission of common administrative and financial transactions such as billing and payment through the establishment and use of standardized formats and codes.
- Having unique health identifiers for individuals, employers, health plans, and health care providers.
- Ensuring privacy and security standards to protect the confidentiality and integrity of individually identifiable health care information.

HIPAA imposes new duties and responsibilities on the country's health care providers.

The Department of Health and Human Services (HHS) is charged with the responsibility of establishing regulations to implement the legislation. Promulgation of rules has taken several years, and they are still a work in progress. It will be necessary for mental health providers to be alert to the possibility of rule changes or new interpretations of existing regulations in the future.

Compliance with the Privacy Rule began on April 14, 2003. The Privacy Rule requires mental health professionals to create and implement procedures, policies, and agreements with business associates to control disclosure and use of an individual's personal health care information.

Compliance with the Security Rule is currently scheduled for April 2005 for most covered entities. This rule deals with a provider's physical space and equipment such as offices, files, and computer equipment and the necessity for secure and private communication and storage of an individual's personal health care information.

The Privacy Rule requires mental health professionals to create and implement procedures, policies, and agreements with business associates to control disclosure and use of an individual's personal health care information.

Who Must Comply with HIPAA?

- Health plans, which include health insurance companies, HMOs, and managed care plans.
- Health care clearinghouses, which are defined as public or private entities that process or facilitate the processing of information received from another entity in a nonstandard format (or containing nonstandard data content) into standard data elements or a standard transaction.
- Health care providers, defined as providers of medical or other health services and any other person who furnishes, bills, or is paid for health care in the normal course of business.

Mental health professionals are clearly health care providers as defined by HIPAA and will be required to comply with HIPAA's security and/or privacy rules.

Why Should a Mental Health Professional Comply with HIPAA Requirements?

Failure to comply is really not an option because serious penalties can result. Therapists who refuse to become familiar with the requirements and to implement them into their mental health practice could face the following consequences:

- Administrative action taken by the HHS Office of Civil Rights.
- Civil penalties of not more than $100 for each violation, with the total amount imposed on the mental health professional for all violations of an identical requirement or prohibition during a calendar year not to exceed $25,000.

Failure to comply is not an option.

- Fines up to $250,000, imprisonment for up to 10 years, or both, for wrongfully disclosing a client's identifiable health information.

In addition, incorrect formatting or coding of billings could result in revenue interruption for the practice.

Legal Lightbulb

- Mental health providerss must be well informed on all privacy and security requirements and implement them in their practices.

- These Rules are new and will undergo judicial and administrative scrutiny in the months and years to come.

- Mental health providerss must be alert to new and revised versions of the Rules in the future.

38

HIPAA Privacy Rule

The full text for HIPAA *Standards for Privacy of Individually Identifiable Health Information* (the Privacy Rule) published by the U.S. Department of Health and Human Services (HHS) on December 28, 2000, and modifications of the Rule adopted on August 14, 2002, can be found at *45 CFR Parts 160 and 164*. The Privacy Rule can be downloaded from the web site of the HHS Office for Civil Rights (http://www.hhs.gov/ocr/hipaa/). Rather than give the specific citation for each rule discussed in this chapter, we refer you to the regulations themselves. It is strongly suggested that mental health professionals obtain a full copy of the regulations and review the Privacy Rule as they would their state licensing acts and ethical canons.

The Privacy Rule provides the first comprehensive federal protection for the privacy of health information.

The Privacy Rule provides the first comprehensive federal protection for the privacy of health information. The Privacy Rule seeks to provide strong privacy protections that do not interfere with patient access to, or the quality of, health care delivery. The Privacy Rule establishes, for the first time, a foundation of federal protections for the privacy of protected health information (PHI). The Rule does not replace other federal or state law that grants individuals even greater privacy protections, and covered entities are free to retain or adopt more protective policies or practices. It creates for the first time national standards to protect an individual's medical records and other personal health information:

- It gives patients more *control* over their health information.
- It sets *boundaries* on the use and release of health records.
- It establishes appropriate *safeguards* that health care providers and others must achieve to protect the privacy of health information.
- It holds violators *accountable*, with civil and criminal penalties that can be imposed if they violate patients' privacy rights.
- It strikes a balance when *public responsibility* supports disclosure of some forms of data, for example, to protect public health.

For patients, it means being able to make informed choices when seeking care and reimbursement for care based on how personal health information may be used:

- It enables patients to find out how their information may be used and about certain disclosures of their information that have been made.
- It generally limits release of information to the minimum reasonably needed for the purpose of the disclosure.
- It generally gives patients the right to examine and obtain a copy of their own health records and request corrections.
- It empowers individuals to control certain uses and disclosures of their health information.

For the average mental health provider, the Privacy Rule requires activities, such as:

- Notifying patients about their privacy rights and how their information can be used.
- Adopting and implementing privacy procedures for the practice.
- Training employees so that they understand the privacy procedures.
- Designating an individual to be responsible for seeing that the privacy procedures are adopted and followed.
- Securing patient records containing individually identifiable health information so that they are not readily available to those who do not need them.
- Keeping an accounting of disclosures of a client's protected health information.

To ease the burden of complying with the new requirements, the Privacy Rule gives needed flexibility for providers to create their own privacy procedures, tailored to fit their size and needs. The scalability of the Rule provides a more efficient and appropriate means of safeguarding protected health information than would any single standard, for example:

- The privacy official at a small mental health practice may be the office manager, who has other nonprivacy-related duties; the privacy official at a large mental health clinic may be a full-time position and may have the regular support and advice of a privacy staff or board; the privacy official for a sole practitioner therapist is obviously that therapist.
- The training requirement may be satisfied by a small mental health practice providing each new member of the workforce with a copy of its privacy policies and documenting that new members have reviewed the policies, whereas a large mental health clinic may provide training through live instruction, video presentations, or interactive software programs.
- The policies and procedures of small providers may be more limited under the Rule than those of a large hospital or clinic, based on the volume of health information maintained and the number of interactions with those within and outside the health care system.

The Privacy Rule gives needed flexibility for providers to create their own privacy procedures, tailored to fit their size and needs.

Health and Human Services determined that its original consent requirement unintentionally prevented health care providers from providing timely, quality health care to individuals in a variety of circumstances. The most troubling and pervasive problem was that health care providers would not have been able to use or disclose protected health information for treatment, payment, or health care operations purposes before the initial face-to-face encounter with the patient, which is routinely done to provide timely access to quality health care. The following are two examples of how the consent requirement would have posed barriers to mental health care:

- Providers who do not provide treatment in person (such as a provider prescribing over the telephone) might have been unable to provide care because they would have had difficulty obtaining prior written consent to use protected health information at the first service delivery.
- Psychiatric emergency room providers were concerned that, in an urgent situation, they would have had to try to obtain consent to comply with the Privacy Rule, even if that would be inconsistent with the appropriate practice of emergency medicine.

To eliminate such barriers to health care, mandatory consent was replaced with the voluntary consent provision that permits health care providers to obtain consent for treatment, payment, and health care operations, at their option, and enables them to obtain consent in a manner that does not disrupt needed treatment. Securing informed consent is a matter that is left to state law, and mental health professionals must comply with all requirements of their respective home states.

Under HIPAA, HHS has the authority to modify the privacy standards as its Secretary may deem appropriate. However, a standard can be modified only once in a 12-month period.

As a general rule, future modifications to the Privacy Rule must be made in accordance with the Administrative Procedure Act (APA). HHS will comply with the APA by publishing proposed rule changes, if any, in the *Federal Register* through a Notice of Proposed Rulemaking and will invite comment from the public. After reviewing and addressing those comments, HHS will issue a modified final rule.

As stated previously, HIPAA and the Privacy Rule should be considered a work in progress, and mental health professionals should endeavor to stay fully informed of all new rules, interpretations, and revisions. Much of the material in this chapter is adapted from information and opinions published by HHS. As with all regulations, their legality and scope will be determined by the courts as legal challenges and defenses are raised over time. HHS will not have the last word, and its opinions, rules, and interpretations will not necessarily prevail.

HIPAA and the Privacy Rule should be considered a work in progress, and mental health professionals should endeavor to stay fully informed of all new rules, interpretations, and revisions.

Privacy Standard

Stated simply, the Privacy Standard provides that protected health information may not be used or disclosed except as permitted under the Privacy Rule. In analyzing this standard and its applicability, mental health professionals must determine (1) if they are covered entities, (2) what constitutes protected health information, and (3) the permitted uses and disclosures of protected health information.

Covered Entities (45 CFR 160.103)

The Privacy Rule covers:

- Health plans.
- Health care clearinghouses.
- Health care providers who conduct certain financial and administrative transactions electronically. These electronic transactions are those for which standards have been adopted by the Secretary under HIPAA, such as electronic billing and fund transfers.

A mental health professional who transmits personal health information electronically is a covered entity and must comply with the Privacy Rule. If the mental health professional does not personally transmit personal health information electronically but contracts with others to perform some essential functions, the mental health professional must be HIPAA compliant. Specialized contracts required by HIPAA are discussed in Chapter 40.

Protected Health Information (45 CFR 164.501)

What constitutes protected health information is found in the following Privacy Act definitions:

Health information (45 CFR 160.103) means any information whether oral or recorded in any form or medium that:

(1) Is created or received by a health care provider . . . ; and
(2) Relates to the past, present, or future physical or mental health or condition of an individual; the provision of health care to an individual; or the past, present, or future payment for the provision of health care to an individual.

Individually identifiable health information is information that is a subset of health information, including demographic information collected from an individual, and:

(1) Is created or received by a health care provider . . . and
(2) Relates to the past, present, or future physical or mental health or condition of an individual; the provision of health care to an individual; or the past,

present, or future payment for the provision of health care to an individual; and
   (i) That identifies the individual; or
   (ii) With respect to which there is a reasonable basis to believe the information can be used to identify the individual.

Protected health information means individually identifiable health information:

(1) . . . that is:
   (i) Transmitted by electronic media; defined as the mode of electronic transmission and includes the Internet (wide-open), Extranet (using Internet technology to link a business with information only accessible to collaborating parties), leased lines, dial up lines, private networks, and those transmissions that are physically moved from one location to another using magnetic tape, disk, or compact disc.
   (ii) Maintained in any medium described in the definition of electronic media . . . or
   (ii) Transmitted or maintained in any other form or medium.

Excluded from the definition of *protected health information* are education records covered by the Family Education Rights and Privacy Act and employment records held by a covered entity in its role as an employer.

The Privacy Act contains special provisions for psychotherapy notes, which constitute protected health information if electronically transmitted or maintained in any medium as set forth in the definition of electronic media. Special use and disclosure rules for psychotherapy notes are discussed later in this chapter.

Psychotherapy notes (45 CFR 164.501) means notes recorded (in any medium) by a health care provider documenting or analyzing the contents of conversations during a private counseling session or a group, joint, or family counseling session and that are separated from the rest of the individual's medical record.

Psychotherapy notes exclude medication prescription and monitoring; counseling session start and stop times; the modalities and frequencies of treatment; furnished results of clinical tests; and any summary of the following items: diagnosis, functional status, the treatment plan, symptoms, prognosis, and progress to date.

All information traditionally contained in a client's file or chart constitutes individually identifiable health information. Even information written on a note when taking a phone call from a client falls within this definition. The information becomes protected health information with restricted use and disclosure when it is electronically transmitted or maintained in a medium such as computer disk, magnetic tape, or compact disk.

Putting It All Together

If a mental health professional electronically transmits or maintains identifiable protected health care information in connection with any of the following transactions (45 CFR 160.103), it becomes protected health information and compliance with the Privacy Rule is required:

- Health care claims.
- Health care payment and remittance advice.
- Coordination of benefits.
- Health care claim status, enrollment, or disenrollment in a health plan.
- Eligibility for a health plan.
- Referral certification and authorization.
- First report of injury.
- Health claims attachments.
- Other transactions that the Secretary may prescribe by regulation.

In addition, if the mental health professional contracts with an entity that electronically transmits individually identifiable health information in connection with one of these transactions, i.e., billing service, the mental health professional must be fully compliant with the Privacy Rule. The mental health professional who directly or indirectly accepts third-party payments for the services provided to a client must comply. It is important to remember that once compliance is triggered, compliance becomes necessary for the therapist's entire operation—not just an isolated electronic transmission.

We have received calls from several therapists who stated that they had an entirely client-direct-pay practice, and they considered themselves exempt from compliance with the Privacy Rule. In theory, it is possible to avoid the wide net of HIPAA, but on further questioning, it was determined that two of these therapists were wrong. One therapist maintained his client records on a computer hard drive and routinely transferred data to a back-up disk that was stored at the therapist's home for security reasons. He was maintaining and transferring data on electronic media, which triggered the necessity for Privacy Rule compliance.

The second therapist admitted to occasionally receiving and answering an e-mail from a client, which triggered compliance. He indicated that he also sometimes receives faxes from a client. Although the original technology of phone-to-phone fax transmission seems to fall outside the definition of electronic media, faxes now often originate on a computer or are sent through a computer. If that occurs, an electronic copy of the fax is created and, even if deleted on the computer, is usually still recoverable. When the therapist received a fax from a client, there was no way to determine if it was created, stored, or sent through the use of a computer with a modem.

The Privacy Rule requires mental health professionals to have a written policy on how the privacy of faxes and e-mails will be handled by the practice and written procedures for implementing the policy including training, monitoring, and auditing.

As a side matter, the Privacy Rule requires mental health professionals to have a written policy on how the privacy of faxes and e-mails will be handled by the practice and written procedures for implementing the policy including training, monitoring, and auditing. Care should also be given to ensure that the recipient of the faxed or electronically transmitted PHI will be protective of its privacy. A confidentiality notice should be included with each fax and e-mailed transmission of PHI (see sample form on page 325).

Consider also sending a fax audit to potential recipients of faxed protected health information (see sample fax audit form on pages 326–327).

Compliance with the Privacy Rules is recommended for all mental health professionals. We cannot envision a sensible scenario where a therapist can safely and realistically practice without being HIPAA compliant. Our home state of Texas requires compliance with the Privacy Rule by all mental health professionals whether they are considered a covered entity (TX Health & Safety Code, Chapter 181) or not, and other states may do so, also. In time, compliance will be unavoidable; therefore, rather than spend time and energy trying to stay out from under HIPAA, a mental health professional should become compliant now and not risk being penalized in the future.

Permitted Uses and Disclosures

The Privacy Rule contains very specific rules with respect to the use and disclosure of PHI. The mental health professional should keep in mind, however, that HIPAA provides that this federal law will not necessarily preempt state law. If a state law is more protective of the privacy of an individual's mental health information, the more protective state law will control. Each permitted use or disclosure under the Privacy Rule should be compared with the state law in the location where the mental health professional is practicing.

For example, the Privacy Rule, consistent with the holding of the *Tarasoff v. Regents of the University of California* (17 Cal. 3d 425, 551 P2d 334, 131 Cal. Rep. 14 [1976]) case, permits disclosure of PHI to "the target of the threat" to prevent or lessen a serious and imminent threat to the health or safety of a person or the public. In a few states, including Texas, mental health professionals are authorized by state law to contact only medical facilities and law enforcement personnel when confronted with such circumstances. This is a much more restrictive and protective approach, which HIPAA presumably would not preempt. It would appear that the mental health professional should comply only with state law and not contact the identified victim.

It is just as important today to be well versed on the state law in which the mental health professional practices as well as all ethical canons and codes that apply to the practice and discipline.

Sample Form

CONFIDENTIALITY NOTICE FROM SUSAN A. JONES, LPC

This fax (or e-mail) and any files transmitted with it are confidential and intended solely for the use of the individual or entity to whom they are addressed. Nothing in this fax (or e-mail) is intended to constitute a waiver of any privilege or the confidentiality of this message. Any dissemination, copying, or use of this information by anyone other than the designated and intended recipient(s) is prohibited. If you have received this fax (or e-mail) in error, please notify me immediately by reply and delete and destroy this message and information immediately.

Sample Form

FAX AUDIT

To: Name: _____

Company: _____

FAX Number: _____

From: Name: Susan A. Jones, LPC

Date: _____ Title: Privacy/Security Officer

FAX Number: _____

REPLY REQUESTED

We are conducting an audit of our fax network to verify if the intended recipient, listed below, is still receiving faxes at the number listed below.

We are asking for your help in assessing the security of our faxes sent to this number by answering a few simple questions. This information can help us improve the confidential and private delivery of protected health information.

Please return your completed fax audit to our office at our fax number listed above. Thank you for your assistance.

_____   _____

Intended Recipient   Fax Number

Is the intended recipient still receiving faxes at this number? Yes _____ No _____

If no, is there a different fax number we should be using? Fax Number: _____

Please Answer the Following Questions

1. Is your fax machine located in a locked room or other secured area? Yes _____ No _____

2. Can nonauthorized visitors to your office view any documents lying on your fax machine? Yes _____ No _____

Sample Form
(continued)

3. During what hours is there always an attendant at your fax machine?

Morning Hours _____ Evening Hours _____

Afternoon Hours _____ Late Night Hours _____

Attendant Never Available _____

4. Do you have another, more secure fax number we may use? Yes _____ No _____
Fax Number: _____

_____ _____
Signature of Intended Recipient   Date

Please sign and date this from and fax it back to us at our number listed above.

THANK YOU.

Incidental Uses and Disclosures (45 CFR 164.502 (a)(1)(iii))

Covered entities should assess potential risks to patient privacy, as well as consider issues such as the potential effects on patient care and any administrative or financial burden to be incurred from implementing particular safeguards.

Many customary health care communications and practices play an important or even essential role in ensuring that individuals receive prompt and effective health care. Due to the nature of these communications and practices, as well as the various environments in which individuals receive health care or other services from covered entities, the potential exists for an individual's health information to be disclosed incidentally. For example, a hospital visitor may overhear a provider's confidential conversation with another provider or a patient or may glimpse a patient's information on a sign-in sheet or nursing station whiteboard. The HIPAA Privacy Rule is not intended to impede these customary and essential communications and practices and, thus, does not require that all risk of incidental use or disclosure be eliminated to satisfy its standards. Rather, the Privacy Rule permits certain incidental uses and disclosures of protected health information to occur when the covered entity has in place reasonable safeguards and minimum necessary policies and procedures to protect an individual's privacy.

The Privacy Rule permits incidental uses and disclosures that occur as a by-product of another permissible or required use or disclosure, as long as the covered entity has applied *reasonable safeguards* and implemented the *minimum necessary standard (45 CFR 164.502(b) and 164.514 (d))*, where applicable, with respect to the primary use or disclosure. An incidental use or disclosure is a secondary use or disclosure that cannot reasonably be prevented, is limited in nature, and that occurs as a result of another use or disclosure that is permitted by the Rule. However, an incidental use or disclosure is not permitted if it is a by-product of an underlying use or disclosure that violates the Privacy Rule.

A covered entity must have in place appropriate administrative, technical, and physical safeguards that protect against uses and disclosures not permitted by the Privacy Rule, as well as limit incidental uses or disclosures. It is not expected that a covered entity's safeguards guarantee the privacy of protected health information from any and all potential risks. Reasonable safeguards will vary from covered entity to covered entity depending on factors such as the size of the covered entity and the nature of its business.

What may be reasonable and permissible in a hospital setting or a pediatrician's office will not be tolerated in a therapist's office. Greater care must be given to privacy when mental health services are provided. In an office where multiple therapists are providing services, it would not be unreasonable to have offices that are designed to prevent the possibility of anyone's overhearing the voices of a therapist and the client. Sound-muffling devices may be necessary if the conversation is audible outside the office walls.

Other reasonable safeguards for a therapist's office might include:

- Isolating or locking file cabinets or records rooms.
- Providing additional security, such as passwords, on computers maintaining personal information.

- Making sure computer screens are not visible to people passing by.
- Although permitted in a larger facility or hospital, it is not unreasonable to prohibit the use of a sign-in sheet in a small therapist office.
- Staggering session start times if there are two or three therapists in the practice location.
- Separate ingress and egress routes from the therapist's office.
- Isolated waiting rooms.

Covered entities must implement reasonable safeguards to limit incidental, and avoid prohibited, uses and disclosures. The Privacy Rule does not require that all risk of protected health information disclosure be eliminated. Covered entities must review their own practices and determine what steps are reasonable to safeguard their patient information. In determining what is reasonable, covered entities should assess potential risks to patient privacy, as well as consider issues such as the potential effects on patient care and any administrative or financial burden to be incurred from implementing particular safeguards. Covered entities also may take into consideration the steps that other prudent health care and health information professionals are taking to protect patient privacy.

Minimum Necessary (45 CFR 164.502(b) and 164.514(d))

The minimum necessary standard, a key protection of the HIPAA Privacy Rule, is derived from confidentiality codes and practices in common use today. It is consistent with the common practice of many mental health professionals to offer a summary when copies of a client's records are requested. It is based on sound current practice that protected health information should not be used or disclosed when it is not necessary to satisfy a particular purpose or carry out a function. The minimum necessary standard requires covered entities to evaluate their practices and enhance safeguards as needed to limit unnecessary or inappropriate access to and disclosure of protected health information. The Privacy Rule's requirements for minimum necessary disclosure are designed to be sufficiently flexible to accommodate the various circumstances of any covered entity.

The Privacy Rule generally requires covered entities to take reasonable steps to limit the use or disclosure of, and requests for, protected health information to the minimum necessary to accomplish the intended purpose. The minimum necessary standard does not apply to the following:

- Disclosures to or requests by a health care provider for treatment purposes.
- Disclosures to the individual who is the subject of the information.
- Uses or disclosures made pursuant to an individual's authorization.
- Uses or disclosures required for compliance with the HIPAA Administrative Simplification Rules.

- Disclosures to HHS when disclosure of information is required under the Privacy Rule for enforcement purposes.
- Uses or disclosures that are required by other law.

The implementation specifications for this provision require a covered entity to develop and implement policies and procedures appropriate for its own organization, reflecting the entity's business practices and workforce. HHS has stated it will continue to monitor the workability of the minimum necessary standard and consider proposing revisions, where appropriate, to ensure that the Rule does not hinder timely access to quality health care.

For uses of protected health information, the covered entity's policies and procedures must identify the persons or classes of persons within the covered entity who need access to the information to carry out their job duties, the categories or types of protected health information needed, and conditions appropriate to such access. A covered entity should implement policies that identify and limit the persons who will be allowed to have access to the entire client file, including psychotherapy notes. Case-by-case review of each use is not required. Where the entire client record is necessary, the covered entity's policies and procedures must state so explicitly and include a justification.

For routine or recurring requests and disclosures, the policies and procedures may be standard protocols and must limit the protected health information disclosed or requested to the minimum necessary for that particular type of disclosure or request. Individual review of each disclosure or request is not required.

For nonroutine disclosures and requests, covered entities must develop reasonable criteria for determining and limiting the disclosure or request to only the minimum amount of protected health information necessary to accomplish the purpose of a nonroutine disclosure or request. Nonroutine disclosures and requests must be reviewed on an individual basis in accordance with these criteria and limited accordingly.

Where protected health information is disclosed to, or requested by, health care providers for treatment purposes, the minimum necessary standard does not apply.

In certain circumstances, the Privacy Rule permits a covered entity to rely on the judgment of the party requesting the disclosure as to the minimum amount of information that is needed. Such reliance must be reasonable under the particular circumstances of the request. This reliance is permitted when the request is made by:

- A public official or agency who states that the information requested is the minimum necessary for a purpose permitted under the Privacy Rule, such as for public health purposes.
- Another covered entity.

- A professional who is a workforce member or business associate of the covered entity holding the information and who states that the information requested is the minimum necessary for the stated purpose.
- A researcher with appropriate documentation from an institutional review board (IRB) or privacy board.

The Rule does not require such reliance, however, and the covered entity always retains discretion to make its own minimum necessary determination for disclosures to which the standard applies.

Legal Lightbulb

- Obtain a copy of the Privacy Rule.

- Designate a privacy officer and guarantee this individual sufficient authority to make the changes required to bring the entity into compliance with the Privacy Rule. Consider appointing one or more workforce members to a privacy committee.

- Create a plan of action that sets out how the entity will bring itself into compliance with the Privacy Rule.

- Conduct an analysis of the entity's operation and determine the need to enter into business associate contracts with persons or entities providing support services to the entity.

- Develop the privacy notice that must be posted and distributed to every client and the business associate contracts needed for support services providers. Seek assistance from a local attorney in developing these documents.

- Create new authorization forms consistent with the Privacy Rule to be used by the entity in its disclosure of PHI.

- Create a form for the accounting of disclosures of PHI that must be maintained for each file.

- Develop and implement training programs for the entity's workforce on privacy matters and sanctions to be imposed for violations by members of the workforce.

- Document training programs as they are provided.

- Stay current with respect to probable modification to the Privacy Rule as the country and HHS have more experience with its actual implementation.

Covered entities are also required to apply the minimum necessary standard to their own requests for protected health information. One covered entity may reasonably rely on another covered entity's request as the minimum necessary and does not need to engage in a separate minimum necessary determination. However, if a covered entity does not agree that the amount of information requested by another covered entity is reasonably necessary for the purpose, it is up to both covered entities to negotiate a resolution of the dispute as to the amount of information needed. Nothing in the Privacy Rule prevents a covered entity from discussing its concerns with another covered entity making a request and negotiating an information exchange that meets the needs of both parties.

39

Personal Representatives (45 CFR 164.502(g))

The HIPAA Privacy Rule establishes a foundation of federally protected rights that permit individuals to control certain uses and disclosures of their protected health information. Along with these rights, the Privacy Rule provides individuals with the ability to access and amend this information and the right to an accounting of certain disclosures. Health and Human Services (HHS) recognized that there may be times when individuals are legally or otherwise incapable of exercising their rights or simply choose to designate another to act on their behalf with respect to these rights. Under the Rule, a person authorized (under state or other applicable law, e.g., tribal or military law) to act on behalf of the individual in making health care-related decisions is the individual's *personal representative*.

With certain exceptions, the Privacy Rule requires covered entities to treat an individual's personal representative as the individual with respect to uses and disclosures of the individual's protected health information, as well as the individual's rights under the Rule.

The personal representative stands in the shoes of the individual and has the ability to act for the individual and exercise the individual's rights. For instance, covered entities must provide the individual's personal representative with an accounting of disclosures (see discussion of accounting rules in Chapter 43) as well as provide the personal representative access to the individual's protected health information in accordance with the extent such information is relevant to such representation. In addition to exercising the individual's rights under the Rule, a personal representative may also authorize disclosures of the individual's protected health information.

The personal representative stands in the shoes of the individual and has the ability to act for the individual and exercise the individual's rights.

In general, the scope of the personal representative's authority to act for the individual under the Privacy Rule derives from his or her authority under applicable law to make health care decisions for the individual. Where the person has broad authority to act on the behalf of a living individual in making decisions related to health care, such as a parent with respect to a minor child or a legal guardian of a mentally incompetent adult, the covered entity must treat the personal representative as the individual for all purposes under the Rule, unless an exception applies. Where the authority to act for the individual is limited or specific to particular health care decisions, the personal representative is to be treated as the individual only with respect to protected health information that is relevant to the representation. For example, a person with an individual's limited health care power of attorney covering only a specific treatment, such as use of artificial life support, is that individual's personal representative only with respect to protected health information that relates to that health care decision. The covered entity should not treat that person as the individual for other purposes, such as to sign an authorization for the disclosure of protected health information for marketing purposes. Finally, where the person has authority to act on the behalf of a deceased individual or his or her estate, which would not include the authority to make decisions related to health care, the covered entity must treat the personal representative as the individual for all purposes under the Rule. State or other law should be consulted to determine the authority of the personal representative to receive or access the individual's protected health information.

The following chart shows who must be recognized as the personal representative for a category of individuals:

If the Individual Is	The Personal Representative Is
An adult or an emancipated minor	A person with legal authority to make health care decisions on behalf of the individual. *Examples:* Health care power of attorney. Court-appointed legal guardian. General power of attorney.
An unemancipated minor	A parent, guardian, or other person acting *in loco parentis* with legal authority to make health care decisions on behalf of the minor child (subject to exceptions).
Deceased	A person with legal authority to act on behalf of the decedent or the estate (not restricted to health care decisions). *Examples:* Executor of the estate. Next of kin or other family member. Durable power of attorney.

The Privacy Rule defers to state or other applicable laws that address the ability of a parent, guardian, or other person acting *in loco parentis* (collectively, "parent") to obtain health information about a minor child. In most cases under the Rule, the parent is the personal representative of the minor child and can exercise the minor's rights with respect to protected health information, because the parent usually has the authority to make health care decisions about his or her minor child. Whether a parent is the personal representative or not, the Privacy Rule permits a covered entity to disclose to a parent, or provide the parent with access to, a minor child's protected health information when and to the extent it is expressly permitted or required by state or other laws (including relevant case law). Likewise, the Privacy Rule prohibits a covered entity from disclosing a minor child's protected health information to a parent or providing a parent with access to such information when and to the extent it is expressly prohibited under state or other laws (including relevant case law). Thus, state and other applicable law governs when such law explicitly requires, permits, or prohibits the disclosure of, or access to, the health information about a minor child.

The Privacy Rule specifies three circumstances in which the parent is not the personal representative with respect to certain health information about his or her minor child. These exceptions generally track the ability of certain minors to obtain specified health care without parental consent under state or other laws or standards of professional practice. In these situations, the parent does not control the minor's health care decisions and, thus, under the Rule, does not control the protected health information related to that care. A parent is not the minor's personal representative in these three exceptional circumstances:

- When state or other law does not require the consent of a parent or other person before a minor can obtain a particular health care service and the minor consents to the health care service; for example, a state law provides an adolescent the right to obtain mental health treatment without the consent of his or her parent, and the adolescent consents to such treatment without the parent's consent.
- When a court determines or other law authorizes someone other than the parent to make treatment decisions for a minor; for example, a court may grant authority to make health care decisions for the minor to an adult other than the parent, to the minor, or the court may make the decision(s) itself.
- When a parent agrees to a confidential relationship between the minor and the physician; for example, a therapist asks the parent of a 16-year-old if the therapist can talk with the child confidentially about a problem and the parent agrees.

Even in these exceptional circumstances, where the parent is not the personal representative of the minor, the Privacy Rule defers to state or other laws

The Privacy Rule prohibits a covered entity from disclosing a minor child's protected health information to a parent or providing a parent with access to such information when and to the extent it is expressly prohibited under state or other laws.

that require, permit, or prohibit the covered entity to disclose to a parent, or provide the parent access to, a minor child's protected health information. Further, in these situations, if state or other law is silent or unclear concerning parental access to the minor's protected health information, a covered entity has discretion to provide or deny a parent with access to the minor's health information, if doing so is consistent with state or other applicable law, and provided the decision is made by a licensed health care professional in the exercise of professional judgment.

If the minor child is permitted, under state law, to consent to mental health care without the consent of a parent and does consent to such care, the mental health professional may notify the parent when the state law explicitly requires or permits the health provider to do so. If state law permits the minor child to consent to such health care without parental consent, but is silent on parental notification, the provider would need the child's permission to notify a parent.

When a physician or other covered entity reasonably believes that an individual, including an unemancipated minor, has been or may be subjected to domestic violence, abuse, or neglect by the personal representative or that treating a person as an individual's personal representative could endanger the individual, the covered entity may choose not to treat that person as the individual's personal representative, if in the exercise of professional judgment, doing so would not be in the best interests of the individual. For example, if a therapist

Legal Lightbulb

- The Privacy Rule requires mental health providers to treat personal representatives as if they were clients with respect to consent for treatment and access to records.

- State law will define who a personal representative will be, so mental health providers should become familiar with the law of personal representatives in their own states.

- Parents of a child can agree to a confidential relationship between the therapist and the child.

- Request and review a copy of the most recent court order establishing a person's right to serve as a personal representative before treating the client or allowing access to records. When in doubt, seek competent legal advice.

- Acting on the consent or authorization of a person without legal authority is unlawful, constitutes a violation of the Privacy Rule, and is sanctionable.

reasonably believes that disclosing information about an incompetent elderly individual to the individual's personal representative would endanger that individual, the Privacy Rule permits the therapist to decline to make such disclosure.

The Privacy Rule does require covered entities to verify a personal representative's authority. If a personal representative has been court appointed, there will be a court order or letter of authority issued by the court that should be reviewed to verify the person's authority. If a child's parents have been divorced or are separated, it is necessary to inquire about the existence of court orders that may impact a parent's right to consent to mental health care or treatment or access the child's mental health records. It is then imperative to obtain and review a copy of the most recent court order that impacts the right to give consent or to access records. Providing records to a parent or personal representative who does not have the right to access the protected health information is a violation of the Privacy Rule.

Providing records to a parent or personal representative who does not have the right to access the protected health information is a violation of the Privacy Rule.

40

Business Associates (45 CFR 164.502(e), 164.504(e), 164.532(d) and (e))

The Privacy Rule allows covered providers and health plans to disclose protected health information to business associates if the providers obtain satisfactory assurances that the business associate will use the information only for the purposes for which it was engaged by the covered entity.

By law, the HIPAA Privacy Rule applies only to covered entities: health plans, health care clearinghouses, and certain health care providers. However, most health care providers and health plans do not carry out all of their health care activities and functions by themselves. Instead, they often use the services of a variety of other persons or businesses. The Privacy Rule allows covered providers and health plans to disclose protected health information to these *business associates* if the providers or plans obtain satisfactory assurances that the business associate will use the information only for the purposes for which it was engaged by the covered entity, will safeguard the information from misuse, and will help the covered entity comply with some of the covered entity's duties under the Privacy Rule. Covered entities may disclose protected health information to an entity in its role as a business associate *only* to help the covered entity carry out its health care functions—not for the business associate's independent use or purposes, except as needed for the proper management and administration of the business associate.

The Privacy Rule requires that a covered entity obtain satisfactory assurances from its business associate that the business associate will appropriately safeguard the protected health information it receives or creates on behalf of the covered entity. The satisfactory assurances must be in writing, whether in the form of a contract or other agreement between the covered entity and the business associate.

Satisfactory assurances must be in writing.

A *business associate* is defined as a person or entity that performs certain functions or activities that involve the use or disclosure of protected health information on behalf of, or provides services to, a covered entity:

- A member of the covered entity's workforce is not a business associate.
- A covered health care provider, health plan, or health care clearinghouse can be a business associate of another covered entity.

The Privacy Rule lists some of the functions or activities, as well as the particular services, that make a person or entity a business associate if the activity or service involves the use or disclosure of protected health information. The types of functions or activities that may make a person or entity a business associate include payment or health care operations activities, as well as other functions or activities regulated by the Administrative Simplification Rules:

- **Business associate functions and activities include:** claims processing or administration; data analysis, processing, or administration; utilization review; quality assurance; billing; benefit management; practice management; and repricing.
- **Business associate services are:** legal, actuarial, accounting, consulting, data aggregation, management, administrative, accreditation, and financial.

The following are examples of business associates:

- A third-party administrator that assists a health plan with claims processing.
- A CPA firm whose accounting services to a health care provider involve access to protected health information.
- An attorney whose legal services to a health plan or a mental health provider involve access to protected health information.
- A consultant that performs utilization reviews for a hospital.
- A health care clearinghouse that translates a claim from a nonstandard format into a standard transaction on behalf of a health care provider and forwards the processed transaction to a payer.
- An independent medical transcriptionist that provides transcription services to a physician.
- A pharmacy benefits manager that manages a health plan's pharmacist network.

A covered entity's contract or other written arrangement with its business associate must contain the elements specified in the Privacy Rule. (See Appendixes E and F for sample business associate contracts.) The contract must:

- Describe the permitted and required uses of protected health information by the business associate.
- Provide that the business associate will not use or further disclose the protected health information other than as permitted or required by the contract or as required by law.
- Require the business associate to use appropriate safeguards to prevent a use or disclosure of the protected health information other than as provided for by the contract.

A covered entity's contract with a business associate may not authorize the business associate to use or further disclose the information in a manner that would violate the HIPAA Privacy Rule if done by the covered entity. Thus, a business associate contract must limit the business associate's uses and disclosures of, as well as requests for, protected health information to be consistent with the covered entity's minimum necessary policies and procedures. Given that a business associate contract must limit a business associate's requests for protected health information on behalf of a covered entity to that which is reasonably necessary to accomplish the intended purpose, a covered entity is permitted to reasonably rely on such requests from a business associate of another covered entity as the minimum necessary.

Where a covered entity knows of a material breach or violation by the business associate of the contract or agreement, the covered entity is required to take reasonable steps to cure the breach or end the violation and, if such steps are unsuccessful, to terminate the contract or arrangement. If termination of the contract or agreement is not feasible, a covered entity is required to report the problem to the Department of Health and Human Services Office for Civil Rights (OCR).

Covered entities (other than small health plans) that have an existing contract (or other written agreement) with a business associate before October 15, 2002, are permitted to continue to operate under that contract for up to one additional year beyond the April 14, 2003, compliance date, provided that the contract is not renewed or modified before April 14, 2003. This transition period applies only to written contracts or other written arrangements. Oral contracts or other arrangements are not eligible for the transition period. Covered entities with contracts that qualify are permitted to continue to operate under those contracts with their business associates until April 14, 2004, or until the contract is renewed or modified, whichever is sooner, regardless of whether the contract meets the Rule's applicable contract requirements. A covered entity must otherwise comply with the Privacy Rule, such as making only permissible disclosures to the business associate and permitting individuals to exercise their rights under the Rule.

The Privacy Rule includes exceptions to the business associate standard.

The Privacy Rule includes the following exceptions to the business associate standard. In these situations, a covered entity is not required to have a business associate contract or other written agreement in place before protected health information may be disclosed to the person or entity:

- Disclosures by a covered entity to a health care provider for treatment of the individual. For example:
  —A social worker is not required to have a business associate contract with the psychiatrist to whom he or she refers a patient and transmits the patient's file for treatment purposes.

—A physician is not required to have a business associate contract with a laboratory as a condition of disclosing protected health information for the treatment of an individual.

—A hospital laboratory is not required to have a business associate contract to disclose protected health information to a reference laboratory for treatment of the individual.

- Disclosures to a health plan sponsor, such as an employer, by a group health plan or by the health insurance issuer or HMO that provides the health insurance benefits or coverage for the group health plan, provided that the group health plan's documents have been amended to limit the disclosures or one of the exceptions has been met.
- The collection and sharing of protected health information by a health plan that is a public benefits program, such as Medicare, and an agency other than the agency administering the health plan, such as the Social Security Administration, that collects protected health information to determine eligibility or enrollment or determines eligibility or enrollment for the government program where the joint activities are authorized by law.

Other situations in which a business associate contract is *not* required are:

- When a health care provider discloses protected health information to a health plan for payment purposes or when the health care provider simply accepts a discounted rate to participate in the health plan's network. A provider that submits a claim to a health plan and a health plan that assesses and pays the claim are both acting on their own behalf as covered entities and not as business associates of the other.
- With persons or organizations (e.g., janitorial service or electrician) whose functions or services do not involve the use or disclosure of protected health information and where any access to protected health information by such persons would be incidental, if at all.
- With a person or organization that acts merely as a conduit for protected health information, for example, the U.S. Postal Service, certain private couriers, and their electronic equivalents.
- Among covered entities who participate in an organized health care arrangement (OHCA) to make disclosures that relate to the joint health care activities of the OHCA.
- Where a group health plan purchases insurance from a health insurance issuer or HMO. The relationship between the group health plan and the health insurance issuer or HMO is defined by the Privacy Rule as an OHCA, with respect to the individuals they jointly serve or have served. Thus, these covered entities are permitted to share protected health information that relates to the joint health care activities of the OHCA.

- Where one covered entity purchases a health plan product or other insurance, for example, reinsurance, from an insurer. Each entity is acting on its own behalf when the covered entity purchases the insurance benefits and when the covered entity submits a claim to the insurer and the insurer pays the claim.
- To disclose protected health information to a researcher for research purposes, either with patient authorization or pursuant to a waiver. Because the researcher is not conducting a function or activity regulated by the Administrative Simplification Rules, such as payment or health care operations, or providing one of the services listed in the definition of *business associate* at 45 CFR 160.103, the researcher is not a business associate of the covered entity, and no business associate agreement is required.
- When a financial institution processes consumer-conducted financial transactions by debit, credit, or other payment card; clears checks; initiates or processes electronic funds transfers; or conducts any other activity that directly facilitates or affects the transfer of funds for payment for health care or health plan premiums. When it conducts these activities, the financial institution is providing its normal banking or other financial transaction services to its customers; it is not performing a function or activity for, or on behalf of, the covered entity.

Any covered mental health provider (or other covered entity) may share protected health information with a health care provider for treatment purposes without a business associate contract.

The HIPAA Privacy Rule explicitly excludes from the business associate requirements disclosures by a covered entity to a health care provider for treatment purposes. Therefore, any covered mental health provider (or other covered entity) may share protected health information with a health care provider for treatment purposes without a business associate contract. For example, a therapist may provide information about a client's behavior to the client's psychiatrist without a business associate contract. However, this exception does not preclude one health care provider from establishing a business associate relationship with another health care provider for some other purpose. For example, a therapist may enlist the services of another mental health care provider to provide supervisory or practice consulting services. In this case, a business associate contract is required before the therapist can allow the mental health care provider access to patient health information.

If the HIPAA Privacy Rule permits a covered entity to share protected health information with another covered entity, the covered entity is permitted to make the disclosure directly to a business associate acting on behalf of that other covered entity.

If a service is hired to do work for a covered entity where disclosure of protected health information is not limited in nature (such as routine handling of records or shredding of documents containing protected health information), it likely would be a business associate. However, when such work is performed under the direct control of the covered entity (e.g., on the covered entity's premises), the Privacy Rule permits the covered entity to treat the service as part of its workforce, and the covered entity need not enter into a business associate contract with the service.

Plumbers, electricians, and photocopy repair technicians who are hired to work in a health professional's office do not require access to protected health information to perform their services, so they do not meet the definition of a business associate. Under the HIPAA Privacy Rule, business associates are contractors or other nonworkforce members hired to do the work of, or for, a covered entity that involves the use or disclosure of protected health information. Any disclosure of protected health information to such technicians that occurs in the performance of their duties (such as may occur walking through or working in file rooms) is limited in nature, occurs as a by-product of their duties, and

Legal Lightbulb

- The treating mental health provider has the ultimate responsibility to safeguard protected health information. Requiring mental health providers to enter into business associate contracts with all nontreatment service providers emphasizes this responsibility.

- Assurances must be obtained that business associates will safeguard protected health information.

- This assurance must be in writing.

- Each provider should have a HIPAA compliant form to be signed by the business associate so there is evidence that the associate is aware of the confidentiality of protected health information.

- Contracts with the business entities need to provide for nonredisclosure to any third parties.

- Material breaches of the business associate agreement must be stopped at once and remedial action taken within a reasonable time.

- Compliance must be assured at the earliest possible time to avoid serious penalties.

- Careful consideration and lawyer consultation is advised in the drafting, implementation, and execution of all HIPAA complaint forms.

cannot be reasonably prevented. Such disclosures are incidental and permitted by the Privacy Rule.

A computer technician who transports to his repair shop a computer hard drive on which protected health information is stored should be required to enter into a business associate contract with the health care entity requesting the repairs.

A mental health professional with hospital privileges and the hospital are not required to enter into a business associate agreement. The hospital and such mental health professionals participate in what the HIPAA Privacy Rule defines as an OHCA. Thus, they may use and disclose protected health information for the joint health care activities of the OHCA without entering into a business associate agreement.

The Privacy Rule requires a covered entity to provide an accounting of certain disclosures, including certain disclosures by its business associates, to the individual upon request. The business associate contract must provide that the business associate will make such information available to the covered entity so that the covered entity can fulfill its obligation to the individual. As with access and amendment, the parties can agree through the business associate contract that the business associate will provide the accounting to individuals, as may be appropriate given the protected health information held by, and the functions of, the business associate.

If a mental health provider is a member of a health plan network (accepted on a managed care company's provider panel) and the only relationship between the health plan (payer) and the provider is one where the provider submits claims for payment to the plan, the provider is not a business associate of the health plan. Each covered entity is acting on its own behalf when a provider submits a claim to a health plan and when the health plan assesses and pays the claim. However, a business associate relationship could arise if the provider is performing another function on behalf of, or providing services to, the health plan (e.g., case management services) that meet the definition of *business associate*.

When in doubt, enter into a business associate contract.

41

Uses and Disclosures for Treatment, Payment, and Health Care Operations (45 CFR 164.506)

The HIPAA Privacy Rule, while establishing a foundation of federal protection for personal health information, attempts to avoid creating unnecessary barriers to the delivery of quality health care. As such, the Rule generally prohibits a covered entity from using or disclosing protected health information (PHI) unless authorized by patients, except where this prohibition would result in unnecessary interference with access to quality health care or with certain other important public benefits or national priorities.

Ready access to treatment and efficient payment for health care, both of which require use and disclosure of protected health information, are essential to the effective operation of the health care system. In addition, certain health care operations (such as administrative, financial, legal, and quality improvement activities) conducted by or for health care providers and health plans are essential to support treatment and payment. Many individuals expect that their health information will be used and disclosed as necessary to treat them, bill for treatment, and, to some extent, operate the covered entity's health care business. To avoid interfering with an individual's access to quality health care or the efficient payment for such health care, the Privacy Rule permits a covered entity to use and disclose protected health information, with certain limits and protections, for treatment, payment, and health care operations activities without client consent (45 CFR 164.502 (a) (1)(ii)).

The core health care activities of *treatment, payment,* and *health care operations* are defined as follows:

The Privacy Rule permits a covered entity to use and disclose protected health information, with certain limits and protections, for treatment, payment, and health care operations activities without client consent.

- **Treatment** generally means the provision, coordination, or management of health care and related services among health care providers or by a health care provider with a third party; consultation between health care providers about a patient; or the referral of a patient from one health care provider to another.

- **Payment** encompasses the various activities of health care providers to obtain payment or be reimbursed for their services and of a health plan to obtain premiums, to fulfill their coverage responsibilities and provide benefits under the plan, and to obtain or provide reimbursement for the provision of health care.

  In addition to the general definition, the Privacy Rule provides examples of common payment activities, which include, but are not limited to:

  —Determining eligibility or coverage under a plan and adjudicating claims.
  —Risk adjustments.
  —Billing and collection activities.
  —Reviewing health care services for medical necessity, coverage, justification of charges, and the like.
  —Utilization review activities.
  —Disclosures to consumer reporting agencies (limited to specified identifying information about the individual, his or her payment history, and identifying information about the covered entity).

- **Health care operations** are certain administrative, financial, legal, and quality improvement activities of a covered entity that are necessary to run its business and to support the core functions of treatment and payment and include:

  —Conducting quality assessment and improvement activities, population-based activities relating to improving health or reducing health care costs, and case management and care coordination.
  —Reviewing the competence or qualifications of health care professionals, evaluating provider and health plan performance, training health care and non-health care professionals, accreditation, certification, licensing, or credentialing activities.
  —Underwriting and other activities related to the creation, renewal, or replacement of a contract of health insurance or health benefits, and ceding, securing, or placing a contract for reinsurance of risk relating to health care claims.
  —Conducting or arranging for medical review, legal, and auditing services, including fraud and abuse detection and compliance programs.
  —Business planning and development, such as conducting cost-management and planning analyses related to managing and operating the entity.
  —Business management and general administrative activities, including those related to implementing and complying with the Privacy Rule and other administrative simplification rules, customer service, resolution of internal grievances, sale or transfer of assets, creating deidentified health information or a limited data set, and fund-raising for the benefit of the covered entity.

Pursuant to the Privacy Rule, a covered entity may, without the individual's authorization:

- Use or disclose protected health information for its own treatment, payment, and health care operations activities, for example:
  —A psychiatric hospital may use protected health information about an individual to provide mental health care to the individual and may consult with other mental health care providers about the individual's treatment.
  —A mental health care provider may disclose protected health information about an individual as part of a claim for payment to a health plan.
- A covered entity may disclose protected health information for the treatment activities of any health care provider (including providers not covered by the Privacy Rule), for example:
  —A primary care provider may send a copy of an individual's medical record to a mental health professional who needs the information to treat the individual.
  —A hospital may send a patient's health care instructions to a psychiatric facility to which the patient is transferred.
- A covered entity may disclose protected health information to another covered entity or a health care provider (including providers not covered by the Privacy Rule) for the payment activities of the entity that receives the information, for example:
  —A physician may send an individual's health plan coverage information to a laboratory that needs the information to bill for services it provided to the physician with respect to the individual.
  —A hospital emergency department may give a patient's payment information to an ambulance service provider that transported the patient to the hospital so the ambulance provider can bill for its treatment services.
- A covered entity may disclose protected health information to another covered entity for certain health care operation activities of the entity that receives the information if:
  —Each entity either has or had a relationship with the individual who is the subject of the information and the protected health information pertains to the relationship.
  —The disclosure is for a permitted quality-related health care operations activity or for the purpose of health care fraud and abuse detection or compliance, for example:
    —A health care provider may disclose protected health information to a health plan for the plan's Health Plan Employer Data and Information Set (HEDIS) purposes, provided that the health plan has or had a relationship with the individual who is the subject of the information.
- A covered entity that participates in an organized health care arrangement (OHCA) may disclose protected health information about an individual to

another covered entity that participates in the OHCA for any joint health care operations of the OHCA, for example:

—The physicians with staff privileges at a hospital may participate in the hospital's training of medical students.

Specific rules apply to the use and disclosure of psychotherapy notes that differ from other PHI and the permitted use for treatment, payment, and health care operations. Use and disclosure of psychotherapy notes (see definition of *psychotherapy notes* in Chapter 38), other than to the client, require a valid authorization (45 CFR 164.508). There are exceptions, however, and an authorization is not required for the following uses or disclosures:

1. Use by the originator of the psychotherapy notes for treatment.
2. Use or disclosure by the covered entity for its own training programs in which students, trainees, or practitioners in mental health learn under supervision to improve their skills in group, joint, family, or individual counseling.
3. Use or disclosure by the covered entity to defend itself in a legal action or other proceeding brought by the individual.
4. Use or disclosure required by the Secretary to investigate a covered entity's compliance.
5. Use or disclosure is required by law and the use or disclosure is limited to the relevant requirements of such law.
6. Disclosure to health oversight agency for oversight activities authorized by law with respect to the oversight of originator of the psychotherapy notes (i.e., licensing board).
7. Disclosure to a coroner or medical examiner for the purpose of identifying a deceased person, determining a cause of death, or other purpose duties authorized by law.
8. Use or disclosure to avert a serious threat to health or safety.

Section h. is the Privacy Rule's attempt to lay a foundation for dealing with threats of harm to the client, other persons, or the general public (45 CFR 164.512 (j)). It provides that a covered entity, consistent with applicable law (i.e., state law) and standards of ethical conduct, may use or disclose PHI (including psychotherapy notes) if the covered entity believes in good faith that the use or disclosure:

is necessary to prevent or lessen a serious and imminent threat to the health or safety of a person or the general public and is made to a person or persons reasonably able to prevent or lessen the threat, including the target of the threat.

or

is necessary for law enforcement authorities to identify or apprehend an individual because of a statement by an individual admitting participation in a violent crime that the covered entity reasonably believes may have caused physical harm to the victim or it appears form all the circumstances that the individual has escaped from a correctional institution or from lawful custody.

There is an exception to the exception, a provision of particular interest to mental health providers who treat sex offenders (CFR 164.512 (j) (2)). The exception states that if an individual admits participating in a violent crime that the covered entity reasonably believes may have caused serious physical harm to the victim, use or disclosure of PHI is *not* permitted if the information is learned (1) in the course of treatment to affect the propensity to commit criminal conduct that is the basis for the disclosures, counseling, or therapy, or (2) through a request by the individual to initiate or to be referred for the treatment, counseling, or therapy.

The intent is to allow people to seek help for psychological problems without fear of being reported for past conduct. This exception, however, does not apply to child abuse or neglect reporting, which is a use or disclosure required by law; notification of the proper authorities is mandatory in those circumstances. However, if after sexually assaulting an *adult* woman, a client sought treatment from a mental health professional to affect his propensity to commit these kinds of offenses, the mental health professional could not disclose this information to law enforcement authorities. This is similar to the protection afforded alcohol and substance abusers who seek treatment.

Clients should feel able to seek help without fear of being reported for past conduct.

It is not clear just how significant this provision will be since the Privacy Rule also requires reporting of other kinds of abuse or matters if required by law, which, by definition, includes state law. Most states have laws protecting other classes of individuals who cannot protect themselves, that is, elderly, mentally challenged, physically disabled, and so on. Violent crimes and acts of abuse and neglect committed against these classes of individuals will probably still require reporting. If there is no reporting statute applicable to healthy adults, mental health professionals may be able to protect the privacy of an offending client.

It is useful to note the difference between consent and authorization as used in the Privacy Rule. The Privacy Rule permits, but does not require, a covered entity to voluntarily obtain patient consent for uses and disclosures of protected health information for treatment, payment, and health care operations. Covered entities that do so have complete discretion to design a process that best suits their needs. The Privacy Rule does not prohibit a covered entity from obtaining an individual's consent to use or disclose his or her health information and, therefore, presents no barrier to the entity's ability to comply with state law requirements.

By contrast, an "authorization" is required by the Privacy Rule for uses and disclosures of protected health information not otherwise allowed by the Rule,

An authorization is a detailed document that gives covered entities permission to use protected health information for specified purposes.

that is, psychotherapy notes. Where the Privacy Rule requires patient authorization, voluntary consent is not sufficient to permit a use or disclosure of protected health information unless it also satisfies the requirements of a valid authorization. An authorization is a detailed document that gives covered entities permission to use protected health information for specified purposes, which are generally other than treatment, payment, or health care operations, or to disclose protected health information to a third party specified by the individual.

An authorization must contain the following core elements (45 CFR 164.508 (c)):

- A description of the information to be used or disclosed that identifies the information in a specific and meaningful way.
- The name or other specific identification of the person(s), or class of persons, authorized to make the requested use or disclosure.
- The name or other specific identification of the person(s), or class of persons, to whom the covered entity may make the requested use or disclosure.
- A description of each purpose of the requested use or disclosure. (*Note:* The statement, "at the request of the individual" is a sufficient description of the purposes when an individual initiates the authorization and does not, or elects not to, provide a statement of the purposes.)
- An expiration date or an expiration event that relates to the individual or the purpose of the use or disclosure. (*Note:* The statement "end of research study," "none," or similar language is sufficient if the PHI is used or disclosed for research.)
- Signature of the individual and date (*Note:* If the signature is signed by a personal representative of the individual, there must be a description of such representative's authority to act for the individual.)

In addition, a valid authorization must include statements adequate to place the individual on notice of *all* of the following:

1. The individual's right to revoke the authorization in writing and either:
   - The exceptions to the right to revoke and a description of how the individual may revoke the authorization, or
   - To the extent that information on the individual's right to revoke and a description of how to do it is included in the covered entity's privacy notice, a reference to the entity's notice. See Appendix L for an example of an authorization revocation form.

2. The ability or inability to condition treatment, payment, enrollment, or eligibility of benefits on the authorization by stating either:

- The covered entity may not condition treatment, payment, enrollment, or eligibility of benefits on whether the individual signs the authorization. (*Note:* Exceptions exist for research-related treatment, when a health plan conditions eligibility for benefits on the signing an authorization for use and disclosure of PHI not including psychotherapy notes and when the health care provided is solely for the purpose of creating PHI for a third party, that is, forensic mental health services.)
- The consequences to the individual for the refusal to sign an authorization when treatment, payment, enrollment, or eligibility can be conditioned on the signing of an authorization pursuant to one of the exceptions set out previously, that is, payer's right to deny payment for the services.

3. The potential for information disclosed pursuant to the authorization subject to redisclosure by the receiving party and no longer protected by the Privacy Rule.

In addition, an authorization must be written in "plain language" and a copy must be given to the individual.

The Privacy Rule requires new language that was not previously typical in authorizations. New forms are required to be in compliance and are especially important when psychotherapy notes are requested. (See Appendix G for an example of an authorization.)

Last, mental health professionals should remember three other elements of the Privacy Rule in analyzing use and disclosures for treatment, payment, or health care operations:

New forms are required to be in compliance and are especially important when psychotherapy notes are requested.

1. **The minimum disclosure rule discussed in Chapter 38 must be followed:** A covered entity must develop policies and procedures that reasonably limit its disclosures of, and requests for, protected health information for payment and health care operations to the minimum necessary. A covered entity also is required to develop role-based access policies and procedures that limit members of its workforce who may have access to protected health information for treatment, payment, and health care operations, based on those who need access to the information to do their jobs. However, covered entities are not required to apply the minimum necessary standard to disclosures to or requests by a health care provider for treatment purposes.

2. **Individuals have the right to request restrictions on how a covered entity will use and disclose protected health information about them for treatment, payment, and health care operations:** A covered entity is not required to agree to an individual's request for a restriction, but is bound by any restrictions to which it agrees. See 45 CFR 164.522(a).

3. **Any use or disclosure of protected health information for treatment, payment, or health care operations must be consistent with the covered entity's notice of privacy practices:** A covered entity is required to provide the individual with adequate notice of its privacy practices, including the uses or disclosures the covered entity may make of the individual's information and the individual's rights with respect to that information. (See Chapter 44, Notice of Privacy Practices for Protected Health Information.)

Answers to Frequently Asked Questions about:

HIPAA Privacy Rule
Disclosures

Question

I am a mental health professional working with other mental health treatment providers in a mid-size mental health clinic. I often treat clients who have been previously treated at this same clinic. When I am requested to produce a copy of a client's

Legal Lightbulb

- The Privacy Rule allows disclosures of PHI without client consent or authorization for treatment, payment, and health care operation purposes. Failure to do so would be highly impractical and negatively impact health care treatment.

- Even if consent or authorization is not required, only the PHI minimally necessary to accomplish the intended purpose of the use or disclosure is permitted.

- Prior consideration must be given to the kinds of uses and disclosures of PHI confronted by the mental health provider to determine the necessity for consent or authorization and the extent of PHI that can be shared that will comply with the "minimally necessary" requirements of the Privacy Rule.

- A specifically worded authorization is required for the use of disclosure of psychotherapy notes.

- All existing releases and authorizations should be scrutinized and revised as necessary in light of the Privacy Rules' requirements.

file, what am I expected to provide? For example, if the file includes notes from a previous therapist, must I provide those notes as well?

❗ Answer

The Privacy Rule permits a provider who is a covered entity to disclose a complete health care record, including portions that were created by another provider, assuming that the disclosure is for a purpose permitted by the Privacy Rule, such as treatment. To produce any psychotherapy notes, the Privacy Rule generally requires a specific authorization from the client. All disclosures require the application of the reasonably necessary rule whereby disclosure must be limited to the minimum amount of information reasonably necessary to comply with the request or to meet the purpose of the request.

42

Disclosures for Public Health Activities and Workers' Compensation

There is an inherent conflict between individual privacy and disclosures that are necessary for the protection of the public. The relationship and duties are clarified in the Privacy Rule, balancing these public and private rights.

Disclosures for Public Health Activities (45 CFR 164.512(b))

The HIPAA Privacy Rule recognizes the legitimate need for public health authorities and others responsible for ensuring public health and safety to have access to protected health information to carry out their public health mission. The Rule also recognizes that public health reports made by covered entities are an important means of identifying threats to the health and safety of the public at large, as well as individuals. Accordingly, the Rule *permits* covered entities to disclose protected health information without authorization for specified public health purposes.

The Privacy Rule keeps alive the mental health professional's duty to comply with existing federal and state reporting requirements. The Privacy Rule permits covered entities to disclose protected health information, without authorization, to public health authorities who are legally authorized to receive such reports for the purpose of preventing or controlling disease, injury, or disability. This includes, for example, the reporting of a disease or injury; reporting vital events, such as births or deaths; and conducting public health surveillance, investigations, or interventions. In addition, covered entities may, at the direction of a public health authority, disclose protected health information to a foreign government agency that is acting in collaboration with a public health authority. Covered entities who are also a public health authority may use, as well as disclose, protected health information for these same public health purposes:

A *public health authority* (45 CFR 164.501) is an agency or authority of the United States government, a state, a territory, a political subdivision of a state or territory, or Indian tribe that is responsible for public health matters as part of its official mandate, as well as a person or entity acting under a grant of authority from, or under a contract with, a public health agency. Examples of a public health authority include state and local health departments (i.e., Child or Adult Protective Services), the Food and Drug Administration (FDA), the Centers for Disease Control and Prevention, and the Occupational Safety and Health Administration (OSHA).

Generally, covered entities are required to reasonably limit the protected health information disclosed for public health purposes to the minimum amount necessary to accomplish the public health purpose. However, covered entities are not required to make a minimum necessary determination for public health disclosures that are made pursuant to an individual's authorization or for disclosures that are required by other law (45 CFR 164.502(b)(2)). For disclosures to a public health authority, covered entities may reasonably rely on a minimum necessary determination made by the public health authority in requesting the protected health information (CFR 164.514(d)(3)(iii)(A)). For routine and recurring public health disclosures, covered entities may develop standard protocols as part of their minimum necessary policies and procedures, which address the types and amount of protected health information that may be disclosed for such purposes (45 CFR 164.514(d)(3)(i)).

Generally, covered entities are required to reasonably limit the protected health information disclosed for public health purposes to the minimum amount necessary to accomplish the public health purpose.

The Privacy Rule recognizes the important role that persons or entities other than public health authorities play in certain essential public health activities. Accordingly, the Rule permits covered entities to disclose protected health information, without authorization, to such persons or entities for the following public health activities:

- **Child abuse or neglect:** Covered entities may disclose protected health information to report known or suspected child abuse or neglect, if the report is made to a public health authority or other appropriate government authority that is authorized by law to receive such reports. For instance, the social services department of a local government might have legal authority to receive reports of child abuse or neglect, in which case, the Privacy Rule would permit a covered entity to report such cases to that authority without obtaining individual authorization. Likewise, a covered entity could report such cases to the police department when the police department is authorized by law to receive such reports. *The same is true concerning disclosures about adult victims of abuse, neglect, or domestic violence that are required by law.*
- **Quality, safety, or effectiveness of a product or activity regulated by the FDA:** Covered entities may disclose protected health information to a person subject to FDA jurisdiction for public health purposes related to the quality, safety, or effectiveness of an FDA-regulated product or activity for

which that person has responsibility. Examples of purposes or activities for which such disclosures may be made include, but are not limited to:

—Collecting or reporting adverse events (including similar reports about food and dietary supplements), product defects or problems (including problems about use or labeling), or biological product deviations.

—Tracking FDA-regulated products.

—Enabling product recalls, repairs, replacement, or lookback (which includes locating and notifying individuals who received recalled or withdrawn products or products that are the subject of lookback).

—Conducting postmarketing surveillance.

The "person" subject to the jurisdiction of the FDA does not have to be a specific individual. Rather, it can be an individual or an entity, such as a partnership, corporation, or association. Covered entities may identify the party or parties responsible for an FDA-regulated product from the product label, from written material that accompanies the product (know as labeling), or from sources of labeling, such as the *Physician's Desk Reference.*

- **Persons at risk of contracting or spreading a disease:** A covered entity may disclose protected health information to a person who is at risk of contracting or spreading a disease or condition if other law authorizes the covered entity to notify such individuals as necessary to carry out public health interventions or investigations. For example, a covered health care provider may disclose protected health information as needed to notify a person that (s)he has been exposed to a communicable disease if the covered entity is legally authorized to do so to prevent or control the spread of the disease (CFR 164.512(b)(1)(iv)).

- **Workplace medical surveillance:** A covered health care provider who provides a health care service to an individual at the request of the individual's employer or provides the service in the capacity of a member of the employer's workforce may disclose the individual's protected health information to the employer for the purposes of workplace medical surveillance or the evaluation of work-related illness and injuries to the extent the employer needs that information to comply with OSHA, the Mine Safety and Health Administration (MSHA), or the requirements of state laws having a similar purpose. The information disclosed must be limited to the provider's findings about such medical surveillance or work-related illness or injury. The mental health professional conducting an examination or evaluation on behalf of an employer must provide the individual with prior written notice that the information will be disclosed to his or her employer. For the protection of the mental health professional as well as the individual, this information should be provided in writing and included in a privacy notice as discussed in Chapter 44.

In summary, the HIPAA Privacy Rule permits disclosures that are required by law including, but not limited to, disclosures to public health authorities that are authorized by law to collect or receive information for public health purposes, without authorization from a client. This rule is mere confirmation of existing requirements under which mental health professionals have long practiced. When required to report by law, mental health professionals should do so and will do so without concern for HIPAA's privacy standard.

Mental health professionals should note that the Privacy Rule's public health provision permits, but does not require, covered entities to make such disclosures. This provision is intended to allow covered entities to continue current permissive as well as mandatory reporting practices that are critically important to public health and safety.

Disclosures for Workers' Compensation Purposes (45 CFR 164.512(l))

The HIPAA Privacy Rule does not apply to entities that are either workers' compensation insurers, workers' compensation administrative agencies, or employers, except to the extent they may otherwise be covered entities. However, these entities need access to the health information of individuals who are injured on the job or who have a work-related illness to process or adjudicate claims or to coordinate care under workers' compensation systems. Generally, this health information is obtained from health care providers who treat these individuals and who may be covered by the Privacy Rule. The Privacy Rule recognizes the legitimate need of insurers and other entities involved in the workers' compensation systems to have access to individuals' health information as authorized by state or other law. Due to the significant variability among such laws, the Privacy Rule permits disclosures of health information for workers' compensation purposes in a number of different ways.

The HIPAA Privacy Rule does not apply to entities that are either workers' compensation insurers, workers' compensation administrative agencies, or employers, except to the extent they may otherwise be covered entities.

Disclosures without Individual Authorization

The Privacy Rule permits covered entities to disclose protected health information to workers' compensation insurers, state administrators, employers, and other persons or entities involved in workers' compensation systems, without the individual's authorization:

- As authorized by and to the extent necessary to comply with laws relating to workers' compensation or similar programs established by law that provide benefits for work-related injuries or illness without regard to fault. This includes programs established by the Black Lung Benefits Act, the Federal Employees' Compensation Act, the Longshore and Harbor Workers' Compensation Act, and the Energy Employees' Occupational Illness Compensation Program Act. See 45 CFR 164.512(l).

- To the extent the disclosure is required by state or other law. The disclosure must comply with and be limited to what the law requires. See 45 CFR 164.512(a).
- For purposes of obtaining payment for any health care provided to the injured or ill worker. See 45 CFR 164.502(a)(1)(ii) and the definition of *payment* at 45 CFR 164.501.

Disclosures with Individual Authorization

In addition, covered entities may disclose protected health information to workers' compensation insurers and others involved in workers' compensation systems where the individual has provided his or her authorization for the release of the information to the entity. The authorization must contain the elements and otherwise meet the requirements specified at 45 CFR 164.508.

Covered entities are required reasonably to limit the amount of protected health information disclosed under 45 CFR 164.512(l) to the minimum necessary to accomplish the workers' compensation purpose. Under this requirement, protected health information may be shared for such purposes to the full extent authorized by state or other law.

In addition, covered entities are required reasonably to limit the amount of protected health information disclosed for payment purposes to the minimum

Legal Lightbulb

- Although the Privacy Rule restricts disclosure of and access to protected health information it does permit disclosures required by law.

- Mental health providers must comply with all state and federal reporting statutes.

- Authorization or consent for the use and disclosure of protected health information is not required when a mental health provider has a duty to report protected health information to authorities.

- A minimal necessary determination is required with respect to the amount of protected health information that is reported to authorities.

- There should be careful and detailed documentation of the steps taken by a mental health provider in complying with the reporting law and in determining the amount of protected health information actually disclosed to authorities.

necessary. Covered entities are permitted to disclose the amount and types of protected health information that are necessary to obtain payment for health care provided to an injured or ill worker.

Where a covered entity routinely makes disclosures for workers' compensation purposes under 45 CFR 164.512(l) or for payment purposes, the covered entity may develop standard protocols as part of its minimum necessary policies and procedures that address the type and amount of protected health information to be disclosed for such purposes.

Where protected health information is requested by a state workers' compensation or other public official, covered entities are permitted to reasonably rely on the official's representations that the information requested is the minimum necessary for the intended purpose. See 45 CFR 164.514(d)(3)(iii)(A).

Covered entities are not required to make a minimum necessary determination when disclosing protected health information as required by state or other law or pursuant to the individual's authorization. See 45 CFR 164.502(b).

Health and Human Services has stated that it will actively monitor the effects of the Privacy Rule and, in particular, the minimum necessary standard, on the workers' compensation systems and consider proposing modifications, where appropriate, to ensure that the Rule does not have any unintended negative effects that disturb these systems.

43

Marketing and Research (Accounting for Disclosures)

Marketing and research are necessary activities for the advancement and success of the health care industry. There can be a legitimate need for the use and disclosure of protected health information (PHI) in furtherance of these activities. The Privacy Rule attempts to balance these needs with patient rights to privacy.

Marketing (45 CFR 164.501, 164.508(a)(3))

The HIPAA Privacy Rule gives individuals important controls over whether and how their protected health information is used and disclosed for marketing purposes. Previously, state law was not very protective of protected health information when it came to marketing uses. With limited exceptions, the Rule requires an individual's written authorization before a use or disclosure of his or her protected health information can be made for marketing. So as not to interfere with core health care functions, the Rule distinguishes marketing communications from those communications about goods and services that are essential for quality health care.

The Privacy Rule addresses the use and disclosure of protected health information for marketing purposes by:

- Defining *marketing* under the Rule.
- Excepting from that definition certain treatment or health care operations activities.
- Requiring individual authorization for all uses or disclosures of protected health information for marketing purposes with limited exceptions.

The Privacy Rule defines marketing as making "a communication about a product or service that encourages recipients of the communication to purchase or use the product or service."

The Privacy Rule defines *marketing* as making "a communication about a product or service that encourages recipients of the communication to purchase or use the product or service." Generally, if the communication is marketing, the communication can occur only if the covered entity first obtains an individual's authorization. This definition of marketing has certain exceptions, as discussed later.

An example of marketing communications requiring prior authorization is a communication from a mental health professional to former clients promoting a company's nutritional supplements when the communication is not for the purpose of providing treatment advice.

The particularly offensive type of marketing is:

> An arrangement between a covered entity and any other entity whereby the covered entity discloses protected health information to the other entity, in exchange for direct or indirect remuneration, for the other entity or its affiliate to make a communication about its own product or service that encourages recipients of the communication to purchase or use that product or service.

This part of the definition of marketing has no exceptions. The individual must authorize these marketing communications before they can occur.

Simply put, a covered entity may not sell protected health information to a business associate or any other third party for that party's own purposes. Moreover, covered entities may not sell lists of patients or enrollees to third parties without obtaining authorization from each person on the list.

For example, it is "marketing" when a drug manufacturer receives a list of patients from a psychiatrist and provides remuneration, then uses that list to send discount coupons for a new antidepressant medication directly to the psychiatrist's patients.

The Privacy Rule carves out exceptions to the definition of marketing under the following three categories:

A covered entity may not sell protected health information to a business associate or any other third party for that party's own purposes.

1. A communication describing available products or services offered by a covered entity, for example:
   - A mental health provider provides clients with information about new or additional therapy programs he or she is offering.
   - An ophthalmologist or health plan sends existing patients or members discounts for eye exams or eyeglasses available only to the patients and members.
2. A communication is not "marketing" if it is made for treatment of the individual. For example, under this exception, it is not "marketing" when:
   - A pharmacy or other health care provider mails prescription refill reminders to patients or contracts with a mail house to do so.
   - A psychiatrist refers an individual to a specialist for a medical evaluation or test or provides free samples of a prescription drug to a patient.
3. A communication is not "marketing" if it is made for case management or care coordination for the individual or to direct or recommend alternative treatments, therapies, health care providers, or settings of care to the individual. For example, under this exception, it is not "marketing" when:
   - An endocrinologist shares a patient's medical record with several behavior management programs to determine which program best suits the ongoing needs of the individual patient.

- A hospital social worker shares medical record information with various nursing homes in the course of recommending that the patient be transferred from a hospital bed to a nursing home.

For any of the three exceptions to the definition of marketing, the activity must otherwise be permissible under the Privacy Rule, and a covered entity may use a business associate to make the communication. As with any disclosure to a business associate, the covered entity must obtain the business associate's agreement to use the protected health information only for the communication activities of the covered entity.

Except as discussed previously, any communication that meets the definition of marketing is not permitted, unless the covered entity obtains an individual's authorization. What constitutes an acceptable authorization is discussed in Chapter 41. If the marketing involves direct or indirect remuneration to the covered entity from a third party, the authorization must state that such remuneration is involved (45 CFR 164.508(a)(3)).

A communication does not require an authorization, even if it is marketing, if it is in the form of a face-to-face communication made by a covered entity to an individual or a promotional gift of nominal value provided by the covered entity.

For example, no prior authorization is necessary when:

It has long constituted an actionable and sanctionable breach of confidentiality for the mental health professional to disclose the identity of the people they treat without client authorization or unless compelled by law.

- A hospital provides a free package of formula and other baby products to new mothers as they leave the maternity ward.
- An insurance agent sells a health insurance policy in person to a customer and proceeds to market a casualty and life insurance policy as well.

In summary, the marketing restrictions imposed by the Privacy Rule do not prohibit mental health professionals from advising current, former, or prospective clients of the kinds of services that they provide. It does require the client's authorization to furnish the client's identity to a third party that will solicit the client for its own products and services. This is not a new rule or consideration for the mental health professional. It has long constituted an actionable and sanctionable breach of confidentiality for the mental health professional to disclose the identity of the people they treat without client authorization or unless compelled by law.

Research (45 CFR 164.501, 164.508, 164.512(i), 164.514(e), 164.528, 164.532)

The HIPAA Privacy Rule establishes the conditions under which protected health information may be used or disclosed by covered entities for research purposes. *Research* (45 CFR 164.501) is defined as "a systematic investigation, including research development, testing, and evaluation, designed to develop or contribute to generalizable knowledge." A covered entity may always use or disclose for research purposes health information that has been deidentified (in accordance with 45 CFR 164.502(d), and 164.514(a)-(c) of the Rule) without regard to the following provisions.

The Privacy Rule also defines the means by which individuals will be informed of uses and disclosures of their medical information for research purposes and their rights to access information about them held by covered entities. Where research is concerned, the Privacy Rule protects the privacy of individually identifiable health information, while at the same time ensuring that researchers continue to have access to medical information necessary to conduct vital research. Currently, most research involving human subjects operates under the Common Rule (45 CFR Part 46, Subpart A) and/or the Food and Drug Administration's (FDA) human subject protection regulations (21 CFR Parts 50 and 56), which have some provisions that are similar to, but separate from, the Privacy Rule's provisions for research. These human subject protection regulations, which apply to most federally funded and to some privately funded research, include protections to help ensure the privacy of subjects and the confidentiality of information. The Privacy Rule builds on these existing federal protections. More importantly, the Privacy Rule creates equal standards of privacy protection for research governed by the existing federal human subject regulations and research that is not.

In the course of conducting research, researchers may obtain, create, use, and/or disclose individually identifiable health information. Under the Privacy Rule, covered entities are permitted to use and disclose protected health information for research with individual authorization or without individual authorization under limited circumstances set forth in the Privacy Rule.

Research Use/Disclosure without Authorization

To use or disclose protected health information without authorization by the research participant, a covered entity must obtain one of the following:

- **Documented Institutional Review Board (IRB) or Privacy Board approval:** Documentation that an alteration or waiver of research participants' authorization for use/disclosure of information about them for research purposes has been approved by an IRB or a Privacy Board (CFR 164.512(i)(1)(i)). This provision of the Privacy Rule might be used, for example, to conduct records research when researchers are unable to use deidentified information, and the research could not practicably be conducted if research participants' authorization were required.

- **Preparatory to research:** Representations from the researcher, either in writing or orally, that the use or disclosure of the protected health information is solely to prepare a research protocol or for similar purposes preparatory to research, that the researcher will not remove any protected health information from the covered entity, *and* representation that protected health information for which access is sought is necessary for the research purpose (45 CFR 164.512(i)(1)(ii)). This provision might be used, for example, to design a research study or to assess the feasibility of conducting a study.
- **Research on protected health information of decedents:** Representations from the researcher, either in writing or orally, that the use or disclosure being sought is solely for research on the protected health information of decedents, that the protected health information being sought is necessary for the research, *and,* at the request of the covered entity, documentation of the death of the individuals about whom information is being sought (45 CFR 164.512(i)(1)(iii)).
- **Limited data sets with a data use agreement:** A data use agreement entered into by both the covered entity and the researcher, pursuant to which the covered entity may disclose a limited data set to the researcher for research, public health, or health care operations (45 CFR 164.514(e)).

Research Use/Disclosure with Individual Authorization

The Privacy Rule also permits covered entities to use or disclose protected health information for research purposes when a research participant authorizes the use or disclosure of information about himself or herself. Today, for example, a research participant's authorization is typically sought for most clinical trials and some records research. In this case, documentation of IRB or Privacy Board approval of a waiver of authorization is not required for the use or disclosure of protected health information.

To use or disclose protected health information with authorization by the research participant, the covered entity must obtain an authorization that satisfies the requirements of 45 CFR 164.508. The Privacy Rule has a general set of authorization requirements that apply to all uses and disclosures, including those for research purposes. However, several special provisions apply to research authorizations:

- Unlike other authorizations (see discussion of authorizations in Chapter 41), an authorization for a research purpose may state that the authorization does not expire, that there is no expiration date or event, or that the authorization continues until the "end of the research study."
- An authorization for the use or disclosure of protected health information for research may be combined with a consent to participate in the research or with any other legal permission related to the research study.

Accounting for Disclosures

In general, the Privacy Rule gives individuals the right to receive an accounting of certain disclosures of protected health information made by a covered entity (45 CFR 164.528). This accounting must include disclosures of protected health information that occurred during the six years prior to the individual's request for an accounting or since the applicable compliance date (whichever is sooner) and must include the following specified information about each disclosure:

- The date of the disclosure.
- The name of the entity or persons who received the public health information and, if known, the address of such entity or person.
- A brief description of the public health information disclosed.
- A brief statement of the purpose of the disclosure that reasonably informs the individual of the basis for the disclosure or, in lieu of such statement, a copy of a written request for a disclosure.

(See Appendixes J and K for examples of a disclosure accounting entry to be maintained by the mental health treatment provider and a request for accounting of disclosures for clients to complete.)

A more general accounting is permitted for subsequent multiple disclosures to the same person or entity for a single purpose (45 CFR 164.528(b)(3)). Research disclosures pursuant to an individual's authorization and disclosures that are part of a limited data set (data that includes no individually identified information, that is, name, address, telephone numbers, fax numbers, e-mail addresses, account numbers, health plan numbers, license numbers) for purposes of research, public health, or health care operations (45 CFR 164.514(e)) are among the types of permitted disclosures pursuant to the Privacy Rule. Other permitted disclosures that are exempt from this accounting requirement are:

In general, the Privacy Rule gives individuals the right to receive an accounting of certain disclosures of protected health information made by a covered entity.

- To carry out treatment, payment, and health care operations.
- To the individual.
- Pursuant to an individual's authorization.
- Incidental uses and disclosures.
- For a facilities directory or to persons involved in an individual's care or for other notification purposes.
- For national security or intelligence purposes.
- To correctional institution or law enforcement.
- That occurred prior to the covered entity's compliance date.

In addition, for disclosures of protected health information for research purposes without the individual's authorization pursuant to 45 CFR164.512(i) that involve at least 50 records, the Privacy Rule allows for a simplified accounting of such disclosures by covered entities. Under this simplified accounting provision, covered entities may provide individuals with a list of all protocols for which the patient's protected health information may have been disclosed under 45 CFR 164.512(i), as well as the researcher's name and contact information. Other requirements related to this simplified accounting provision are found in 45 CFR 164.528(b)(4).

If an individual revokes his or her authorization for research, covered entities may continue to use and disclose protected health information that was obtained before the time of the revocation as necessary to maintain the integrity of the research study. An individual may not revoke an authorization to the extent the covered entity has acted in reliance on the authorization. For research uses and disclosures, this reliance exception at 45 CFR 164.508(b)(5)(i) permits the continued use and disclosure of protected health information already obtained pursuant to a valid authorization to the extent necessary to preserve the integrity of the research study.

If a health oversight agency or law enforcement official provides a covered entity with a written statement that an individual's requested accounting would be reasonably likely to impede the agency's activities, the covered entity must temporarily suspend the individual's right to receive the accounting for the time period designated by the agency or official. Otherwise, a covered entity must act on the individual's request for an accounting no later than the 60th day after receipt of such request (45 CFR 160.528(c)). If the covered entity is unable to comply within the 60 days, the time period for compliance can be extended for no more than another 30 days if the individual is provided within the first 60-day period a written statement of the reasons for the delay and the date by which the covered entity will provide the accounting.

Copies of all accounting disclosures, requests, and notices must be kept as part of the client file for a minimum of six years.

An individual is entitled to one accounting in any 12-month period free of charge. A reasonable cost-based charge may be imposed for each subsequent request for an accounting in a 12-month period as long as the individual is informed in advance of the charge and given an opportunity to withdraw or modify the request for a subsequent accounting. Copies of all accounting disclosures, requests, and notices must be kept as part of the client file for a minimum of six years. This is true for all health information that is protected or otherwise compiled by a mental health professional. The information may be written or electronic but must be securely maintained for at least a six-year period.

The law in many states requires records for certain mental health disciplines to be maintained for only five years. Six years is now the minimum period for record retention; where state law requires records to be maintained for longer periods, the mental health professional should comply with the longer state law requirement.

Under the Privacy Rule, a covered entity may use and disclose protected health information that was created or received for research, either before or after the compliance date, if the covered entity obtained any one of the following before the compliance date:

- An authorization or other express legal permission from an individual to use or disclose protected health information for the research.
- The informed consent of the individual to participate in the research.
- A waiver of informed consent by an IRB in accordance with the Common Rule or an exception under FDA's human subject protection regulations at 21 CFR 50.24.

However, if a waiver of informed consent was obtained before the compliance date, but informed consent is subsequently sought after the compliance date, the covered entity must obtain the individual's authorization as required at 45 CFR 164.508. For example, if there was a temporary waiver of informed consent for emergency research under the FDA's human subject protection regulations and informed consent was later sought after the compliance date, individual authorization would be required before the covered entity could use or disclose protected health information for the research after the waiver of informed consent was no longer valid.

The Privacy Rule allows covered entities to rely on such express legal permission, informed consent, or IRB-approved waiver of informed consent, which they create or receive before the applicable compliance date, to use and disclose protected health information for specific research studies, as well as for future unspecified research that may be included in such permission.

With few exceptions, the Privacy Rule gives patients the right to inspect and obtain a copy of health information about themselves that is maintained by a covered entity or its business associate in a "designated record set." A designated record set is basically a group of records that a covered entity uses to make decisions about individuals—includes a health care provider's medical and billing records and a health plan's enrollment, payment, claims adjudication, and case or medical management record systems. While it may be unlikely that a researcher would be maintaining a designated record set, any research records or results that are actually maintained by the covered entity as part of a designated record set would be accessible to research participants unless one of the Privacy Rule's permitted exceptions applies.

One of the permitted exceptions applies to protected health information created or obtained by a covered health care provider/researcher for a clinical trial. The Privacy Rule permits the individual's access rights in these cases to be suspended *while the clinical trial is in progress,* provided the research participant agreed to this denial of access when consenting to participate in the clinical trial. In addition, the health care provider/researcher must inform the research participant that the right to access protected health information will be reinstated at the conclusion of the clinical trial.

A researcher, however, can be a covered entity if he or she furnishes health care services to individuals, including the subjects of research, and transmits any health information in electronic form in connection with a transaction covered by the Transactions Rule (CFR 160.102, 160.103). For example, a researcher who conducts a clinical trial that involves the delivery of routine health care, such as an MRI or liver function test, and transmits health information in electronic form to a third-party payer for payment, would be considered a covered health care provider under the Privacy Rule. Researchers who provide health care to the subjects of research or other individuals would be covered health care providers even if they do not themselves electronically transmit information in connection with a HIPAA transaction but have other entities, such as a hospital or billing service, conduct such electronic transactions on their behalf. As a covered entity, the researcher would have to allow an individual access to his or her protected health information.

Legal Lightbulb

- The Privacy Rule, consistent with preexisting law, prohibits the sale of a client's PHI to a third person for that third person's own purposes without the client's authorization (e.g., the sale of client lists).

- Mental health providers can provide clients with information about their own professional services, but marketing activities involving the disclosure of protected health information require client authorization.

- The Privacy Rule establishes conditions under which protected health information may be used or disclosed by covered entities for research purposes.

- PHI that has been deidentified in the manner prescribed by the Privacy Rule may be used or disclosed for research purposes with client authorization.

- To use or disclose protected health information that has not been deidentified for research purposes requires documented approval by an Institutional Review Board or Privacy Board or client authorization.

- Specific, written client authorization is required for use or disclosure of protected health information for research purposes.

- Marketing and research activities that require the use or disclosure of protected health information should be undertaken only with careful consideration of the legalitites involved and with competent legal advice.

44

Notice of Privacy Practices for Protected Health Information (45 CFR 164.520)

The HIPAA Privacy Rule gives individuals a fundamental new right to be informed of the privacy practices of their health plans and of most of their health care providers, as well as to be informed of their privacy rights with respect to their personal health information. Health plans and covered health care providers are required to develop and distribute a notice that provides a clear explanation of these rights and practices. The notice is intended to focus individuals on privacy issues and concerns and to prompt them to have discussions with their health plans and health care providers and exercise their rights.

The Privacy Rule provides that an individual has a right to adequate notice of how a covered entity may use and disclose protected health information (PHI) about the individual, as well as his or her rights and the covered entity's obligations with respect to that information. Most covered entities must develop and provide individuals with this notice of their privacy practices. Health care clearinghouses, correctional institutions, and group health plans are not required to develop a notice.

Covered entities are required to provide a notice in *plain language* that contains (45 CFR 164.520 (b)):

- The following statement, prominently displayed, as a header:

  THIS NOTICE DESCRIBES HOW MEDICAL INFORMATION ABOUT YOU MAY BE USED AND DISCLOSED AND HOW YOU CAN GET ACCESS TO THIS INFORMATION. PLEASE REVIEW IT CAREFULLY.

- A description, including at least one example, of the types of uses and disclosures that the covered entity is permitted to make for treatment, payment, and health care operations. The description must include sufficient detail to place the individual on notice of such permitted or required uses and disclosures.

The Privacy Rule provides that an individual has a right to adequate notice of how a covered entity may use and disclose protected health information (PHI) about the individual, as well as his or her rights and the covered entity's obligations with respect to that information.

- A description of each of the other purposes for which the covered entity is permitted or required to use or disclose protected health information without the individual's authorization. This description must also include sufficient detail to place the individual on notice of such permitted or required uses and disclosures.
- A statement that the covered entity may contact the individual to provide appointment reminders or information about treatment alternatives or other health-related benefits and services that may be of interest to the individual. (This statement is required only if the covered entity intends to engage in these kinds of activities.)
- A statement of the individual's right to request restrictions on certain uses and disclosures of protected health information, including a statement that the covered entity is not required to agree to the requested restriction.
- A statement of the individual's right to receive confidential communication of protected health information.
- A statement of the individual's right to inspect and copy protected health information.
- A statement of the individual's right to amend protected protected health information. (See Appendix H for an example of a Client Information Amendment form.)
- A statement of the individual's right to receive an accounting of disclosures of protected health information. (See Appendix K for an example of a request for accounting of disclosures.)
- A statement of an individual's right, including an individual who has agreed to receive the notice electronically, to obtain a paper copy of the notice from the covered entity upon request.
- A statement that the covered entity is required by law to maintain the privacy of protected health information and to provide individuals with notice of its legal duties and privacy practices with respect to protected health information.
- A statement that the covered entity is required to abide by the terms of the notice currently in effect.
  - —If the covered entity wishes to change or revise its privacy notice, a statement that it reserves the right to change the terms of its notice and to make the new notice provisions effective to all protected health information that it maintains. The statement must also describe how it will provide individuals with a revised notice.
  - —A statement that individuals may complain to the covered entity and to the Secretary of HHS if they believe their privacy rights have been violated, including a brief description of how they may file a complaint with the covered entity and a statement that individuals will not be retaliated against for filing a complaint.
  - —Information on whom individuals can contact for further information about the covered entity's privacy policies.

The notice must include an effective date, and a covered entity is required to promptly revise and distribute its notice whenever it makes material changes to any of its privacy practices.

A covered entity must make its notice available to any person who asks for it (45 CFR 164.520(c)). In addition, a covered entity must prominently post and make available its notice on any web site it maintains that provides information about its customer services or benefits. A covered entity may e-mail the notice to an individual if the individual agrees to receive an electronic notice. An individual who is the recipient of an electronic notice retains the right to obtain a paper copy of the notice from a covered entity on request.

Covered direct treatment providers must:

- Provide the notice to the individual no later than the date of first service delivery (after the April 14, 2003, compliance date of the Privacy Rule) and, except in an emergency treatment situation, make a good faith effort to obtain the individual's written acknowledgment of receipt of the notice. If an acknowledgment cannot be obtained, the provider must document his or her efforts to obtain the acknowledgment and the reason it was not obtained.
- When first service delivery to an individual is provided over the Internet, through e-mail, or otherwise electronically, the provider must send an electronic notice automatically and contemporaneously in response to the individual's first request for service. The provider must make a good faith effort to obtain a return receipt or other transmission from the individual in response to receiving the notice.
- When first service delivery to an individual is provided over the telephone, the provider must mail a copy of the privacy notice to the individual. The provider must make a good faith effort to obtain the individual's acknowledgment of receipt of the notice. (A suggested technique is to include a card for the individual to sign and an addressed return envelope.)
- In an emergency treatment situation, provide the notice as soon as it is reasonably practicable to do so after the emergency situation has ended. In these situations, providers are not required to make a good faith effort to obtain a written acknowledgment from individuals.
- Make the latest notice (i.e., the one that reflects any changes in privacy policies) available at the provider's office or facility for individuals to request to take with them, and *post it in a clear and prominent location at the facility.*

If treatment is provided to a minor or an adult person for whom a personal representative has been appointed, copy of the notice must be given to a parent of the child or the personal representative of the treated adult. Acknowledgment of receipt of the privacy notice must be obtained from the parent or the personal representative.

A covered entity must make its notice available to any person who asks for it.

Any covered entity may choose to develop more than one notice, such as when an entity performs different types of covered functions.

Any covered entity may choose to develop more than one notice, such as when an entity performs different types of covered functions (i.e., the functions that make it a health plan, a health care provider, or a health care clearing-house), and there are variations in its privacy practices among these covered functions. Covered entities are expected to provide individuals with the most specific notice possible.

Mental health professionals must develop and disseminate a privacy notice with all the information set forth in the Privacy Rule. A defective privacy notice could subject the mental health professional to onerous sanctions. (See Appendix I for an example of a Notice of Privacy Practices.)

Answers to Frequently Asked Questions about:

HIPAA Privacy Rule

Records

? Question

I am a mental health professional in private practice and need to run a very cost-efficient operation to be profitable. If a client requests a copy of his or her file, including my psychotherapy notes, is the client required to pay for the copy?

Legal Lightbulb

- Documentation has always been a critical responsibility of the mental health provider.

- The Notice of Privacy Practices adds a new piece of documentation to be included in every client file after April 14, 2003.

- The Notice must be in plain language and prominently displayed in a common area of the practice and made available to every person who asks to see a copy.

- Old intake and consent forms are not adequate and must be rewritten in light of the Privacy Rule requirements.

- An inadequate Notice will subject the mental health provider to sanctions and is easily policed by the Office of Civil Rights.

❗ Answer

The Privacy Rule permits a covered entity to impose reasonable, cost-based fees. The fee may include only the cost of copying (including supplies and labor) and postage if the client requests that the copy be mailed. You are required to advise clients in your Notice of Privacy Practices of the client's right to access and copy protected health information. If the client has agreed to receive a summary or explanation of his or her protected health information, a covered entity may also charge a fee for preparation of the summary or explanation. The fee may not include costs associated with searching for and retrieving the requested information. (See 45 CFR 164.524.)

45

Restrictions on Government Access to Health Information (45 CFR Part 160, Subpart C; 164.512(f))

Under the HIPAA Privacy Rule, government-operated health plans and health care providers must meet substantially the same requirements as private ones for protecting the privacy of individual identifiable health information.

Under the HIPAA Privacy Rule, government-operated health plans and health care providers must meet substantially the same requirements as private ones for protecting the privacy of individually identifiable health information. For instance, government-run health plans, such as Medicare and Medicaid, must take virtually the same steps to protect the claims and health information that they receive from beneficiaries as private insurance plans or health maintenance organizations (HMOs). In addition, all federal agencies must meet the requirements of the Privacy Act of 1974, which restricts the information about individual citizens (including any personal health information) that can be shared with other agencies and with the public.

The Rule does not require a covered entity to send health information to the government for a government database or similar operation. The Rule does not require or allow any new government access to medical information, with one exception: There is new authority for government access for enforcement of the protections in the Privacy Rule itself. To ensure that covered entities protect patients' privacy, the Rule requires that health plans, hospitals, and other covered entities cooperate with efforts by the Department of Health and Human Services (HHS) Office for Civil Rights (OCR) to investigate complaints or otherwise ensure compliance.

For enforcement purposes, OCR may need to look at how a covered entity handled protected health information, as is typical in many enforcement settings. This investigative authority is needed so that the Rule can be enforced and to ensure the independent review of consumers' concerns over privacy violations. Even so, the Privacy Rule limits disclosures to OCR to information that is "pertinent to ascertaining compliance." The OCR is expected to maintain stringent controls to safeguard any individually identifiable health information that it receives. The concern is that if covered entities could avoid or ignore enforcement requests, consumers would not have a way to ensure an independent review of their concerns about privacy violations under the Rule.

Examples of investigations that may require OCR to have access to protected health information include:

- Allegations that a covered entity refused to note a request for correction in a patient's mental health treatment record.
- Allegations that a covered entity did not provide complete access to an individual's mental health treatment record to that individual when there was no issue that disclosure would be harmful to the individual.

Specifically covered entities must (45 CFR 160.310):

- Keep such records and submit such reports in such time and manner and containing such information as the Secretary may determine to be necessary to enable the Secretary to ascertain whether the covered entity has complied or is complying with the Privacy Rule.
- Cooperate with the Secretary, if the Secretary undertakes an investigation or compliance review of the policies, procedures, or practices of a covered entity to determine whether the covered entity is complying with the Privacy Rule.
- Permit access by the Secretary during normal business hours to its facilities, books, records, accounts, and other sources of information, including protected health information, that are pertinent to ascertaining compliance with the Privacy Rule. If the Secretary determines that exigent circumstances exist, such as when documents may be hidden or destroyed, a covered entity must permit access by the Secretary at any time without notice.

Most mental health professionals are familiar with the oversight powers of their state licensing boards. The Privacy Rule now adds a new dimension in terms of oversight by the federal government. "Big Brother" will now be looking over their shoulders.

Current law enforcement access to individually identifiable health information has not been expanded. In fact, it limits access to a greater degree than currently exists because the Rule establishes new procedures and safeguards that restrict the circumstances under which a covered entity may give such information to law enforcement officers. It is important to remember that the applicable section (45 CFR 164.512(f)) is a permissive section that provides that a covered entity *may* disclose protected health information:

- As required by law, including laws that require the reporting of certain types of wounds or other physical injuries.

- In compliance with and as limited by the relevant requirements of a court-ordered warrant, a subpoena or summons issued by a judicial officer, a grand jury subpoena, or an administrative subpoena or summons, provided that the information sought is relevant and material to a legitimate law enforcement inquiry, the request is specific and limited in scope to the extent reasonably practicable in light of the purpose for which the information is sought, and deidentified information could not be used.
- In response to a law enforcement official's request for such information for the purpose of identifying or locating a suspect, fugitive, material witness, or missing person, provided that the covered entity disclose only the following information:
  —Name and address.
  —Date and place of birth.
  —Social security number.
  —ABO blood type and rh factor.
  —Type of injury.
  —Date and time of treatment.
  —Date and time of death.
  —A description of physical characteristics (height, weight, gender, hair and eye color, scars, etc.).
  Note: The Rule prohibits the disclosure of DNA information, dental records, or samples or analysis of body fluids or tissue information for this purpose, absent some other legal requirements such as a warrant.
- If a crime victim agrees, in response to a law enforcement official's request for information about the victim.
- If a law enforcement official is unable to obtain the crime victim's agreement because of incapacity or other emergency circumstance, provided that the disclosure is in the best interest of the victim and the law enforcement official:
  —Represents that the information is needed to determine whether a violation of law by a person other than the victim has occurred and such information is not intended to be used against the victim; and
  —Represents that immediate law enforcement activity that depends on the disclosure would be materially and adversely affected by waiting until the victim is able to agree to the disclosure.
- About an individual who has died to a law enforcement official for the purpose of alerting law enforcement of the death of the individual if the covered entity has suspicion that such death may have resulted from criminal conduct.
- That the covered entity believes in good faith constitutes evidence of criminal conduct that occurred on the premises of the covered entity.

Where state law imposes additional restrictions on disclosure of health information to law enforcement, those state laws continue to apply. Even in

Legal Lightbulb

- Although the Privacy Rule is designed to protect the privacy of protected health information, it creates a new exception to a patient's right to privacy. The Office of Civil Rights has the right to access protected health information for investigations of alleged violations, compliance verification, and enforcement of the Privacy Rule.

- The Privacy Rule addresses law enforcement rights to access protected health information.

- The Privacy Rule contains *permissive* provisions with respect to mental health provider's right to share protected health information with law enforcement personnel. However, mental health providers need to be mindful of their state reporting laws and duties in making determinations about what information is disclosed to law enforcement authorities.

circumstances when disclosure to law enforcement is permitted by the Rule, the Privacy Rule does not require covered entities to disclose any information. Other federal or state law may require a disclosure, and the Privacy Rule does not interfere with the operation of these other laws. However, unless the disclosure is required by some other law, covered entities should use their professional judgment to decide whether to disclose information, reflecting their own policies and ethical principles. Mental health professionals could continue to follow their own policies to protect privacy in such instances.

46

HIPAA Security Rule

The word security should not be confused with either privacy or confidentiality.

On February 20, 2003, the U.S. Department of Health and Human Services (HHS) published the final form of the HIPAA Security Rules. When the HIPAA statute was passed in 1996, it mandated the creation of standards to ensure the security and integrity of health information that is maintained or transmitted electronically. *Security* or *security measures* encompass all of the administrative, physical, and technical safeguards in an information system whereas *integrity* is defined as "the property that data or information have not been altered or destroyed in an unauthorized manner" (45 CFR 164.304).

The word *security* should not be confused with either *privacy* or *confidentiality*. Privacy refers to a person's right to control his or her personal health care information and to prevent its unauthorized disclosure. Confidentiality comes into play once disclosure has been made to a health care provider and refers to the means of protecting and safeguarding the information from unauthorized disclosures. Security represents the tools and safeguards by which confidentiality is ensured.

While the Privacy Rule applies to protected health information in all media (written, electronic, and oral), the Security Rule applies only to protected health information in electronic form. It specifically states that its "standards, requirements, and implementation specifications" apply to "a health care provider who transmits any health information in electronic form . . ." (45 CFR 162.104). As discussed earlier with respect to the Privacy Rule, it will become increasingly rare and difficult for mental health professionals to position themselves outside the scope of HIPAA's Privacy and Security Rules. Even the occasional e-mail communication to or from a client or the sending of client information via the Internet from the therapist's office to a home computer will require the mental health professional to be compliant with the Security Rule. Eventually, billing a payor for services will have to be accomplished electronically.

The compliance dates for the Security Rule are the same for each covered entity except small health plans (45 CFR 164.318):

- *Large health plans:* 26 months after the date of publication in the *Federal Register* (4/20/05).

- *Small health plans:* 38 months after the date of publication in the *Federal Register* (4/20/06).
- *Health care clearinghouse:* 26 months after the date of publication in the *Federal Register* (2/20/05).
- *Health care provider:* 26 months after the date of publication in the *Federal Register* (4/20/05).

Although mental health professionals who are covered entities may have until April 20, 2005, to come into compliance with the Security Rule, they would be well served to initiate efforts to become compliant as quickly as possible. The comprehensive implementation provisions will take time and effort to develop, document, and put into practice. The Security Rule is process oriented, which should begin with a risk assessment to identify risks to confidentiality, integrity, and availability of protected health information and to identify existing measures to guard against them. The Rule contains approximately 22 standards of administrative, physical, and technical safeguards.

Once the risk assessment is completed, a covered entity must implement a risk management plan that addresses each standard. The Security Rule sets out "implementation specifications" actions or processes that safeguard against the risks identified in the standard (45 CFR 164.306 (c)). The Rule contains two types of implementation specifications: required and addressable. A required implementation specification *must* be implemented, whereas an addressable implementation specification is not mandatory but must be implemented unless it is reasonable and appropriate to implement an alternative that addresses the risks.

The Rule does not make addressable implementation specifications completely discretionary for the covered entity. It states that a covered entity must first assess whether the implementation specification "is a reasonable and appropriate safeguard in its environment, when analyzed with reference to the likely contribution to protecting the electronic protected health information."

If the covered entity determines that the implementation specification is reasonable and appropriate, it should implement the same specification. If it determines that it is not reasonable and appropriate, the covered entity must:

1. Document why it would not be reasonable and appropriate to implement the implementation specification.
2. Implement an equivalent alternative measure if reasonable and appropriate.
3. Retain the documentation for the decision and its basis for six years from the last date on which the decision was made the effective policy.

As with the Privacy Rule, covered entities making decisions concerning addressable implementation specifications may make *scalable* choices. This means that the specific details may appropriately vary depending on the size, operational needs, and resources of the covered entity. As a general rule, the larger the organization, the more financial and administrative burden it will be expected to bear. A counselor in a solo practice will not need or be expected to finance the security measures a large psychiatric hospital will be required to fund and implement.

The Security Rule is intended to create a minimum level of security, and organizations are encouraged to implement security standards and measures that exceed HIPAA's requirements.

The Security Rule is intended to create a minimum level of security, and organizations are encouraged to implement security standards and measures that exceed HIPAA's requirements. All covered entities must ensure that all staff members comply with the safeguards implemented to protect against threats to protected health information security, integrity, and its unauthorized use and disclosure.

The Security Rule lists several general standards, followed by three categories of safeguards that in turn are followed by organizational requirements, policies, procedures, and documentation requirements. The most important standards are set forth and discussed in the following sections. As with the Privacy Rule, the Security Rule should be reviewed by the mental health professional in its entirety. In addition, the mental health professional should look for substantive modifications and additions to the Rule by the Department of Health and Human Services as time passes and experience or judicial rulings require change.

General Security Standards (45 CFR 164.306)

These standards apply to all covered entities. The Security Rule states that all covered entities must do the following:

1. Ensure the confidentiality, integrity, and availability of all electronic protected health information the covered entity creates, receives, maintains, or transmits.
2. Protect against any reasonably anticipated threats or hazards to the security or integrity of such information.
3. Protect against any reasonably anticipated uses or disclosures of such information that are not permitted or required.
4. Ensure compliance with these standards by its workforce.

Although, at first review, the Security Rule may appear to be a little overwhelming, its standards specifically provide for flexibility in the approach chosen by the health care provider.

The standards should not seem unusual or burdensome to most mental health professionals. Historically, mental health professionals have been required to provide a greater degree of security and confidentiality for their client files than other health care professionals. Although, at first review, the Security Rule may appear to be a little overwhelming, its standards specifically provide for flexibility in the approach chosen by the health care provider. "Covered entities may use any security measures that allow the covered entity to reasonably and appropriately implement the standards and implementation specifications . . ."

In deciding on which security measures to use, a covered entity must take the following factors into account:

1. The size, complexity, and capabilities of the covered entity.
2. The covered entity's technical infrastructure, hardware, and software security capabilities.
3. The costs of the security measures.
4. The probability and criticality of potential risks to electronic protected health information.

As previously stated, these rules are "scalable," and a mental health professional in a solo practice with a desktop computer will not be expected to implement the same sophisticated security measures of a large health plan or health care clearinghouse.

Administrative Safeguards (45 CFR 164.308)

These safeguards are designed to limit protected health information access to appropriate parties and prevent use or disclosure by all others. There are nine standards in this section, each with its own implementation specifications.

Standard One

A covered entity must implement policies and procedures to prevent, detect, contain, and correct security violations.

The following implementation specifications are *required* of all covered entities under this standard:

A. **Risk analysis:** Conduct an accurate and thorough assessment of the potential risks and vulnerabilities to the confidentiality, integrity, and availability of electronic protected health information held by the covered entity.
B. **Risk management:** Implement security measures sufficient to reduce risks and vulnerabilities to a reasonable and appropriate level.
C. **Sanction policy:** Apply appropriate sanctions against workforce members who fail to comply with the security policies and procedures of the covered entity.
D. **Information system information review:** Implement procedures to regularly review records of information system activity, such as audit logs, access reports, and security incident tracking reports.

It is important for mental health professionals to remember to thoroughly document compliance with each standard of the Security Rule. A security log

Thoroughly document compliance with each standard of the Security Rule. A security log or manual should be created and maintained for this purpose.

or manual should be created and maintained for this purpose. For a mental health professional in a small or individual practice with a desktop computer on which protected health information is stored, risk analysis might show that through its modem connection, the hard drive is at risk of being accessed by outsiders. Purchasing firewall software and periodically testing its effectiveness would be an appropriate security measure. This compliance with the standard should be documented in the security file.

Standard Two

A covered entity must identify the security official who is responsible for the development and implementation of the policies and procedures for the entity.

Just as the Privacy Rule required the designation of a privacy officer, the Security Rule mandates the appointment of a security officer. The same person may serve in both capacities. The intent is to have one individual to whom persons within and from outside the covered entity can go to with security questions or issues.

Standard Three

A covered entity must implement policies and procedures to ensure that all members of its workforce have appropriate access to electronic protected health information and to prevent those workforce members who do not have access from obtaining access to electronic protected health information.

There are no *required* implementation specifications for this standard. The following implementation specifications are *addressable* by all covered entities under this standard:

A. **Authorization and/or supervision:** Implement procedures for the authorization and/or supervision of workforce members who work with electronic protected health information or in locations where it might be accessed.
B. **Workforce clearance procedures:** Implement procedures to determine that the access of a workforce member to electronic protected health information is appropriate.
C. **Termination procedures:** Implement procedures for terminating access to electronic protected health information when the employment of a workforce member ends or when access to electronic protected health information by a workforce member is no longer appropriate.

The goal here, consistent with the Privacy Rule, is to allow access to protected health information only to those with a need to access and prevent all others from gaining access. Appropriate procedures may include assigning an individual password to those workforce members who need access to protected health information and to create separate electronic files for different components of a client's protected health information. For example, a client's psychotherapy notes may be kept in a separate computer file with access restricted to fewer members of the workforce by password.

Standard Four

A covered entity must implement policies and procedures for authorizing access to electronic protected health information.

The only *required* implementation specification applies just to health care clearinghouses that are part of a larger organization. These covered entities must implement policies and procedures that protect the electronic protected health information of the clearinghouse from unauthorized access by the larger organization.

The following implementation specifications are *addressable* by all covered entities under this standard:

A. Access authorization: Implement policies and procedures for granting access to electronic protected health information, for example, through access to a workstation, transaction, program, process, or other mechanism.

B. Access establishment and modification: Implement policies and procedures that, based on the entity's access authorization policies, establish, document, review, and modify a user's right of access to a workstation, transaction, program, or process.

An example of a policy and procedure is placing workforce members who are not authorized to access protected health information at workstations where the computers are not networked with the computer system that stores protected health information. The goal is to determine which workforce members should be allowed access to protected health information and to prevent those who aren't from obtaining access. As stated, password-protecting access to protected health information will be essential.

Standard Five

A covered entity must implement a security awareness and training program for all members of its workforce, including management. This program should be documented.

There are no *required* implementation specifications for this standard. The following implementation specifications are *addressable* by all covered entities under this standard:

A. **Security reminders:** Implement periodic security updates.
B. **Protection from malicious software:** Implement procedures for guarding against, detecting, and reporting malicious software. (Malicious software is defined as software, e.g., a virus, which is designed to damage or disrupt a system.)
C. **Log-in monitoring:** Implement procedures for monitoring log-in attempts and reporting discrepancies.
D. **Password management:** Implement procedures for creating, changing, and safeguarding passwords.

Remember that these are addressable implementation specifications; if they don't make sense, as may be true for a mental health practitioner who is a solo practitioner, it is still necessary to document why these specifications are not reasonable and appropriate. Every computer system, however, should be installed with virus protection software that should be updated as often as its creator or distributor provides updating. The entity's policies and procedures should document the person responsible for this updating and how verification of compliance with the policy and procedure will be documented. (For example, a note in the security log or manual may read, "Virus protection software update downloaded 4/15/2003.")

Generally, it is the security officer's duty to adequately train and monitor the workforce and oversee security compliance. The security officer should be placed in charge of issuing, modifying, and deleting employee passwords. An entity will be well served to give the designated security officer sufficient authority to keep the entity in compliance and to make necessary changes to policies and procedures.

Standard Six

A covered entity must implement policies and procedures to address security incidents.

There are no *required* implementation specifications for this standard. The following implementation specifications are *addressable* by all covered entities under this standard:

A. **Response and reporting:** Identify and respond to suspected or known security incidents; mitigate, to the extent practicable, harmful effects to security incidents that are known to the covered entity; and document security incidents and their outcome.

A *security incident* means "the attempted or successful unauthorized access, use, disclosure, modification, or destruction of information or interference with system operations in an information system." If the mental health professional's hard drive crashes or a virus alters software and prevents access to client files, a security incident occurs, and policies and procedures must be in place to address these problems. An acceptable policy and procedure may be to contract with a computer consultant (see Chapter 40 concerning business associate contracts) who is ready to come in on short notice to restore the hard drive, delete virus software, or reinstall needed software.

Standard Seven

A covered entity must establish and implement, as needed, policies and procedures for responding to an emergency or other occurrences (e.g., fire, vandalism, system failure, and natural disaster) that damage systems containing electronic protected health information.

The following implementation specifications are *required* of all covered entities under this standard:

A. **Data backup plan:** Establish and implement procedures to create and maintain retrievable exact copies of electronic protected health information.
B. **Disaster recovery plan:** Establish and implement as needed procedures to restore any loss of data.
C. **Emergency mode operation plan:** Establish and implement as needed procedures to enable continuation of critical business processes for protection of the security of electronic protected health information while operating in emergency mode.

The following implementation specifications are *addressable* by all covered entities under this standard:

A. **Testing and revision procedures:** Implement procedures for periodic testing and revision of contingency plans.
B. **Applications and data criticality analysis:** Assess the relative criticality of specific applications and data in support of other contingency components.

A mental health professional backing up all client files on CD-ROMs may wish to consider making multiple backup CD-ROMs and keeping one at a different location, for example, his or her home. Consideration must be given to how often the files should be backed up. It would not be unreasonable to back up files at the conclusion of each day. The mental health professional would back up the hard drive, make the extra copy, and take it home at the end of each day. If a fire destroys the office, a recovery plan could be as simple as bringing in a new desktop and keeping the backup CD-ROM at the therapist's home. The CD-ROM taken home must be adequately secured as well. It is not hard to imagine how much more complicated and difficult compliance with this standard becomes for large covered entities.

Standard Eight

A covered entity must perform a periodic technical and nontechnical evaluation, based initially on the standards implemented under this rule and, subsequently, in response to environmental or operational changes affecting the security of electronic protected health information, which establishes the extent to which an entity's security policies and procedures meet the requirements of the Security Rule.

It is imperative to document that such evaluations have occurred. If a security log or manual is maintained, it would be appropriate to record the date, findings, and actions taken with respect to the evaluation. It may be wise to create a policy that requires the designated security officer to conduct an evaluation at specified intervals, that is, monthly, quarterly, semiannually, and at the time of any environmental or operational changes.

Standard Nine

A covered entity may permit a business associate to create, receive, maintain, or transmit electronic protected health information on the covered entity's behalf only if the covered entity obtains satisfactory assurances that the business associate will appropriately safeguard the information. (This standard does not apply to a covered entity that transmits electronic protected health information to a health care provider concerning the treatment of an individual.)

The following implementation specification is *required* of all covered entities under this standard:

A. **Written contract:** Document the satisfactory assurances required by this standard through a written contract or other arrangement with the business associate.

The Privacy Rule requires business associate contracts (discussed in Chapter 40) for all business associates who by necessity will have access to protected health information. The Security Rule establishes standards for business associate contracts for all covered entities and a separate standard applicable for health plans in 45 CFR 164.314, organizational requirements. This first standard in this section states that a covered entity is not in compliance with both the Privacy Rule and Security Rule if the entity knew of a material breach of a business associate contract by a business associate and failed to: (a) take reasonable steps to cure the breach or end the violation, and (b) if unsuccessful in doing so, terminate the contract if feasible, and (c) if not, to report the problem to the Secretary of HHS.

The *required* implementation provision of this standard states that a contract between a covered entity and a business associate must provide that the business associate will:

A. Implement administrative, physical, and technical safeguards that reasonably and appropriately protect the confidentiality, integrity, and availability of the electronic protected health information that it creates, receives, maintains, or transmits on behalf of the covered entity.

B. Ensure that any agent, including a subcontractor, to whom it provides such information agrees to implement reasonable and appropriate safeguards to protect it.

C. Report to the covered entity any security incident of which it becomes aware.

D. Authorize termination of the contract by the covered entity if the covered entity determines that the business associate has violated a material term of the contract.

See Appendixes E and F for examples of business associate contracts.

Physical Safeguards (45 CFR 164.310)

There are four standards in the physical safeguard section. They address the integrity and security of the physical locations where protected health information is stored and accessed.

Standard Ten

A covered entity must implement policies and procedures to limit physical access to its electronic information systems and the facility or facilities in which they are housed, while ensuring that properly authorized access is allowed.

There are no *required* implementation specifications for this standard. The following implementation specifications are *addressable* by all covered entities under this standard:

A. **Contingency operations:** Establish and implement as needed procedures that allow facility access in support of restoration of lost data under the disaster recovery plan and emergency mode operations plan in the event of an emergency.

B. Facility security plan: Implement policies and procedures to safeguard the facility and the equipment therein from unauthorized physical access, tampering, and theft.

C. Access control and validation procedures: Implement policies and procedures to control and validate a person's access to facilities based on their role or function, including visitor control and control of access to software programs for testing and revisions.

D. Maintenance records: Implement policies and procedures to document repairs and modifications to the physical components of a facility related to security (i.e., hardware, walls, doors, and locks).

Larger health care entities may wish to provide each employee with a name or security badge with different levels of security clearance.

Locking down individual PCs and, with larger systems, allowing only limited access to network servers located in locked rooms are examples of policies and procedures that could be implemented under this standard. In an all-paper world, keeping locked file cabinets in locked rooms provided an adequate level of security for client files. Requiring a double-lock approach may be a reasonable requirement in today's electronic age.

Larger health care entities may wish to provide each employee with a name or security badge with different levels of security clearance, similar to procedures of a defense contractor or a governmental agency. Repairs to hardware and facilities should be documented by the security officer in the security log or manual.

Standard Eleven

A covered entity must implement policies and procedures that specify the proper functions to be performed, the manner in which those functions are to be performed, and the physical attributes of the surroundings of a specific workstation or class of workstation that can access electronic protected health information.

Close attention must be given to each member of the workforce's workstation, its design, and functions. If a function of a workstation is to allow access to a network system and protected health information, greater thought must be given to security. Limiting use to a limited class of employee will be a given, and limiting access to certain times of the day may be required as well.

Standard Twelve

A covered entity must implement physical safeguards for all workstations that access electronic protected health information to restrict access to authorized users.

Password protecting the PC and requiring the employee to further lock down the PC with a locking system for the PC at the end of the work day might be adequate. Workstations should be positioned so that persons who are not authorized to access protected health information cannot view protected health information displayed on the workstation's monitor. Enclosed cubicles for each workstation may be necessary.

Standard Thirteen

A covered entity must implement policies and procedures that govern the receipt and removal of hardware and electronic media that contain electronic protected health information into and out of a facility and the movement of these items within a facility.

The following implementation specifications are *required* of all covered entities under this standard:

A. **Disposal:** Implement policies and procedures to address the final disposition of electronic protected health information and/or hardware or electronic media on which it is stored.
B. **Media reuse:** Implement policies and procedures for removal of electronic protected health information from electronic media before the media are made available for reuse.

The following implementation specifications are *addressable* by all covered entities under this standard:

A. **Accountability:** Maintain a record of the movements of hardware and electronic media and any person responsible therefor.
B. **Data backup and storage:** Create a retrievable, exact copy of electronic protected health information, when needed, before movement of equipment.

Mental health professionals have always taken careful steps to destroy client files when maintaining the file was no longer required or desired. Shredding is a common approach. Equal care must be given to obliterating electronic files to be sure that the information is not recoverable, especially if the media will be reused. Physical destruction of the disk, tape, or other media rather than reuse may still be the safest alternative. The security officer will have to keep up with hardware and media at all times and must document their movement within or outside the entity.

Technical Safeguards (45 CFR 164.312)

Five standards are contained in the technical safeguard section. They mandate policies and procedures to protect against unauthorized access to protected health information.

Standard Fourteen

A covered entity must implement technical policies and procedures for electronic information systems that maintain electronic protected health information to allow access only to those persons or software programs that have been granted access rights in accordance with Standard Four.

The following implementation specifications are *required* of all covered entities under this standard:

A. **Unique user identification:** Assign a unique name and/or number for identifying and tracking user identity.
B. **Emergency access procedures:** Establish and implement as needed procedures for obtaining necessary electronic protected health information during an emergency.

The following implementation specifications are *addressable* by all covered entities under this standard:

A. **Automatic logoff:** Implement electronic procedures that terminate an electronic session after a predetermined time of inactivity.
B. **Encryption and decryption:** Implement a mechanism to encrypt and decrypt electronic protected health information.

It will be necessary to establish a tracking system to keep track of employees and contractors who will access protected health information. This may be accomplished through the development or acquisition of tracking software or, in a smaller organization, with a sign-in log and with the security officer giving out a new password for access each day to any employee who legitimately needs to access protected health information.

Everyone who is familiar with Internet access software has experienced the automatic sign-off because of inactivity. This same software can be used to shut down access to protected health information if a computer sits idle for a proscribed time period. Certainly, encryption and decryption software should be considered when transmitting electronic protected health information via the Internet. As discussed in Chapter 36, "Internet Therapy," this software is recommended for distance therapy as well.

Standard Fifteen

A covered entity must implement hardware, software, and/or procedural mechanisms that record and examine activity in information systems that contain or use electronic protected health information.

Before you can transmit electronic protected health information, it has to be recorded, and the entity has to have the software, hardware, and procedures in place to do so. It may be as simple as a desktop PC and Microsoft Word; as files are saved to the hard drive, the time and date can be recorded on the hard drive.

Standard Sixteen

A covered entity must implement policies and procedures to protect electronic protected health information from alteration or destruction.

There are no *required* implementation specifications for this standard. The following implementation specification is *addressable* by all covered entities under this standard:

A. Mechanism to authenticate electronic protected health information: Implement electronic mechanisms to corroborate that electronic protected health information has not been altered or destroyed in an unauthorized manner.

Larger entities may have the resources to invest in software and hardware that can automatically scan and identify corrupted electronic protected health information and perhaps correct it. Less sophisticated software (e.g., ScanDisk) comes standard with most operating programs used on desktop PCs. A solo practitioner may also want to randomly access old client data to determine that it is not corrupted and is retrievable. If there are problems, data from a backup medium can be used to restore the file to its original form.

Standard Seventeen

A covered entity must implement procedures to verify that a person or entity seeking access to electronic protected health information is the one claimed.

Only persons or entities authorized to access or to receive disclosure of protected health information should be able to do so. Password protecting access is one means of complying with this standard, but a mental health entity may consider requiring additional log-in data beyond a password (e.g., driver's license number) before access is granted or disclosure made.

Standard Eighteen

A covered entity must implement technical security measures to guard against unauthorized access to electronic protected health information that is being transmitted over an electronic communications network.

There are no *required* implementation specifications for this standard. The following implementation specifications are *addressable* by all covered entities under this standard:

Mental health professionals must sit down and devise a plan on how implementation specifications will be developed and implemented, document them, and carry them through.

A. Integrity controls: Implement security measures to ensure that electronically transmitted electronic protected health information is not improperly modified without detection until disposed of.
B. Encryption: Implement a mechanism to encrypt electronic protected health information whenever deemed appropriate.

Transmitting electronic protected health information over the Internet may require encryption to comply with this standard. There may be no other way to ensure that an unauthorized person who captures protected health information at least cannot easily decipher it. If electronic protected health information is transmitted to a third party, there should be assurances given that it will not be modified by the recipient and that it will be returned or destroyed when no longer needed.

Policies and Procedures and Documentation Requirements (45 CFR 164.316)

This section contains two standards designed to ensure compliance with all requirements of the Security Rule.

Standard Nineteen

A covered entity must implement reasonable and appropriate policies and procedures to comply with all the standards, implementation specifications, or other requirements of the Security Rule, taking into account those factors listed previously in deciding on which security measures to use. This standard is not to be construed to permit or excuse an action that violates any other standard, implementation specification, or other requirement of the Security Rule. A covered entity may change its policies and procedures at any time, provided that the changes are documented and are implemented in accordance with the Security Rule.

Covered mental health professionals must not only create and establish policies and procedures on how to comply with each standard of the Security Rule but also implement policies and procedures on how to create the necessary policies and procedures to implement the standards. A mental health professional must sit down and devise a plan determining how implementation specifications will be developed and implemented, document them, and carry them through.

Standard Twenty

A covered entity must maintain policies and procedures implemented to comply with the Security Rule in written (which may be electronic) form and, if any activity or assessment is required to be documented, maintain a written (which may be electronic) record of the action, activity, or assessment.

The following implementation specifications are *required* of all covered entities under this standard:

A. **Time limit:** Retain the documentation required by this standard for six years from the date of its creation or the date when it last was in effect, whichever is later.

B. **Availability:** Make documentation available to those persons responsible for implementing the procedures to which the documentation pertains.

C. **Updates:** Review documentation periodically and update as needed in response to environmental or operational changes affecting the security of the electronic protected health information.

We have suggested that mental health professionals develop a security log or security manual in which to document compliance with the Security Rule. It should be a multipart file that contains a section for each standard and the policies and procedures developed to implement the standard. Particular attention should be given to each *required* implementation specification, which should be set forth in the log or manual under the applicable standard with a discussion on how the entity has met the specification. To develop workable measures for compliance, efforts should begin immediately. Mental health professionals will want to have sensible and tested measures in place by April 20, 2005. The security manual or log will always be a work in progress and should be maintained and kept current by one individual, preferably the security officer for the entity. Each employee and all new employees should be required to read the security log or manual and acknowledge in writing that they have done so and understood what they have read.

❓ Question

I am a social worker. In my state, I am required to keep client files for only five years. How long must I retain written documentation of my security policies and procedures, and in what form must this information be retained?

Legal Lightbulb

- Obtain a copy of the Security Rule.

- Designate a security officer and guarantee this individual sufficient authority to make the changes required to bring the entity into compliance with the Security Rule. Consider appointing one or more workforce members to a security committee.

- Create a security log or manual listing each standard of the Security Rule and each required implementation specification under each standard. Require each employee and all new employees to read the security manual or log and acknowledge in writing that they have done so and understood what they have read.

- Create a plan of action that sets out how the entity will bring itself into compliance with the Security Rule and document this plan in the security log or manual.

- Conduct a risk analysis of electronic systems, protected health information, facilities, hardware, and workforce.

- Develop specific measures to ensure compliance with the standard and each required implementation specification. Document the adopted policies and procedures in the security log or manual.

- Review each addressable implementation specification for every standard; if the decision is made not to adopt an addressable standard, document the decision in accordance with the Security Rule.

- Develop and implement training programs for the entity's workforce on security matters and sanctions to be imposed for violations by members of the workforce.

- Conduct routine audits of protected health information and inspection of all hardware, software, and facilities documenting the date, findings, and actions taken.

- Stay current on hardware and software technological developments that can enhance your entity's security capabilities. Don't be afraid or hesitant to make beneficial changes.

- Take HIPAA seriously.

! *Answer*

The Security Rule requires a covered entity to maintain documentation of each policy and procedure for six years from the date of its creation or the date when it last was in effect, whichever is later. The five-year rule applicable to client records under your state law would not be applicable. The Privacy Rule requires information to be retained for six years as well. You should maintain your client files for at least six years. The documentation of your security policies and procedures must be in written form and may be maintained electronically.

? *Question*

I am a licensed counselor and a solo practitioner. I have a small office and occasionally electronically bill third-party payers for my services. I understand that the Security Rule contains implementation specifications for its many standards. Must I comply with each implementation specification?

! *Answer*

The Security Rule contains two types of implementation specifications: required and addressable. A required implementation specification *must* be implemented whereas an addressable implementation specification is not mandatory but must be implemented unless it is reasonable and appropriate to implement an alternative that addresses the risks. The Security Rule is scalable, however, and the security measures you will be expected to implement will be those appropriate to the size of your practice.

Appendix A

Bylaws for an IPA

MPH BEHAVIORAL HEALTH SERVICES, INC.
(A Texas Corporation)*

BYLAWS
ARTICLE ONE: NAME AND OFFICES

1.01 Name: The name of the Corporation is MPH Behavioral Health Services, Inc., hereinafter referred to as the "Corporation."

1.02 Registered Office and Agent: The Corporation shall establish, designate, and maintain a registered office and agent in the State of Texas. The registered office of the Corporation shall be at 350 Highway 183, Suite 206, Bedford, Texas 76022. The name of the registered agent at such address is Helen S. Shackowsky.

1.03 Change of Registered Office or Agent: The Corporation may change its registered office or change its registered agent, or both, by following the procedure set forth in Article 2.10 of the Texas Business Corporation Act. Any such change shall constitute an amendment to these Bylaws.

1.04 Other Offices: The Corporation may have offices at such places both within and without the State of Texas as the Board of Directors may from time to time determine or the business of the Corporation may require.

ARTICLE TWO: SHAREHOLDERS

2.01 Place of Meetings: All meetings of the Shareholders for the election of Directors and for any other purpose may be held at such time and place, within or without the State of Texas, as stated in the notice of the meeting or in a duly executed waiver of notice thereof.

2.02 Annual Meeting: An annual meeting of the Shareholders for the election of Directors and for the transaction of such other business as may properly come before the meeting shall be held each year on the first Monday in February, beginning in 20__, or such other date as may be selected by the Board of Directors from time to time. At the meeting, the Shareholders shall elect Directors and transact such other business as may properly be brought before the meeting.

2.03 Special Meetings: Special meetings of the Shareholders, for any purpose or purposes, unless otherwise prescribed by statute or by the Articles of Incorporation, or by these Bylaws, may be called by the President, the Secretary, the Board of Directors, or the holders of not less than one-tenth of all the shares

---

* *Authors' Note:* Each state has its own incorporation statute, and the statutes vary slightly. Every lawyer has computer-generated forms available. The only special wrinkle is that certain professional disciplines have some corporate requirements that must be considered, and these requirements vary slightly from state to state.
  Section 8.09 discusses the inclusiveness intended by use of masculine nouns and pronouns.

entitled to vote at the meeting. Business transacted at a special meeting shall be confined to the subjects stated in the notice of the meeting.

2.04   Notice: Written or printed notice stating the place, day, and hour of the meeting and, in case of a special meeting, the purpose or purposes for which the meeting is called, shall be delivered not less than ten nor more than sixty days before the date of the meeting, either personally or by mail, by or at the direction of the person calling the meeting, to each Shareholder of record entitled to vote at the meeting. If mailed, such notice shall be deemed to be delivered when deposited in the United States mail addressed to the Shareholder at his address as it appears on the stock transfer books of the Corporation, with postage thereon prepaid.

2.05   Voting List: At least ten days before each meeting of Shareholders, a complete list of the Shareholders entitled to vote at such meeting, arranged in alphabetical order and setting forth the address of each and the number of voting shares held by each, shall be prepared by the officer or agent having charge of the stock transfer books. Such list, for a period of ten days prior to such meeting, shall be kept on file at the registered office of the Corporation and shall be subject to inspection by any Shareholder at any time during usual business hours. Such list shall also be produced and kept open at the time and place of the meeting during the whole time thereof, and shall be subject to inspection by any Shareholder during the whole time of the meeting.

2.06   Quorum: The holders of a majority of the shares issued and outstanding and entitled to vote thereat, present in person or represented by proxy, shall be requisite and shall constitute a quorum at all meetings of the Shareholders for the transaction of business except as otherwise provided by statute, by the Articles of Incorporation, or by these Bylaws. If a quorum is not present or represented at a meeting of the Shareholders, the Shareholders entitled to vote thereat, present in person or represented by proxy, shall have power to adjourn the meeting from time to time, without notice other than announcement at the meeting, until a quorum is present or represented. At such adjourned meeting at which a quorum is present or represented, any business may be transacted which might have been transacted at the meeting as originally notified.

2.07   Majority Vote; Withdrawal of Quorum: When a quorum is present at any meeting, the vote of the holders of a majority of the shares having voting power, present in person or represented by proxy, shall decide any question brought before such meeting, unless the question is one upon which, by express provision of the statutes or of the Articles of Incorporation or of these Bylaws, a different vote is required, in which case such express provision shall govern and control the decision of such question. The Shareholders present at a duly organized meeting may continue to transact business until adjournment, notwithstanding the withdrawal of enough Shareholders to leave less than a quorum.

2.08   Method of Voting: Each outstanding share, regardless of class, shall be entitled to one vote on each matter subject to a vote at a meeting of Shareholders, except to the extent that the voting rights of the shares of any class or classes are limited or denied by the Articles of Incorporation. The Board of Directors may, in the future, at their discretion, direct that voting be cumulative, according to any plan adopted by the Board. At any meeting of the Shareholders, every Shareholder having the right to vote may vote either in person or by proxy executed in writing by the Shareholder or by his duly authorized attorney-in-fact. No proxy shall be valid after eleven months from the date of its execution, unless otherwise provided in the proxy. Each proxy shall be revocable unless expressly provided therein to be irrevocable or unless otherwise made irrevocable by law. Each proxy shall be filed with the Secretary of the Corporation prior to, or at the time of, the meeting. Voting for Directors shall be in accordance with Section 3.06 of these Bylaws. Any vote may be taken viva voce or by show of hands unless someone entitled to vote objects, in which case written ballots shall be used. Cumulative voting is not prohibited.

2.09   Record Date—Closing Transfer Books: The Board of Directors may fix in advance a record date for the purpose of determining Shareholders entitled to notice of, or to vote at, a meeting of Shareholders, such record date to be not less than ten nor more than sixty days prior to such meeting; or the Board of Directors may close the stock transfer books for such purpose for a period of not less than ten nor more than sixty days prior to such meeting. In the absence of any action by the Board of Directors, the date upon which the notice of the meeting is mailed shall be the record date.

2.10   Action without Meeting: Any action required to be taken at any annual or special meeting of Shareholders, or any action which may be taken at any annual or special meeting of Shareholders, may be taken without a meeting, without prior notice, and without a vote, if a consent or consents in writing, setting forth the action so taken, is signed by the holder or holders of shares having not less than the minimum number of votes that would be necessary to take such action at a meeting at which the holders of all shares entitled to vote on the action were present and voted. Such consent or consents shall have the same force and effect as the requisite vote of the Shareholders at a meeting. The signed consent or consents, or a copy or copies thereof, shall be placed in the minute book of the Corporation. Such consents may be signed in multiple counterparts, each of which shall constitute an original for all purposes, and all of which together shall constitute the requisite written consent or consents of the Shareholders, if applicable. A telegram, telex, cablegram, or similar transaction by a Shareholder, or a photographic, photostatic, facsimile or similar reproduction of a writing signed by a Shareholder, shall be regarded as signed by the Shareholder for purposes of this Section 2.10.

2.11   Order of Business at Meetings: The order of business at annual meetings, and so far as practicable at other meetings of Shareholders, shall be as follows unless changed by the Board of Directors:

    (a) Call to order.

    (b) Proof of due notice of meeting.

    (c) Determination of quorum and examination of proxies.

    (d) Announcement of availability of voting list (see Bylaw 2.05).

    (e) Announcement of distribution of annual reports (see Bylaw 8.03).

    (f) Reading and disposing of minutes of last meeting of shareholders.

    (g) Reports of officers and committees.

    (h) Appointment of voting inspectors.

    (i) Unfinished business.

    (j) New business.

    (k) Nomination of directors.

    (l) Opening of polls for voting.

    (m) Recess.

    (n) Reconvening; closing of polls.

    (o) Report of voting inspectors.

    (p) Other business.

    (q) Adjournment.

2.12 Credentialing Committee: Each and every individual who, from time to time, is a Shareholder in the Corporation, shall automatically be a member of a committee of all of the Shareholders of the Corporation to be called the Credentialing Committee of the Corporation. The Credentialing Committee shall be chaired by the President of the Corporation and shall be governed by the Articles of Incorporation and Bylaws of the Corporation and *Robert's Rules of Order, Newly Revised*. The duty of the Credentialing Committee shall be to meet from time to time, as convened by the President or at the written request of any three or more Shareholders, to determine for the Corporation which service providers the Corporation will contract for the providing of services. It is expressly understood and agreed that participation of the Shareholders on the Credentialing Committee shall not be deemed to be participation by the Shareholders in the operational management of the Corporation.

ARTICLE THREE: DIRECTORS

3.01 Management: The business and affairs of the Corporation shall be managed by the Board of Directors, which may exercise all such powers of the Corporation and do all such lawful acts and things as are not, by statute or by the Articles of Incorporation or by these Bylaws, directed or required to be exercised or done by the Shareholders.

3.02 Number: Qualification; Election—Term: The Board of Directors shall consist of not less than one member nor more than nine members; provided however, the Board of Directors in effect as of the date of effectiveness of these Bylaws consists of seven members. A Director need not be a Shareholder or resident of any particular state or country. The Directors shall be elected at the annual meeting of the Shareholders, except as provided in Bylaws 3.03 and 3.05. Each Director elected shall hold office until his successor is elected and qualified. Each person elected as a Director shall be deemed to have qualified unless he states his refusal to serve shortly after being notified of his election.

3.03 Change in Number: The number of Directors may be increased or decreased from time to time by amendment to these Bylaws, but no decrease shall have the effect of shortening the term of any incumbent Director. Any directorship to be filled by reason of an increase in the number of Directors shall be filled by the Board of Directors for a term of office continuing only until the next election of one or more Directors by the Shareholders; provided that the Board of Directors may not fill more than two such directorships during the period between any two successive annual meetings of Shareholders.

3.04 Removal: Any Director may be removed either for or without cause at any special or annual meeting of Shareholders by the affirmative vote of a majority, in number of shares, of the Shareholders present in person or by proxy at such meeting and entitled to vote for the election of such Director if notice of intention to act upon such matter is given in the notice calling such meeting.

3.05 Vacancies: Any unfilled directorship position, or any vacancy occurring in the Board of Directors (by death, resignation, removal, or otherwise), shall be filled by an affirmative vote of a majority of the remaining Directors though less than a quorum of the Board of Directors. A Director elected to fill a vacancy shall be elected for the unexpired term of his predecessor in office, except that a vacancy occurring due to an increase in the number of Directors shall be filled in accordance with Section 3.03 of these Bylaws.

3.06 Election of Directors: Directors shall be elected by majority vote.

3.07 Place of Meeting: Meetings of the Board of Directors, regular or special, may be held either within or without the State of Texas.

3.08 First Meeting: The first meeting of each newly elected Board of Directors shall be held without further notice immediately following the annual meeting of Shareholders, and at the same place, unless the Directors change such time or place by unanimous vote.

3.09 Regular Meetings: Regular meetings of the Board of Directors may be held without notice at such time and place as determined by the Board of Directors.

3.10 Special Meetings: Special meetings of the Board of Directors may be called by the President or by any Director on three days' notice to each Director, given either personally or by mail or by telegram. Except as otherwise expressly provided by statute, or by the Articles of Incorporation, or by these Bylaws, neither the business to be transacted at, nor the purpose of, any special meeting of the Board of Directors need be specified in a notice or waiver of notice.

3.11 Quorum—Majority Vote: At all meetings of the Board of Directors, a majority of the number of Directors then elected and qualified shall constitute a quorum for the transaction of business. The act of a majority of the Directors present at any meeting at which a quorum is present shall be the act of the Board of Directors, except as otherwise specifically provided by statute or by the Articles of Incorporation or by these Bylaws. If a quorum is not present at a meeting of the Board of Directors, the Directors present thereat may adjourn the meeting from time to time, without notice other than announcement at the meeting, until a quorum is present. Each Director who is present at a meeting will be deemed to have assented to any action taken at such meeting unless his dissent to the action is entered in the minutes of the meeting, or unless he files his written dissent thereto with the Secretary of the meeting or forwards such dissent by registered mail to the secretary of the Corporation immediately after such meeting.

3.12 Compensation: By resolution of the Board of Directors, the Directors may be paid their expenses, if any, of attendance at each meeting of the Board of Directors and may be paid a fixed sum for attendance of each meeting of the Board of Directors, or a stated salary as Director. No such payment shall preclude any Director from serving the Corporation in any other capacity and receiving compensation therefor. Members of any executive, special, or standing committees established by the Board of Directors, may, by resolution of the Board of Directors, be allowed like compensation and expenses for attending committee meetings.

3.13 Procedure: The Board of Directors shall keep regular minutes of its proceedings. The minutes shall be placed in the minute book of the Corporation.

3.14 Interested Directors, Officers, and Shareholders:

(a) If Paragraph (b) is satisfied, no contract or other transaction between the Corporation and any of its Directors, Officers, or Shareholders (or any corporation or firm in which any of them are directly or indirectly interested) shall be invalid solely because of such relationship or because of the presence of such Director, Officer, or Shareholder at the meeting authorizing such contract or transaction, or his participation in such meeting or authorization.

(b) Paragraph (a) shall apply only if:

(1) The material facts of the relationship or interest of each such Director, Officer, or Shareholder are known or disclosed:

(A) To the Board of Directors and it nevertheless authorizes or ratifies the contract or transaction by a majority of the Directors present, each such interested Director to be counted in determining whether a quorum is present but not in calculating the majority necessary to carry the vote; or

(B) To the Shareholders and they nevertheless authorize or ratify the contract or transaction by a majority of the shares present, each such interested person to be counted for a quorum and voting purposes; or

(2) The contract or transaction is fair to the Corporation as of the time it is authorized or ratified by the Board of Directors, a committee of the Board, or the Shareholders.

(c) This provision shall not be construed to invalidate a contract or transaction which would be valid in the absence of this provision.

3.15 Certain Officers: The President shall be elected from among the members of the Board of Directors.

3.16 Action without Meeting: Any action required or permitted to be taken at a meeting of the Board of Directors may be taken without a meeting if a consent in writing, setting forth the action so taken, is signed by all members of the Board of Directors. Such consent shall have the same force and effect as unanimous vote of the Board of Directors at a meeting. The signed consent, or a signed copy thereof, shall be placed in the minute book of the Corporation. Such consents may be signed in multiple counterparts, each of which shall constitute an original for all purposes, and all of which together shall constitute the unanimous written consent of the Directors.

ARTICLE FOUR: EXECUTIVE COMMITTEE

4.01 Designation: The Board of Directors may, by resolution adopted by a majority of the whole Board, designate an Executive Committee from among its members.

4.02 Number—Qualification; Term: The Executive Committee shall consist of one or more Directors. The Executive Committee shall serve at the pleasure of the Board of Directors.

4.03 Authority: The Executive Committee shall have and may exercise the authority of the Board of Directors in the management of the business and affairs of the Corporation except where action of the full Board of Directors is required by statute or by the Articles of Incorporation, and shall have power to authorize the seal of the Corporation to be affixed to all papers which may require it; except that the Executive Committee shall not have authority to: amend the Articles of Incorporation; approve a plan of merger or consolidation; recommend to the Shareholders the sale, lease, or exchange of all or substantially all of the property and assets of the Corporation other than in the usual and regular course of its business; recommend to the Shareholders the voluntary dissolution of the Corporation; amend, alter, or repeal the Bylaws of the Corporation or adopt new Bylaws for the Corporation; fill any vacancy in the Board of Directors or any other corporate committee; fix the compensation of any member of any corporate committee; alter or repeal any resolution of the Board of Directors; declare a dividend; or authorize the issuance of shares of the corporation. Each Director shall be deemed to have assented to any action of the Executive Committee unless, within seven days after receiving actual or constructive notice of such action, he delivers his written dissent thereto to the secretary of the Corporation.

4.04 Change in Number: The number of Executive Committee members may be increased or decreased (but not below one) from time to time by resolution adopted by a majority of the Board of Directors.

4.05 Removal: Any member of the Executive Committee may be removed by the Board of Directors by the affirmative vote of a majority of the Board of Directors whenever in its judgment the best interests of the Corporation will be served thereby.

4.06 Vacancies: A vacancy occurring in the Executive Committee (by death, resignation, removal, or otherwise) shall be filled by the Board of Directors in the manner provided for original designation in Section 4.01.

4.07 Meetings: Time, place, and notice, if any, of Executive Committee meetings shall be as determined by the Executive Committee.

4.08 Quorum; Majority Vote: At meetings of the Executive Committee, a majority of the members shall constitute a quorum for the transaction of business. The act of a majority of the members present at any meeting at which a quorum is present shall be the act of the Executive Committee, except as otherwise specifically provided by statute or by the Articles of Incorporation or by these Bylaws. If a quorum is not present at a meeting of the Executive Committee, the members present thereat may adjourn the meeting from time to time, without notice other than announcement at the meeting, until a quorum is present.

4.09 Compensation: By resolution of the Board of Directors, the members of the Executive Committee may be paid their expenses, if any, of attendance at each meeting of the Executive Committee and may be paid a fixed sum for attendance at each meeting of the Executive Committee or a stated salary as a member thereof. No such payment shall preclude any member from serving the Corporation in any other capacity and receiving compensation therefor.

4.10 Procedure: The Executive Committee shall keep regular minutes of its proceedings and report the same to the Board of Directors when required. The minutes of the proceedings of the Executive Committee shall be placed in the minute book of the Corporation.

4.11 Action without Meeting: Any action required or permitted to be taken at a meeting of the Executive Committee may be taken without a meeting if a consent in writing, setting forth the action so taken, is signed by all the members of the Executive Committee. Such consent shall have the same force and effect as a unanimous vote at a meeting. The signed consent, or a signed copy thereof, shall be placed in the minute book. Such consents may be signed in multiple counterparts, each of which shall constitute an original for all purposes, and all of which together shall constitute the unanimous written consent of the Directors.

4.12 Responsibility: The designation of an Executive Committee and the delegation of authority to it shall not operate to relieve the Board of Directors, or any member thereof, of any responsibility imposed by law.

ARTICLE FIVE: NOTICE

5.01 Method: Whenever by statute or the Articles of Incorporation or these Bylaws notice is required to be given to any Director or Shareholder and no provision is made as to how such notice shall be given, it shall not be construed to mean personal notice, but any such notice may be given:

(a) In writing, by mail, postage prepaid, addressed to such Director or Shareholder at such address as appears on the books of the Corporation; or

(b) By any other method permitted by law.

Any notice required or permitted to be given by mail shall be deemed to be given at the time it is deposited, postage prepaid, in the United States mail.

5.02 Waiver: Whenever, by statute or the Articles of Incorporation or these Bylaws, notice is required to be given to a Shareholder or Director, a waiver thereof in writing signed by the person or persons entitled to such notice, whether before or after the time stated in such notice, shall be equivalent to the giving of such notice. Attendance of a Director at a meeting shall constitute a waiver of notice of such meeting except where a Director attends for the express purpose of objecting to the transaction of any business on the grounds that the meeting is not lawfully called or convened.

5.03 Telephone Meetings: Shareholders, Directors, or members of any committee may hold any meeting of such Shareholders, Directors, or committee by means of conference telephone or similar communications equipment which permits all persons participating in the meeting to hear each other. Actions taken at such meeting shall have the same force and effect as a vote at a meeting in person. The secretary shall prepare a memorandum of the actions taken at conference telephone meetings.

ARTICLE SIX: OFFICERS AND AGENTS

6.01 Number—Qualification; Election: Term:

(a) The Corporation shall have:

(1) A Chairman of the Board (should the Board of Directors so choose to select), a President, a Vice President, a Secretary, and a Treasurer, and

(2) Such other Officers (including one or more Vice Presidents, and assistant Officers and agents) as the Board of Directors authorizes from time to time.

(b) No Officer or agent need be a Shareholder, a Director, or a resident of Texas, except as provided in Sections 3.15 and 4.02 of these Bylaws.

(c) Officers named in Section 6.01(a) (I) above shall be elected by the Board of Directors on the expiration of an Officer's term or whenever a vacancy exists. Officers and agents named in Section 6.01 (a) (2) may be elected by the Board of Directors at any meeting.

(d) Unless otherwise specified by the Board at the time of election or appointment, or in an employment contract approved by the Board, each Officer's and agent's term shall end at the first meeting of Directors after the next annual meeting of Shareholders. He shall serve until the end of his term or, if earlier, his death, resignation, or removal.

(e) Any two or more offices may be held by the same person.

6.02 Removal and Resignation: Any Officer or agent elected or appointed by the Board of Directors may be removed with or without cause by a majority of the Directors at any regular or special meeting of the Board of Directors. Any Officer may resign at any time by giving written notice to the Board of Directors or to the President or Secretary. Any such resignation shall take effect upon receipt of such notice if no date is specified in the notice, or, if a later date is specified in the notice, upon such later date; and unless otherwise specified in the notice, the acceptance of such resignation shall not be necessary to make it effective. The removal of any Officer or agent shall be without prejudice to the contract rights, if any, of the person so removed. Election or appointment of an Officer or agent shall not of itself create contract rights.

6.03 Vacancies: Any vacancy occurring in any office of the Corporation (by death, resignation, removal, or otherwise) may be filled by the Board of Directors.

6.04 Authority: Officers shall have full authority to perform all duties in the management of the Corporation as are provided in these Bylaws or as may be determined by resolution of the Board of Directors from time to time not inconsistent with these Bylaws.

6.05 Compensation: The compensation of Officers and agents shall be fixed from time to time by the Board of Directors.

6.06 Chairman of the Board: The Chairman of the Board, if any, shall preside at all meetings of the Board of Directors and shall exercise and perform such other powers and duties as may be assigned to him by the Board of Directors or prescribed by these Bylaws.

6.07 Executive Powers: The Chairman of the Board, if any, and the President of the Corporation respectively, shall, in the order of their seniority, unless otherwise determined by the Board of Directors or otherwise are positions held by the same person, have general and active management of the business and affairs of the Corporation and shall see that all orders and resolutions of the Board are carried into effect. They shall perform such other duties and have such other authority and powers as the Board of Directors may from time to time prescribe. Within this authority and in the course of their respective duties, the Chairman of the Board, if any, and the President of the Corporation, respectively, shall have the general authority to:

(a) *Conduct Meetings.* Preside at all meetings of the Shareholders and at all meetings of the Board of Directors, and shall be ex officio members of all the standing committees, including the Executive Committee, if any.

(b) *Sign Share Certificates.* Sign all certificates of stock of the corporation, in conjunction with the Secretary or Assistant Secretary, unless otherwise ordered by the Board of Directors.

(c) *Execute Instruments.* When authorized by the Board of Directors or if required by law, execute, in the name of the Corporation, deeds, conveyances, notices, leases, checks, drafts, bills of exchange, warrants, promissory notes, bonds, debentures, contracts, and other papers and instruments in writing, and unless the Board of Directors orders otherwise by resolution, make such contracts as the ordinary conduct of the Corporation's business requires.

(d) *Hire and Discharge Employees.* Subject to the approval of the Board of Directors, appoint and remove, employ and discharge, and prescribe the duties and fix the compensation of all agents, employees, and clerks of the Corporation other than the duly appointed Officers, and, subject to the direction of the Board of Directors, control all of the Officers, agents, and employees of the Corporation.

6.08 Vice Presidents: The Vice Presidents, if any, in the order of their seniority, unless otherwise determined by the Board of Directors, shall, in the absence or disability of the President, perform the duties and have the authority and exercise the powers of the President. They shall perform such other duties and have such other authority and powers as the Board of Directors may from time to time prescribe or as the senior Officers of the Corporation may from time to time delegate.

6.09 Secretary: The Secretary shall attend all meetings of the Board of Directors and all meetings of the Shareholders and record all votes and minutes of all proceedings in a book to be kept for that purpose, and shall perform like duties for the Executive Committee when required. He shall give, or cause to be given, notice of all meetings of the Shareholders and special meetings of the Board of Directors. He shall keep in safe custody the seal of the Corporation and, when authorized by the Board of Directors or the Executive Committee, affix the same to any instrument requiring it, and when so affixed, it shall be attested by his signature or by the signature of the Treasurer or an Assistant Secretary. He shall be under the supervision of the senior Officers of the Corporation. He shall perform such other duties and have such other authority and powers as the Board of Directors may from time to time prescribe or as the senior Officers of the Corporation may from time to time delegate.

6.10 Assistant Secretaries: The Assistant Secretaries, if any, in the order of their seniority, unless otherwise determined by the Board of Directors, shall, in the absence or disability of the Secretary, perform the duties and have the authority and exercise the powers of the Secretary. They shall perform such other duties and have such other powers as the Board of Directors may from time to time prescribe or as the senior Officers of the Corporation may from time to time delegate.

6.11 Treasurer: The Treasurer shall have the custody of the corporate funds and securities and shall keep full and accurate accounts of all income, expenses, receipts, and disbursements of the Corporation and shall deposit all moneys and other valuable effects in the name and to the credit of the Corporation in such depositories as may be designated by the Board of Directors. He shall disburse the funds of the Corporation as may be ordered by the Board of Directors, taking proper vouchers for such disbursements, and shall render to the senior Officers of the Corporation and Directors, at the regular meeting of the Board, or whenever they may request it, accounts of all his transactions as Treasurer and of the financial condition of the Corporation. If required by the Board of Directors, he shall give the Corporation a bond in such form, in such sum, and with such surety or sureties as satisfactory to the Board, for the faithful performance of the duties of his office and for the restoration to the Corporation, in case of his death, resignation, retirement or removal from office, of all books, paper, vouchers, money, and other property of whatever kind in his possession or under his control belonging to the Corporation. He shall perform such other duties and have such other authority and powers as the Board of Directors may from time to time prescribe or as the senior Officers of the Corporation may from time to time delegate.

6.12 Assistant Treasurers: The Assistant Treasurers, if any, in the order of their seniority, unless otherwise determined by the Board of Directors, shall, in the absence or disability of the Treasurer, perform the duties and exercise the powers of the Treasurer. They shall perform such other duties and have such other powers as the Board of Directors may from time to time prescribe or as the senior Officers of the Corporation may from time to time delegate.

ARTICLE SEVEN: CERTIFICATE AND TRANSFER REGULATIONS

7.01 Certificates: Certificates in such form as may be determined by the Board of Directors shall be delivered, representing all shares to which Shareholders are entitled. Certificates shall be consecutively numbered and shall be entered in the books of the Corporation as they are issued. Each certificate shall state on the face thereof that the Corporation is organized under the laws of the State of Texas, the holder's name, the number and class of shares, the par value of such shares or a statement that such shares are without par value, and such other matters as may be required by law. They shall be signed by the President or a Vice President and either the Secretary or Assistant Secretary or such other Officer or Officers as the Board of Directors designates, and may be sealed with the seal of the Corporation or a facsimile thereof. If any certificate is countersigned by a transfer agent, or an assistant transfer agent, or registered by a registrar (either of which is other than the Corporation or an employee of the Corporation), the signature of any such Officer may be a facsimile thereof.

7.02 Issuance of Certificates: Shares (both treasury and authorized but unissued) may be issued for such consideration (not less than par value) and to such persons as the Board of Directors determines from time to time. Shares may not be issued until the full amount of the consideration, fixed as provided by law, has been paid. In addition, Shares shall not be issued or transferred until such additional conditions and documentation as the Corporation (or its transfer agent, as the case may be) shall reasonably require, including without limitation, the delivery with the surrender of such stock certificate or certificates of proper evidence of succession, assignment, or other authority to obtain transfer thereof, as the circumstances may require, and such legal opinions with reference to the requested transfer as shall be required by the Corporation (or its transfer agent) pursuant to the provisions of these Bylaws and applicable law, shall have been satisfied.

7.03 Legends on Certificates:

(a) *Shares in Classes or Series.* If the Corporation is authorized to issue shares of more than one class, the certificates shall set forth, either on the face or back of the certificate, a full or summary statement of all of the designations, preferences, limitations, and relative rights of the shares of such class and, if the Corporation is authorized to issue any preferred or special class in series, the variations in the relative rights and preferences of the shares of each such series so far as the same have been fixed and determined, and the authority of the Board of Directors to fix and determine the relative rights and preferences of subsequent series. In lieu of providing such a statement in full on the certificate, a statement on the face or back of the certificate may provide that the Corporation will furnish such information to any Shareholder without charge upon written request to the Corporation at its principal place of business or registered office and that copies of the information are on file in the office of the Secretary of State.

(b) *Restriction on Transfer.* Any restrictions imposed by the Corporation on the sale or other disposition of its shares and on the transfer thereof may be copied at length or in summary form on the face, or so copied on the back and referred to on the face, of each certificate representing shares to which the restriction applies. The certificate may, however, state on the face or back that such a restriction exists pursuant to a specified document and that the Corporation will furnish a copy of the document to the holder of the certificate without charge upon written request to the Corporation at its principal place of business, or refer to such restriction in any other manner permitted by law.

(c) *Preemptive Rights.* Any preemptive rights of a Shareholder to acquire unissued or treasury shares of the Corporation which are or may at any time be limited or denied by the Articles of Incorporation may be set forth at length on the face or back of the certificate representing shares subject thereto. In lieu of providing such a statement in full on the certificate, a statement on the face or back of the certificate may provide that the Corporation will furnish such information to any Shareholder without charge upon written request to the Corporation at its principal place of business, and that a copy of such information is on file in the office of the Secretary of State, or refer to such denial of preemptive rights in any other manner permitted by law.

(d) *Unregistered Securities.* Any security of the Corporation, including, among others, any certificate evidencing shares of the Common Stock or warrants to purchase Common Stock of the Corporation, which is issued to any person without registration under the Securities Act of 1933, as amended, or the securities laws of any state, shall not be transferrable until the Corporation has been furnished with a legal opinion of counsel with reference thereto, satisfactory in form and content to the Corporation and its counsel, if required by the Corporation, to the effect that such sale, transfer, or pledge does not involve a violation of the Securities Act of 1933, as amended, or the securities laws of any state having jurisdiction. The certificate representing the security shall bear substantially the following legend:

"THE SECURITIES REPRESENTED BY THIS CERTIFICATE HAVE NOT BEEN REGISTERED UNDER THE SECURITIES ACT OF 1933, AS AMENDED, OR UNDER THE SECURITIES LAWS OF ANY STATE AND MAY NOT BE OFFERED, SOLD, OR TRANSFERRED UNLESS SUCH OFFER, SALE, OR TRANSFER WILL NOT BE IN VIOLATION OF THE SECURITIES ACT OF 1933, AS AMENDED, OR ANY APPLICABLE

BLUE SKY LAWS. ANY OFFER, SALE, OR TRANSFER OF THESE SECURITIES MAY NOT BE MADE WITHOUT THE PRIOR WRITTEN APPROVAL OF THE CORPORATION."

7.04   Payment of Shares:

(a)   *Kind.* The consideration for the issuance of shares shall consist of money paid, labor done (including services actually performed for the Corporation), or property (tangible or intangible) actually received. Neither promissory notes nor the promise of future services shall constitute payment for shares.

(b)   *Valuation.* In the absence of fraud in the transaction, the judgment of the Board of Directors as to the value of consideration received shall be conclusive.

(c)   *Effect.* When consideration, fixed as provided by law, has been paid, the shares shall be deemed to have been issued and shall be considered fully paid and nonassessable.

(d)   *Allocation of Consideration.* The consideration received for shares shall be allocated by the Board of Directors, in accordance with law, between Stated Capital and Capital Surplus accounts.

7.05   Subscriptions: Unless otherwise provided in the subscription agreement, subscriptions for shares shall be paid in full at such time or in such installments and at such times as determined by the Board of Directors. Any call made by the Board of Directors for payment on subscriptions shall be uniform as to all shares of the same series. In case of default in the payment on any installment or call when payment is due, the Corporation may proceed to collect the amount due in the same manner as any debt due to the Corporation.

7.06   Lien: For any indebtedness of a Shareholder to the Corporation, the Corporation shall have a first and prior lien on all shares of its stock owned by him and on all dividends or other distributions declared thereon.

7.07   Lost, Stolen, or Destroyed Certificates: The Corporation shall issue a new certificate in place of any certificate for shares previously issued if the registered owner of the certificate:

(a)   *Claim.* Submits proof in affidavit form that it has been lost, destroyed, or wrongfully taken; and

(b)   *Timely Request.* Requests the issuance of a new certificate before the Corporation has notice that the certificate has been acquired by a purchaser for value in good faith and without notice of an adverse claim; and

(c)   *Bond.* Gives a bond in such form, and with such surety or sureties, with fixed or open penalty, if the Corporation so requires, to indemnify the Corporation (and its transfer agent and registrar, if any) against any claim that may be made on account of the alleged loss, destruction, or theft of the certificate; and

(d)   *Other Requirements.* Satisfies any other reasonable requirements imposed by the Corporation.

When a certificate has been lost, apparently destroyed, or wrongfully taken, and the holder of record fails to notify the Corporation within a reasonable time after he has notice of it, and the Corporation registers a transfer of the shares represented by the certificate before receiving such notification, the holder of record shall be precluded from making any claim against the Corporation for the transfer or for a new certificate.

7.08   Registration of Transfer: The Corporation shall register the transfer of a certificate for shares presented to it for transfer if:

(a) *Endorsement.* The certificate is properly endorsed by the registered owner or by his duly authorized attorney; and

(b) *Guaranty and Effectiveness of Signature.* If required by the Corporation, the signature of such person has been guaranteed by a national banking association or member of the New York Stock Exchange, and reasonable assurance is given that such endorsements are effective; and

(c) *Adverse Claims.* The Corporation has no notice of an adverse claim or has discharged any duty to inquire into such a claim; and

(d) *Collection of Taxes.* Any applicable law relating to the collection of taxes has been complied with.

7.09 Registered Owner: Prior to due presentment for registration of transfer of a certificate for shares, the Corporation may treat the registered owner or holder of a written proxy from such registered owner as the person exclusively entitled to vote, to receive notices, and otherwise exercise all the rights and powers of a Shareholder.

7.10 Preemptive Rights: No Shareholder or other person shall have any preemptive rights of any kind to acquire additional, unissued, or treasury shares of the Corporation, or securities of the Corporation convertible into, or carrying rights to subscribe to or acquire, shares of any class or series of the Corporation's capital stock, unless, and to the extent that, such rights may be expressly granted by appropriate action.

ARTICLE EIGHT: GENERAL PROVISIONS

8.01 Dividends and Reserves:

(a) *Declaration and Payment.* Subject to statute and the Articles of Incorporation, dividends may be declared by the Board of Directors at any regular or special meeting and may be paid in cash, in property, or in shares of the Corporation. The declaration and payment shall be at the discretion of the Board of Directors.

(b) *Record Date.* The Board of Directors may fix in advance a record date for the purpose of determining Shareholders entitled to receive payment of any dividend, such record date to be not more than sixty days prior to the payment date of such dividend, or the Board of Directors may close the stock transfer books for such purpose for a period of not more than sixty days prior to the payment date of such dividend. In the absence of any action by the Board of Directors, the date upon which the Board of Directors adopts the resolution declaring such dividend shall be the record date.

(c) *Reserves.* By resolution, the Board of Directors may create such reserve or reserves out of the Earned surplus of the Corporation as the Directors from time to time, in their discretion, think proper to provide for contingencies, or to equalize dividends, or to repair or maintain any property of the Corporation, or for any other purpose they think beneficial to the Corporation. The Directors may modify or abolish any such reserve in the manner in which it was created.

8.02 Books and Records: The Corporation shall keep correct and complete books and records of account and shall keep minutes of the proceedings of its Shareholders and Board of Directors, and shall keep at its registered office or principal place of business, or at the office of its transfer agent or registrar, a record of its Shareholders, giving the names and addresses of all Shareholders and the number and class of the shares held by each.

8.03   Annual Reports: The Board of Directors shall cause such reports to be mailed to Shareholders as the Board of Directors deems to be necessary or desirable from time to time.

8.04   Checks and Notes: All checks or demands for money and notes of the Corporation shall be signed by such Officer or Officers or such other person or persons as the Board of Directors designates from time to time.

8.05   Fiscal Year: The fiscal year of the Corporation shall be the calendar year.

8.06   Seal: The Corporation Seal (of which there may be one or more examples) may contain the name of the Corporation and the name of the state of incorporation. The Seal may be used by impressing it or reproducing a facsimile of it, or otherwise. Absence of the Corporation Seal shall not affect the validity or enforceability or any document or instrument.

8.07   Indemnification:

(a)   The Corporation shall have the right to indemnify, to purchase indemnity insurance for, and to pay and advance expenses to, Directors, Officers and other persons who are eligible for, or entitled to, such indemnification, payments, or advances, in accordance with and subject to the provisions of Article 2.02–1 of the Texas Business Corporation Act and any amendments thereto, to the extent such indemnification, payments, or advances are either expressly required by such provisions or are expressly authorized by the Board of Directors within the scope of such provisions. The right of the Corporation to indemnify such persons shall include, but not be limited to, the authority of the Corporation to enter into written agreements for indemnification with such persons.

(b)   Subject to the provisions of Article 2.02–1 of the Texas Business Corporation Act and any amendments thereto, a Director of the Corporation shall not be liable to the Corporation or its shareholders for monetary damages for an act or omission in the Director's capacity as a Director, except that this provision does not eliminate or limit the liability of a Director to the extent the Director is found liable for:

(1)   A breach of the Director's duty of loyalty to the Corporation or its shareholders;

(2)   An act or omission not in good faith that constitutes a breach of duty of the Director to the Corporation or an act or omission that involves intentional misconduct or a knowing violation of the law;

(3)   A transaction from which the Director received an improper benefit, whether or not the benefit resulted from an action taken within the scope of the Director's office; or

(4)   An act or omission for which the liability of a Director is expressly provided by an applicable statute.

8.08   Amendment of Bylaws: These Bylaws may be altered, amended, or repealed at any meeting of the Board of Directors at which a quorum is present, by the affirmative vote of a majority of the Directors present thereat, provided notice of the proposed alteration, amendment, or repeal is contained in the notice of such meeting.

8.09   Construction: Whenever the context so requires, the masculine shall include the feminine and neuter, and the singular shall include the plural, and conversely. If any portion of these Bylaws is ever finally determined to be invalid or inoperative, then, so far as is reasonable and possible:

(a)   The remainder of these Bylaws shall be valid and operative; and

(b)   Effect shall be given to the intent manifested by the portion held invalid or inoperative.

8.10 Table of Contents; Headings: The table of contents and headings are for organization, convenience, and clarity. In interpreting these Bylaws, they shall be subordinated in importance to the other written material.

MPH Behavioral
Health Services, Inc.,
A Texas Corporation

By: _____
Helen S. Shackowsky, President

Appendix B

Partnership Agreement

This agreement is made on February 1, 20__ between James Hathaway of 3638 Ridgecove, Rockwall, Rockwall County, Texas 75032, Sylvia Wainright of 1467 Royal Lane, Apt. 645, Dallas, Dallas County, Texas 75210, and Benjamin Stickle of 14679 Allenway, Plano, Collin County, Texas 75462, who are referred to in this agreement as "partners."

The partners form a partnership under the Texas Revised Partnership Act as a registered limited liability partnership per § 3.08 of the Texas Revised Partnership Act pursuant to the following terms and conditions which are stated in this partnership agreement.

RECITALS

1. The partners are mental health professionals licensed to practice as professional counselors in Texas.

2. The partners have each been sole practitioners in their respective mental health specialties.

3. The partners desire to enter into a partnership for the practice of counseling. (Practice of: Psychology, Social Work, Marriage and Family Therapy, Addictions Therapy, Play Therapy, etc.)

In consideration of the mutual covenants contained in this agreement, the parties agree as follows:

I. PURPOSE AND NAME

A partnership is created and shall be known as 3P Wellness Center, LLP, and shall be for the practice of counseling as regulated by the laws of the State of Texas, and the Code of Ethics of the American and Texas Counseling Associations.

II. DURATION

The partnership commences on February 1, 20 __ and continues in effect until terminated by operation of law or by the agreement of the partners as provided in Article XX.

III. CONTRIBUTIONS

The partnership shall be capitalized at $45,000.00, consisting of the contribution of their existing three counseling practices, with values stipulated at $10,000.00 each and a cash contribution of $5,000.00 each, receipt of which is hereby acknowledged.

IV. OFFICE EQUIPMENT

All office equipment that presently is on the premises to be occupied by the partnership belongs to Benjamin Stickle but shall remain on the premises for use by the partnership.

The equipment shall remain the personal property of Benjamin Stickle and the partnership shall pay him $250.00 per month rental for the use of the equipment.

V. SHARES IN PARTNERSHIP

The partners are entitled to share in the partnership profits and losses, as follows:

James Hathaway   33 ⅓ percent

Sylvia Wainright   33 ⅓ percent

Benjamin Stickle   33 ⅓ percent

VI. FEES

All fees received by any partner, whether for counseling services rendered, grants, consultation fees, or any other service, shall be the property of the partnership and shall be treated as ordinary partnership income. Personal property received as a gift by a partner may be retained by that partner as his or her separate property.

VII. DUTIES OF PARTNERS

Each partner shall contribute his or her full time and all of his or her skills to the partnership business. Each partner is responsible for the consultation, evaluation, and treatment of those clients desiring care in that partner's mental health specialty area as follows:

James Hathaway specializing in addiction/chemical dependency therapy

Sylvia Wainright specializing in children/play therapy

Benjamin Stickle specializing in adolescents/family therapy

Each partner may be called on to consult with any other partner regarding the consultation, evaluation, and treatment for any client of the other partner, for any purpose whatever.

VIII. LIMITATIONS ON DUTIES

The partners shall not engage in the practice of counseling in any manner or form except for the benefit of the partnership unless the prior written consent of the remaining partners is obtained. This prohibition shall apply equally to services performed without a fee.

A partner shall not obligate the partnership by acting as guarantor or surety on a note, discharging any debts owed to the partnership for less than full consideration, loaning partnership money to third parties, or contracting any indebtedness for the partnership in excess of $150.00 ($ _____._____) without the prior written approval of the remaining partners.

IX. PRIVATE DEBTS

Each partner shall hold the partnership harmless on any private debt that he or she has incurred, and should the partnership be held liable for any personal indebtedness of a partner, that partner's share of the annual profits shall be debited a corresponding amount.

X. EXPENSES

The partnership shall pay all expenses incurred by the partnership and those of each partner incurred in the course of partnership business, except as follows:

Each partner shall obtain, maintain, and use an automobile of his or her personal selection for performing the duties required in the partnership business. The costs and expenses for obtaining, operating, and maintaining the automobiles shall be the personal obligations of each partner, and the partner shall hold the partnership harmless for such expenses.

XI. PROFITS AND LOSSES

A monthly profit and loss statement shall be prepared for the partnership by a certified public accountant selected by the partners, reporting the monthly partnership net profits or losses for distribution. These figures shall be controlling on all parties, and the reported net profit or loss shall be distributed proportionately to partners based on their percentage interest in the partnership on the 30th day of each month. All errors in the statements must be noted and corrected within 2 months after release of the statement figures, or they shall be binding.

XII. DRAWS

The partners are entitled to obtain advance disbursements of money from the partnership to meet anticipated business expenses. A draw shall be made on the basis of a voucher submitted by the partner, and each partner shall file a monthly expense account statement, reconciling all expenses with draws he or she has obtained during the reporting period. (Alternatively, periodic draws can be agreed on in advance in a specific sum.)

XIII. GOOD FAITH

The duties of each partner are of a fiduciary nature relating to the remaining partners in the partnership, and each partner owes a duty of complete disclosure of all business transactions and good faith in his or her dealings on behalf of and with the partnership and the remaining partners.

XIV. BANKING

The partnership shall maintain a business banking account at Bank One located at 4625 Main Street, Richardson, Texas. All the receipts of the partnership shall be deposited in this account, and all partnership and partners' authorized business expenses shall be disbursed from this account.

XV. BOOKS OF ACCOUNTS

A complete set of books of accounts, organized and maintained using approved accounting practices, shall be established by the partnership's accounting firm. The books shall be retained at the principal place of the partners' business and shall be open for inspection by any partner at all reasonable hours.

XVI. ACCOUNTING

The fiscal year of the partnership is from January 1 to December 31, each year, a date corresponding to the fiscal year used by the partners in their former individual practices. The accounting basis used shall be cash. The accounting firm shall prepare, in addition to the monthly profit and loss statements, the annual profit and loss statements, financial statements, annual audits, and valuations of partners' interests.

XVII. INSURANCE

The partnership shall procure and maintain a policy of liability insurance providing malpractice insurance for each of the partners for $2,000,000.00 for each occurrence and $5,000.000.00 total coverage per partner.

XVIII. NEGLIGENCE

Each partner is personally and individually liable for repayment to the partnership of any sum paid out by the partnership in excess of insurance coverage provided in Article XVII where the negligence or misconduct of the partner has been determined to be the cause of the insurance settlement or suit.

XIX. TERMINATION

The partnership is terminated either by operation of law or on written notice from any partner desiring to terminate the partnership to the remaining partners. A notice of termination must be given at least six months prior to the intended date of termination.

XX. LIQUIDATION

On the termination of the partnership, either by operation of law or election of a partner, the existing business of the partnership shall be completed with special consideration being given to appropriate referral and termination of all existing clients of the partnership. Client files shall be maintained by the partner providing services to a client. The office equipment shall be returned to Benjamin Stickle and all assets of the partnership shall be liquidated. After discharging all obligations of the partnership, all remaining proceeds shall be distributed to the partners on a basis proportionate to their interest in the partnership. In the event there are insufficient assets to discharge all obligations of the partnership, the partners shall be liable for the remaining obligations on a basis proportionate to their interest in the partnership.

Dated February 1, 20__

_____

James Hathaway

_____

Sylvia Wainright

_____

Benjamin Stickle

Appendix C

ARTICLES OF INCORPORATION: PROFESSIONAL CORPORATION

ARTICLES OF INCORPORATION OF CARL DAVIDSON, JR., PHD, PC

The undersigned, acting as incorporator of a professional corporation under the Texas Professional Corporation Act, adopts the following articles of incorporation:

ARTICE 1. NAME AND TYPE OF CORPORATION

The corporation's name is Carl Davidson, Jr., PhD, PC. The corporation is a professional corporation, as that term is defined in law.

ARTICLE 2. DURATION

The duration of the corporation's existence is perpetual or until dissolved on a vote of the shareholders as later provided for in these articles.

ARTICLE 3. PURPOSE

The purposes for which this corporation is formed are:

1. To engage in the practice of psychology; to counsel with individuals, families, and groups; to do psychological testing; to employ knowledge of psychological techniques, human capabilities, and conscious and unconscious motivation to assist people to achieve more adequate, satisfying, and productive emotional adjustments and improved emotional and mental health; and to do research related to these endeavors.

2. To own property, enter into contracts, and carry on the business that is necessary or incidental to the accomplishment or furtherance of the professional service to be rendered by the corporation.

3. The professional services of the corporation shall be carried on only through officers, employees, and agents who are licensed in the State of Texas to render professional psychological services.

ARTICLE 4. PRINCIPAL OFFICE

The address of the corporation's current principal office is 600 Meadow Rd., Suite 104, Dallas, TX 75231.

ARTICLE 5. CORPORATE POWERS

The corporation has all of the rights and powers now or hereafter conferred on professional corporations by the laws of the State of Texas, including: to own property, enter into contracts and carry on the business that is necessary or incidental to the accomplishment or furtherance of the professional service to be rendered by the corporation.

ARTICLE 6. INCORPORATOR

The name and address of the incorporator is:

Name   Address
Carl Davidson, Jr., PhD   5826 Dondo Drive
                              Dallas, TX 75218

ARTICLE 7. DIRECTORS

The number of directors constituting the initial board of directors is one, and the name and address of the initial director is:

Name   Address
Carl Davidson, Jr., PhD   5826 Dondo Drive
                              Dallas, TX 75218

The initial director shall hold office until his successor(s) are elected and qualify as provided in the bylaws. Thereafter, the term of office of each director is one year, and each director shall remain in office until the election and qualification of a successor.

The number of directors set forth in these articles and constituting the initial board of directors is the authorized number of directors until that number is changed by a bylaw duly adopted by the shareholders.

The initial director and each subsequent director of the corporation are licensed or otherwise duly authorized to perform the professional service that the corporation may render.

ARTICLE 8. BYLAWS

The initial director shall submit the proposed bylaws to the shareholders at a meeting to be held for that purpose not more than thirty (30) days following the issuance of the Certificate of Incorporation. Following the adoption of bylaws by the affirmative vote of three-fourths of the shareholders, the internal affairs of the corporation are to be regulated and managed in accordance with such bylaws.

ARTICLE 9. SHAREHOLDERS

The name and address of the individual who is to be the shareholder of the corporation is:

Name   Address
Carl Davidson, Jr., PhD   5826 Dondo Drive
                              Dallas, TX 75218

The initial shareholder and each subsequent shareholder of the corporation are licensed or otherwise duly authorized to perform the professional service that the corporation shall render.

ARTICLE 10. SHARES AND REQUIRED CAPITAL

The total number of shares and the par value, if any, of each class of stock that the corporation is authorized to issue are as follows: 10,000 shares of $00.01 par value.

The amount of the stated capital with which the corporation shall begin business is $1,000.00

No shares may be sold, transferred, or owned by any person who is not licensed or otherwise duly authorized to perform the professional service that the corporation renders.

Each outstanding share of ownership in the corporation shall be entitled to one vote. Cumulative voting is not allowed. All questions shall be determined by a majority vote of shares present in person or by proxy, unless otherwise provided in these Articles or in the bylaws of the corporation. All voting matters shall be governed by the bylaws of the corporation.

The shareholders of this corporation shall have the preemptive right to subscribe to any issue of shares or securities of the corporation.

Any shareholder who becomes disqualified to perform the services to be rendered by the corporation or if a person succeeds to shares of the corporation and that person is not licensed or otherwise duly authorized to perform the professional service that the corporation shall render, he or she shall immediately transfer the shares to the corporation or other shareholders for the consideration stated in the shareholder's stock purchase agreement or in any other manner allowed by law if the shares cannot be transferred by the shareholder agreement.

ARTICLE 11. DISSOLUTION

The corporation may be dissolved at any time by the affirmative vote of the holders of three-fourths of the outstanding shares of the corporation at a meeting called for that purpose or by unanimous written consent of all the shareholders without a meeting.

In the event of such dissolution, the corporate property and assets shall, after payment of all debts of the corporation, be distributed to the shareholders, each shareholder to participate in such distribution in direct proportion to the number of shares held by such shareholder.

If there are two or more shareholders of record, then no one shareholder may cause the dissolution of the corporation by his or her own independent action.

ARTICLE 12. REGISTERED OFFICE AND REGISTERED AGENT

The name and address of the initial registered agent is:

Name   Address
Carl Davidson, Jr., PhD   5826 Dondo Drive
                                  Dallas, TX 75218

ARTICLE 13. LICENSED PROFESSIONALS

The director and shareholder is duly licensed or otherwise legally authorized to render in Texas the specific kind of professional service to be rendered by the corporation.

ARTICLE 14. INDEMNIFICATION

The corporation shall indemnify any director or officer, former director or officer of the corporation, or any person who may have served in the capacity of director or officer of another corporation in which it owns shares of stock or of which it is a creditor, against expenses actually and necessarily incurred by that person in connection with the defense of any action, suit, or proceeding in which he or she is made a party by reason of being or having been such director or officer. The corporation may purchase and maintain liability insurance for such persons. The corporation will not indemnify any such director or officer in relation to matters as to which he or she shall be adjudged liable for negligence or misconduct in the performance of his or her duty. Indemnification will not be deemed exclusive of any other rights to which such director or officer may be entitled under any bylaw, agreement, vote of shareholders, or otherwise.

In witness whereof, I, the undersigned incorporator of this corporation, have executed these articles of incorporation on March _____, 20__.

_____
Carl Davidson, Jr., PhD

The State of Texas
County of Dallas

I, the undersigned Notary Public, do hereby certify that on the _____ day of March, 20__, personally appeared before me Carl Davidson, Jr., PhD, who being by me first duly sworn, declared that he is the person who signed the foregoing document, and that the statements therein contained are true and correct.

_____
Notary Public, State of Texas
My commission expires:_____

Appendix D

ARTICLES OF INCORPORATION: GENERAL CORPORATION

ARTICLES OF INCORPORATION OF MPH BEHAVIORAL HEALTH SERVICES, INC.

We, the undersigned natural persons of the age of 18 years or more, acting as incorporators of a corporation under the Texas Business Corporation Act, adopt the following Articles of Incorporation for the corporation:

ARTICLE I. NAME

The name of this corporation is MPH Behavioral Health Services, Inc.

ARTICLE II. DURATION

The period of its duration is perpetual.

ARTICLE III. PURPOSE OR PURPOSES

The purposes for which the corporation is organized are as follows:

(a) The transaction of any or all lawful business for which corporations may be incorporated under the Texas Business Corporation Act and which is authorized or approved by the board of directors of this corporation;

(b) To carry on any other trade or business which can, in the opinion of the board of directors of the company, be advantageously carried on in connection with or auxiliary to those described in clause (a) of this Article III, and to do all such things as are incidental or conducive to the attainment of these objects or any of them;

(c) To enter into any lawful arrangements for sharing profits and/or losses in any transaction or transactions, and to promote and organize other corporations;

(d) To have and to exercise all rights and powers that are now or may subsequently be granted to a corporation by law.

The above shall be construed as objects, purposes, and powers and their enumeration shall not limit or restrict in any manner the powers now or subsequently conferred on this corporation by the laws of Texas.

The objects, purposes, and powers specified in these articles of incorporation shall, except as otherwise expressed, be in no way limited or restricted by reference to or inference from the terms of any other clause or paragraph of these articles.

The objects, purposes, and powers specified in each of the clauses or paragraphs of these articles of incorporation shall be regarded as independent objects, purposes, or powers.

The corporation may in its bylaws confer powers, not in conflict with law, upon its directors in addition to the foregoing and in addition to the powers and authorities expressly conferred upon them by statute.

ARTICLE IV. CAPITALIZATION

The aggregate number of shares which the corporation shall have authority to issue is one hundred thousand (100,000) shares of $00.01 par value. The corporation is authorized to issue only one class of stock. All issued stock shall be held of record by not more than 35 persons. Stock shall be issued and transferred only to (1) natural persons, (2) estates, or (3) a trust as defined in the Internal Revenue Code provision defining a qualified "small business corporation."

ARTICLE V. ISSUANCE OF SHARES

The corporation will not commence business until it has received for the issuance of its shares consideration of the value of One Thousand Dollars ($1,000.00), consisting of money, labor done, or property actually received, which sum is not less than One Thousand Dollars ($1,000.00).

The shareholders of this corporation shall have the preemptive right to subscribe to any and all issues of shares or securities of this corporation but shall not have the right to cumulative voting.

ARTICLE VI. REGISTERED OFFICE

The street address of its initial registered office is 600 Preston Avenue, Suite 520, Dallas, Dallas County, Texas 75210, and the name and address of the initial registered agent is:

Name   Address
Shirley Jameson   600 Preston Avenue
                                 Suite 520
                                 Dallas, TX 75210

ARTICLE VII. DIRECTORS

(a) The number of directors constituting the initial board of directors is three (3), and the names and addresses of the persons who are to serve as directors until the first annual meeting of the shareholders or until their successors are elected and qualified are:

Name   Address
Shirley Jameson   600 Preston Avenue
                                 Suite 520
                                 Dallas, Texas 75210

Adrian Burns   600 Preston Avenue
                                 Suite 520
                                 Dallas, Texas 75210

Cynthia Reynolds   600 Preston Avenue
                                 Suite 520
                                 Dallas, Texas 75210

(b) The number of directors of the corporation set forth in clause (a) of this article shall constitute the authorized number of directors until changed by an amendment or a bylaw adopted by the vote or written consent of the holders of a majority of the then outstanding shares of stock of the corporation.

ARTICLE VIII. INDEMNIFICATION

The corporation shall indemnify any director or officer, former director or officer of the corporation, or any person who may have served in the capacity of director or officer of another corporation in which it owns shares of stock or of which it is a creditor, against expenses actually and necessarily incurred by that person in connection with the defense of any action, suit, or proceeding in which he or she is made a party by reason of being or having been such director or officer. The corporation will not indemnify any such director or officer in relation to matters as to which he or she shall be adjudged liable for negligence or misconduct in the performance of his or her duty. Indemnification will not be deemed exclusive of any other rights to which such director or officer may be entitled under any bylaw, agreement, vote of shareholders, or otherwise.

ARTICLE IX. INCORPORATORS

The names and addresses of the incorporators are:

Name	Address
Shirley Jameson	600 Preston Avenue Suite 520 Dallas, Texas 75210
Adrian Burns	600 Preston Avenue Suite 520 Dallas, Texas 75210
Cynthia Reynolds	600 Preston Avenue Suite 520 Dallas, Texas 75210

For the purpose of forming this corporation under the laws of Texas, we, the undersigned, constituting the incorporators of this corporation, have executed these Articles of Incorporation on this _____ day of January, 20__ .

_____
Shirley Jameson
Incorporator

_____
Adrian Burns
Incorporator

_____
Cynthia Reynolds
Incorporator

The State of Texas
County of Dallas

I, the undersigned Notary Public, do hereby certify that on the _____ day of January, 20__, personally appeared before me SHIRLEY JAMESON, who being by me first duly sworn, declared that she is the person who signed the foregoing document, and that the statements therein contained are true and correct.

_____
Notary Public, State of Texas
My commission expires: _____

The State of Texas
County of Dallas

I, the undersigned Notary Public, do hereby certify that on the _____ day of January, 20__, personally appeared before me ADRIAN BURNS, who being by me first duly sworn, declared that he is the person who signed the foregoing document, and that the statements therein contained are true and correct.

_____
Notary Public, State of Texas
My commission expires: _____

The State of Texas
County of Dallas

I, the undersigned Notary Public, do hereby certify that on the _____ day of January, 20__, personally appeared before me CYNTHIA REYNOLDS, who being by me first duly sworn, declared that she is the person who signed the foregoing document, and that the statements therein contained are true and correct.

_____
Notary Public, State of Texas
My commission expires: _____

Appendix E

Sample Business Associate Contract

This sample contract incorporates suggested language by HHS and more general contractual language in an effort to provide a form contract that is more complete. This form should be used as a starting or reference point for contracts needed by a mental health professional. Specific state law contractual requirements may vary and individual practice issues will require specialized provisions. This form combines service contract language with business associate provisions suggested by HHS and HIPAA. A mental health provider may wish to separate these agreements into two separate contracts: (1) Services Agreement and (2) Business Associate Contract that incorporates by reference the Services Agreement. The authors however recommend developing single contracts for each Business Associate that includes the required Privacy Rule language. Consultation and review by a local attorney is recommended for each contract developed by a mental health professional for practice use.

Business Associate Contract (Billing Services)

This agreement is entered into on the _____ day of _____, 20___, between Susan A. Jones, LPC of Richardson, Texas hereinafter referred to as "Covered Entity" and ABC Billing Agency, Inc., of Dallas, Texas, hereinafter referred to as "Business Associate."

ENGAGEMENT

Covered Entity owns and operates a mental health services business with its principal offices located at 220 Abrams Rd., Suite 32, Richardson, Texas 75081. Covered Entity agrees to engage Business Associate to perform billing services on a continuing basis and Business Associate agrees to perform such services under the terms and conditions set forth in this contract.

DEFINITIONS

a. *Individual:* "Individual" shall have the same meaning as the term "individual" in 45 CFR §§ 164.501 and shall include a person who qualifies as a personal representative in accordance with 45 CFR §§ 164.502(g). Individual shall also mean "client" as used in this agreement.
b. *Privacy Rule:* "Privacy Rule" shall mean the Standards for Privacy of Individually Identifiable Health Information at 45 CFR Part 160 and Part 164, Subparts A and E.
c. *Protected Health Information:* "Protected Health Information" shall have the same meaning as the term "protected health information" in 45 CFR §§ 164.501, limited to the information created or received by Business Associate from or on behalf of Covered Entity.
d. *Required by Law:* "Required By Law" shall have the same meaning as the term "required by law" in 45 CFR §§ 164.501.

e. *Secretary:* "Secretary" shall mean the Secretary of the Department of Health and Human Services or his designee.
f. *HIPAA:* "HIPAA" shall mean the Health Insurance Portability & Accountability Act.

OBLIGATIONS AND ACTIVITIES OF BUSINESS ASSOCIATE

a. Business Associate agrees to prepare and forward billing invoices for the professional services provided by Covered Entity to clients or third party payers and where appropriate use standard electronic coding and formatting as required by HIPAA and each third party payer. All billing invoices shall be generated and forwarded within seven business (7) days of receipt of the client's information from Covered Entity with copies or confirmation of each billing provided to Covered Entity at the same time.
b. Business Associate agrees not to use or disclose Protected Health Information other than as necessary to bill clients or third party payers for services provided by Covered Entity to clients of Covered Entity or as Required by Law.
c. Business Associate agrees to use or disclose the minimum amount of Protected Health Information necessary to accomplish its billing services.
d. Business Associate agrees to use appropriate safeguards to prevent use or disclosure of the Protected Health Information other than as provided for by this Agreement.
e. Business Associate agrees to mitigate, to the extent practicable, any harmful effect that is known to Business Associate of a use or disclosure of Protected Health Information by Business Associate in violation of the requirements of this Agreement.
f. Business Associate agrees to report to Covered Entity any use or disclosure of the Protected Health Information not provided for by this Agreement of which it becomes aware.
g. Business Associate agrees to ensure that any agent, including a subcontractor, to whom it provides Protected Health Information received from, or created or received by Business Associate on behalf of Covered Entity agrees to the same restrictions and conditions that apply through this Agreement to Business Associate with respect to such information.
h. Business Associate agrees to make internal practices, books, and records, including policies and procedures and Protected Health Information, relating to the use and disclosure of Protected Health Information received from, or created or received by Business Associate on behalf of, Covered Entity available to the Covered Entity, or to the Secretary, or such person designated by the Secretary within five (5) business days of request, for purposes of the Secretary in determining Covered Entity's compliance with the Privacy Rule.
i. Business Associate agrees to document such disclosures of Protected Health Information and information related to such disclosures as would be required for Covered Entity to respond to a request by an Individual for an accounting of disclosures of Protected Health Information in accordance with 45 CFR §§ 164.528.
j. Business Associate agrees to provide to Covered Entity or an Individual, within five (5) business days of request, information collected in accordance with paragraph h of this subsection, to permit Covered Entity to respond to a request by an Individual for an accounting of disclosures of Protected Health Information in accordance with 45 CFR §§ 164.528.
k. Business Associate agrees to provide to Covered Entity or, to an Individual as directed by Covered Entity, within five (5) business days of request by Covered Entity, Protected Health Information necessary to permit Covered Entity to respond to a request by an Individual for PHI in accordance with 45 CFR §§ 164.524.

l. Business Associate agrees to make any amendment to Protected Health Information that is requested by Covered Entity or by an Individual and agreed to by Covered Entity pursuant to 45 CFR 164.526 within five (5) business days of request by Covered Entity.

PERMITTED USES AND DISCLOSURES BY BUSINESS ASSOCIATE

a. Except as otherwise limited in this Agreement, Business Associate may use or disclose Protected Health Information on behalf of, or to provide billing services to, Covered Entity if such use or disclosure of Protected Health Information would not violate the Privacy Rule if done by Covered Entity or the minimum necessary policies and procedures of the Covered Entity.

b. Except as otherwise limited in this Agreement, Business Associate may use Protected Health Information for the proper management and administration of the Business Associate or to carry out the legal responsibilities of the Business Associate. Except as otherwise limited in this Agreement, Business Associate may disclose Protected Health Information for the proper management and administration of the Business Associate, provided that disclosures are Required By Law, or Business Associate obtains reasonable assurances from the person to whom the information is disclosed that it will remain confidential and used or further disclosed only as Required By Law or for the purpose for which it was disclosed to the person, and the person notifies the Business Associate of any instances of which it is aware in which the confidentiality of the information has been breached.

c. Except as otherwise limited in this Agreement, Business Associate may use Protected Health Information to provide billing services to Covered Entity as permitted by 45 CFR §§ 164.504(e)(2)(i)(B).

d. Business Associate may use Protected Health Information to report violations of law to appropriate Federal and State authorities, consistent with 42 CFR §§ 164.502(j)(1).

OBLIGATIONS OF COVERED ENTITY

a. Covered Entity shall provide to Business Associate sufficient client information to allow Business Associate to process, prepare and forward billing invoices to clients or proper third party payers.

b. Pay the sum of $5.00 per each client billing invoice generated and forwarded by Business Associate in accordance with this agreement within five (5) days of receipt from Business Associate of the copies or confirmation of each billing prepared and forwarded by Business Associate on Covered Entity's behalf.

c. Covered Entity shall notify Business Associate of any limitation(s) in Covered Entity's notice of privacy practices in accordance with 45 CFR §§ 164.520, to the extent that such limitation may affect Business Associate's use or disclosure of Protected Health Information.

d. Covered Entity shall notify Business Associate of any changes in, or revocation of, permission by Individual to use or disclose Protected Health Information, to the extent that such changes may affect Business Associate's use or disclosure of Protected Health Information.

e. Covered Entity shall notify Business Associate of any restriction to the use or disclosure of Protected Health Information that Covered Entity has agreed to in accordance with 45 CFR §§ 164.522, to the extent that such restriction may affect Business Associate's use or disclosure of Protected Health Information.

PERMISSIBLE REQUESTS BY COVERED ENTITY

Covered Entity shall not request Business Associate to use or disclose Protected Health Information in any manner that would not be permissible under the Privacy Rule if done by Covered Entity.

TERM AND TERMINATION

Term: The Term of this Agreement shall be effective as of the _____ day of _____, 20___, and shall terminate thirteen (13) months from that date, unless the parties agree to extend the agreement for another thirteen (13) month period, and thereafter until all of the Protected Health Information provided by Covered Entity to Business Associate, or created or received by Business Associate on behalf of Covered Entity, is destroyed or returned to Covered Entity, or, if it is infeasible to return or destroy Protected Health Information, protections are extended to such information, in accordance with the termination provisions in this Section.

TERMINATION FOR CAUSE

Upon Covered Entity's knowledge of a material breach by Business Associate, Covered Entity shall either:

a. Provide an opportunity for Business Associate to cure the breach or end the violation and terminate this Agreement if Business Associate does not cure the breach or end the violation within the time specified by Covered Entity;
b. Immediately terminate this Agreement if Business Associate has breached a material term of this Agreement and cure is not possible; or
c. If neither termination nor cure are feasible for Privacy Rule violations, Covered Entity shall report the violation to the Secretary.

EFFECT OF TERMINATION

a. Except as provided in paragraph (b) of this section, upon termination of this Agreement, for any reason, Business Associate shall return or destroy all Protected Health Information received from Covered Entity, or created or received by Business Associate on behalf of Covered Entity. This provision shall apply to Protected Health Information that is in the possession of subcontractors or agents of Business Associate. Business Associate shall retain no copies of the Protected Health Information.
b. In the event that Business Associate determines that returning or destroying the Protected Health Information is infeasible, Business Associate shall provide to Covered Entity notification of the conditions that make return or destruction infeasible. Upon determination that return or destruction of Protected Health Information is infeasible, Business Associate shall extend the protections of this Agreement to such Protected Health Information and limit further uses and disclosures of such Protected Health Information to those purposes that make the return or destruction infeasible, for so long as Business Associate maintains such Protected Health Information.

RELATIONSHIP OF PARTIES

The parties intend that Business Associate, in performing the specified services, shall act as an independent contractor and shall have control of the work and the manner in which it is performed. Business Associate shall be free to contract for similar services to be performed for other health care providers while Business Associate is under contract with Covered Entity. Business Associate is not to be considered an agent or employee of Covered Entity and is not entitled to participate in any pension plans, bonus, stock, or similar benefits that Covered Entity provides for its employees.

LIABILITY

All work shall be performed entirely at Business Associate's risk. Business Associate shall indemnify and hold Covered Entity harmless from all claims, assessments, suits and charges arising from Business Associate's billing services and activities and Business Associate agrees to carry, for the duration of this contract, professional liability insurance in an amount, and with an insurer, acceptable to Covered Entity. This agreement shall not take effect until such time as Business Associate provides Covered Entity with proof of acceptable professional liability insurance.

MISCELLANEOUS

a. *Regulatory References:* A reference in this Agreement to a section in the Privacy Rule means the section as in effect or as amended.
b. *Amendment:* The Parties agree to take such action as is necessary to amend this Agreement from time to time as is necessary for Covered Entity to comply with the requirements of the Privacy Rule and the Health Insurance Portability and Accountability Act of 1996, Pub. L. No. 104-191.
c. *Survival:* The respective rights and obligations of Business Associate under the "Effect of Termination" Section of this Agreement shall survive the termination of this Agreement.
d. *Interpretation:* Any ambiguity in this Agreement shall be resolved to permit Covered Entity to comply with the Privacy Rule.

GENERAL PROVISIONS

a. This agreement shall be binding upon and inure to the benefit of the parties hereto, their successors, heirs and assigns. The parties agree to execute any instruments and take any other reasonable measure necessary for the successful completion of this agreement.
b. In the event any provision hereof is determined to be invalid, or unlawful, such provision shall be severed hereof without affecting the validity, lawfulness or effectiveness of the remaining portion of this agreement.
c. Waiver of any breach of this agreement shall not constitute a waiver of any recurring, subsequent or other breach.
d. All matters affecting the interpretation, form or validity, and performance of this agreement shall be decided under the laws of the State of Texas. This agreement is performable in Dallas County, Texas.

e. Business Associate agrees that in the event any action, proceeding or investigation, administrative, legal or otherwise, is initiated against Business Associate in connection with or arising out of Business Associate's affiliation with Covered Entity or Business Associate's performance under this Agreement, Business Associate shall not (i) implead Covered Entity in any such action, proceeding or investigation, (ii) initiate any proceeding or file any action, administrative, legal or otherwise, against Covered Entity or (iii) otherwise seek to recover from Covered Entity any losses or seek to obtain contribution or indemnity from Covered Entity with respect to any such losses. For purposes of this paragraph, the term Covered Entity includes any parent, subsidiary or affiliate of Covered Entity, Covered Entity's insurers and the officers, director, employees, agents and Business Associates of each of the foregoing. Without compromising any rights of either Business Associate or Covered Entity under common law, this section is not intended to be and shall not be construed as, an obligation on the part of either party to indemnify the other and will not preclude either party from taking any action for breach of contract to enforce its rights under this Agreement.

f. In the event it is necessary to file suit to enforce this agreement, the prevailing party shall recover court costs and reasonable attorney fees from the other party.

g. Neither party may assign this agreement without the written consent of the other party; provided, however, that Covered Entity may assign this agreement to an affiliate corporation of Covered Entity or may assign this agreement in connection with a merger or acquisition involving Covered Entity and another entity.

h. The parties agree that all addresses used for the processing of client claims and billing invoices shall be those of Covered Entity. All payments on accounts of clients assigned to Business Associate for billing are to be made to SUSAN A. JONES, LPC, 220 Abrams Rd., Suite 32, Richardson, Texas 75081, or such other address determined by Covered Entity.

The parties have executed this agreement at Richardson, Texas on this _____ day of _____, 20___ .

By: _____
Susan A. Jones, LPC
Covered Entity

ABC BILLING AGENCY, INC.

By: _____
Carolyn Hennessey, President
Business Associate

Appendix F

Business Associate Contract (Attorney Services)

This agreement is entered into on the _____ day of _____, 20___, between Susan A. Jones, LPC, of Richardson, Texas, Texas hereinafter referred to as "Covered Entity" and Thomas L. Hartsell, Jr., of Dallas, Texas hereinafter referred to as "Business Associate."

ENGAGEMENT

Covered Entity owns and operates a mental health services business with its principal offices located at 220 Abrams Rd., Suite 32, Richardson, Texas 75081. Covered Entity agrees to engage Business Associate to perform legal services on a continuing basis and Business Associate agrees to perform such services under the terms and conditions set forth in this contract.

DEFINITIONS

a. *Individual:* "Individual" shall have the same meaning as the term "individual" in 45 CFR §§ 164.501 and shall include a person who qualifies as a personal representative in accordance with 45 CFR §§ 164.502(g). Individual shall also mean "client" as used in this agreement.
b. *Privacy Rule:* "Privacy Rule" shall mean the Standards for Privacy of Individually Identifiable Health Information at 45 CFR Part 160 and Part 164, Subparts A and E.
c. *Protected Health Information:* "Protected Health Information" shall have the same meaning as the term "protected health information" in 45 CFR §§ 164.501, limited to the information created or received by Business Associate from or on behalf of Covered Entity.
d. *Required By Law:* "Required By Law" shall have the same meaning as the term "required by law" in 45 CFR §§ 164.501.
e. *Secretary:* "Secretary" shall mean the Secretary of the Department of Health and Human Services or his designee.
f. *HIPAA:* "HIPAA" shall mean the Health Insurance Portability And Accountability Act.

OBLIGATIONS AND ACTIVITIES OF BUSINESS ASSOCIATE

a. Business Associate agrees to provide legal services to Covered Entity.
b. Business Associate agrees not to use or disclose Protected Health Information other than as necessary to bill clients or third party payers for services provided by Covered Entity to clients of Covered Entity or as Required by Law.
c. Business Associate agrees to use or disclose the minimum amount of Protected Health Information necessary to accomplish its legal services.
d. Business Associate agrees to use appropriate safeguards to prevent use or disclosure of the Protected Health Information other than as provided for by this Agreement.

e. Business Associate agrees to mitigate, to the extent practicable, any harmful effect that is known to Business Associate of a use or disclosure of Protected Health Information by Business Associate in violation of the requirements of this Agreement.

f. Business Associate agrees to report to Covered Entity any use or disclosure of the Protected Health Information not provided for by this Agreement of which it becomes aware.

g. Business Associate agrees to ensure that any agent, including a subcontractor, to whom it provides Protected Health Information received from, or created or received by Business Associate on behalf of Covered Entity agrees to the same restrictions and conditions that apply through this Agreement to Business Associate with respect to such information.

h. Business Associate agrees to make internal practices, books, and records, including policies and procedures and Protected Health Information, relating to the use and disclosure of Protected Health Information received from, or created or received by Business Associate on behalf of, Covered Entity available to the Covered Entity, or to the Secretary, or such person designated by the Secretary within five (5) business days of request, for purposes of the Secretary in determining Covered Entity's compliance with the Privacy Rule.

i. Business Associate agrees to document such disclosures of Protected Health Information and information related to such disclosures as would be required for Covered Entity to respond to a request by an Individual for an accounting of disclosures of Protected Health Information in accordance with 45 CFR §§ 164.528.

j. Business Associate agrees to provide to Covered Entity or an Individual, within five (5) business days of request, information collected in accordance with paragraph h of this subsection, to permit Covered Entity to respond to a request by an Individual for an accounting of disclosures of Protected Health Information in accordance with 45 CFR §§ 164.528.

k. Business Associate agrees to provide to Covered Entity or, to an Individual as directed by Covered Entity, within five (5) business days of request by Covered Entity, Protected Health Information necessary to permit Covered Entity to respond to a request by an Individual for PHI in accordance with 45 CFR §§ 164.524.

l. Business Associate agrees to make any amendment to Protected Health Information that is requested by Covered Entity or by an Individual and agreed to by Covered Entity pursuant to 45 CFR §§ 164.526 within five (5) business days of request by Covered Entity.

PERMITTED USES AND DISCLOSURES BY BUSINESS ASSOCIATE

a. Except as otherwise limited in this Agreement, Business Associate may use or disclose Protected Health Information on behalf of, or to provide legal services to, Covered Entity if such use or disclosure of Protected Health Information would not violate the Privacy Rule if done by Covered Entity or the minimum necessary policies and procedures of the Covered Entity.

b. Except as otherwise limited in this Agreement, Business Associate may use Protected Health Information for the proper management and administration of the Business Associate or to carry out the legal responsibilities of the Business Associate. Except as otherwise limited in this Agreement, Business Associate may disclose Protected Health Information for the proper management and administration of the Business Associate, provided that disclosures are Required By Law, or Business Associate obtains reasonable assurances from the person to whom the information is disclosed that it will remain confidential and used or further disclosed only as Required By Law or for the purpose for which it was disclosed to the person, and the person notifies the Business Associate of any instances of which it is aware in which the confidentiality of the information has been breached.

c. Except as otherwise limited in this Agreement, Business Associate may use Protected Health Information to provide legal services to Covered Entity as permitted by 45 CFR §§ 164.504(e)(2)(i)(B).

d. Business Associate may use Protected Health Information to report violations of law to appropriate Federal and State authorities, consistent with 45 CFR §§ 164.502(j)(1).

OBLIGATIONS OF COVERED ENTITY

a. Covered Entity shall provide to Business Associate sufficient client information to allow Business Associate to process, prepare and forward billing invoices to clients or proper third party payers.

b. Covered Entity shall pay the sum of $225.00 per hour to Business Associate for all legal services provided to Covered Entity.

c. Covered Entity shall notify Business Associate of any limitation(s) in Covered Entity's notice of privacy practices in accordance with 45 CFR §§ 164.520, to the extent that such limitation may affect Business Associate's use or disclosure of Protected Health Information.

d. Covered Entity shall notify Business Associate of any changes in, or revocation of, permission by Individual to use or disclose Protected Health Information, to the extent that such changes may affect Business Associate's use or disclosure of Protected Health Information.

d. Covered Entity shall notify Business Associate of any restriction to the use or disclosure of Protected Health Information that Covered Entity has agreed to in accordance with 45 CFR §§ 164.522, to the extent that such restriction may affect Business Associate's use or disclosure of Protected Health Information.

PERMISSIBLE REQUESTS BY COVERED ENTITY

Covered Entity shall not request Business Associate to use or disclose Protected Health Information in any manner that would not be permissible under the Privacy Rule if done by Covered Entity.

TERM AND TERMINATION

Term: The Term of this Agreement shall be effective as of the 14th day of April, 2003, and shall terminate thirteen (13) months from that date, unless the parties agree to extend the agreement for another thirteen (13) month period, and thereafter until all of the Protected Health Information provided by Covered Entity to Business Associate, or created or received by Business Associate on behalf of Covered Entity, is destroyed or returned to Covered Entity, or, if it is infeasible to return or destroy Protected Health Information, protections are extended to such information, in accordance with the termination provisions in this Section.

TERMINATION FOR CAUSE

Upon Covered Entity's knowledge of a material breach by Business Associate, Covered Entity shall either:

a. Provide an opportunity for Business Associate to cure the breach or end the violation and terminate this Agreement if Business Associate does not cure the breach or end the violation within the time specified by Covered Entity;

b. Immediately terminate this Agreement if Business Associate has breached a material term of this Agreement and cure is not possible; or

c. If neither termination nor cure are feasible for Privacy Rule violations, Covered Entity shall report the violation to the Secretary.

EFFECT OF TERMINATION

a. Except as provided in paragraph (b) of this section, upon termination of this Agreement, for any reason, Business Associate shall return or destroy all Protected Health Information received from Covered Entity, or created or received by Business Associate on behalf of Covered Entity. This provision shall apply to Protected Health Information that is in the possession of subcontractors or agents of Business Associate. Business Associate shall retain no copies of the Protected Health Information.

b. In the event that Business Associate determines that returning or destroying the Protected Health Information is infeasible, Business Associate shall provide to Covered Entity notification of the conditions that make return or destruction infeasible. Upon determination that return or destruction of Protected Health Information is infeasible, Business Associate shall extend the protections of this Agreement to such Protected Health Information and limit further uses and disclosures of such Protected Health Information to those purposes that make the return or destruction infeasible, for so long as Business Associate maintains such Protected Health Information.

RELATIONSHIP OF PARTIES

The parties intend that Business Associate, in performing the specified services, shall act as an independent contractor and shall have control of the work and the manner in which it is performed. Business Associate shall be free to contract for similar services to be performed for other health care providers while Business Associate is under contract with Covered Entity. Business Associate is not to be considered an agent or employee of Covered Entity and is not entitled to participate in any pension plans, bonus, stock, or similar benefits that Covered Entity provides for its employees.

LIABILITY

All work shall be performed entirely at Business Associate's risk. Business Associate shall indemnify and hold Covered Entity harmless from all claims, assessments, suits and charges arising from Business Associate's legal services and activities and Business Associate agrees to carry, for the duration of this contract, professional liability insurance in an amount, and with an insurer, acceptable to Covered Entity. This agreement shall not take effect until such time as Business Associate provides Covered Entity with proof of acceptable professional liability insurance.

MISCELLANEOUS

a. *Regulatory References:* A reference in this Agreement to a section in the Privacy Rule means the section as in effect or as amended.

b. *Amendment:* The Parties agree to take such action as is necessary to amend this Agreement from time to time as is necessary for Covered Entity to comply with the requirements of the Privacy Rule and the Health Insurance Portability and Accountability Act of 1996, Pub. L. No. 104-191.

c. *Survival:* The respective rights and obligations of Business Associate under the "Effect of Termination" Section of this Agreement shall survive the termination of this Agreement.

d. *Interpretation:* Any ambiguity in this Agreement shall be resolved to permit Covered Entity to comply with the Privacy Rule.

GENERAL PROVISIONS

a. This agreement shall be binding upon and inure to the benefit of the parties hereto, their successors, heirs and assigns. The parties agree to execute any instruments and take any other reasonable measure necessary for the successful completion of this agreement.

b. In the event any provision hereof is determined to be invalid, or unlawful, such provision shall be severed hereof without affecting the validity, lawfulness or effectiveness of the remaining portion of this agreement.

c. Waiver of any breach of this agreement shall not constitute a waiver of any recurring, subsequent or other breach.

d. All matters affecting the interpretation, form or validity, and performance of this agreement shall be decided under the laws of the State of Texas. This agreement is performable in Dallas County, Texas.

e. Business Associate agrees that in the event any action, proceeding or investigation, administrative, legal or otherwise, is initiated against Business Associate in connection with or arising out of Business Associate's affiliation with Covered Entity or Business Associate's performance under this Agreement, Business Associate shall not (i) implead Covered Entity in any such action, proceeding or investigation, (ii) initiate any proceeding of file any action, administrative, legal or otherwise, against Covered Entity or (iii) otherwise seek to recover from Covered Entity any losses or seek to obtain contribution or indemnity from Covered Entity with respect to any such losses. For purposes of this paragraph, the term Covered Entity includes any parent, subsidiary or affiliate of Covered Entity, Covered Entity's insurers and the officers, director, employees, agents and Business Associates of each of the foregoing. Without compromising any rights of either Business Associate or Covered Entity under common law, this section is not intended to be and shall not be construed as, an obligation on the part of either party to indemnify the other and will not preclude either party from taking any action for breach of contract to enforce its rights under this Agreement.

f. In the event it is necessary to file suit to enforce this agreement, the prevailing party shall recover court costs and reasonable attorney fees from the other party.

g. Neither party may assign this agreement without the written consent of the other party; provided, however, that Covered Entity may assign this agreement to an affiliate corporation of Covered Entity or may assign this agreement in connection with a merger or acquisition involving Covered Entity and another entity.

The parties have executed this agreement at Dallas, Texas, on this _____ day of _____, 20____ .

By: _____   By: _____
    Susan A. Jones, LPC   Thomas L. Hartsell, Jr.
    Covered Entity   Business Associate

Appendix G

Authorization for the Use and Disclosure
of Protected Health Information

I, Harold Cross (Social Security No. 123-45-6789, Date of Birth 6/4/59) the undersigned client of Susan A. Jones, LPC, do hereby authorize Susan A. Jones LPC, my treating mental health provider, to disclose **any and all** protected health information in my file, including but not limited to her psychotherapy notes, to the following persons:

Thomas L. Hartsell, Jr., Attorney at Law, who represents me in connection with my divorce case, Cause #2003-1456-Y, now pending in the 330th Judicial District court of Dallas County, Texas; and Barton E. Bernstein, Attorney at Law, who represents my wife, Sharon Cross in this same divorce suit.

This information is to be provided at my request for use by said attorneys **only** in connection with the child related issues presented in my above referenced divorce suit. This authorization shall expire upon the entry of a final decree of divorce in my above referenced divorce suit and the conclusion of any and all appeals.

I acknowledge that I have the right to revoke this authorization in writing at any time to the extent Susan A. Jones, LPC has not taken action in reliance on this authorization. I further acknowledge that even if I revoke this authorization, the use and disclosure of my protected health information could possibly still be compelled by court Order under state law as indicated in the copy of the Notice of Privacy Practices of Susan A. Jones, LPC that I have received and reviewed.

I acknowledge that I have been advised by Susan A. Jones, LPC of the potential of the redisclosure of my protected health information by the authorized recipients and that it will no longer be protected by the federal Privacy Rule.

I further acknowledge that the treatment provided to me by Susan A. Jones, LPC was not conditioned on my signing this authorization.

Signed this _____ day of _____, 20____

_____
Harold Cross, Client

_____
Social Security Number

_____
Address

_____
Phone Number

I acknowledge that I received a copy of this signed authorization from Susan A. Jones, LPC on this _____ day of _____, 20___ .

_____
Harold Cross

Appendix H

Client Information Amendment Form

I, Harold Cross request that information kept in the records of Susan A. Jones, LPC be amended.

Information to Be Amended: The following information needs to be amended:

- Item to be changed: _____
- Data source: _____
- Change: _____

  _____

- Reason for change: _____

  _____

  _____

If you need help with this form, please contact:

Susan A. Jones, LPC, Privacy Officer at (972) 000-0000. Attach additional copies of this form as needed.

Please sign and date this form below:

Harold Cross
Name of Client (Print or Type)

_____   _____
Signature of Client   Date

This section to be filled out by Susan A. Jones, LPC, Privacy Officer

Approved/Disapproved Amendments:

The following requirements for amendment of information have been

_____ Approved.   The information will be corrected and other organizations to which this information has been disclosed will be notified as required by federal regulations.

_____ Denied.   The request is denied for the following reasons:

_____

_____

_____

The information will be not amended in our records. If you disagree with this decision, you may submit a written statement of disagreement. Your statement of disagreement must be limited to one standard letter-sized page per correction. Your statement of disagreement will be included in my records and it, or an accurate summary of it that I will prepare, will be transmitted to any entity the affected information is disclosed to in the future. I also may include my own comments regarding your statement of disagreement. If I include such comments you will be sent a copy of these comments.

Susan A. Jones, Privacy Officer

_____   _____
Signature   Date

Appendix I

Notice of Privacy Practices of Susan A. Jones, LPC
Effective April 14, 2003

THIS NOTICE DESCRIBES HOW MENTAL HEALTH INFORMATION ABOUT YOU MAY BE USED AND DISCLOSED AND HOW YOU CAN GET ACCESS TO THIS INFORMATION. PLEASE REVIEW IT CAREFULLY.

I am required by law to maintain the privacy of your protected health information (PHI) and to provide you with notice of your privacy rights and my legal duties and privacy practices with respect to your PHI. I am required to abide by the terms of this notice with respect to your PHI but reserve the right to change the terms of this notice and make the new notice provisions effective for all PHI that I maintain. I will provide you with a copy of the revised notice sent by regular mail to the last address you have provided to me for this communication purpose.

UNDERSTANDING YOUR PERSONAL HEALTH INFORMATION

Each time you visit a hospital, physician, mental health professional or other health care provider, a record of your visit is made. Typically, this record contains your symptoms, examination and test results, diagnoses, treatment, in the case of a mental health professional, psychotherapy notes, and a plan for future care or treatment. This information, often referred to as your health or medical record, serves as a:

- Basis for planning your care and treatment.
- Means of communication among the many health professionals who contribute to your care.
- Legal document describing the care you received.
- Means by which you or a third-party payer can verify that services billed were actually provided a tool in educating heath professionals.
- A source of data for medical research.
- A source of information for public health officials charged with improving the health of the nation a source of data for facility planning and marketing.
- A tool with which we can assess and continually work to improve the care we render and the outcomes we achieve.

Understanding what is in your record and how your health information is used helps you to:

- Ensure its accuracy.
- Better understand who, what, when, where, and why others may access your health information.
- Make more informed decisions when authorizing disclosure to others.

YOUR HEALTH INFORMATION RIGHTS

Although your health record is the physical property of my practice, the facility that compiled it, the information belongs to you. You have the following privacy rights:

1. The right to request restrictions on the use and disclosure of your PHI to carry out treatment, payment or health care operations.

   You should note that I am not required to agree to be bound by any restrictions that you request but am bound by each restriction that I do agree to.

2. In connection with any patient directory, the right to request restrictions on the use and disclosure of your name, location at this treatment facility, description of your condition and your religious affiliation. (I do not maintain a patient directory.)

3. To receive confidential communication of your PHI unless I determine that such disclosure would be harmful to you.

4. To inspect and copy your PHI unless I determine in the exercise of my professional judgment that the access requested is reasonably likely to endanger your life or physical safety (*Note:* if state law allows, "emotional safety" may be included as well) or that of another person.

   You may request copies of your PHI by providing me with a written request for such copies. I will provide you with copies within ten (10) business days of your request at my office. You will be charged $.25 for each page copied and you will be expected to pay for the copies at the time you pick them up.

5. To amend your PHI upon your written request to me setting forth your reasons for the requested amendment. I have the right to deny the request if the information is complete or has been created by another entity.

   I am required to act on your request to amend your PHI within sixty (60) days but this deadline may be extended for another thirty (30) days upon written notice to you. If I deny your requested amendment I will provide you with written notice of my decision and the basis for my decision. You will then have the right to submit a written statement disagreeing with my decision which will be maintained with your PHI. If you do not wish to submit a statement of disagreement you may request that I provide your request for amendment and my denial with any future disclosures of your PHI.

6. Upon request to receive an accounting of disclosures of your PHI made within the past 6 years of your request for an accounting. Disclosures that are exempted from the accounting requirement include the following:

   - Disclosures necessary to carry out treatment, payment and health care operations.
   - Disclosures made to you upon request.
   - Disclosures made pursuant to your authorization.
   - Disclosures made for national security or intelligence purposes.
   - Permitted disclosures to correctional institutions or law enforcement officials.
   - Disclosures that are part of a limited data set used for research, public health or health care operations.

   I am required to act on your request for an accounting within sixty (60) days but this deadline may be extended for another thirty (30) days upon written notice to you of the reason for the delay and the date by which I will provide the accounting. You are entitled to one (1) accounting in any twelve (12) month period free of charge. For any subsequent request in a twelve (12) month period you will be charged $.25 for each page copied and you will be expected to pay for the copies at the time you pick them up.

7. To receive a paper copy of this privacy notice even if you agreed to receive a copy electronically.

8. The right to complain to me and to the Secretary of the U.S. Department of Health and Human Services (HHS) if you believe your privacy rights have been violated. You may submit your complaint to me in writing setting out the alleged violation. I am prohibited by law from retaliating against you in any way for filing a complaint with me or HHS.

Uses and Disclosures

Your written authorization is required before I can use or disclose my psychotherapy notes which are defined as my notes documenting or analyzing the contents of our conversations during our counseling sessions and that are separated from the rest of your clinical file. Psychotherapy notes do not include medication prescription and monitoring, counseling session start and stop times, the modalities and frequencies of treatment furnished, results of clinical tests and any summary of the following items: diagnosis, functional status, the treatment plan, symptoms, prognosis and progress to date.

It is my policy to protect the confidentiality of your PHI to the best of my ability and to the extent permitted by law. There are times however, when use or disclosure of your PHI including, psychotherapy notes, is permitted or mandated by law even without your authorization.

Situations where I am not required to obtain your consent or authorization for use or disclosure of your PHI psychotherapy notes include the following circumstances:

- By myself or my office staff for treatment, payment or health care operations as they relate to you.

  For example: Information obtained by me will be recorded in your record and used to determine the course of treatment that should work best for you. I will document in your record our work together and when appropriate I will provide a subsequent counselor or health care provider with copies of various reports that should assist him or her in treating you once we have terminated our therapeutic relationship.

  For example: A bill may be sent to you or a third-party payer. The information on or accompanying the bill may include information that identifies you, as well as your diagnosis, procedures, and supplies used.

- In the event of an emergency to any treatment provider who provides emergency treatment to you.
- To defend myself in a legal action or other proceeding brought by you against me.
- When required by the Secretary of the Department of Health and Human Services in an investigation to determine my compliance with the privacy rules.
- When required by law in so far as the use or disclosure complies with and is limited to the relevant requirements of such law.

  Examples:
  To a public health authority or other government authority authorized by law to receive reports of child abuse or neglect.

If I reasonably believe an adult individual to be the victim of abuse, neglect or domestic violence, to a governmental authority, including a social services agency authorized by law to receive such reports to the extent the disclosure is required by or authorized by law or you agree to the disclosure and I believe in the exercise of my professional judgment disclosure is necessary to prevent serious harm to you or other potential victims. If I make such a report I am obligated to inform you unless I believe informing the adult individual will place the individual at risk of serious injury.

In the course of any judicial or administrative proceeding in response to:

- An order of a court or administrative tribunal so long as only the PHI expressly authorized by such order is disclosed, or
- A subpoena, discovery request or other lawful process, that is not accompanied by an order of a court or administrative tribunal so long as reasonable efforts are made to give you notice that your PHI has been requested or reasonable efforts are made to secure a qualified protective order, by the person requesting the PHI.

- Child custody cases and other legal proceedings in which your mental health or condition is in issue are the kinds of suits in which you PHI may be requested.
- In addition I may use your PHI in connection with a suit to collect fees for my services.
- In compliance with a court order or court ordered warrant, or a subpoena or summons issued by a judicial officer, a grand jury subpoena or summons, a civil or an authorized investigative demand or similar process authorized by law provided that the information sought is relevant and material to a legitimate law enforcement inquiry, the request is specific and limited in scope to the extent reasonably practicable in light of the purpose for which the information is sought and de-identified information could not reasonably be used.
- To a health oversight agency for oversight activities authorized by law as they may relate to me (i.e., audits; civil, criminal or administrative investigations, inspections, licensure or disciplinary actions; civil, administrative, or criminal proceedings or actions).
- To a coroner or medical examiner for the purpose of identifying a deceased person, determining a cause of death, or other duties as authorized by law.
- To funeral directors consistent with applicable law as necessary to carry out their duties with respect to the decedent.
- To the extent authorized by and the extent necessary to comply with laws relating to workers compensation or other similar programs established by law.
- If use or disclosure is necessary to prevent or lessen a serious and imminent threat to the health or safety of a person or the public and the disclosure is made to a person or persons reasonably able to prevent or lessen the threat, including the target of the threat.
- To a public health authority that is authorized by law to collect or receive such information for the purposes of preventing or controlling a disease, injury or disability, including, but not limited to, the reporting of disease, injury, vital events such as birth, death, and the conduct of public surveillance, public health investigations, and public health interventions.
- To a person who may have been exposed to a communicable disease or may otherwise be at risk of contracting or spreading a disease or condition, if the covered entity or public health authority is authorized by law to notify such persons as necessary in the conduct of a public health intervention or investigation.
- To a public health authority or other appropriate governmental authority authorized by law to receive reports of child abuse or neglect.
- To a law enforcement official if I believe in good faith that the PHI constitutes evidence of criminal conduct that occurs on my premises.
- Using my best judgment, to a family member, other relative or close personal friend or any other person you identify, I may disclose PHI that is relevant to that person's involvement in your care or payment related to your care.
- To authorized federal officials for the conduct of lawful intelligence, counter-intelligence, and other national security activities authorized by the National Security Act and implementing authority.
- To Business Associates under a written agreement requiring Business Associates to protect the information. Business Associates are entities that assist with or conduct activities on my behalf including individuals or organizations that provide legal, accounting, administrative, and similar functions.

I may contact you with appointment reminders or information about treatment alternatives or other health related benefits and services that may be of interest to you.

If you have any questions and would like additional information you should bring this to my attention at the first opportunity. I am the designated Privacy Officer for my practice and will be glad to respond to your questions or request for information.

Client Consent Form

I understand that as part of my health care, the undersigned therapist originates and maintains health records describing my health history, symptoms, evaluations and test results, diagnosis, treatment, psychotherapy notes, and any plans for future care or treatment. I understand that this information is utilized to plan my care and treatment, to bill for services provided to me, to communicate with other health care providers and other routine health care operations such as assessing quality and reviewing competence of health care professionals.

The *Notice of Privacy Practices* for SUSAN A. JONES, LPC, provides specific information and a thorough description of how my personal health information may be used and disclosed. I have been provided a copy of or access to the *Notice of Privacy Practices* and I have been given the opportunity to review the notice prior to signing this consent. Before implementation of any revised *Notice of Privacy Practices,* the revised *Notice* will be mailed to me at the address I designate below. I understand that I have the right to restrict the use and/or disclosure of my personal health information for treatment, payment, or health care operations and that I am not required to agree to the restrictions requested. I may revoke this consent at any time in writing except to the extent that SUSAN A. JONES, LPC has already taken action in reliance on my prior consent. This consent is valid until revoked by me in writing.

I request the following restrictions on the use and/or disclosure of my personal health information.

_____

Therapist response: Agree to restriction/Do not agree to restriction

_____

Therapist response: Agree to restriction/Do not agree to restriction

I further understand that any and all records, whether written, oral or in electronic format, are confidential and cannot be disclosed without my prior written authorization, except as otherwise provided by law.

I have been provided and have received SUSAN A. JONES', LPC *Notice of Privacy Practices* dated April 14, 2003.

_____   _____
Signature of Client or Legal Representative   Date

_____   _____
Signature of Client or Legal Representative   Date

I request that changes to the *Notice of Privacy Practices* be sent to me at this address:

_____

_____

_____

Witnessed: _____   Date: _____
            Susan A. Jones, LPC

Appendix J

Accounting of Disclosures of Protected Health Information

Client: Harold Cross

Date: May 1, 2003

Recipient of information: 330th Judicial District Court, Dallas County, Texas
600 Commerce Street, Dallas, Texas 75206

Description of the protected health information disclosed:

A copy of the entire contents of this file including psychotherapy notes together with my responses to questions from counsel regarding the file, the therapy, and my opinions regarding the client's parenting ability.

Description of the purpose of the disclosure:
Compliance with a subpoena, a copy of which is attached to this accounting log.

_____   _____

Susan A. Jones, LPC   Date

Appendix K

**Request for Accounting of Protected
Health Information Disclosures**

I, Harold Cross, request an accounting of disclosures made containing my protected health information. I understand that, consistent with federal regulations, Susan A. Jones, LPC will provide me with an accounting of certain disclosures of my protected health information. I further understand that Susan A. Jones, LPC will not provide me with a copy of the following:

- Uses and disclosures or my protected health information permitted by the Health Insurance Portability and Accountability Act of 1996 for the purposes of treatment, payment, or health care operations.
- Disclosures to law enforcement or correctional institutions.
- Disclosures that occurred prior to April 14, 2003, the effective date of the federal privacy rules.
- Disclosures that occurred six or more years prior to the date of this request.

I will expect to hear from Susan A. Jones, LPC within sixty (60) days of this request. If you have any questions, I can be reached at the address below.

_____
Name of Client (Print or Type)

_____
Signature of Client

_____
Date

_____
Telephone Number

_____
Street Address

_____
City, State, Zip Code

Appendix L

Authorization Revocation Form

This notice revokes the authorization for the use and disclosure of protected health information for

Harold Cross_____ that was signed on _____.
Client Name   Date

Effect of Revocation

Protected health information that is maintained on or after the date on which this revocation is received by Susan A. Jones, LPC will not be disclosed by Susan A. Jones, LPC for the purposes specified in the authorization that is revoked. This revocation of authorization will not limit the ability Susan A. Jones, LPC to seek payment for services she provided under an earlier authorization, nor to meet legal obligations related to those services, nor will it affect uses or disclosures under the revoked authorization that occurred prior to the effective date of this revocation.

Other consequences of revoking the authorization:

- _____
- _____
- _____

Effective Date of Revocation

This revocation of authorization to use or disclose protected health information is effective _____.
                                                                                          Date

Client name: Harold Cross_____

Street Address: _____

City, State, ZipCode: _____

Signature of Client _____ Date _____

References and Reading Materials

I. CURRENT INFORMATION

FMS (False Memory) Foundation
3401 Market Street, Suite 130, Philadelphia, PA 19104-3318; 215-387-1865

Mental Health Law Reporter
Bonnie Becker, Editor, 951 Pershing Drive, Silver Spring, MD 20910-4464; 301-587-6300

Practice Strategies
A Business Guide for Behavioral Health Care Providers, 442½ East Main Street, Suite 2, Clayton, NC 27520; 919-553-0637

Psychotherapy Finances
Managing Your Practice and Your Money, P.O. Box 33468-8979, Jupiter, FL 33468-8979; 800-869-8450; 561-748-7816

II. REFERENCE BOOKS

Lawless, Linda L.
Therapy, Inc—A Hands-On Guide to Developing, Positioning, and Marketing Your Mental Health Practice in the 1990s (John Wiley & Sons, Inc., 1997)

Psychotherapy Finance Managed Care Handbook—The Practitioner's Guide to Behavioral Managed Care (Ridgewood Financial Institute, Inc., 1995)

Martinez, Julie, Sponsoring Editor
Codes of Ethics for the Helping Professions (Brooks/Cole, 2003)

Roach, William H., Jr., and The Aspen Health Law Center
Medical Records and the Law (Aspen Publishing, Inc., 1994)

Stout, Chris E., Editor-in-Chief
The Complete Guide to Managed Behavioral Healthcare (John Wiley & Sons, Inc., 1996)

Wiger, Donald E.
The Clinical Documentation Sourcebook—A Comprehensive Collection of Mental Health Practice Forms, Handouts, and Records (John Wiley & Sons, Inc., 1997)

III. ORGANIZATIONS WITH PERIODIC PUBLICATIONS ON LAW AND MENTAL HEALTH

American Association of Marriage and Family Therapists

American Association of Pastoral Counselors

American Bar Association (Especially mental health or hospital law sections)

American Counseling Association

American Medical Association

American Mental Health Counselors Association

American Psychiatric Association

American Psychological Association

National Association of Social Workers

Note: All state licensing boards publish lists of licensed practitioners who have been disciplined by the boards. Usually, the names of the individuals who have been disciplined are given, together with the rule allegedly violated.

IV. LIBRARY LIST FOR BACKGROUND

Banton, Ragnhild, *The Politics of Mental Health* (1985)

Beis, Edward B., *Mental Health and the Law* (1984)

Corey, Gerald, Maryann Schneider Corey, and Patrick Callahan, *Issues & Ethics in the Helping Professions,* sixth edition (2003)

Dutton, Mary Ann, *Empowering and Healing the Battered Woman* (1992)

Hunter, Edna J., Editor, *Professional Ethics and Law in the Health Sciences* (1990)

Kermani, Ebrahim J., *Handbook of Psychiatry and the Law* (1989)

Lidz, Charles W., *Informed Consent, a Study of Decision Making in Psychiatry* (1984)

Nadelson, Carol C., Editor, *Marriage and Divorce* (1984)

National Institute of Mental Health, *Handbook of Mental Health Consultation* (1986)

Pederson, Paul, *Handbook of Cross-Cultural Counseling and Therapy* (1985)

Pollack, Daniel, *Social Work and the Courts, a Case Study,* second edition (2002)

Rosner, Richard, MD, Editor, *Ethical Practice in Psychiatry and the Law* (1990)

Shuman, Daniel W., *Law and Mental Health Professionals* (1990)

Stout, Chris E., Editor, *The Complete Guide to Managed Behavioral Healthcare* (1996)

U.S. Department of Health and Human Services, *Legal Opinions on the Confidentiality of Alcohol and Drug Abuse Patient Records, 1975–1978* (1980)

Weiner, Myron F., and Anne M. Lipton, *The Dementias, Diagnosis, Treatment and Research* (2003)

Index